THE NEUROSCIENCE OF EMPATHY, COMPASSION, AND SELF-COMPASSION

THE NEUROSCIENCE OF EMPATHY, COMPASSION, AND SELF-COMPASSION

Edited by

LARRY STEVENS
Northern Arizona University, Flagstaff, AZ, United States

C. CHAD WOODRUFF
Northern Arizona University, Flagstaff, AZ, United States

ACADEMIC PRESS
An imprint of Elsevier

Academic Press is an imprint of Elsevier
125 London Wall, London EC2Y 5AS, United Kingdom
525 B Street, Suite 1650, San Diego, CA 92101, United States
50 Hampshire Street, 5th Floor, Cambridge, MA 02139, United States
The Boulevard, Langford Lane, Kidlington, Oxford OX5 1GB, United Kingdom

Notices
Knowledge and best practice in this field are constantly changing. As new research and experience
broaden our understanding, changes in research methods, professional practices, or medical treatment
may become necessary.

Practitioners and researchers must always rely on their own experience and knowledge in evaluating
and using any information, methods, compounds, or experiments described herein. In using such
information or methods they should be mindful of their own safety and the safety of others, including
parties for whom they have a professional responsibility.

To the fullest extent of the law, neither the Publisher nor the authors, contributors, or editors, assume
any liability for any injury and/or damage to persons or property as a matter of products liability,
negligence or otherwise, or from any use or operation of any methods, products, instructions, or ideas
contained in the material herein.

Library of Congress Cataloging-in-Publication Data
A catalog record for this book is available from the Library of Congress

British Library Cataloguing-in-Publication Data
A catalogue record for this book is available from the British Library

ISBN: 978-0-12-809837-0

For information on all Academic Press publications visit our website at
https://www.elsevier.com/books-and-journals

Working together
to grow libraries in
developing countries

www.elsevier.com • www.bookaid.org

Publisher: Nikki Levy
Acquisition Editor: Emily Ekle
Editorial Project Manager: Barbara Makinster
Production Project Manager: Priya Kumaraguruparan
Designer: Victoria Pearson

Typeset by Thomson Digital

To My Beautiful and Brilliant Children
Samantha
Sean
Summer
Erik
Shannon
The Stitches in My Robes
The Beat in My Heart
The Stars in My Firmament
I Love You Each and All
paPa

- Larry Charles Stevens

I dedicate this book to my wife Stacy, and kids Carson and Sierra, who put up with the worst in me because they see the best in me.
Thank you.

- C. Chad Woodruff

Contents

Contributors

Todd Ahern Quinnipiac University, Hamden, CT, United States

Jasmine Benjamin University of Arizona, Tucson, AZ, United States

Melissa Birkett Department of Psychological Sciences, Northern Arizona University, Flagstaff, AZ, United States

Martin Brüne Ruhr-University Bochum, Bochum, Germany

Benjamin Bush Northern Arizona University, Flagstaff, AZ, United States

Adam Calderon Quinnipiac University, Hamden, CT, United States

Kristina Chepak University of California, San Diego, CA, United States

Vera Flasbeck Ruhr-University Bochum, Bochum, Germany

Mark Gauthier-Braham Northern Arizona University, Flagstaff, AZ, United States

Cristina Gonzalez-Liencres Institut d'Investigacions Biomèdiques August Pi i Sunyer (IDIBAPS), Barcelona, Spain

Robert J. Goodman Northern Arizona University, Flagstaff, AZ, United States

Jaime A. Pineda University of California, San Diego, CA, United States

Paul E. Plonski Northern Arizona University, Flagstaff, AZ, United States

Thomas Pruzinsky Quinnipiac University, Hamden, CT, United States

Joni Sasaki Department of Psychology, University of Hawaii, Manoa, HI, United States

Leah Savery Northern Arizona University, Flagstaff, AZ, United States

Fiza Singh University of California, San Diego, CA, United States

Larry Stevens Northern Arizona University, Flagstaff, AZ, United States

Taylor N. West Northern Arizona University, Flagstaff, AZ, United States

C. Chad Woodruff Northern Arizona University, Flagstaff, AZ, United States

Preface

Since the summer of 2008, the Department of Psychological Sciences at Northern Arizona University (NAU) has conducted its own independent (of other Departments) Research Experiences for Undergraduates (REU) summer intensive research internships. REU Site Programs are sponsored by the National Science Foundation (NSF) across the United States for the purpose of creating a new generation of young scientists from diverse cultural backgrounds and supporting their development into doctoral-level careers in the *Professoriate*, that is, teaching and conducting their own research primarily in university settings. The lofty and visionary aim is to cross-fertilize science in this country with exciting new perspectives and creative ideas, ultimately toward the advancement of knowledge and of society. Each summer, and for some throughout the academic year, under-graduate students from across the country spend 8–10 weeks apprenticed for 40 h per week to faculty mentors at selected US universities conduct-ing the interns' own, but faculty supervised, research in a specific topic area. The NSF generously supports the travel, housing, dining, and mod-est research costs, and even provides a stipend, for these fortunate REU Research Interns.

NAU is uniquely positioned to offer such creative science programs not only because of its strong academic foundation and research productivity in the sciences but also because of its proximity to two culturally excit-ing, diverse, and developing Native American nations, the Hopi and the Dine (Navajo), the latter the largest Native American nation in the United States. Prior to the summer of 2008 and continuously for approximately 15 years, the Department had joined with the Department of Biological Sciences to offer REU internships in the broad arena of neural and behav-ioral sciences, but in 2005 the two departments decided to offer indepen-dent REUs in their respective specialty areas. Over the next 2 years, the Department of Psychological Sciences began the quest for development of a unique new standalone REU experience in a specialty area that fit with the general research interests of a majority of our faculty and was of con-temporary value to society. The general theme of Compassion was identi-fied and grant proposals were offered to the National Science Foundation for the funding of an REU Site Program in the Social Psychophysiology of

Compassion. And, given our interests and growing academic involvement with the Dine and Hopi Nations, we titled our REU program, *"Hojooba' bee la' hooniil, Undergraduate Studies into the Social Psychophysiology of Compassion."* Perhaps to best explain the Navajo origin of this title and our excitement with this research theme, we will quote from the original grant proposal:

> *In ancient Navajo lore, there is a story of a time long ago when children who were damaged or unwanted were placed in a pit beneath the Hogan where they would be cared for but also out of sight so as not to offend people. And the one who cared for these children was called "Twilight Boy", one of the four Navajo Deities, representing the evening light in the West. Twilight Boy possessed the attribute of "Hojooba' bee la' hooniil", translated from Navajo as "the expression of loving kindness as healing for the suffering of society", what in English we call "Compassion". From their origins in ancient stories and in the self-less behaviors of many of our ancestors, such acts of compassion have long captured the interests of social scientists. And even today, in contemporary psychological research, few ideas have won the attention of both academic researchers and the broad international community like current research into the construct of compassion. Perhaps of most remarkable focus has been the neuroimaging studies of Dr. Richard Davidson and colleagues at the University of Wisconsin who have placed 256-electrode arrays on the heads of Tibetan monk students of the Dali Lama meditating on compassion and have found striking elevations and synchrony of gamma EEG activity in neural circuitries related to empathy (Lutz et al., 2004; Brefczynski-Lewis et al., 2007), earning cover-story attention in the March 2005 National Geographic. And since these studies compared accomplished meditators with novices, there are reported implications for the ability to actually alter brain functioning with meditative compassion training, to actually train skills that promote happiness and compassion. In Developmental Psychology, Meltzoff's and others' formulations on the development of social cognition and empathy have illuminated how compassionate behaviors can be acquired in young children (Meltzoff, 2002; Meltzoff & Brooks, 2008). Similarly, Shaver and colleagues (Mikulincer & Shaver, 2005) have studied how attachment styles in children and adults relate to the development of compassion and altruism across the lifespan. Many of these ideas have been crystallized in a contemporary seminal text on this area by Gilbert (2005) entitled, Compassion: Conceptualisations, Research, and Use in Psychotherapy. And, more recently, the Center for Compassion and Altruism Research and Education (CCARE) has been established at the Stanford University School of Medicine for the purposes of fostering multidisciplinary studies of compassion.*

From this humble but exciting beginning, our REU program has received two 3-year cycles of funding and is now at the beginning of its third cycle under the able direction of Dr. Woodruff. And, in keeping with progress in compassion research, the program has evolved in exciting new directions, including mediators and moderators of relationships among critical psychological constructs and compassion, the role of mirror neurons in the manifestation of empathy and compassion, the neurological and psychosocial effects of compassion and meditation training, and the neuroscience of self-compassion.

One of the important components of our REU program each year has been the submission of proposals for compassion symposia to the Annual Meetings of the American Psychological Association (APA). These meetings represent the largest gathering of psychological researchers and practitioners in the world and provide a forum for the presentation of our REU interns' research. We have been most honored to have presented symposia nearly every year of funding to the APA conventions across the United States and Canada, most often to standing-room-only crowds. These presentations have been not only a culminating reward for our Interns and their hard work to generate quality research in this area but also allow communication with other researchers from around the world on this critical societal topic.

In August 2016 at the Toronto, Canada APA convention, we were approached by two book publishers and were invited to prepare an edited textbook on the neuroscience of compassion, directly taken from our REU research presentations and as a review of the current literature in this area. Following negotiations with both publishers and on the basis of goodness-of-fit between parties, we opted for the present relationship with Elsevier/Academic Press. This book represents the outcomes of that formative and highly rewarding relationship. We hope that you find our work together enjoyable, informative, illuminating, and stimulating of your own personal or professional pursuits into the neuroscience of empathy, compassion, and self-compassion.

The purpose of this is book is to inform the upper division undergraduate and the graduate student about the current neuroscience of empathy, compassion, and self-compassion. As an academic neuroscience textbook, it is loaded with neuroanatomy, more specifically the neurological sites involved in processes related to these critical mammalian prosocial constructs. At times, the content may seem tedious and pedantic, but we want the academic reader to understand the justification in the established literature and the important functionality and localizations for such statements as, "Given the rather established roles of dlPFC in selective attention and working memory, of vlPFC in response selection and inhibition, of dmPFC in the monitoring and processing of changing emotional states, of posterior temporal cortex (PTC) in perceptual and semantic representations of information, and of AMG as the repository of affective states, a model begins to emerge for the processing and regulation of emotions, including those experienced in compassion." We hope that such detailed descriptions serve to engage the reader in the neurological mechanisms underlying our everyday experiencing of these states of consciousness and to motivate our charges, and perhaps even yourselves, in some day conducting their/your own research to further advance our understanding and to perhaps help the world to become a more compassionate place. Our hope also is that this textbook will serve as a starting point for such academic inquiry through university courses involving *The Neuroscience of Empathy, Compassion, and Self-Compassion*. We have done so at our university to the popular acclaim of our students; we sincerely hope that you will witness the same rewards.

Toward this objective, we have assembled a collection of chapters overviewing the current neuroscience of the important psychosocial concepts of and related to empathy, compassion, and self-compassion. In Chapter 1, *What is this feeling that I have for myself and for others? Contemporary perspectives on empathy, compassion, and self-compassion, and their absence*, Stevens and Woodruff introduce the reader to important phylogenetic and ontogenetic discoveries in the origins of these constructs prosocially across a variety of animal species and some spiritual foundations in humans, to current understandings and controversies in defining empathy, compassion, and self-compassion, and to an engagement of the reader in a series of questions and debates regarding the finer details and inter-relationships of these ideas. In Chapter 2, *The brain that feels into others: Toward a neuroscience of empathy*, Flasbeck, Gonzalez-Liencres, and Brune explore in greater depth the definitional, phylogenetic, and contextual understandings of empathy, review current neurochemical, neuroimaging, and neurophysiological investigations, present manifestations of diminished empathy in neuropsychiatric disorders, and offer a clear and concise model of empathy as well as directions for future research. In Chapter 3, *The brain that longs to care for others: The current neuroscience of compassion*, Stevens and Benjamin start with defining compassion by presenting some personalized examples of compassion expression and erosion and then advance an argument based on current neuroscience research for the hierarchical and temporal organization of the experience of compassion and how it may, by this mechanism, be diminished. Research directions are then offered around this integrated theory for continued explorations into the neuroscience of compassion. In Chapter 4, *The brain that longs to care for itself: The current neuroscience of self-compassion*, Stevens, Gauthier-Braham, and Bush tackle the challenging rather pervasive absence of neuroscience research into the popular construct of self-compassion by examining current research findings on related subcomponents of self-compassion, those being self-kindness, mindfulness, and common humanity. On the basis of this review, a preliminary framework for the neuroscience of self-compassion, with suggested directions for future research, is offered that follows a delineated progression along cortical midline structures anteriorly to posteriorly during a prescribed meditation on these subcomponents.

Chapter 5, *Sometimes I get so mad I could . . . : The neuroscience of cruelty*, by West, Savery, and Goodman, examines neurologically and neuropsychiatrically what happens in the brain and behaviorally when empathy and compassion go away, both acutely and chronically. Such constructs as dehumanization, otherization, in-group/out-group prejudices, threat responses, moral judgments, anger, aggression, hatred, jealousy, envy, schadenfreude, social rejection, Machiavellianism, conduct disorders, personality disorders, psychopathy, and sexual violations are all considered in this chapter from a current neuroscience research perspective. In Chapter 6, *Reflections of others and of self: The mirror neuron system's relationship to empathy*, Woodruff takes the reader on an exciting journey into the new field of mirror neuron research, from the discovery of apparent mirroring neurons in the brains of macaque monkeys over two and a half decades ago, through the development and refinement of an extensive body of research inquiry into the manifestations, relationships, and neurological characteristics of mirroring in primate cortices, and up to the current status, controversies, and directions for future research in mirror neurons, mu-suppression, beta EEG rhythms, and their relationships to empathy. Chapter 7, *Why does it feel so good to care for others and for myself? Neuroendocrinology and prosocial behavior*, examines research investigating the critical, pervasive, but only recently understood role of neurohormones in the expression of empathic, compassionate, and self-compassionate behaviors. Birkett and Sasaki present current translational research from rodent studies to human clinical trials supporting the role of the neuropeptides oxytocin and vasopressin in the manifestation of these important prosocial behaviors, also with specific suggestions for continued research in this developing arena.

The past decade has seen a proliferation of compassion training programs, several directed at establishing neurological markers for the enhancement of compassionate behaviors. Chapter 8, *Can we change our mind about caring for others? The neuroscience of systematic compassion training*, by Calderon, Ahern, and Pruzinsky, reviews the current neuroscience literature on the neurobiological correlates and effects of some of the more popular of these interventions, including Cognitively Based Compassion Training (CBCT) and Compassion Cultivation Training (CCT), spotlights effects of long-term compassion meditation in highly experienced Tibetan meditators, and presents a newer program developed expressly for the inculcation of compassion in the primary and secondary educational setting, Project for Empathy and Compassion Education (PEACE). Existing neuroscience studies that examine neurological changes that occur across these developed training programs are presented, with colorful, detailed, integrative brain maps provided, and with methodological limitations and directions for future research offered. In Chapter 9, *Compassion training from an Early Buddhist perspective: The neurological concomitants of the*

Brahmaviharas, Goodman, Plonski, and Savery begin by conceptually distinguishing compassion from similar contemplative practices described in Early Buddhist scholarship known as the Brahmaviharas — loving-kindness, altruistic joy, and equanimity — as well as other contemplative practices that are foundational to the deliberate cultivation of compassion, such as focused attention and mindfulness. Weaving together Early Buddhist scholarship and evidence from the field of contemplative neuroscience, changes in neural activity that result from the deliberate cultivation of compassion are identified and differentiated from their contemplative cousins. In Chapter 10, *The language and structure of social cognition: An integrative process of becoming the other,* Pineda, Singh, and Chepak present empathy as a socially and neurologically profound "becoming" or knowing the other and offer psychosocial and neuroscience evidence to support this notion. A hierarchical/heterarchical model of social cognition is presented with higher order components more frontally localized and modulated by lower level processes. And Chapter 11, *Where caring for self and others lives in the brain, and how it can be enhanced, and diminished: Observations on the neuroscience of empathy, compassion, and self-compassion,* by Woodruff and Stevens, attempts to organize and to summarize all of the above chapter content into an integrative theory for the neuroscience of these constructs and a new model for the process of coming to understand and to care for another. We hope that across these chapters, we have satisfactorily represented the current state of the neuroscience of empathy, compassion, and self-compassion, but most importantly, have stimulated the reader's thinking about these complex concepts toward continued neuroscience research in these exciting areas.

Certainly this book, the REU program on Compassion, our most stimulating relationships with many undergraduate interns from across the United States, and the continued development of faculty collaborations, not only at NAU but also across the country, in the general research themes of empathy, compassion, and self-compassion would have been much more difficult and even formidable without the visionary support and continued encouragement of the staff at the National Science Foundation. We would particularly like to express our heartfelt gratitude to Dr. Fahmida Chowdhury, former Program Director, Multi-Disciplinary Activities, Social, Behavioral, and Economic Sciences and her outstanding Program Review Panels at the NSF. Dr. Chowdhury was always an available, highly professional and knowledgeable, and inspiring mentor who showed outstanding courage in supporting such an innovative REU program as ours, particularly, and perhaps with remarkable vision indeed, for a US federal agency that finds its roots in the military defense of our country.

And speaking of remarkable, the staff at Elsevier have been so indeed, particularly in suffering with us through the protracted and painful delays in the preparation, editing, and final proofing of each chapter in this book.

They stood with us patiently toward the ultimate completion of each component, offering understanding, guidance, and encouragement where needed. We are particularly grateful to Ms. Emily Ekles, Senior Acquisitions Editor, Ms. Barbara Makinster, Senior Editorial Project Manager, and Ms. Priya Kumaraguruparan, Production Project Manager at Elsevier.

REU programs hinge on the generosity of Faculty Mentors who give of their time, and in many cases sacrifice their summer holidays, in order to shepherd their wide-eyed charges through the often turbulent sea of psychosocial and neurophysiological research. This guidance includes collaborating with their Intern(s) on the selection of a doable research project, co-participating in review of relevant literature, precision design of a suitable study, laborious recruitment of research participants, painstaking data collection, processing, and analysis, creative preparation of research outcomes for oral and visual (posters and graphics) presentations, and eventual preparation and submission of scholarly manuscripts of the Interns' research. Needless to say, this is a lengthy and complicated process that is more often than not punctuated by interruptions, delays, disappointments, discoveries, personal and mechanical crises and failures, and a host of other impediments that such research is heir to. And, to add intensity and excitement to the process, all has to be completed for public oral dissemination at our own local REU Conference held at the end of the summer, after only 8–10 weeks! Sound formidable? It indeed is, but somehow our cadre of Faculty Mentors manages to pull it off. They make it all possible.

Over these past 7 years of our NSF-NAU REU, the following Faculty Mentors have somehow made it all happen: (2008) Drs. Melissa Birkett, Meliksah Demir, Andrew Gardner, Ann Huffman, Andy Walters, and Chad Woodruff; (2010) Drs. Meliksah Demir, Steven Funk, Ann Huffman, Larry Stevens, Andy Walters, Heidi Wayment, and Chad Woodruff; (2011) Drs. Steven Funk, Michael Rader, Larry Stevens, and Andy Walters; (2012) Drs. Melissa Birkett, Meliksah Demir, Larry Stevens, Daniel Weidler, and Chad Woodruff; (2014)[1] Drs. Melissa Birkett, Dana Donohue, Larry Stevens, Viktoria Tidikis, Daniel Weidler, and Chad Woodruff; (2015) Drs. Melissa Birkett, Dana Donohue, Robert Goodman, Daniel Weidler, and Chad Woodruff; (2016) Drs. Meliksah Demir, Robert Goodman, Larry Stevens, Daniel Weidler, and Chad Woodruff.

We have been most fortunate over these 7 years of NSF funding to be provided an Assistant Program Coordinator each year. The Assistant Program Coordinator works closely with the Program Coordinator/

---

[1] Due to federal budgetary uncertainties in the summer of 2013 culminating in the US government shutdown of October 2013, the second 3-year cycle of funding for our REU was delayed, preventing the start of the funding cycle in summer 2013. Consequently, the second 3-year cycle started in the summer of 2014.

Principal Investigator on the grant to implement all components of the project, including the logistical issues of travel to and from NAU, setting up housing and dining arrangements, organizing and implementing twice-weekly professional development luncheons and workshops and twice-monthly Northern Arizona cultural experiences (including a 3-day campout and tour of Navajo sacred sites and rituals in Monument Valley Navajo Tribal Park), organizing weekend social activities, and generally serving as "Mother Hen" for our flock of precious Interns each year. These indispensable operational activities have been most skillfully carried out each year by the following cadre of Department of Psychological Science Graduate Research Assistants: (2008) Ms. Donna Pisano, (2010) Ms. Amanda Berman, (2011) Ms. Kateryna Boyce, (2012) Ms. Kateryna Sylaska, (2014) Mr. David Avram, (2015) Ms. Andrea Brockman, and (2016) Mr. Anthony Stenson.

And, for the past 3 years of the REU grant, NAU has generously funded four Department of Psychological Sciences Graduate Research Assistants to co-mentor, co-supervise, and collaborate in each Intern's research activities. This Co-Mentor program has strategically incorporated students enrolled in our graduate program in the everyday activities of all components of conducting quality psychosocial and neuroscience research in our Department, not only providing our Interns with peer-supervision but also further training our graduate students in the critical skill set of teaching and conducting research. Our most able, highly skilled, and committed Co-Mentors for these past 3 years have been, (2014) Mr. Anthoni Goodman, Ms. Jessica Moschetto, Mr. Gavin Parsons, Mr. Max Williamson, (2015) Ms. Kristina Brookshire, Mr. Timothy Broom, Ms. Victoria VanPuyvelde, Mr. Jordan Wilkins, (2016) Ms. Alyssa Billington, Mr. Matt Brunskill, Mr. Michael Esposito, and Ms. Taylor West.

Certainly managing a nearly $1/2 million federal grant requires precise accounting, web design, and diverse administrative responsibilities. Keeping the financial wheels of this complex machine well-greased and seamlessly turning from week to week from year to year has been the responsibilities of Mrs. Janina Burton, Ms. Delfina Rodriguez, and Mrs. Denise Stippick. We shall always be deeply appreciative of and amazed at their diligence, attention to detail, and fiscal artistry in so skillfully managing this wonderful REU program.

And finally, the real heavy lifting, the future of social and neurological science in this country has fallen on the shoulders of a group of courageous and creative young people from across this land who chose to follow a very different path for their summer between academic semesters, for many a choice of leaving for the first time the predictability and familiarity of home for a distant, culturally unique, and environmentally spectacular oasis atop the Kaibab Plateau in Northern Arizona, that path being the quest for knowledge, the acquisition of psychophysiological research skills, the pursuit of careers in science, and the adventure of discovery of new ideas, of different peoples, and of diverse cultures. These Interns and their journeys are the reasons we Faculty Mentors have chosen the same path. We share their excitement of discovery and are honored to have been able to travel this path with them.

Our REU Interns for these past 7 years of funding are: (2008) Ms. Stephanie Antman (University of Arizona), Ms. Siomara Enriquez (NAU), Ms. Shaness Grenald (St. Johns University), Mr. Sean Guillory (Texas State University), Ms. Jophina Joe (NAU), Ms. Janelle Matthews (NAU), and Mr. Anthony Smallcanyon (Dine College);

(2010) Ms. Ashanti Bragg (Norfolk State University), Mr. Michael Brower (NAU), Mrs. Lynnette Cuellar (University of New Mexico), Ms. Janeen Denny (Dine College), Ms. Michelle Harris (University of Arizona), Mr. Akiee Mayon (NAU), Mr. Ivan Valenzuela (NAU), and Ms. Christine Villasenor (Fort Lewis College);

(2011) Ms. Dibely Acosta (University of New Mexico), Mrs. Kristina Bell (Fort Lewis College), Ms. Jasmine Benjamin (NAU), Ms. Taylor Fellbaum (The College of St. Scholastica), Ms. Jazmin Johnson (Howard University), Ms. Mica McGriggs (NAU), Ms. Sara Mouhktar (Carnegie Mellon University), and Ms. Alanna Pugliese (University of Miami);

(2012) Ms. Courtney Allen (University of Wisconsin), Mr. Joseph Bonner (Villanova University), Mr. Jonathan Gordils (University of Connecticut), Ms. Jasmine Johnson (Norfolk State University), Ms. Marissa Martinez (University of New Mexico), Ms. Haley Pruitt (Fort Lewis College), Mr. Brett Velez (Glendale Community College), and Mrs. Dawn Whinnery (Arizona Western College);

(2014) Ms. Imani Belton (North Carolina Agricultural & Technical State University), Ms. Hannah Brown (Macalester College), Ms. Amanda Garcia (NAU), Ms. Anastasia Gusakova (Beloit College), Mr. Tyrone McCullough (Charleston Southern University), Ms. Christina Rico (NAU), Ms. Alyssa Sanchez (Occidental College), Ms. Misty Stevens (Old Dominion University), and Ms. Rebecca von Oepen (California State University, Monterey Bay);

(2015) Mr. Toe Aung (Albright College), Ms. Cheyenne Begay (NAU), Ms. Stephanie Esquivel (California State University, Northridge), Ms. Tiana Hans (NAU), Ms. Katherine Ilecki (NAU), Mr. Tyler Jimenez (Fort Lewis College), Ms. Joan Paul (Coconino Community College), and Ms. Ariel Shirley (Northland Pioneer College);

(2016) Ms. Danielle Adams (NAU), Mr. Adam Calderon (Quinnipiac University), Ms. Caeli Diamond (Cleveland State University), Ms. Claire Grant (State University of New York, Geneseo), Ms. Lorena Lechuga Gutierrez (NAU), Ms. Emma Nettles (University of South Carolina, Aiken), Mr. Jeremy Petty (Alabama A&M University), and Ms. Taylor Pondy (NAU).

And, as we close the Preface to this book, we would like to leave the reader with a fitting affirmation for the completion of any laborious work.

The Buddhist Prayer on the Completion of 100,000 Prostrations

By this effort,
May all sentient beings
Be free of suffering.

May their minds be filled
With the Nectar of Virtue.

In this way,
May all causes resulting in suffering
Be extinguished.

And only the light of Compassion
Shine throughout all realms.

—Jetsunma

Larry C. Stevens
C. Chad Woodruff
Northern Arizona University

1

What Is This Feeling That I Have for Myself and for Others? Contemporary Perspectives on Empathy, Compassion, and Self-Compassion, and Their Absence

Larry Stevens, C. Chad Woodruff

Northern Arizona University, Flagstaff, AZ, United States

Our comprehension of the concepts of Empathy, Compassion, and Self-Compassion is by no means settled at this stage of scientific and public discourse. This realization is particularly striking within the context of compassion, as this idea has been around for well over 2500 years. Even more remarkable, perhaps, is our understanding of the expression of empathy, which according to de Waal can be traced back well beyond the emergence of humans and our closest ape and chimpanzee primate ancestors to its earliest vestiges in the expressions of self-other differentiation, emotional contagion, and preconcern in dolphins, whales, and elephants (de Waal, 2009). The notion of self-compassion, which also finds its origin in early Buddhist teachings, is perhaps the most clearly understood of the three, largely due to the contemporary formulations of Neff (2003a,b). In this chapter, we will explore the origins and definitions of these three concepts by engaging in a stream of polemical encounters between the authors of this narrative. We shall also consider consequences of the absence of each of these expressions in human behavior. In so departing from the more typical manner of only academically introducing and discussing important concepts in the introductory chapter of this textbook, we hope to engage the reader in not only the depth, complexity, and implications

The Neuroscience of Empathy, Compassion, and Self-Compassion. http://dx.doi.org/10.1016/B978-0-12-809837-0.00001-5

of these terms, but perhaps more importantly in a creative exploration and beginning consensus toward their meanings in and ultimate ramifications for contemporary culture.

ORIGINS

As noted above, we can trace the origin of empathic behavior to the actions of nonprimate mammals, most remarkably to elephants, dolphins, and whales. De Waal estimates that the neurological vestiges of empathy stretch back over a hundred million years and can be witnessed in motor mimicry and emotional contagion in primitive mammalian species (de Waal, 2009). We rather commonly see these manifestations in mockingbirds imitating the whistles and calls of other birds and even of humans (*mimicry*), in dogs howling to the plaintive cries of coyotes in the distance or, perhaps more compelling, in human infants in a nursery joining in after one starts to cry (*emotional contagion*). And perhaps in a more advanced but still primitive vestige of empathy, the expression of what de Waal calls *preconcern* may be seen in the seemingly automatic approach behavior of young rhesus monkeys to an injured peer, when the comfort of mother is also closely available. There are numerous compelling examples of nonhuman primates manifesting behavior which clearly appears to be empathic. Such behavior is hypothesized to have emerged because of its evolutionarily selective, prosocial, protective, and survival value (Decety, Norman, Berntson, & Cacioppo, 2012; de Waal, 2008, 2009; Gonzalez-Liencres, Shamay-Tsoory, & Brüne, 2013; Preston & de Waal, 2002).

A perhaps most telling example of apparently fully developed empathy in animals even lower on the phylogenetic scale, in elephants, is the following account from de Waal:

> I saw an incredible act of targeted helping. An older female, perhaps close to 65, fell down in the middle of the night. It was a very rainy, muddy jungle environment, difficult for us to walk around, I can only imagine how difficult it was for a tired old female to get up. For hours, mahouts and volunteers alike tried to lift her. In the meantime, her close companion, Mae Mai, an unrelated female of about 45, refused to leave her side. I say refused because mahouts were trying to get her out of the way (tempting her with food). She may have sensed that they were trying to help, because after repeated tries to lift the fallen female with human hands and with another elephant tethered to her, Mae Mai, in a rather agitated state, got alongside the old female, and with her head, tried to push her up. She repeatedly tried to do so, ending each failed attempt with frustrated trunk smacks to the ground and rumbling. She seemed highly committed to staying with her friend.
>
> When the old female died, a few days later, Mae Mai urinated uncontrollably, and started bellowing loudly. When the mahouts tried to take down a large wooden frame to try and raise the old female, Mae Mai got in the way and wouldn't let the wood

anywhere near her dead friend. Mae Mai then spent the next two days wandering around the park bellowing at the top of her voice every few minutes, causing the rest of the herd to respond with similar sounds (de Waal, 2009, 133–134).

We see in this retelling of an observation of elephant behavior in Thailand the preconcern, emotional contagion, and even what de Waal calls *insightful assistance* in Mae Mai's emotional response to her friend's demise. Such behavior bears a remarkable resemblance to the experience of loss of a dear friend or relative and bereavement in more advanced mammals, including humans, perhaps in the above story with a painful failure to sufficiently differentiate self from other and with subsequent prolonged emotional distress.

Compassion evolutionarily is a much more recent concept and may require the emergence of higher order executive processing not available to nonprimate mammals. Nonetheless, it is important to note evidence of apparent compassionate and altruistic behavior in animals other than primates, as the example above suggests. In studies of fossilized remains of ancient hominins, anthropological evidence indicates that compassionate/altruistic behavior has likely been around in early humans for well over a million years. For example, remains of cranial, brain, dental, and mandible congenital deformities and injuries indicate that these individuals survived sometimes for decades when to do so would be impossible without the care of others (Hublin, 2009).

Wang (2005) has presented a compelling and detailed explanation for the evolution of such acts of compassion in the relatively recent development of a physiologically based, largely parasympathetic/vagal, prosocial species-preservative system, in direct juxtaposition to the more ancient sympathetic-dominated self-preservative system. This more contemporary neurohormonal network evolved from maternal instincts to protect the vulnerable human infant and to promote its welfare through its fragile growth, ultimately leading to the recruitment of support from clan conspecifics toward this objective, and led to the creation of the physiological infrastructure for the emergence of compassion. This species-preservative system comprises (1) an enlarged neocortex including intricately interconnected and bilaterally differentiated prefrontal and thalamocingulate pathways allowing an improved differentiation of self from other and the experience of *receptive emotional prosody*, or the ability to understand the emotional information conveyed by another (Davidson, 2002; MacLean, 1990); (2) a newly evolved ventral vagal complex (Porges, 1995, 2003) which allows an immediate, moment-to-moment fine-tuning of physiological and affect regulation, further promoting social engagement behaviors including "looking, listening, facial expression, vocalizing, filtering of low-frequency sounds for the discrimination of human voices from background sounds, head gestures, & ingestion;" and (3) the elaboration of the posterior pituitary hormone oxytocin from its original role in parturition and nursing to the facilitation of kinship and clan emotional bonding. In this manner, mother–infant bonding, caregiving, and familiarity behaviors emerged as an evolutionary template for the development of a constellation of social engagement, species-preservative behaviors leading to the emergence of compassion (Goetz, Keltner, & Simon-Thomas, 2010; Wang, 2005). The underpinnings of this evolutionary model for the development of compassion in (1) the care of vulnerable offspring, (2) sexual selection theory, and (3) the formation of protective, prosocial kinship bonds has been supported in a more recent empirical review by Goetz et al. (2010).

While very early dating of hominin acts of compassion and the evolution of an elaborate species-preservative prosocial system are largely inferential, more recently but still thousands of years ago, we see the written emergence of compassion. Some of these earliest writings encouraging the practice of compassion may be found in ancient Vedic Upanishads dated to the fifth to sixth centuries BCE and in the earliest of Buddhist meditations on the Four Noble Truths circa 500 BCE. Later we see it emerge in the Islamic Qur'an in the recitations of Rahman, in the ideals of Tzedakah in the Jewish Torah, across the Christian Bible in stories, sermons, and prayers, and passed down in the aural history of Native Peoples in the Americas for hundreds of years. Today, compassion is championed across many religious institutions, but its most prolific proponent and enthusiastic advocate is His Holiness Tenzin Gyatso, the 14th Dalai Lama (Lama, 1984, 1995, 1997, 2011).

Self-compassion also finds its roots in early Buddhism but may even be traceable to primate self-grooming behavior (de Waal, 2009). The Buddha is reported to have said, "It is possible to travel the whole world in search of one who is more worthy of compassion than oneself. No such person can be found" (Tatia & Upasak, 1973). In the early stages of the ancient practice of *Metta*, or loving-kindness, Meditation, the aspirant is advised to first feel loving-kindness toward the self, then in a progressive sequence toward various others (Analayo, 2015; Gethin, 1998; Kornfield, 1993, 2009). Notwithstanding its objective of relieving suffering in others, Buddhism has long extolled the virtue of compassion toward the self.

More recently, this concept has been popularized in the writings and research of Kristin Neff, who differentiates self-compassion from the long-standing Western focus on self-esteem as an important marker for psychological health. Neff explains that self-esteem is based in social comparisons and judgments of self-worth and is often associated with self-absorption, self-centeredness, narcissism, diminished concern for others, out-group prejudice, and even aggression and violence (Neff, 2003a). Self-compassion, on the other hand, is associated with feelings of loving kindness (*Metta*) toward one's self, with mindfulness, balance, or equanimity and nonjudgment and receptivity toward one's thoughts, feelings, and experiences, and with a sense of common-humanity or belongingness to the family of personkind. Neff and colleagues have established a considerable body of contemporary research attesting to the psychological and physical well-being of such feelings of compassion toward the self (Neff, 2003b).

DEFINITIONS

Empathy

There are clearly as many definitions of empathy as there are "fish in the sea," that is, philosophers and researchers investigating this complex concept. Origins of the expression may be found in the ancient Greek term *empatheia*, literally en (in) pathos (passion). However, in 1873 the philosopher, Robert Vischer, was the first to use in print the German expression *Einfühlung*, meaning "feeling into" as an expression for analyzing works of art. In 1909, Edward Bradford Titchener, the student of Wilhelm Wundt, one of the founding fathers of the discipline of Psychology and of the school of Structural Psychology, translated this German expression into the English term, *Empathy*, and applied it to the experience of analyzing human behavior (Stueber, 2017).

From these origins, empathy has retained the notion of *feeling into* the experiences of another. However, considerable variability has developed in the elaborations of this concept. The eminent German philosopher and psychologist, Theodor Lipps, highlighted the notion of projecting oneself into another and feeling the passion of their experiences. More recently, de Waal (2009) incorporated Lipp's notion by explaining empathy as unconsciously merging oneself with another and feeling their experiences within ourselves. De Waal further traces the ontogeny and phylogeny of empathy to the involuntary, bottom-up process of *emotional contagion* described earlier. From this perspective on empathy, the neuroscientist might expect to see brain regions involved in the more pure, even unconscious experiencing of emotions.

Tania Singer and colleagues have retained the preeminence of an automatic shared affective response but have identified four components, comprising (1) an affective sharing, (2) an isomorphism of this affective sharing, (3) a mental representation of the other's affective state, and (4) the differentiation of self from other, enabling the observer to understand the affective state as belonging to the other rather than to the self (Singer & Lamm, 2009). A critical component of this elaborated definition is the fourth, top-down discrimination of self from other, allowing a more contextually-, interpersonally-, and perceptually-rich representation of the other's affective response. Though one could argue about whether empathy is a discrete variable that either is or is not present, or whether it is a continuous variable ranging from primitive components such as emotional contagion to more sophisticated empathy involving self-other discrimination, without the fourth component, the observer is vulnerable to reacting to a shared affective state as though it were her own affective state that she were experiencing (e.g., leading to personal distress).

This recognition of a four-stage process of empathic responding has led to the more contemporary understanding of empathy as composed of at least two components, *emotional empathy* and *cognitive empathy* (Decety & Jackson, 2004). Such a differentiation may be seen in the writings of *Simulation Theorists* who suggest that we infer the internal states of others by projecting ourselves into their states and then reading the other's internal experiences from our own. This notion stands in contrast to those of *Theory Theorists* who speculate that we develop cognitive theories about others' mental states from our own experiences and constructions (Batson, 2011b; See the Theory of Mind section in Chapter 3 for further explanation of these concepts). Similar understandings of empathy may be seen in the extrapolations of Decety and Jackson (2004) who propose three interacting functional components of human empathy, comprising (1) affective sharing, (2) self-other awareness, and (3) mental flexibility combined with regulatory processes. Eisenberg and Eggum (2009), from a more developmental perspective, also conceptualize empathy as composed of an affective sharing coupled with self-other differentiation and necessary cognitive regulation in order to avoid over-identification and personal distress. And, Baron-Cohen (2011) defines empathy as the identification of another's feelings and thoughts and the appropriately modulated emotional response to that experience. Thus, we see an evolution of our understanding of empathic responding from an original, more automatic "feeling into" the experiences of another to increasing attention to the cognitive modulation of such affective sharing coupled with necessary differentiation of self from other.

Compassion

The word compassion derives from the Latin expression *compati*, meaning literally to suffer with. Considered among all of the world's major religious traditions as one of the most cherished of virtues, compassion is widely accepted as a sensitivity to the suffering of another and a desire to alleviate that suffering (Goetz et al., 2010). Implicit in this definition are several components. One is first the presence of empathy, the ability to understand another's feelings and experiences, including the ability to take perspective on another and to engage in self-other differentiation. But with compassion, one "feels into" the negative experience of another only enough to understand that they are suffering. One then cognitively identifies that the other is suffering and directs one's attention to the alleviation of that suffering. With compassion, there is a more immediate self-other differentiation and shifting (perhaps as a personally—lessens emotional distress—and prosocially adaptive process) to a recognition of general suffering and to attention to helping. For example, another may feel sadness at the loss of a friend, but the observer experiences this sadness only briefly, cognitively identifies this sadness as suffering, and experiences the desire to help in some way. This "feeling with" nature of compassion differentiates it from the "feeling into" characteristic of empathy and suggests a more top-down processing dominance in the experience of compassion relative to the lingering automatic experiencing of the other's sadness that occurs with empathy. On the assumption that compassion recruits higher level control processes, one might expect to see more frontal lobe activity to occur during compassion.

Compassion is thus composed of three components: (1) (brief) affective empathy, (2) a cognitive labeling of the experience as "sadness," and so on, and (3) a desire to help (see Singer & Lamm, 2009 for a similar understanding). The third component of compassion which differentiates it from empathy is the desire to alleviate the suffering of the other. One does not have to actually help the other but only to have the desire to do so. In fact, the Buddha was asked by a disciple how one can truly practice compassion by meditating in seclusion. The Buddha replied that retreating into compassionate meditation is an integral part of the cultivation of compassion, as long as the aspirant possesses the desire and motivation to benefit others, and in fact such practice better lays the foundation for a compassionate life by purifying the mind of defilements. Doing so actually leads to "sympathetic joy" in the delight of preparing for the alleviation of suffering in others (Analayo, 2015). This desire to lessen suffering also represents a likely frontal, top-down planning, rehearsal, and anticipated execution of helping behaviors and accordingly may also involve prefrontal motor components. An additional outcome of compassion meditation and practice is the potential creation of more positive affective states than one might experience in pure empathic responding. Thus, overall, neurological manifestations of compassion contemplation may well be quite different from those of empathy, recruiting cortical regions more involved in information processing, planning, and execution of motor behaviors.

Definitions of altruism span the gamut from a mere motivational state designed to help others (Batson, 2011a) to the actual engagement in helping behaviors (Monroe, 1996). Ricard (2015) defines authentic altruism as the motivational state having the objective of advancing the welfare of another. According to Ricard, altruism can occur in the presence of pure joy and happiness, in contrast to compassionate helping which follows suffering (although true compassion-motivated helping is associated with "sympathetic joy" in the alleviation of another's suffering; see Analayo, 2015 above). Both are thus associated with approach behaviors and prosocial motivation.

Compassion, empathic concern, and sympathy are often used interchangeably, thus confusing their meanings. Empathic concern seems more similar to empathy, with the exception that empathy involves more affective sharing, a "feeling into" the other whereas empathic concern indicates a more "feeling for" or other-oriented focus of the observer's feelings (Singer & Lamm, 2009). Sympathy remains difficult to disentangle from compassion, as they are often considered synonyms (de Waal, 2009; Eisenberg & Strayer, 1990). Sympathy derives from the Latin expression, *sympatheia*, meaning literally "feeling (patheia) together (sym)." In common parlance, however, sympathy lacks the desire to help component that is found more typically in use of the term compassion. Pity, derived from the Latin *"pietas"* or pious, not only suggests a feeling of sorrow or distress over one's suffering but also a subtle elevation of the observer, or feeling of superiority, over the sufferer (Goetz et al., 2010; Ricard, 2015).

With a slightly different take on the relationship between empathy and compassion, Singer and Klimecki, who have written and researched most extensively about the neuroscience of empathy, consider compassion to be a sub-type of the empathic response to suffering (Singer & Klimecki, 2014). According to their model, one can experience either of two responses to the observation of suffering in another, empathic distress or empathic concern, the latter they call "compassion" (or sympathy). These two responses are distinguished by either self-focused, aversive, and avoidant perspectives and behavior, for empathic distress, or other-focused, more positive, and approach perspectives and behavior, for empathic concern (compassion). Thus, a critical component of these differential responses is the success of self-other differentiation; the over-involvement, or over-identification, of self in the perception of another's suffering produces personal distress, while the ability to separate one's self-perception from that of another allows the experiencing of more compassionate, prosocial helping motivation and behaviors. Such a differentiation of self from other has been operationalized in one of the more popular measures of empathy, the Interpersonal Reactivity Index, which measures perspective-taking, empathic concern, fantasy, and personal distress (Davis, 1980).

Self-Compassion

Self-compassion is quite simply compassion for oneself, or a sensitivity to one's own suffering and a desire to alleviate that suffering. Although self-compassion finds it roots in early Buddhist meditative practices, the concept has been more recently elaborated, as mentioned above, in the extensive works of Neff (2003a,b). Neff conceptualizes self-compassion as composed of three bipolar subcomponents: (1) Self-Kindness versus Self-Judgment, (2) Mindfulness versus Over-Identification, and (3) Common Humanity versus Isolation (Neff, 2003b). Therefore, self-compassion is feeling the same loving kindness toward oneself that a compassionate person would feel toward another coupled with the desire to alleviate any suffering one may feel, a sense of equanimity toward all things, or being in the moment without undue attention to any one thing over another, and an awareness of membership in the community of personkind with all of the joys, successes, disappointments, losses, and tribulations of the rest of humanity, a sense of all of us being in this process of living together. From a neuroscience perspective, one might predict rather diffuse involvement of cognitive and affective processes across the cortex during the experience of true self-compassion. (See Chapter 4 for a presentation of the neuroscience of self-compassion.)

AND THEIR ABSENCE: A WORLD WITHOUT EMPATHY, COMPASSION, OR SELF-COMPASSION

It is a sobering thought indeed to consider a world void of the ability to "feel into" or "with" others or to feel loving-kindness toward oneself. There are tragically a few examples of human and even nonhuman primate subcultural and species groups that appear to lack empathy. For example, among monkeys, there are numerous indicators of an abject lack of empathic concern. de Waal (2009) recounts compelling episodes of mother baboons crossing a river leaving their offspring on the other side to either drown or be eaten by predators, seemingly oblivious to their cries. Fortunately, in our Western culture, we have only isolated examples, some think too many, of individuals or groups who seem to be void of empathy. Baron-Cohen (2011) considers the erosion and absence of empathy to be the sources of cruelty in our culture. According to Baron-Cohen, empathy erosion results from (1) the objectification of others; (2) temporary states of mind such as conformity to subgroup norms, obedience to authority, or vengeful, protective, resentful, or hateful behaviors; and (3) more permanent psychological traits, such as Psychopathy, Borderline Personality Disorders, and Narcissism. A similar empathy valence, or gradient, explanation for the neurological basis of moral cognition has been offered by Blair and Blair (2011), Moll, Zahn, de Oliveira-Souza, Krueger, and Grafman (2005), and others. Certainly given the close connection between empathy and compassion, we can assume that similar pathologies, insensitivities, and cruelties result from the absence of compassion as well. One need only reference the horrid atrocities that occurred in this country during the 18th and 19th centuries against primarily Africans and African-Americans during slavery to witness the consequences of a suspension of compassion.

Regarding a dearth of self-compassion, Neff and colleagues (MacBeth & Gumley, 2012; Neff, 2003b; Neff, Kirkpatrick, & Rude, 2007a; Neff, Rude, & Kirkpatrick, 2007b; Neff & Vonk, 2009) have established negative relationships between this psychological construct and depression, anxiety, neurotic perfectionism, rumination, avoidance of unwanted thoughts, and negative mood, and positive relationships with self-esteem, self-acceptance, self-determination, autonomy, competence, relatedness, happiness, optimism, positive mood, reflective wisdom, personal initiative, curiosity and exploration, agreeableness, extroversion, conscientiousness, and numerous other positive psychological constructs. Positive relationships have also been found between self-compassion and multiple physical measures as well (Arch, Landy, & Brown, 2016; Breines et al., 2014, 2015; Friis, Johnson, Cutfield, & Consedine, 2015; Hall, Row, Wuensch, & Godley, 2013; Petrocchi, Ottaviani, & Couyoumdijian, 2017; Svendsen et al., 2016; Zessin, Dickhauser, & Garbade, 2015). Clearly, an absence of self-compassion can have pervasive deleterious effects on psychological and physiological well-being.

We will not elaborate further the impacts of an absence of empathic, compassionate, and self-compassionate attitudes and responding on individuals and society, as these effects, and their neurological correlates, are detailed in Chapter 5 in this book. Let it suffice here to say that individuals and societies lacking in these important psychosocial constructs suffer in a multitude of ways in modern society.

INTERROGATIVES AND POLEMICS

Certainly our understandings of the complexities inherent in the concepts of empathy, compassion, and self-compassion are limited at this stage of the science. Many questions remain and we hope to address some of these puzzlements in the remainder of this chapter. We will do so by presenting a number of these questions and then engage in a dialogue and sometimes debate regarding potential answers. By no means do we pretend to have all of these answers, and we hope that this discussion will stimulate students of these important, yes even critical, social constructs to consider their answers, to ask more questions, and to begin their own research toward our further understandings.

Should compassion be defined as simply a mental state or should the definition entail a requisite and corresponding behavior?

Woodruff: Compassion is often described as something one experiences for a target object/entity. The experience is often described as a feeling for another person involving an interest in that person's well-being. Framed as such, compassion is purely mental. Though it may motivate helping behavior, if it is just a mental state, then there would be no requirement that a behavior follow. Compassion happens when a person feels it, whether or not one acts on it.

Stevens: I disagree somewhat: I believe, as stated above, that compassion is affective, cognitive, and, at least implicitly, behavioral, but to different degrees for the first two components than empathy (empathy alone does not involve the third component). That is, compassion involves a brief period of affective empathy but is quickly followed by a more cognitive appraisal of the victim's status, suffering (with well-developed self-other differentiation) coupled with the affective experience of that suffering, then followed by further mentalizing about how to help, with implicit motor efferents related to the nature of the desired assistance. Empathy, on the other hand, involves a much larger affective component involving the "sharing" of the other's experiences, with or without subsequent mentalizing, especially concerning self-other differentiation. Therefore, we should see affective and cognitive valence differences between empathy and compassion, with the addition of motor efferents with compassion. This hypothesis would certainly be testable in a research context.

Woodruff: Then, what about the occasions in which one feels compassion for someone(s) that s/he does not even know, or groups of suffering individuals not individually known? How can we feel compassion for common humanity?

Stevens: As a partial answer to this question, I would fall back on the explanation of the Projective Hypothesis, that when presented with ambiguous stimuli and the social pressure to interpret these stimuli, humans will project their own "implicit motivations," values, and perspectives into those ambiguous stimuli (Rapaport, 1942, 1967). So, when I hear impassioned news reports of the tragic personal losses from Hurricane Harvey flooding in South Texas, I recall my own frightening experiences with flooding, project those affective states and memories onto South Texans, feel my pain and suffering as their pain and suffering, consider how I can possibly help, and thus feel compassion for people with whose personal suffering I have no direct experience.

Woodruff: Your definition of compassion above may miss something important about this social construct. To employ a reductio ad absurdum, by this definition, we would have to call a sadistic torturer compassionate if, despite his cruel actions, his mental state were one of compassion. Indeed, it has been reported that some who have sexually assaulted children actually felt something akin to sympathy for their victims. That is, they seemed to regret the harmful impacts on the child while at the same time, deriving some sense of reward from the action causing that harm. Is this mental state of concern for the victim compassion?

Stevens: Your sadistic torturer question is an interesting one. If the torturer is a sadist, then by definition, s/he cannot be compassionate, because s/he is putting his/her pleasure over that of another, is causing their suffering for his/her own reward and is not directing his/her actions at the relief of their suffering. Now, if the person is "just" a torturer, and they believe that their torture will lessen the suffering of others, then I would claim that they are indeed being compassionate. (I am not sanctioning torture here and I would hope that one would search far and wide to find alternative ways of caring for others, certainly ways that are more effective and do not involve harming anyone.) The first argument would hold for the pedophile, since they clearly put their own pleasure over the suffering of the victim. So, the answer is in the purpose of their behavior, their mentalizing. Was Robert Oppenheimer being compassionate in heading up the creation of the atomic bomb, especially given its use on Japan to end that part of WWII? I think yes, but I was not in his head at the time. It likely was more compassion-less, or acompassionate, if that is a word, more excited and perhaps dissociated mentalizing about the possibilities of nuclear physics, with a huge "Oh Shit" later. "I am become Death," he said afterward, "the destroyer of worlds." So, again, the mentalizing component of compassion is an essential and definitive part of this process.

Does compassion require empathy? Must one feel another's bodily state, and/or must one have cognitive awareness of another's perspective in order to experience compassion for that person?

Woodruff: One possible answer is no. Compassion meditation can involve compassion for individuals whom the meditator does not know. For example, one could have compassion for all living beings, as mentioned above.

Stevens: As I suggest earlier, yes, compassion requires empathy, but only briefly, after which the observer moves on to the above-described mentalizing. I think we impute/project our own affective experiences onto others with whom we are less familiar, believe that we are feeling their affect, realize that they are suffering, and engage in relief desires/ planning. Singer and colleagues' (de Vignemont & Singer, 2006; Singer & Lamm, 2009) notion of "shared neural representations" suggests that it is *our* pain that we are feeling when we empathize with another, not theirs. That pain may actually be very different from the other's pain, but we "project" it onto the other in order to understand their suffering.

Woodruff: I think you and/or Singer are looking at self-other relationships as a binary choice—you are either focused on self or on other. But I think representations of others' affect can be classified as ones that are recognized as belonging to the other and ones that are falsely seen as belonging to the self when in fact they belong to the other. Put differently, there is the self feeling the self's feelings. There's the self feeling his body's best simulation of the other's feelings as though it were the self's feelings (if negative feelings, you would have personal distress). And then, there's the self feeling his body's best simulation of the other's feelings as being the other's feelings. Put more simplistically:

1. Self represents self,
2. Self represents other as self,
3. Self represents other as other.

It is number 2 that I think Singer confuses as empathy when it is not—under my definition. It is not empathy because it is a failure to recognize that the experienced affect is not one's own, and therefore, attention will be focused on those representations motivated by the belief that these are one's own affectations. Empathy requires that the self not only experience the other's affect, but that the self be motivated to focus on the fact that these are the affective states (he believes) the other is experiencing. In this latter case, mental representations are about the other. In the former case, mental representations are about the self and therefore could not be considered empathic.

Stevens: I agree; I think we often are too categorical in answering such probing questions. Doubtlessly, empathic responding falls on a continuum, or some multidimensional space, that better represents the process of self-other differentiation. Your formulations seem philosophically tenable, if not empirically testable.

Stevens: Now, coming back to the question of whether one has to be able to empathize in order to be compassionate? I think the answer is more complex, because of the presence of both affective and cognitive empathy. We could engage the "projective hypothesis," experience affective empathy for the other, and then move on to a mentalizing about their suffering. But also one could cognitively empathize, for example, *know* that someone is in pain, without feeling their pain, realize that they are suffering, and then desire to alleviate their suffering, thus being compassionate without affective empathy. As long as we define empathy as affective and/or cognitive, then one generally engages some form of empathy when being compassionate. However, if all that is required in our definition of compassion is that we know, cognitively, that someone is suffering and we desire to alleviate their suffering, then we *could* experience compassion without any emotional empathy. That seems satisfactory to me, since the objective of compassion is the ultimate alleviation of the suffering of others.

Woodruff: And, one can be compassionate toward others without any recognition of any specific suffering. Isn't that true? We really have to nail that one down. Because if it is true, that indicates immediately that no specific instance of empathizing is necessary for compassion because you can be compassionate toward individuals about whom you know nothing, other than that they are citizens of the universe.

Stevens: Consider my comments above regarding the projective hypothesis. I think this process is more pervasive and nuanced in our perceptions of other's behavior than we give it credit. I have a dear friend who feels considerable, very affective, compassion for me because he "knows" that I will not experience the rapture some day because I do not share his religious beliefs. He also knows that I am not presently suffering in this regard, but his experiences of his own previous suffering are projected into the future onto my pending suffering and he "knows" that this suffering will be pretty severe. His compassion for me is salient and quite genuine and I cherish him for this caring for me and for others. Yet, there is no suffering presently. Isn't compassion wonderful!

Woodruff: Of course, this also begs the question of whether compassion requires a behavior or whether it is simply a mental state that can be associated with helping behavior, but need not necessarily.

Stevens: I'll refer you to my and Jasmine Benjamin's Chapter 3 on the neuroscience of compassion. We argue that there must be an at least implicit motor component to compassion in the desire to help and we suggest that one manifestation of this component may be the mirror neuron system in the brain.

Does empathy necessarily lead to compassion?

Woodruff: The answer to this question is highly dependent on a precise definition of empathy, which we explored above. Speaking in broad terms however, it is likely that empathy can facilitate compassion. While it might be possible to experience compassion for an individual without knowledge of her experiences, it seems plausible that embodied simulation of her experiences and/or allocentric spatial representation of her experiences would lead to compassion in the observer. Note, that we are not arguing that empathy would be a sufficient cause, or even a necessary cause.

Stevens: I believe that empathy does not necessarily lead to compassion, but may, depending on the mental set of the observer. The "pure" empath shares the neural representations of the other; that's it in some cases. The subsequent mentalizing, to the extent that it occurs, determines whether they feel empathic distress, cognitively regulated empathic concern, or compassion. (We have elaborated this idea into a figure that we present in Chapter 11 which attempts to capture the differences among empathic concern, empathy, sympathy, and compassion. But, we hope that the reader will savor the ensuing chapters before reviewing this figure in order to appreciate the ideas and research findings that have gone into its development.)

Is empathy Feeling Into or Reasoning Into? Are there two types of Empathy: Emotional vs. Cognitive Empathy?

Woodruff: Some (e.g., Lamm & Singer, 2010; Singer & Lamm, 2009) suggest that the primary sense of empathy involves feeling what another person feels. Given that the German word from which empathy was derived, *einfühlung*, is translated into English as "to feel into," it seems reasonable to suggest that this is simply what empathy is—feeling what another feels. According to Singer and Lamm (2009), this seems to entail that the feelings are felt as belonging to the other person. Some have called this perspective-taking (and self-other discrimination). However, some additionally consider perspective-taking a cognitive function. Now the question being begged is whether this cognitive component is part of empathy, or, because it lacks the necessary feeling component implied by einfühlung, is something distinct from empathy? Those who argue that empathy involves primarily the feeling aspect of knowing another's experience call the more cognitive means to this end mentalizing. Mentalizing is generally considered to result in a Theory of Mind. This is a process whereby one infers the mental state of another deduced form behavioral observations.

Stevens: As mentioned above, I would argue that "pure" feeling into another's affect would involve, at its extreme, complete absorption into their feelings, an approximation of what Singer calls a "shared neural representation." This would not necessarily be healthy and would lead to empathic distress in most cases. (Read Le Guin's (1978) story of the Empath in *The Wind's Twelve Quarters*, 1978.) Furthermore, it would not seem to be neurologically possible, to identically share another's feelings or experiences. However, we can approximate their feelings by invoking our own very contextually similar feelings. For example, if you have sciatic nerve and muscle pain and I have experienced a state labeled the same, I can "share" your pain by remembering neurologically and muscularly my experience. But there is no way of knowing just how closely my experience matches yours. I only know how you feel by how I feel. So, as Singer suggests, my experience is a mere representation of yours, not a neurological identity.

Cognitive empathy subsequent to emotional empathy would not be required, but would be more in one's mental health interests (and more in the other's interest as well), what I call above "regulated empathic concern." If this mentalizing leads to desires and plans to help, then it is called Compassion, and, according to Monroe (1996), if we act on those plans, it is called Altruism. But, the mentalizing (Cognitive Empathy) is phenomenologically and neurologically distinct from affective empathy. Now, the question is, is there such a state as pure cognitive empathy, thoughts without feelings? The Psychopath! Yes, but I would not call it empathy, and Singer probably wouldn't either, as there is no feeling into it. I might call it "understanding," or how about "Cognitive Empathy?" Interesting idea.

What are the Roles of Personal Distress and Perspective-Taking in the Expression of Empathy and Compassion?

Woodruff: As is implied by the term personal distress, when experiencing it, one's attention is necessarily focused on the self. Differences in attentional allocation between conditions of personal distress and conditions of perspective-taking may help in the effort to define empathy. Some have suggested that empathy need not entail perspective-taking but only the feeling of another's feelings. By this definition, empathy is happening even if the empathizer is experiencing personal distress.

We suggest, however, that the preferred definition of empathy includes the locus of attention. It seems reasonable to suggest that, if the observer's attention is on himself, as is the case if he is experiencing personal distress rather than perspective-taking, then he is not empathizing with the other. We suggest that empathy be used to refer only to those instances in which the observer's attention is focused on the target of that empathy.

Stevens: But I would argue, elaborating on a point above, that self-other differentiation is not categorical nor static, but is continuous (on a continuum) and dynamic, with neither extreme realizable, healthful, nor prosocially viable. Is self-empathy tautological? All empathy would be self-empathy (neural representation), but for projection (self-other perspective-taking); the latter is ToM. So, a man walks into my office with a left leg limp. I immediately, for 5 ms, feel a cramping pain in my left thigh (pure empathy). I say, "Steve, what is wrong with *your* leg (beginning self-other differentiation)?" He says, "I am having sciatic leg pain." I immediately feel my left leg sciatic pain, but I think automatically, "Steve, not I, is having sciatic leg pain but I've had that before and I know how painful that is!" (continuing and enhanced self-other differentiation). I ask him, in so many words, what he is doing to alleviate the pain and perhaps I make some suggestions. I no longer feel my own pain, but I felt "his" pain as a projection of my own pain, realized (cogitated) that it was his pain, not mine, and then felt compassion for his suffering. That's the process! Also, I don't have to feel the cramp nor the neural representation/memory of my own sciatic leg pain, but doing so increases "empathic resonance" or "receptive and expressive emotional prosody" (MacLean, 1990; Porges, 1995) and my expressed compassion.

Woodruff: "Is self-empathy tautological?" Well Mr. Fancy Pants, if we must talk about tautologies, I don't think so. I feel I'm standing on a shaky branch atop a tall pine tree when I say this, but it seems that a psychological experience and the understanding of that experience (e.g., *What was I thinking? Why was I thinking it? Why did I have that emotional reaction?*) are dissociable. Formally, a tautology is A = A. Self-empathy would be expressed as *my experience = my knowledge of it*. As long as my experience of empathy does not equal my knowledge of it, there's no tautology.

"All empathy would be self-empathy (neural representation), but for projection (self-other perspective-taking); the latter is ToM." Whoa Nelly! I see some conflation here that, as far as I can tell, is a universal problem in empathy research. The field has got to decide whether empathy and mentalizing (ToM) are two sides of the same coin or different denominations. My bias is toward a single-process model whereby empathy is what happens when one comes to understand another, either emotionally, cognitively, or both. Indeed, I would argue they perfectly co-occur, somewhat like electricity and magnetism. So, I see no reason to see them as two independent systems.

Later you say that, in response to another's sciatic pain, you "immediately, for 5 milliseconds, feel a cramping pain in [your] left thigh (pure empathy)" How is that pure empathy? At best, I'd call it a rudimentary precursor which may or may not evolve into empathy in a couple of more processing steps. We both seem to agree that self-other differentiation is a necessary prerequisite of empathy, but the vicarious pain you experience in the hypothetical scenario seems more akin to emotional contagion, which de Waal, rightly I think, considers a precursor to empathy—an evolutionary precursor as well as an information processing precursor, which precedes an individual occurrence of empathy. After emotional contagion, if the observer proceeds to represent the emotional experience as belonging to the other, attention to allocentric representations highlights details of the other's experience and the observer has now entered what *I* would call "pure empathy."

Stevens: You got me there, Kemosabe. I would have to agree with you, and de Waal, that my immediate 5 ms left thigh flinch is a good example of emotional contagion. I consider emotional contagion to be an automatic precursor of empathic responding and often blur the two. You are correct in differentiating them and I agree that we may need to do so particularly as we explore their neurological underpinnings.

Woodruff: Regarding cognitive empathy, if we say that self-other differentiation is a prerequisite to empathy, aren't we saying that cognition is a prerequisite for cognition? I argue that self-other differentiation is an inferential process and that inferential processes are cognitive insofar as they represent propositions about the world. Therefore, cognition is a prerequisite of empathy. However, according to some, empathy and mentalizing/ToM are distinct psychological constructs with the former referring to feelings and the latter referring to cognitions. But, if cognition (i.e., the inferential process of self-other differentiation) is a *prerequisite* of empathy, then cognition cannot be used to distinguish mentalizing/ToM from empathy. This argument would extend to the distinction of cognitive and emotional empathy, which seems to be an equivalent distinction to mentalizing/ToM and empathy distinction, as well. From all this, I favor a model that describes empathy as a process of coming to understand another through all means available, cognition and emotion.

Stevens: I would argue that empathy starts, if only very briefly and on a millisecond time scale, as a purely affective reaction to stimulus input, more emotional contagion, expressed in deeper brain structures of amygdala, anterior cingulate cortex, and insular cortex. In the model that we present in Chapter 3 for compassion, it is followed almost immediately by implicit premotor efferents (probably so for empathy as well as for compassion) and then later by frontal and posterior higher order self-other processing. It is this later top-down processing that allows for self-other differentiation, ToM mentalizing. So, I don't believe that cognition is a prerequisite for empathy but is most frequently paired with the experience on a millisecond timescale, so much so that they appear to be inseparable. This is certainly a testable hypothesis.

Is Empathy Necessarily Prosocial?

Stevens: I would direct the reader to my above statements as well as to the earlier brief comments about the prosocial evolution of empathy. Additionally, Preston and de Waal (2002) exquisitely present the differentiation between the ultimate (evolutionary) and proximate (immediate environmental) causes of empathy within the context of their Perception-Action Model and argue for the evolutionary sharpening of perception and response selection to maximize inclusive fitness. On the basis of this evolutionary argument, we conclude inferentially that empathy is necessarily prosocial. However, it is also likely that it has become "functionally autonomous," that is, freed of its phylogenetic prosocial developmental origins and operational now from a more purely ontogenetic understanding. In other words, I may, in complete isolation without ramifications for conspecifics, experience the feelings of another and even mentalize about those experiences, without ever sharing those feelings or their ramifications with another. I would still claim that I am experiencing empathy for others, and I would claim that many in our culture do just this, although not in seclusion. For example, I believe that many in this country would be able to experience the fear or anxiety of 22 million fellow citizens who might lose their health care, but those many observers would still implicitly support the dissolution of the Affordable Care Act!

Woodruff: I'm not sure that I agree. I suspect that among the natural selective pressures generating empathy, one is the selection of Machiavellian (see Chapter 5) traits that enable an observer to manipulate the social target. So I wouldn't argue that empathy was selected solely for its prosocial consequences.

Stevens: Preston and de Waal (2002) agree that ultimate arguments for the origin of empathy are "notorious for being cursory and speculative" and to some extent, given our difficulty with time travel except through the "macroscope" of evolutionary biology, must remain so. And, it is clear that this discussion regarding the finer natures of empathy and compassion could go on for decades, as it has thus far among very many more studied (and perhaps "steadied") minds than ours. So let us call a halt to these polemics for now, look at the neuroscience of empathy, compassion, and self-compassion through the lenses of our chapter authors, and then return to our attempt at a reconciliation of this debate and to an integration of the many ideas and research findings of our panel of contributors.

References

Analayo, B. (2015). *Compassion and emptiness in early Buddhist meditation*. Cambridge, UK: Windhorse Publications.

Arch, J. J., Brown, K. W., Dean, D. J., Landy, L. N., Brown, K. D., & Laudenslager, M. L. (2014). Self-compassion training modulates alpha-amylase, heart rate variability, and subjective responses to social evaluative threat in women. *Psychoneuroendocrinology, 42*, 49–58.

Arch, J. J., Landy, L. N., & Brown, K. W. (2016). Predictors and moderators of biopsychological social stress responses following brief self-compassion meditation training. *Psychoneuroendocrinology, 69*, 35–40.

Baron-Cohen, S. (2011). *The science of evil: On Empathy and the origins of cruelty*. New York, NY: Basic Books.

Batson, C. (2011a). *Altruism in humans*. New York, NY: Oxford University Press.

Batson, C. (2011b). These things called empathy: Eight related but distinct phenomena. In J. Decety, & W. Ickes (Eds.), *The social neuroscience of empathy* (pp. 3–15). Cambridge, MA: The MIT Press.

Blair, R. J. R., & Blair, K. S. (2011). Empathy, morality, and social convention: Evidence from the study of psychopathology and other psychiatric disorders. In J. Decety, & W. Ickes (Eds.), *The social neuroscience of empathy* (pp. 139–152). Cambridge, MA: The MIT Press.

Breines, J. G., Thoma, M. V., Gianferante, D., Hanlin, L., Chen, X., & Rohleder, N. (2014). Self-compassion as a predictor of interleukin-6 response to acute psychosocial stress. *Brain, Behavior, and Immunity, 37*, 109–114.

Breines, J. G., McInnis, C. M., Kuras, Y. I., Thoma, M. V., Gianferante, D., Hanlin, L., et al. (2015). Self-compassionate young adults show lower salivary alpha-amylase responses to repeated psychosocial stress. *Self and Identity, 14*(4), 390–402.

Davidson, R. J. (2002). Toward a biology of positive affect and compassion. In R. J. Davidson, & A. Harrington (Eds.), *Visions of compassion: Western scientists and Tibetan Buddhists examine human nature* (pp. 107–130). New York, NY: Oxford University Press.

Davis, M. (1980). A multidimensional approach to individual differences in empathy. *JSAS Catalogue of Selected Documents in Psychology, 10*, 1–19.

de Vignemont, F., & Singer, T. (2006). The empathic brain: How, when and why? *Trends in Cognitive Science, 10*, 435–441.

de Waal, F. B. M. (2009). Putting the altruism back into altruism: The evolution of empathy. *Annual Review of Psychology, 59*, 279–300.

de Waal, F. (2009). *The age of empathy*. New York, NY: Three Rivers Press.

Decety, J., & Jackson, P. L. (2004). The functional architecture of human empathy. *Behavioral and Cognitive Neuroscience Reviews, 3*(2), 71–100.

Decety, J., Norman, G. J., Berntson, G. G., & Cacioppo, J. T. (2012). A neurobehavioral evolutionary perspective on the mechanisms underlying empathy. *Progress in Neurobiology, 98*, 38–48.

Eisenberg, N., & Eggum, N. D. (2009). Empathic responding: Sympathy and personal distress. In J. Decety, & W. Ickes (Eds.), *The social neuroscience of empathy* (pp. 71–83). Cambridge, MA: The MIT Press.

Eisenberg, N., & Strayer, J. (1990). *Empathy and its development*. New York, NY: Cambridge University Press.

Friis, A. M., Johnson, M. H., Cutfield, R. G., & Consedine, N. S. (2015). Does kindness matter: Self-compassion buffers the negative impact of diabetes-distress on HbA1c. *Diabetic Medicine, 32*, 1634–1640.

Gethin, R. (1998). *The foundations of Buddhism*. Oxford: Oxford University Press.

Goetz, J. L., Keltner, D., & Simon-Thomas, E. (2010). Compassion: An evolutionary analysis and empirical review. *Psychological Bulletin, 136*, 351–374.

Gonzalez-Liencres, C., Shamay-Tsoory, S. G., & Brüne, M. (2013). Towards a neuroscience of empathy: Ontogeny, phylogeny, brain mechanisms, context and psychopathology. *Neuroscience and Biobehavioral Reviews, 37*, 1537–1548.

Hall, C. W., Row, K. A., Wuensch, K. L., & Godley, K. R. (2013). The role of self-compassion in physical and psychological well-being. *The Journal of Psychology, 147*(4), 311–323.

Hublin, J. -J. (2009). The prehistory of compassion. *Proceedings of the National Academy of Sciences, 106*(16), 6429–6430.

Kornfield, J. (1993). *A path with heart: A guide through the perils and promises of spiritual life.* New York, NY: Bantam Books.

Kornfield, J. (2009). *The wise heart: A guide to the universal teachings of Buddhist psychology.* New York, NY: Bantam Books.

Lama, D. (1984). *Kindness, clarity, and insight.* Boston, MA: Snow Lion.

Lama, D. (1995). *The world of Tibetan Buddhism: An overview of its philosophy and practice.* Somerville, MA: Wisdom.

Lama, D. (1997). *Sleeping, dreaming, and dying.* Somerville, MA: Wisdom.

Lama, D. (2011). *How to be compassionate: A handbook for creating inner peace and a happier world.* New York, NY: Atria.

Lamm, C., & Singer, T. (2010). The role of anterior insular cortex in social emotions. *Brain Structure and Function, 214*, 579–591.

Le Guin, U. K. (1978). *The wind's twelve quarters.* London: Granada Publishers.

MacBeth, A., & Gumley, A. (2012). Exploring compassion: A meta-analysis of the association between self-compassion and psychopathology. *Clinical Psychology Review, 32*, 545–552.

MacLean, P. (1990). *The triune brain in evolution: Role in paleocerebral functions.* New York, NY: Plenum Press.

Moll, J., Zahn, R., de Oliveira-Souza, R., Krueger, F., & Grafman, J. (2005). The neural basis of human moral cognition. *Nature Reviews Neuroscience, 6*, 799–809.

Monroe, K. R. (1996). *The heart of altruism: Perceptions of a common humanity.* Princeton, NJ: Princeton University Press.

Neff, K. (2003a). Self-compassion: An alternative conceptualization of a healthy attitude toward oneself. *Self and Identity, 2*, 85–101.

Neff, K. (2003b). The development and validation of a scale to measure self-compassion. *Self and Identity, 2*, 223–250.

Neff, K., & Vonk, R. (2009). Self-compassion versus global self-esteem: Two different ways of relating to oneself. *Journal of Personality, 77*(1), 23–50.

Neff, K. D., Kirkpatrick, K. L., & Rude, S. S. (2007a). Self-compassion and adaptive psychological functioning. *Journal of Research in Personality, 41*, 139–154.

Neff, K. D., Rude, S. S., & Kirkpatrick, K. L. (2007b). An examination of self-compassion in relation to positive psychological functioning and personality traits. *Journal of Research in Personality, 41*, 908–916.

Petrocchi, N., Ottaviani, C., & Couyoumdijian, A. (2017). Compassion at the mirror: Exposure to a mirror increases the efficacy of a self-compassion manipulation in enhancing soothing positive affect and heart rate variability. *The Journal of Positive Psychology, 12*(6), 525–536.

Porges, S. (1995). Orienting in a defensive world: Mammalian modification of our evolutionary heritage. A polyvagal theory. *Psychophysiology, 32*, 301–318.

Porges, S. W. (2003). The polyvagal theory: Phylogenetic contributions to social behavior. *Physiology and Behavior, 79*, 503–513.

Preston, S., & de Waal, F. B. M. (2002). Empathy: Its ultimate and proximate bases. *Behavioral and Brain Sciences, 25*, 1–72.

Rapaport, D. (1942/1967). Principles underlying projective techniques. In M. M. Gill (Ed.), *Collected papers of David Rapaport* (pp. 91–97). New York, NY: Basic Books.

Ricard, M. (2015). *Altruism: The power of compassion to change yourself and the world.* New York, NY: Little, Brown, & Company.

Singer, T., & Klimecki, O. M. (2014). Empathy and compassion. *Current Biology, 24*(18), R875–R878.

Singer, T., & Lamm, C. (2009). The social neuroscience of empathy. *Annals of the New York Academy of Sciences, 1156,* 81–96.

Stueber, K. (2017). Empathy. In E. N. Zalta (Ed.), *The Stanford encyclopedia of philosophy (Spring 2017 Edition).* Stanford: Stanford University, Metaphysics Research Lab https://plato.stanford.edu/archives/spr2017/entries/empathy/.

Svendsen, J. L., Osnes, B., Binder, P. -E., Dundas, I., Visted, E., Nordby, H., et al. (2016). Trait self-compassion reflects emotional flexibility through an association with high vagally mediated heart rate variability. *Mindfulness, 7*(5), 1103–1113.

Tatia, N., & Upasak, C. S. (1973). In *The Dhammapada—Atthakatha* (1–11). Nalanda, Bihar: Nava Nalanda Mahavihara.

Wang, S. (2005). A conceptual framework for integrating research related to the physiology of compassion and the wisdom of Buddhist teachings. In P. Gilbert (Ed.), *Compassion: Conceptualisations, research, and use in psychotherapy* (pp. 75–120). New York, NY: Routledge.

Zessin, U., Dickhauser, O., & Garbade, S. (2015). The relationship between self-compassion and well-being: A meta-analysis. Applied Psychology Health and Well-Being, 7(3), 340–364.

2

The Brain That Feels Into Others: Toward a Neuroscience of Empathy

Vera Flasbeck*, Cristina Gonzalez-Liencres**, Martin Brüne*

*Ruhr-University Bochum, Bochum, Germany; **Institut d'Investigacions Biomèdiques August Pi i Sunyer (IDIBAPS), Barcelona, Spain

The way humans socially interact is highly influenced by their capacity to empathize with others. "Empathy" is a multifaceted construct of emotional experiences and behavioral responses based on these experiences that arise as a consequence of perceiving another individual's emotional state. Accordingly, there is no generally accepted definition of what empathy actually is. A relatively broad conceptualization describes empathy as the ability to feel and to understand what another individual feels and understands. This is thought to occur through a process involving the semi-automatic copying or mirroring of another's emotional state, which induces a similar emotional state in the observer, referred to as emotional empathy (Nummenmaa, Hirvonen, Parkkola, & Hietanen, 2008; Singer & Lamm, 2009) Aside from such matching of another's emotional state, empathy, as we prefer to define it, also entails an understanding of the causality of the emotions displayed by the observed individual, awareness of contextual factors and distinction of self and other (Gonzalez-Liencres, Shamay-Tsoory, & Brüne, 2013). This cognitive facet of empathy can then serve as a basis to engage in truly prosocial behaviors including sympathy and compassion. We contend that this narrower functional definition of empathy allows distinguishing it from related, but phylogenetically or ontogenetically simpler, forms of sharing emotions—such as emotional contagion—and from instinct-driven prosocial behavior involved in nurturance and offspring protection. In the following sections, we therefore

The Neuroscience of Empathy, Compassion, and Self-Compassion. http://dx.doi.org/10.1016/B978-0-12-809837-0.00002-7

briefly highlight definitional boundaries and the fuzziness of the concept, "empathy." We then describe, in a nutshell, the phylogenetic development of empathy. This is meant to serve as a basis to understand the neuro-scientific research of empathy that has utilized animal models, or empathy in human subjects at different levels of complexity. We subsequently summarize studies of empathy in people with neuropsychiatric disorders. Finally, we propose future lines of potential interest in empathy research.

DEFINITIONAL QUANDARIES OF EMPATHY

Aside from the distinction between the emotional and the cognitive facets of empathy, it is important to differentiate empathy from a number of other mechanisms that are either developmental precursors of empathy or based on the representation of empathy. To begin with, more than 80 years ago, Lorenz (1935) described the phenomenon of "Stimmungsüber-tragung" ("emotional transference or contagion") in corvids which led to the execution of another individual's "instinct-bound" behavior by an observer based on shared emotions. Lorenz explicitly distinguished emotional contagion (or "social facilitation") from imitation, because it lacks insight into a common goal. That is, emotional contagion does not require a causal understanding of the observed emotional reactions. Hence, its behavioral correlate is restricted to the display of the same behavior as that perceived in the initiating individual. For example, wolves howling when hearing another wolf howl may be emotionally affected and thus join in, yet without awareness of the wolf's motivation to start howling or the ability to disengage from copying the behavior based on a causal understanding of the contextual factors.

In contrast, "imitation" does not entail shared feelings, but refers to an intentional act aimed at achieving a goal by copying another's observable behavior. "Emulation," while being similar to imitation, is defined as the ability to accomplish a goal-directed action based on observed behavior, but without copying the means of the observed individual. Emulating behaviors in the animal kingdom includes nut-cracking or termite-fishing techniques in chimpanzees (Byrne, 1995).

"Sympathy" is an emotion driven by empathy which often requires the perception of another's distress and the motivation to reduce the distress of the other (Kristjansson, 2004). Sympathy can, however, also be evoked by physical or psychological attractiveness or similarity and may therefore even be decoupled from sharing emotions.

"Compassion" describes caring or helping behavior based on empathic concern (Goetz, Keltner, & Simon-Thomas, 2010; Singer & Lamm, 2009). In contrast to empathy, however, compassion involves the ability of the observer to disengage from the shared or imagined feeling of the other, and to act upon his willingness to help and ameliorate the other's distress. For example, observing an individual who is afraid of spiders does not necessarily induce spider-phobia in the observer but may instead induce prosocial behavior in the observer motivated to ameliorate the other's fear and reduce his or her emotional distress (see Chapter 3). Fig. 2.1 summarizes the most relevant aspects in relation to definitional boundaries of empathy.

PHYLOGENY AND COMPARATIVE ETHOLOGY OF EMPATHY

Evidence suggests that empathy, as we conceptualize it, evolved in animals that extensively invest in parenting and nurturing or protecting offspring (Preston, Hofelich, & Stansfield, 2013). As living creatures differ in their life cycles, those species experiencing relatively long lifespans, having few offspring and maturing ontogenetically late, tend to invest more in offspring survival compared to species that mature quickly, produce large numbers of offspring per litter, or reproductive cycle and have short lifespans. These differences in "life history" patterns have been described long ago by MacArthur and Wilson (1967), whereby the slower life cycle has been referred to as "K-strategy" while the faster life cycles have been called "r-strategies." Stearns (1992) has elaborated on this research such that nowadays, one can make predictions about how and why species differ with regard to their life history strategies (LHS). While there is no space to

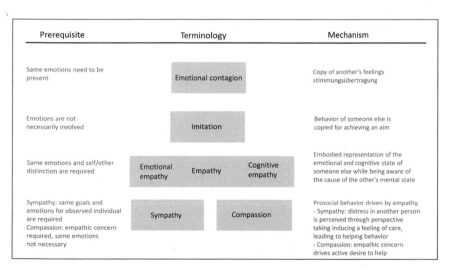

FIGURE 2.1 **Definitional boundaries of empathy: description of distinct mechanisms (right column).** Emotional contagion, imitation, empathy, sympathy, and compassion differ in regard of the presence or absence of shared emotions and goals (left column).

outline this in greater detail, for the purpose of this chapter, it is important to note that mammals tend to have evolved slower LHS compared to plants, unicellular organisms, insects, fishes, reptiles, etc., though vast differences exist between, say, mice and elephants or between rabbits and humans.

So, clearly, parental care in offspring is higher in slowly developing species that grow large bodies, enjoy longevity, and face relatively few deaths in infancy, because higher parental investment entails the necessity to protect reproductively "costly" offspring from premature death through starvation, exposure to extreme hot or cold temperatures, and predation (Gonzalez-Liencres et al., 2013; Gross, 2005; Magnhagen, 1992; McDiarmid, 1978; Sargent & Gross, 1985; Tullberg, Ah-King, & Temrin, 2002; Wesolowski, 1994). Accordingly, several authors have argued that extensive parental care has selected for attention to the needs of offspring, which entails emotional states as potential precursors of empathic concern (Preston & De Waal, 2002; Provine, 2005). Furthermore, parental care arguably evolved into empathy for kin in order to facilitate cooperation in social groups in gregarious animal species (Decety, Bartal, Uzefovsky, & Knafo-Noam, 2015; Trivers, 1971).

When looking at brain anatomy, it was MacLean (1990) who suggested that mammalian brains differ from those of reptiles by a peculiar structure that he referred to as the "palaeomammalian" brain. The palaeomammalian brain is roughly equivalent to the limbic system, which comprises the hippocampus, the amygdala (AMG), the insula, and the cingulate cortex (Zilles, 1987). These brain structures, as we now know, are essentially involved in the processing of complex emotions, including empathy, while, in addition, cortical structures are involved in "mirroring" another's behavior and are engaged in the processing of the causal understanding of emotions in context (for more details, see below).

This phenomenon is extremely difficult to study in nonhuman animals, especially in the context of positive emotions. Thus, most nonhuman animal research on empathy or related processes has focused on responses to another individual's stress. Laboratory animals such as mice and rats display freezing behavior when frightened or otherwise distressed (LeDoux, 2000). An interesting research question that arose from this observation was, then, whether or not a mouse or rat would freeze when observing a conspecific in a frightening or otherwise stressful situation. One of the first reports examining this was published by Kavaliers and colleagues (2003) who exposed a target mouse to biting flies while an observer mouse witnessed the event (Kavaliers, Colwell, & Choleris, 2003). Mice usually react to the presence of biting flies by engaging in self-burying behaviors in order to avoid the bites and, neurochemically, by releasing corticosterone as a stress response. The authors found that observer mice that had never been exposed to biting flies also engaged in self-burying behavior and had an increased corticosterone response even when they were exposed to flies whose mouth parts had been removed and could therefore not bite. Along similar lines, other studies showed that mice treated with acetic acid writhe more when they see another mouse also treated with acetic acid than when they observe a nonwrithing mouse or when they are placed in isolation (Langford et al., 2006). An observer mouse can also learn a classical fear conditioning task just by mere observation: after learning the tone-shock pairing from a target mouse, the observer freezes in response to a tone although it had never been exposed to the tone-shock pairing (Chen, Panksepp, & Lahvis, 2009). Moreover, several reports have demonstrated the ability of mice to perceive and be affected by a conspecific's distress. That is, observer mice freeze when they see another mouse receiving electric foot shocks in an adjacent compartment (Gonzalez-Liencres, Juckel, Tas, Friebe, & Brüne, 2014; Jeon et al., 2010). More recently, it has been shown that the presence of a cagemate suffering from chronic pain increases the nociceptive response and anxiety-like behavior of observer mice (Baptista-de-Souza, Nunes-de-Souza, & Canto-de-Souza, 2016). Nonetheless, some authors have raised the possibility that the sharing of affective states between target and observer mice might be due to observers perceiving the target's fear as a threatening cue (Grenier & Lüthi, 2010). However, most of the above-mentioned studies also showed that the empathy-like responses in mice were amplified by increasing familiarity and genetic relatedness between target and observer (Chen et al., 2009; Gonzalez-Liencres et al., 2014; Jeon et al., 2010; Langford et al., 2006). In any case, these studies highlight that suffering mice have a strong impact on the distress of observers and, as we will see later on, the extent to which observers show distress is modulated by contextual factors.

Rats, which are usually much more social compared to mice, show even more sophisticated responses to a conspecific's distress. A series of experiments have revealed that a rat, in order to free another caged rat, learns to open a door of a restrainer where the caged rat is enclosed (Bartal, Decety, & Mason, 2011; Bartal, Rodgers, Sarria, Decety, & Mason, 2014). Moreover, a free rat will open the restrainer where the other rat is enclosed as often as it will open another restrainer that contains chocolate chips (a highly desirable food for rats), and it will share the chocolate chips with the liberated rat (Bartal et al., 2011). Such complex behavior almost certainly did not occur by chance, because a free rat would not open an empty restrainer or a restrainer that contains a plastic rat. Another interesting observation is that a white rat (Sprague–Dawley strain) will free a black-hooded rat (Long–Evans strain) only if the white rat had previously lived with the black-hooded rat strain (Bartal et al., 2014). Finally, rats will free caged conspecifics even if social interaction after the release is impeded (Bartal et al., 2011). Taken together, these findings indicate that rats engage in prosocial behavior upon the detection of another's distress, that prosocial behavior takes place even if the subsequent rewarding social interaction is prevented, and that familiarity is essential for prosocial behavior to occur. Therefore, it is reasonable to assume that rats possess advanced social skills that allow them to perceive and to react to their conspecifics' distress.

Primate research in the 1960s has already demonstrated that rhesus monkeys will consistently starve to avoid the suffering of another monkey that would receive electric shocks if the first accepted the food (Masserman, Wechkin, & Terris, 1964). Similar to mice and rats, this response was stronger the more familiar both monkeys were with one another. Related to this, another study has shown that capuchin monkeys have a sense of fairness and become angry when another monkey receives a higher reward for the same action (Brosnan & de Waal, 2003). It is not clear whether this behavior can be called "envy" and how it relates to empathy, even though theoretically such a connection might exist. In any event, what nonhuman animal research shows is that contextual factors such as familiarity and kinship play an important role in the expression of empathic concern for others. Accordingly, we highlight some state and trait-dependent issues that impact on empathy in quite profound ways.

CONTEXTUAL FACTORS CONCERNING EMPATHY

Even though many animal species have developed the ability to detect and to respond to the affective state of their conspecifics, empathy and related processes such as emotional contagion, observational fear learning, etc. are clearly modulated by the context in which observer and target act. Ultimately, as discussed above, empathy most likely evolved because it increases survival of offspring and other close kin by facilitating protection and nurturance, and caregiving in general. From a proximate perspective, perceiving the affective state of a target individual activates autonomic responses in the observer that may (or may not) result in empathy (Preston & De Waal, 2002). These responses arise from the combination of multiple factors that modulate the perception of our environment and of our own physical and affective state. Some of these factors concern transient states and include the observer's stress level and the salience of the target individual's needs, whereas other factors are more pervasive in nature, including personality factors and occupation, as well as ingroup–outgroup membership, though the distinction between state and trait dependent factors seems, at times, to be arbitrary.

State-Dependent Aspects

An individual's stress level is central to his or her ability to perceive the affective state of another and resonate accordingly. For example, when emotionally relaxed, an observer is able to detect and to respond appropriately to the surrounding environment, while this may not work for situations associated with higher subjective distress. In terms of empathy, mouse and human observers show more emotional contagion and empathy when the target individual is familiar or genetically related, that is, when the target is not perceived as dangerous or threatening and thus does not engender a stress response. Generating a stress response in observer mice reduces their ability to show emotional contagion even if the target mouse is a cagemate (Martin et al., 2015). Conversely, mice and humans are less affected by the distress of strangers. Moreover, when the stress response is pharmacologically attenuated in an observer, the empathic response to the distress of a stranger is enhanced (Martin et al., 2015). Our own work in psychologically healthy subjects suggests, however, that (mild) psychosocial stress induces an increase in the subjective unpleasantness one feels when watching images of hands exposed to painful stimuli. Stress also enhances negative affect and reduces the degree to which people consider themselves as socially desirable (Gonzalez-Liencres, Brown, Tas, Breidenstein, & Brüne, 2016a). Along similar lines, Tomova et al. (2016) reported, using functional brain imaging, that stress increases activation of the anterior insula (AI), the anterior midcingulate cortex, and the primary somatosensory cortex, all regions involved in empathy-for-pain processing, which mediated the expression of prosocial behavior. Conversely, the same study revealed that stressed individuals have difficulties in adequately taking into account contextual information, suggesting that increased empathy by stress may come at the cost of poor cognitive appraisal of the other's factual exposure to pain (Tomova et al., 2016). What we currently do not properly understand is whether stress, if exceeding a certain amount, and depending on individual resilience to stress, can also diminish empathic concern for others. The most plausible model, in our view, is that excessive stress levels attenuate empathic responses, while mild stress may intensify empathy for another's pain.

Aside from the relevance of stress for empathic responses, the ability of an individual to perceive the affective state of another is also modulated by the salience of the target's needs. That is, observers will not help a distressed target individual when the target's needs are not overtly expressed (Zaki, Bolger, & Ochsner, 2008). Similarly, observers will not help a target in need when this need is exceedingly expressed and causes significant distress in the observer to a degree that difficulties in regulating one's own emotional reaction emerge. Such a situation precludes empathy and helping behavior, in favor of avoidance or flight (Eisenberg et al., 1994). As regards humans, a recent study showed that participants' empathic responses varied when viewing videos of hospital patients with chronic or terminal illnesses according to the target's behavior (Preston et al., 2013). In this study, patients were classified into five types depending on their emotional behavior (distraught, resilient, sanguine, reticent, and wistful).

Based on this classification, participants showed distinct behaviors to each patient type; for example, they tended to empathize more with resilient and wistful patients (i.e., positive and likeable or quietly sad), although some participants empathized most with patients who did not express need or distress, that is, who were reticent or sanguine. The authors proposed that their results are compatible with empathy–altruism theories, in which intermediate levels of distress elicit the most optimal empathic response (Preston et al., 2013). Together, studies of stress in the observer and the salience of signals of distress sent by target individuals seem to follow an inverted U-shaped curve, where too little or too much of either impairs the expression of empathy.

Trait-Dependent Aspects

While transient states can modulate the observer's appraisal of another individual in distress, there are more permanent factors that greatly modulate our perception and reaction to others' affective states. A vast body of research suggests that several personality traits are key to the experience and expression of empathic concern. It is beyond the scope of this chapter to give an exhaustive overview of this literature. However, it is necessary to note that when researchers use the five-factor model of personality ("big five"), the most convincing associations between empathy (using a self-rating scale, the Interpersonal Reactivity Index [IRI]; for details, see below) and personality dimensions (as assessed using the NEO-FFI) emerge for "agreeableness," "conscientiousness" and, in part, "openness to new experiences" (Habashi, Graziano, & Hoover, 2016). This effect seems to be similar across cultures (Melchers et al., 2016).

Another huge body of research has examined the association of psychopathic traits with empathy. By definition, psychopathy is associated with a lack of emotional empathy, absence of guilt, shallow affect, manipulation of other people, and antisocial behavior (Viding, McCrory, & Seara-Cardoso, 2014). Similarly, narcissism has been linked to empathy deficits (Ritter et al., 2011), though this has recently been called into question (Baskin-Sommers, Krusemark, & Ronningstam, 2014). Related to this, the term "Machiavellianism" concerns essentially noncooperative, exploitative, and interpersonally manipulative strategies (Wilson, Near, & Miller, 1998). People scoring high on a scale measuring such attitudes (Mach-IV scale; Christie & Geis, 1970) manipulate others more and are often cynical and unempathic, even though some "high-Machs" can appear superficially charming. Machiavellianism overlaps, to a certain degree, with the concept of "psychopathy" (Hare, 2006). Together, pathological narcissism, Machiavellianism, and psychopathy have been deemed "the dark triad," sharing a common core of "disagreeableness" (i.e., akin to low empathy; Paulhus & Williams, 2002).

Aside from personality factors, dozens of research articles have focused on the impact of occupation on empathy, which is certainly a highly relevant issue for the health sciences. In fact, it is obvious that clinician empathy has beneficial effects on patient (and physician) health (Decety & Fotopoulou, 2015). Conversely, there is growing evidence that physicians often struggle with expressing empathy for their patients, and that training doctors in experiencing more empathic concern is an important issue (Kelm, Womer, Walter, & Feudtner, 2014). Here, we emphasize that it can be sometimes mandatory to suppress one's empathic reactions in clinical interaction, particularly in situations where clinicians' interventions inflict pain on their patients. For example, Cheng and colleagues were among the first to describe that clinicians who apply acupuncture to their patients actively suppress the activation of their empathy-for-pain neural network, particularly the AI, somatosensory cortex, periaqueductal gray, and anterior cingulate cortex (ACC), as revealed in a functional brain imaging study. Instead they displayed activation of the medial and superior prefrontal cortex and the temporoparietal junction, which are known to be relevant for perspective-taking (Cheng et al., 2007; for details about the neural network of empathy, see sections below). In line with this, another study examined the event-related potential (ERP) responses to painful and neutral stimuli in physicians and a matched control group of participants with a distinct occupation. Differences in an early (N110) component occurred only in the control subjects, but not in the clinician group, again suggesting that physicians process painful stimuli differently from people with other occupations (Decety, Yang, & Cheng, 2010). Moreover, Jensen et al. (2014) reported, using neuroimaging, that physicians activate brain regions during painful treatment of patients that have been associated with the processing of pain-relief expectations and reward. Together, these studies suggest that physicians sometimes seem to suppress their empathic responses, particularly when pain-inducing procedures are necessary.

Another trait-dependent factor that impacts on the expression of empathic concern for others is familiarity, or ingroup versus outgroup membership. In mice, for example, empathy-like behaviors ensue between familiar and genetically closely related individuals, whereas strangers or nonkin may express no such behaviors (Chen et al., 2009; Gonzalez-Liencres et al., 2014; Jeon et al., 2010; Langford et al., 2006). Likewise, as described above, rats engage in prosocial behaviors with a clear preference for familiar conspecifics (Bartal et al., 2011). In humans, the situation is more complex. People not only show empathic concern for family, kin, and friends, they may also do so for strangers, depending on personality traits, xenophobia, and contextual factors like economic wealth. For example, De Dreu et al. (2010) have shown that social orientation impacts upon how people perform in intergroup conflict. Compared to more self-oriented subjects, prosocially oriented individuals showed stronger ingroup trust and ingroup love (but not more or less outgroup hate or distrust), which is arguably related to empathy. These differential attitudes toward in- and outgroups can be enhanced by oxytocin that is known to increase trust and reciprocity, as well as empathy (De Dreu, Greer, Van Kleef, Shalvi, & Handgraaf, 2011; see Chapter 7). In addition, empathetic responses to one's suffering also seem to be clearly skewed to ingroup members, whereas suffering of outgroup members more likely elicits gloating or *Schadenfreude* (Cikara, Bruneau, & Saxe, 2011), which probably reflects an emotional pattern that was ecologically important enough in ancestral environments to be selected. (See Chapter 5 for a more in-depth discussion of these concepts.)

MEASURING EMPATHY IN HUMANS

Historical Aspects

In the 1960s and 1970s, Stanley Milgram conducted experiments investigating the sense of responsibility we take for our own acts. Milgram's ideas developed in the context of World War II, where soldiers committed all kinds of atrocities, and he wondered how this could have occurred. More specifically, he was interested in investigating how far people would go in obeying orders if these entailed harm to other persons. As he put it, "could it be that Eichmann and his million accomplices in the Holocaust were just following orders?" (Milgram, 1974). Following up on this, male participants were assigned the role of a Teacher who instructed a fictive Learner (a confederate, of which participants were not aware) by giving them electric shocks of increasing voltage every time the Learner made a mistake. A Researcher (an actor) stayed in the same room as the Teacher (the participant). The fictive Learner screamed each time when a shock was delivered and asked the Teacher to stop. The Researcher, in contrast asked the Teacher to continue applying shocks by pointing out that it was essential for the success of the procedure and that there was no other choice. The results showed that 65% of participants continued to give shocks to the Learners up to the highest level of 450 V, and that all participants continued to apply up to 300 V (Milgram, 1963). Milgram's studies demonstrated that obedience to an authority can critically alter one's behavior to the extent that empathic responses are overridden and suppressed.

Novel Experimental Procedures

More recent approaches to measure empathy in human subjects entail a number of procedures including behavioral observation, self-ratings, and experimental studies of empathy for another's bodily or psychological pain. Early studies involving the observation of emotional responses of young infants have shown that even newborns respond to facial expressions of another individual by imitating simple movements (Meltzoff & Moore, 1977). Emotional contagion occurs shortly after birth, as newborns start crying when hearing another infant cry (Simner, 1971). More specifically, listening to another infant's cry causes more distress in the listener as compared to hearing one's own recorded crying. Martin and Clark further demonstrated that the infant's response to someone else's crying was peer- and species-specific, insofar as infants responded to the crying of other infants, but not to their own recorded crying or to crying displayed by older children or chimpanzees (Dondi, Simion, & Caltran, 1999; Martin & Clark, 1982). Other research has shown that infants at the age of 10 weeks are able to discriminate their mother's facial expressions when coupled with vocal expressions of happiness, sadness, and anger and also show matching behavior for joy and anger (Haviland & Lelwica, 1987). While a detailed review of infant development of empathy is beyond the scope of this chapter, it is important to emphasize that the ontogenetic development of empathy is complex and critically depends on the quality of the child's interaction with early caregivers, particularly concerning the caregivers' emotional responsiveness to the infant's emotional needs and the caregivers' ability to help the child regulate its emotions when stressed (Decety & Svetlova, 2012; Panfile & Laible, 2012; Zahn-Waxler, Radke-Yarrow, & King, 1979).

The caregiver's consistent mirroring and responsiveness to an infant's emotional needs help the child develop more sophisticated empathic abilities (Fonagy, Steele, Steele, Moran, & Higgitt, 1991), which also depend on the maturation of joint attention mechanisms (Carpenter, Nagell, Tomasello, Butterworth, & Moore, 1998), self-awareness (Bischof-Köhler, 2012), self-other distinction (Rochat & Striano, 2000), and "mentalizing" (the ability to appreciate the mental lives of others as distinct from one's own, also known as Theory of Mind (ToM); see Chapter 3 for a more detailed description of ToM; Leslie, 1987). All of this is quintessential for the development of empathy-based prosocial behavior (Decety & Jackson, 2004), which in its earliest form appears in infants who help other distressed children associated with their ability to recognize themselves in a mirror (Bischof-Köhler, 2012, see also Svetlova, Nichols, & Brownell, 2010; Zahn-Waxler, Radke-Yarrow, Wagner, & Chapman, 1992).

In adult humans, self-rating questionnaires have been widely employed to examine an individual's cognitive and affective empathy. For example, the Interpersonal Reactivity Index IRI (Davis, 1983) is a tool consisting of two cognitive subscales, namely "perspective taking" and "fantasy," and two affective subscales called "empathic concern" and "personal distress." Participants are asked to rate 32 statements describing their empathic abilities with scores ranging from zero ("that does not describe me well") to four ("that describes me very well"). Other empathy questionnaires include the Empathy Scale, The Questionnaire Measure of Emotional Empathy, and a plethora of other measures for specific populations such as physicians, nurses, or people with autism (summarized in Spreng, McKinnon, Mar, & Levine, 2009).

More objective approaches in the study of empathy have utilized experiments requiring imagining the intensity of another's bodily pain. In other words, in such experimental designs, pictures of others in somatically painful situations, for example, a hand shown pinched in a door, are presented to participants, whereby their task is to rate the pain intensity (e.g., Fan & Han, 2008; Jackson, Meltzoff, & Decety, 2005; for a meta-analysis see Lamm, Decety, & Singer, 2011). Our own group recently developed a novel task ("Social Interaction Empathy Task" [SIET]) examining empathy for both bodily and psychological pain, based on considerations that empathy for psychological pain may differ from empathy for bodily pain. Psychological pain has hitherto been examined from a first-person perspective only by employing a so-called "cyberball game" (Williams, Cheung, & Choi, 2000). In the cyberball game, two virtual players and the participant pass a ball among them, whereby unexpectedly, the participant is excluded from the game at some point (Eisenberg, 2012). This task taps into the domain of rejection sensitivity or responses to ostracism but is not necessarily related to empathy.

In contrast, in our SIET participants are asked to judge the pain intensity of images depicting different social interactions. The interactions show either psychologically (social) or somatically painful interactions (as well as neutral situations as control conditions). To examine the impact of perspective, participants are asked to rate pain intensity either from a first-person or a third-person perspective. Preliminary findings have revealed that healthy participants rated somatically painful images as more painful than psychologically painful and neutral pictures, whereby psychologically painful pictures were judged as more painful than neutral pictures. Interestingly, there was no difference between the first and the third-person perspective (Flasbeck, Enzi, & Brüne, 2017). Such empathy-for-pain tasks have the advantage that they are relatively simple in design and therefore suitable for studies of biological and psychological correlates of empathy using neuroimaging or electrophysiological techniques.

BRAIN MECHANISMS INVOLVED IN EMPATHY

Nonhuman animal research suggests that the neural circuits and the neurotransmitter systems necessary to perceive, to be affected by, and to respond to others' distress rely on evolutionarily conserved structures

(MacLean, 1990). Above all, the limbic system is critical in the study of empathy-related processes, as revealed in humans in neurochemical, neuroimaging, and neurophysiological studies. As regards the former, oxytocin, an evolutionarily conserved nonapeptide, plays a fundamental role in this regard. In addition to its well-known role in parturition and lactation, oxytocin promotes social behavior across mammalian species including mating and offspring care (Donaldson & Young, 2008; Knobloch & Grinevich, 2015). In vertebrates, oxytocin is made available by secretion into the cerebro-spinal fluid and via axonal release (especially in mammals). Even though the number of oxytocin axons in forebrain structures is relatively small, the high receptor affinity of oxytocin and its supposed action on interneurons allows rapid modification of neuronal activity, preferentially in the AMG, which is a key region involved in empathy-related processes (Knobloch, Charlet, Stoop, & Grinevich, 2014).

Experimental evidence in nonclinical human subjects has shown that intranasal application of oxytocin improves empathy, mentalizing, trust, cooperation, and the experience of social reward, as well as ingroup favoritism (Domes, Heinrichs, Michel, Berger, & Herpertz, 2007; Kosfeld, Heinrichs, Zak, Fischbacher, & Fehr, 2005). At the neurobiological level, oxytocin seems to downregulate AMG responsivity, to dampen the action of stress hormones (Evans, Shergill, & Averbeck, 2010; Heinrichs, Baumgartner, Kirschbaum, & Ehlert, 2003; Labuschagne et al., 2010) and to modulate brain activity in neural networks involved in empathy (Lancaster et al., 2015). With regard to empathy for pain, Shamay-Tsoory and colleagues (2013) found that lower empathy for out-group members in the frame of a political conflict can be overcome by administration of intranasal oxytocin (Shamay-Tsoory et al., 2013). Moreover, another study reported an increase in empathy for pain under oxytocin treatment when participants were asked to adopt a third-person perspective (Abu-Akel, Palgi, Klein, Decety, & Shamay-Tsoory, 2015). Thus, oxytocin seems to enhance the perception of social agents and therefore increase empathy for others.

Another important aspect concerning the neurochemical correlates of empathy refers to the fact that social interaction can have rewarding effects in its own right (Dölen, Darvishzadeh, Huang, & Malenka, 2013). That is, it can be pleasurable to empathize with others. Social reward, in general, seems to be linked to oxytocin metabolism in the brain, yet nonhuman animal studies suggest interactions between the oxytocinergic and the serotonergic system (5-HT) in reward-processing areas of the brain, foremost the nucleus accumbens (Dölen et al., 2013), as well as with dopamine, whereby nonhuman animal studies corroborate the link of these circuits with parental (maternal) care for offspring (Shahrokh, Zhang, Diorio, Gratton, & Meaney, 2010; see Chapter 7 for a more detailed presentation of the role of hormones in prosocial behavior).

Neuroimaging research has revealed overlapping brain areas that are activated during empathy for another's pain and during the first-hand experience of pain. Research regarding neural mechanisms of processing painful experiences found three main modules, namely a sensory-discriminative (or somatosensory), an affective-motivational (or affective), and a cognitive-evaluative (or cognitive) dimension (Melzack & Casey, 1968; Treede, Kenshalo, Gracely, & Jones, 1999). The sensory–discriminatory dimension recruits the primary (S1) and secondary (S2) somatosensory cortices, as well as the ventroposteriomedial, and the ventroposterolateral nuclei of the thalamus. The activation of these brain regions seems to be linked to the processing of the intensity, localization, and quality of the perceived pain (Craig, 2003a; Treede et al., 1999). In contrast, the affective-motivational pain component, which entails the perception of the painful stimulus as unpleasant, activates the medial nociceptive system including the medial thalamus. Moreover, the AMG, the ACC, and the AI, all parts of the "palaeomammalian" limbic system, contribute to the processing of complex emotions (Grenier & Lüthi, 2010; Langford et al., 2006; Singer et al., 2004; Treede et al., 1999). Conscious appraisal of experiencing pain, that is, the cognitive component of pain perception, recruits frontal and limbic brain areas such as the bilateral medial prefrontal cortex (mPFC), ACC, dorsolateral prefrontal cortex, orbitofrontal cotex (OFC), and the bilateral AI and frontal operculum. Several parietal regions are also involved, namely the right superior parietal cortex and the inferior parietal lobule (Kong et al., 2006).

Similar to the brain activation during first-hand experience of physical pain, the affective parts of the pain matrix become activated when observing someone else in pain (Jackson, Rainville, & Decety, 2006; Lamm et al., 2011; Singer et al., 2004). Moreover, the magnitude of activation of these brain regions correlates with self-rated empathic abilities and with the judgment of pain intensity (Jackson et al., 2005; Saarela et al., 2007).

Aside from neuroimaging research into empathy for pain, a surprisingly small number of studies have focused on empathy for emotions. Morelli and Lieberman (2013) conducted an fMRI study using pictures showing individuals in happy, sad, and anxious conditions. Participants were asked to simply observe, actively empathize, or memorize a number, while looking at the images. In the empathizing condition, a core set of neural regions was activated comprising the dorsomedial prefrontal cortex (dmPFC), the mPFC, the temporoparietal junction (TPJ), the AMG, the AI, and the septal area (Sep). Distraction by a cognitive task was not only accompanied by lower empathy ratings, but also by a diminished activation of the dmPFC, the mPFC, the TPJ, and the AMG. In contrast, the AI and Sep areas were recruited in all conditions, suggesting that they were automatically activated by more bottom-up processes (Morelli & Lieberman, 2013; Rameson, Morelli, & Lieberman, 2012). Our own study has aimed to more specifically distinguish between cognitive and emotional empathy, showing that cognitive empathy involves activity of the precuneus and cuneus, while emotional empathy recruits more strongly prefrontal structures, the posterior cingulate cortex and the basal ganglia (Schlaffke et al., 2015).

As regards empathy for positive emotions such as happiness and joy, the researchers found that empathy for positive emotions activated those regions involved in mentalizing (i.e., vmPFC), while empathy for negative affect selectively recruited limbic brain areas including the AI and the dACC. Notably, the Sep area was activated in all empathy conditions, and the magnitude of its activation was predictive of daily helping behavior, supporting the assumption that the Sep area is linked to the display of prosocial behavior (Morelli, Rameson, & Lieberman, 2012). Overall, these outcomes suggest task-dependent overlap of recruitment of brain regions involved in cognitive and emotional empathy.

In addition to neuroimaging studies, neurophysiological research using electroencephalography (EEG) to determine ERP can be informative with regard to the time-course of neural processes. Fan and Han (2008) were the first to develop an empathy-for-pain paradigm that employs the presentation of images of hands in neutral or painful situations. The participants' attention was in some conditions required and in another condition intentionally withdrawn from the painful stimuli (Fan & Han, 2008). ERP investigation showed that painful cues, compared to neutral cues, evoked positive shifts at short-latencies over frontal and central regions and at long-latencies over central-parietal areas. In addition, a modulatory effect of the attention and stimulus reality (cartoon or pictures) of the painful stimuli was found (more detailed description below). The finding that painful stimuli elicited a positive shift of ERP components relative to neutral stimuli was replicated in further studies (Han, Fan, & Mao, 2008; Li & Han, 2010).

Aside from attentional factors that potentially influence empathic responses, a crucial question is whether or not perspective matters in this regard. Accordingly, researchers have designed paradigms to examine differences between a first-person perspective and a third-person perspective on the execution of an empathy-for-pain task. Put another way, participants were asked to imagine how *they* would feel in a given situation (first-person perspective) and how an observed character would feel (i.e., third-person perspective). Findings have been mixed, so far. While several studies reported higher pain ratings and faster reactions in the first-person perspective compared to the third-person perspective (Li & Han 2010; van der Heiden, Scherpiet, Konicar, Birbaumer, & Veit, 2013), others did not find any difference. For example, Jackson et al. (2006) demonstrated that empathy for pain activated overlapping brain activity in both perspectives. The group further reported a higher recruitment of the secondary somatosensory cortex, ACC, and insula during the first-person perspective and a higher involvement of the right TPJ during the third-person perspective condition, possibly implying some involvement of cognitive empathic processes (Jackson et al., 2006). These results suggest that empathic processing could be modulated by the task itself or strength of identification with the painful situations.

In our own SIET experiments we found a condition-specific response, with greater magnitude of ERPs to bodily and psychological pain compared to neutral interactions both at an early and a late phase. Furthermore, significant differences were found between the two painful conditions with greater ERPs during somatically painful pictures compared to the psychologically painful condition. Results indicated that the painful pictures used in the SIET were processed in similar ways compared to the work of Han and colleagues, though it is important to note that psychological and bodily pain were not processed equally. Another finding of the study was that the activity over frontal regions for painful and neutral interactions was lateralized to the right hemisphere and that the ERPs correlated with self-rated empathic perspective taking abilities. This finding suggests that the right hemisphere may be specifically involved in the processing of empathy-related stimuli (Flasbeck & Brüne, 2017).

Aside from neuroimaging and ERP findings with regard to empathy for pain research, another line of research has focused on the role of the mirror neuron system (MNS) for empathy. Mirror neurons (MNs) are a subset of cross-modal sensorimotor neurons that were discovered in area F5 of the macaque brain (Di Pellegrino, Fadiga, Fogassi, Gallese, & Rizzolatti, 1992). These neurons fire not only when an action is performed but also when the same action is observed. The discharge of MNs is reinforced by goal-oriented, pragmatically meaningful actions that have a distinctive role in a certain context (Rizzolatti, Fadiga, Gallese, & Fogassi, 1996).

According to the "Simulation Theory," empathic responses occur due to the activation of mental processes in the observer, which simulate the observed action, emotion, or cognition mentally by utilizing a specialized neural system (i.e., the MNS) for action–observation matching (Gallese & Goldman, 1998; Rizzolatti et al., 1996). This activation occurs unconsciously and automatically and is supposed to be the basis of a direct form of action understanding (Gallese, Eagle, & Migone, 2007). Hence, the MNS might be a neural correlate recruited during empathic processes comparable to the representation of goal-directed actions that is referred to as motor resonance (Carr, Iacoboni, Dubeau, & Mazziotta, 2003; Mitchell, 2009). In humans, MN activity can be inferred, albeit tenuously, by electroencephalographic recording of mu-rhythm desynchronization (Altschuler, Vankov, Wang, Ramachandran, & Pineda, 1997). During resting state EEG, mu-rhythm oscillations can be measured over the primary premotor- and motor cortex with EEG or motorencephalography with frequencies in alpha

(8–13 Hz) and beta bands (around 20 Hz) (Pineda, 2005). EEG studies reported that performing a goal-directed action and observing someone else' goal-directed action both lead to mu-rhythm desynchronization (Rizzolatti & Craighero, 2005; Salmelin & Hari, 1994). Importantly, not only action execution and witnessing but also preparation and motion-imagination lead to the desynchronization of mu-oscillation leading to a suppression of up to 60% relative to the resting state (Pineda, 2005).

The relationship between mu-suppression and empathy is, however, obscure to some degree. In a study using hypnosis to modulate mu-suppression, we found that hypnosis was able to increase mu-suppression, at least in highly suggestible individuals, possibly by enhancing bottom-up activation of the MNS (Neufeld, Brown, Lee-Grimm, Newen, & Brüne, 2016). The study also showed, in line with previous work (Horan, Pineda, Wynn, Iacoboni, & Green, 2014; Perry, Troje, & Bentin, 2010; Woodruff, Martin, & Bilyk, 2011), a relationship between subjective measures of empathy and mu-rhythm suppression in the lower alpha band, whereby participants with greater mu-rhythm suppression reported *less* empathy. This finding seems to be counter-intuitive, because suggestibility values correlated both with higher mu-suppression and higher scores in empathy. However, whereas suggestibility correlated with mu-suppression in the beta frequency band, empathy traits correlated inversely with mu-suppression in the lower alpha band, suggesting that the different frequency components of the mu-rhythm need to be analyzed separately (Neufeld et al., 2016).

In fact, with regard to subjective empathy ratings, several studies found an inverse relationship between empathy and mu-suppression, that is, individuals with high empathy scores showed less mu-suppression (Brown, Wiersema, Pourtois, & Brüne, 2013; Perry et al., 2010). Similarly, Milston, Vanman, and Cunnington (2013) reported that participants rating higher in perspective taking exhibited less suppression in the beta band when observing actions. Another experiment demonstrated both enhancement and suppression in the beta band when subjects were asked to judge facial emotions (other-perspective) or imagine the presented emotion (self-perspective). In fact, while the "self" task was associated with enhancement, the "other" task was associated with suppression, suggesting a functional dissociation of the two frequency bands (Woodruff, Barbera, & von Oepen, 2016; for further details, see Chapter 6). Since mu-suppression also occurs when using empathy-for-pain paradigms (Mu, Fan, Mao, & Han, 2008), facial emotion recognition tasks (Moore, Gorodnitsky, & Pineda, 2012), or stimuli involving contagious yawning (Cooper et al., 2012), the MNS does not seem to be specific for empathy or empathy-related processes. This observation must be kept in mind when interpreting findings from studies of mu-suppression in clinical conditions such as autism or schizophrenia, in which empathy deficits may be part of the clinical picture (see below).

EMPATHY IN NEUROPSYCHIATRIC DISORDERS

Clinical work with neuropsychiatric patients suggests that empathy deficits or altered expressions of empathy are important issues across a range of diagnoses. Differences between disorders in terms of empathy are multifaceted and include onset of the disorder, chronicity, and coping strategies. An exhaustive review of the vast literature on empathy in neuropsychiatric conditions is beyond the scope of this overview, but a few examples may illustrate how complicated the study of empathy in relation to psychopathological syndromes can be. For example, antisocial traits in children with conduct disorder are often associated with a lack of empathic concern for others and are predictive of antisocial behavior later in life (Decety et al., 2015; Rhee et al., 2013). Adults with psychopathy are unable to experience distress of others as aversive, although their cognitive empathy seems at least to be intact. That is, psychopathy entails a good cognitive understanding of others' feelings ("I know how you feel") but does not entail the sharing of affective states ("I do not feel what you feel"), which can in part explain their callous and unemotional attitude toward others and experience of others' distress as pleasurable (Blair, 2005). In line with these clinical observations, neuroimaging studies have revealed that psychopathic traits in children, adolescents and adults are associated with less activation of brain regions involved in empathy for pain such as the ACC, AI, and AMG compared to unaffected individuals (Lockwood et al., 2013; Marsh et al., 2013). Adults with psychopathy display decreased activation in the vmPFC, lateral OFC and periaqueductal grey, as well as atypical functional and anatomical connectivity between the AMG, insula, and vmPFC (Decety, Chen, Harenski, & Kiehl, 2013a; Decety, Skelly, & Kiehl, 2013b).

A dissociation between cognitive and affective empathy also seems to be involved in neuropsychiatric diseases such as frontotemporal lobar degeneration, bipolar disorder and borderline personality disorder (BPD) (Cusi, Macqueen, & McKinnon, 2010; Harari, Shamay-Tsoory, Ravid, & Levkovitz, 2010; Minzenberg, Poole, & Vinogradov, 2006; Rankin, Kramer, & Miller, 2005; Shamay-Tsoory, Aharon-Peretz, & Perry, 2009), though the picture might be more complex. For example in BPD, we found altered empathy depending on the pain quality when compared to healthy control participants by using the SIET. Patients with BPD showed higher pain ratings for psychologically painful interactions and neutral interactions, whereas there was no difference regarding bodily pain (Flasbeck et al., 2017). In addition, patients rated psychologically painful interaction as more painful and bodily painful interactions as less painful in the first-person perspective when compared to the third-person perspective. The psychological pain rating was associated with Borderline symptom severity and with alexithymia, which was related to childhood trauma.

Moreover, alexithymia, traumatization, and pain ratings correlated with personal distress and perspective taking abilities, suggesting that empathy in BPD cannot simply be considered to be a "deficit" but highly dependent on biographical experiences and identification processes (Flasbeck et al., 2017).

Autism spectrum disorder (ASD) is another group of clinical syndromes associated with alterations in empathy. There is some evidence to suggest that people with ASD have difficulties in cognitive empathy, while evidence for emotional empathy deficits is more mixed with some studies reporting preserved emotional empathy (Capps, Kasari, Yirmiya, & Sigman, 1993; Dziobek et al., 2008; Sigman & Capps, 1997; Smith, 2006, 2009; Tams, 1998). Others have found reduced emotional empathy in ASDs (Minio-Paluello, Baron-Cohen, Avenanti, Walsh, & Aglioti, 2009; Shamay-Tsoory, Tomer, Yaniv, & Aharon-Peretz, 2002). Neuroimaging research reported dysfunction of the MNS in children with ASD (Dapretto et al., 2006) and in adults (Williams et al., 2006). Williams and colleagues found differences in the activity of the right TPJ which is a region involved in ToM during an imitation task. Moreover, patients with ASD showed no modulation of left AMG activity, suggesting altered patterns of brain activity during imitation, which may affect the development of mentalizing and empathic abilities. In addition to differences in the MNS, further neuroimaging studies in ASD demonstrated lower activation of brain areas involved in mentalizing (Castelli, Frith, Happé, & Frith, 2002; Happé et al., 1996), supporting the findings of dysfunctional cognitive empathy in autism. Regarding empathy for pain, participants with ASD showed altered hemodynamic responses of the pain matrix, heightened empathic arousal but impaired social understanding when perceiving others' distress (Fan, Chen, Chen, Decety, & Cheng, 2014).

Similar to ASDs, patients with schizophrenia present difficulties in all facets of empathy. Theoretical considerations have suggested that cognitive empathy is higher in patients with schizophrenia than in controls, partly, because paranoid patients seem to over-attribute mental states to others (Crespi & Badcock, 2008). On the other hand, experimental studies have revealed deficits in emotional and cognitive empathy in schizophrenia and these deficits affect processes including emotion recognition, feeling affected by others' emotions, and understanding others' mental states (Bora, Gökçen, & Veznedaroglu, 2008; Haker & Rössler, 2009). Neuroimaging studies investigating empathy in schizophrenia showed hypoactivation in frontal, temporal, and parietal regions, as well as hyperactivation in occipital regions compared with control subjects (Derntl et al., 2012; Smith et al., 2014). A meta-analysis also reported medial prefrontal hypoactivation and ventrolateral prefrontal dysfunction during the execution of empathy tasks. Moreover, facial emotion recognition has been found to be associated with AMG hypoactivation in schizophrenia. Also, there seems to be reduced activation of the superior temporal sulcus during cognitive empathy tasks (Sugranyes, Kyriakopoulos, Corrigall, Taylor, & Frangou, 2011). Together, these neuroimaging studies suggest that the neural network involved in empathy and related processes is functionally altered in individuals with ASD or schizophrenia.

SUMMARY AND FUTURE DIRECTIONS

The term "empathy" refers to a multifaceted construct involved in social relatedness to others. Its definitional boundaries are, in part, fuzzy, and different researchers have adopted different definitions, which needs to be taken into account when contrasting and comparing the various lines of research in nonhuman animals and humans. Our own take is that empathy involves the matching of another's emotional state *and* an understanding of the causality of the emotions displayed by the observed individual (Gonzalez-Liencres et al., 2013). Empathy also entails awareness of contextual factors and the ability to distinguish oneself from others. In the present chapter, we have argued that an understanding of the phylogeny of empathy is relevant for the interpretation of comparative nonhuman animal research on this topic. That is, empathy evolved as a mechanism that facilitates offspring survival, benefits close kin (genetically related) and more distantly related individuals belonging to the same social group (ingroup favoritism).

Showing empathic concern for others clearly depends on the availability of one's emotional resources. Put another way, expressing empathy is "costly" and may therefore vary with current affect, stability of emotional bonds, perceived stress, and more pervasive factors such as genetic variation, personality dimensions, and gender (or sex).

The neural pathway by which empathy is processed in the human brain seems to rely on a shared network comprising parts of the pain matrix, at least as far as empathy evoked by exposure to bodily or psychologically painful situations is concerned. Furthermore, this pathway may have "coopted" the MNS as a biological basis for matching one's own with another's emotional state. Measuring mu-rhythm suppression offers a neurophysiological window into the MNS, yet recent research has demonstrated that the relationship between the suppression of the brain's electrical activity in the alpha and beta band and empathy is more complex than initially thought. Accordingly, more research is needed to obtain a better understanding of the association of the subcomponents of mu-suppression and different facets of empathy in psychologically healthy subjects and in people with neuropsychiatric disorders.

Current research has focused on empathy as a trait marker. In addition, another line of research, however relatively unexplored, aims to investigate distinct dimensions of state-empathy, namely affective, cognitive, and associative state-empathy (Shen, 2010). Future studies may also need to explore more extensively state-empathy and the impact of psychosocial stress and other state-dependent factors, as for example the emotional state on trait-empathy (Kawakami & Katahira, 2015).

Psychopathological conditions are often associated with impoverished expression of empathy. This does not necessarily always imply a deficit in this domain, but can also rely on functional impairment or inaccessibility of empathic responses to another's distress. We have highlighted just a few neuropsychiatric conditions in which one or more facets of empathy seem to be compromised. Again, we consider it mandatory to examine in future studies how individuals with neuropsychiatric disorders respond to stress-inducing manipulations with regard to empathy. Such research could provide important insights for therapeutic approaches that aim to improve empathy or related processes such as compassion for others or being compassionate for oneself, including ones that employ novel psychotherapeutic techniques or pharmacological treatment (see additional chapters in this book). There is hope that empathy, compassion, and self-compassion are responsive to therapy, and seeing these emotional domains as a prime target for psychological treatment reflects their importance for humaneness.

References

Abu-Akel, A., Palgi, S., Klein, E., Decety, J., & Shamay-Tsoory, S. (2015). Oxytocin increases empathy to pain when adopting the other-but not the self-perspective. *Social Neuroscience, 10*(1), 7–15.

Altschuler, E., Vankov, A., Wang, V., Ramachandran, V., & Pineda, J. (1997). Person see, person do: Human cortical electrophysiological correlates of monkey see monkey do cells. *Society for Neuroscience, 23*(2), 1848.

Baptista-de-Souza, D., Nunciato, A. C., Pereira, B. C., Fachinni, G., Zaniboni, C. R., & Canto-de-Souza, A. (2015). Mice undergoing neuropathic pain induce anxiogenic-like effects and hypernociception in cagemates. *Behavioural Pharmacology, 26*, 664–672 (7-Special Issue Pharmacological Approaches To The Study Of Social Behaviour. Part 2: Social Module).

Baptista-de-Souza, D., Nunes-de-Souza, R., & Canto-de-Souza, A. (2016). Empathy for pain: Hyper or hypoalgesia in mice living with a conspecific in chronic pain? *The Journal of Pain, 17*(4), S58 (331).

Barnett, M. A. (1987). Empathy and related responses in children. In N. Eisenberg, & J. Strayer (Eds.), *Cambridge studies in social and emotional development. Empathy and its development* (pp. 146–162). New York: Cambridge University Press.

Bartal, I. B. A., Decety, J., & Mason, P. (2011). Empathy and pro-social behavior in rats. *Science, 334*(6061), 1427–1430.

Bartal, I. B. A., Rodgers, D. A., Sarria, M. S. B., Decety, J., & Mason, P. (2014). Pro-social behavior in rats is modulated by social experience. *Elife, 3*, e01385.

Baskin-Sommers, A., Krusemark, E., & Ronningstam, E. (2014). Empathy in narcissistic personality disorder: From clinical and empirical perspectives. *Personality Disorders: Theory, Research, and Treatment, 5*(3), 323.

Bischof-Köhler, D. (2012). Empathy and self-recognition in phylogenetic and ontogenetic perspective. *Emotion Review, 4*(1), 40–48.

Blair, R. J. R. (2005). Responding to the emotions of others: Dissociating forms of empathy through the study of typical and psychiatric populations. *Consciousness and Cognition, 14*(4), 698–718.

Bora, E., Gökçen, S., & Veznedaroglu, B. (2008). Empathic abilities in people with schizophrenia. *Psychiatry Research, 160*, 23–29.

Botvinick, M., Jha, A. P., Bylsma, L. M., Fabian, S. A., Solomon, P. E., & Prkachin, K. M. (2005). Viewing facial expressions of pain engages cortical areas involved in the direct experience of pain. *NeuroImage, 25*(1), 312–319.

Brosnan, S. F., & de Waal, F. B. M. (2003). Monkeys reject unequal pay. *Nature,*(425), 297–299.

Brown, E., Wiersema, J., Pourtois, G., & Brüne, M. (2013). Modulation of motor cortex activity when observing rewarding and punishing actions. *Neuropsychologia, 51*, 52–58.

Byrne, R. W. (1995). *The thinking ape: Evolutionary origins of intelligence*. Oxford: Oxford University Press on Demand.

Capps, L., Kasari, C., Yirmiya, N., & Sigman, M. (1993). Parental perception of emotional expressiveness in children with autism. *Journal of Consulting and Clinical Psychology, 61*, 475–484.

Carpenter, M., Nagell, K., Tomasello, M., Butterworth, G., & Moore, C. (1998). Social cognition, joint attention, and communicative competence from 9 to 15 months of age. *Monographs of the society for research in child development*, i-174.

Carr, L., Iacoboni, M., Dubeau, M. C., Mazziotta, J. C., & Lenzi, G. L. (2003). Neural mechanisms of empathy in humans: A relay from neural systems for imitation to limbic areas. *Proceedings of the National Academy of Sciences of the United States of America, 100*(9), 5497–5502.

Castelli, F., Frith, C., Happé, F., & Frith, U. (2002). Autism, Asperger syndrome and brain mechanisms for the attribution of mental states to animated shapes. *Brain, 125*(8), 1839–1849.

Chen, Q., Panksepp, J. B., & Lahvis, G. P. (2009). Empathy is moderated by genetic background in mice. *PLoS ONE, 4*(2), e4387.

Cheng, Y., Lin, C. P., Liu, H. L., Hsu, Y. Y., Lim, K. E., Hung, D., et al. (2007). Expertise modulates the perception of pain in others. *Current Biology, 17*(19), 1708–1713.

Christie, R., & Geis, F. L. (1970). *Studies in Machiavellianism*. New York, NY: Academic Press.

Cikara, M., Bruneau, E. G., & Saxe, R. R. (2011). Us and them intergroup failures of empathy. *Current Directions in Psychological Science, 20*(3), 149–153.

Cooper, N. R., Puzzo, I., Pawley, A. D., Bowes-Mulligan, R. A., Kirkpatrick, E. V., Antoniou, P. A., et al. (2012). Bridging a yawning chasm: EEG investigations into the debate concerning the role of the human mirror neuron system in contagious yawning. *Cognitive, Affective, & Behavioral Neuroscience, 2*, 393–405.

Craig, A. (2003a). Pain mechanisms: Labeled lines versus convergence in central processing. *Annual Review of Neuroscience, 26*, 1–30.

Craig, A. (2003b). A new view of pain as a homeostatic emotion. *Trends in Neurosciences, 26*, 303–307.

Crespi, B., & Badcock, C. (2008). Psychosis and autism as diametrical disorders of the social brain. *The Behavioral and Brain Sciences, 31*, 241–320.

Cusi, A., Macqueen, G. M., & McKinnon, M. C. (2010). Altered self-report of empathic responding in patients with bipolar disorder. *Psychiatry Research, 178*, 354–358.

Dapretto, M., Davies, M. S., Pfeifer, J. H., Scott, A. A., Sigman, M., Bookheimer, S. Y., et al. (2006). Understanding emotions in others: Mirror neuron dysfunction in children with autism spectrum disorders. *Nature Neuroscience, 9*(1), 28–30.

Davis, M. H. (1983). Measuring individual differences in empathy: Evidence for a multidimensional approach. *Journal of Personality and Social Psychology, 44*(1), 113–126.

Decety, J. (2011). The neuroevolution of empathy. *Annals of the New York Academy of Sciences,* *1231,* 35–45.

Decety, J., & Fotopoulou, A. (2015). Why empathy has a beneficial impact on others in medicine: Unifying theories. *Frontiers in Behavioral Neuroscience, 8,* 457.

Decety, J., & Jackson, P. L. (2004). The functional architecture of human empathy. *Behavioral and Cognitive Neuroscience Reviews, 3*(2), 71–100.

Decety, J., & Svetlova, M. (2012). Putting together phylogenetic and ontogenetic perspectives on empathy. *Developmental Cognitive Neuroscience, 2*(1), 1–24.

Decety, J., Yang, C. Y., & Cheng, Y. (2010). Physicians down-regulate their pain empathy response: An event-related brain potential study. *NeuroImage, 50*(4), 1676–1682.

Decety, J., Chen, C., Harenski, C., & Kiehl, K. A. (2013a). An fMRI study of affective perspective taking in individuals with psychopathy: Imagining another in pain does not evoke empathy. *Frontiers in Human Neuroscience, 7,* 489.

Decety, J., Skelly, L. R., & Kiehl, K. A. (2013b). Brain response to empathy-eliciting scenarios involving pain in incarcerated individuals with psychopathy. *JAMA Psychiatry, 70,* 638.

Decety, J., Bartal, I. B. -A., Uzefovsky, F., & Knafo-Noam, A. (2015). Empathy as a driver of prosocial behaviour: Highly conserved neurobehavioural mechanisms across species. *Philosophical Transactions of the Royal Society of London: Series B, Biological sciences* (371).

De Dreu, C. K., Greer, L. L., Handgraaf, M. J., Shalvi, S., Van Kleef, G. A., Baas, M., et al. (2010). The neuropeptide oxytocin regulates parochial altruism in intergroup conflict among humans. *Science, 328*(5984), 1408–1411.

De Dreu, C. K., Greer, L. L., Van Kleef, G. A., Shalvi, S., & Handgraaf, M. J. (2011). Oxytocin promotes human ethnocentrism. *Proceedings of the National Academy of Sciences, 108*(4), 1262–1266.

Derntl, B., Finkelmeyer, A., Toygar, T. K., Hülsmann, A., Schneider, F., Falkenberg, D. I., et al. (2009). Generalized deficit in all core components of empathy in schizophrenia. *Schizophrenia Research, 108,* 197–206.

Derntl, B., Finkelmeyer, A., Voss, B., Eickhoff, S. B., Kellermann, T., Schneider, F., et al. (2012). Neural correlates of the core facets of empathy in schizophrenia. *Schizophrenia Research, 136*(1), 70–81.

Di Pellegrino, G., Fadiga, L., Fogassi, L., Gallese, V., & Rizzolatti, G. (1992). Understanding motor events: A neurophysiological study. *Experimental Brain Research, 91*(1), 176–180.

Dölen, G., Darvishzadeh, A., Huang, K. W., & Malenka, R. C. (2013). Social reward requires coordinated activity of nucleus accumbens oxytocin and serotonin. *Nature, 501*(7466), 179–184.

Domes, G., Heinrichs, M., Michel, A., Berger, C., & Herpertz, S. C. (2007). Oxytocin improves "mind-reading" in humans. *Biological Psychiatry, 61*(6), 731–733.

Donaldson, Z. R., & Young, L. J. (2008). Oxytocin, vasopressin, and the neurogenetics of sociality. *Science, 322*(5903), 900–904.

Dondi, M., Simion, F., & Caltran, G. (1999). Can newborns discriminate between their own cry and the cry of another newborn infant? *Developmental Psychology, 35*(2), 418–426.

Dziobek, I., Rogers, K., Fleck, S., Bahnemann, M., Heekeren, H. R., Wolf, O. T., et al. (2008). Dissociation of cognitive and emotional empathy in adults with Asperger syndrome using the Multifaceted Empathy Test (MET). *Journal of Autism and Developmental Disorders, 38,* 464–473.

Eibl-Eibesfeldt, I. (1975). *Ethology: Biology of behaviour* (2nd ed.). Boston, MA: Thomson Learning.

Eisenberg, N. I. (2012). The neural bases of social pain: Evidence for shared representations with physical pain. *Psychosomatic Medicine, 74*(2), 126–135.

Eisenberg, N., Fabes, R. A., Murphy, B., Karbon, M., Maszk, P., Smith, M., et al. (1994). The relations of emotionality and regulation to dispositional and situational empathy-related responding. *Journal of Personality and Social Psychology, 66*(4), 776.

Evans, S., Shergill, S. S., & Averbeck, B. B. (2010). Oxytocin decreases aversion to angry faces in an associative learning task. *Neuropsychopharmacology*, *35*(13), 2502–2509.

Fan, Y., & Han, S. (2008). Temporal dynamic of neural mechanisms involved in empathy for pain: An event-related brain potential study. *Neuropsychologia*, *46*(1), 160–173.

Fan, Y. T., Chen, C., Chen, S. C., Decety, J., & Cheng, Y. (2014). Empathic arousal and social understanding in individuals with autism: Evidence from fMRI and ERP measurements. *Social Cognitive and Affective Neuroscience*, *9*(8), 1203–1213.

Flasbeck, V., & Brüne, M. (2017). Neural correlates of empathy for physical and psychological pain. *Journal of Psychophysiology*.

Flasbeck, V., Enzi, B., & Brüne, M. (2017). Altered empathy for psychological and physical pain in Borderline Personality Disorder. *Journal of Personality Disorders*, *31*(5), 689–708.

Fogassi, L., Ferrari, P. F., Gesierich, B., Rozzi, S., Chersi, F., & Rizzolatti, G. (2005). Parietal lobe: From action organization to intention understanding. *Science*, *308*(5722), 662–667.

Fonagy, P., Steele, M., Steele, H., Moran, G. S., & Higgitt, A. C. (1991). The capacity for understanding mental states: The reflective self in parent and child and its significance for security of attachment. *Infant Mental Health Journal*, *12*(3), 201–218.

Gallese, V. (2009). Mirror neurons, embodied simulation, and the neural basis of social identification. *Psychoanalytic Dialogues*, *19*, 519–536.

Gallese, V., & Goldman, A. (1998). Mirror neurons and the simulation theory of mind-reading. *Trends in Cognitive Sciences*, *2*(12), 493–501.

Gallese, V., Eagle, M., & Migone, P. (2007). Intentional attunement: Mirror neurons and the neural underpinnings of interpersonal relations. *Journal of the American Psychoanalytic Association*, *55*, 131–175.

Goetz, J. L., Keltner, D., & Simon-Thomas, E. (2010). Compassion: An evolutionary analysis and empirical review. *Psychological Bulletin*, *136*, 351–374.

Gonzalez-Liencres, C., Shamay-Tsoory, S. G., & Brüne, M. (2013). Towards a neuroscience of empathy: Ontogeny, phylogeny, brain mechanisms, context and psychopathology. *Neuroscience and Biobehavioral Reviews*, *37*, 1537–1548.

Gonzalez-Liencres, C., Juckel, G., Tas, C., Friebe, A., & Brüne, M. (2014). Emotional contagion in mice: The role of familiarity. *Behavioural Brain Research*, *263*, 16–21.

Gonzalez-Liencres, C., Brown, E. C., Tas, C., Breidenstein, A., & Brüne, M. (2016a). Alterations in ERP responses to empathy for pain in schizophrenia. *Psychiatry Research*, *241*, 14–21.

Gonzalez-Liencres, C., Juckel, G., Esslinger, M., Wachholz, S., Manitz, M. P., Brüne, M., et al. (2016b). Emotional contagion is not altered in mice prenatally exposed to poly(I:C) on gestational day 9. *Frontiers in* Behavioral Neuroscience, *10*, 134.

Grenier, F., & Lüthi, A. (2010). Mouse brains wired for empathy? *Nature Neuroscience*, *13*, 406–408.

Groppe, S. E., Gossen, A., Rademacher, L., Hahn, A., Westphal, L., Gründer, G., et al. (2013). Oxytocin influences processing of socially relevant cues in the ventral tegmental area of the human brain. *Biological Psychiatry*, *74*(3), 172–179.

Gross, M. R. (2005). The evolution of parental care. *The Quarterly Review of Biology*, *80*, 37–45.

Habashi, M. M., Graziano, W. G., & Hoover, A. E. (2016). Searching for the prosocial personality a big five approach to linking personality and prosocial behavior. *Personality and Social Psychology Bulletin* 0146167216652859.

Haker, H., & Rössler, W. (2009). Empathy in schizophrenia: Impaired resonance. *European Archives of Psychiatry and Clinical Neuroscience*, *259*, 352–361.

Han, S., Fan, Y., & Mao, L. (2008). Gender difference in empathy for pain: An electrophysiological investigation. *Brain Research*, *1196*, 85–93.

Happé, F., Ehlers, S., Fletcher, P., Frith, U., Johansson, M., Gillberg, C., et al. (1996). 'Theory of mind' in the brain evidence from a PET scan study of Asperger syndrome. *NeuroReport*, *8*(1), 197–201.

Harari, H., Shamay-Tsoory, S. G., Ravid, M., & Levkovitz, Y. (2010). Double dissociation between cognitive and affective empathy in borderline personality disorder. *Psychiatry Research*, *175*, 277–279.

Hare, R. D. (2006). Psychopathy: A clinical and forensic overview. *Psychiatric Clinics of North America, 29*, 709–724.

Haviland, J. M., & Lelwica, M. (1987). The induced affect response: 10-week-old infants' responses to three emotion expressions. *Developmental Psychology, 23*(1), 97–104.

Heinrichs, M., Baumgartner, T., Kirschbaum, C., & Ehlert, U. (2003). Social support and oxytocin interact to suppress cortisol and subjective responses to psychosocial stress. *Biological Psychiatry, 54*(12), 1389–1398.

Horan, W. P., Pineda, J. A., Wynn, J. K., Iacoboni, M., & Green, M. F. (2014). Some markers of mirroring appear intact in schizophrenia: Evidence from mu suppression. *Cognitive, Affective, & Behavioral Neuroscience, 14*(3), 1049–1060.

Iacoboni, M. (2009). Imitation, empathy, and mirror neurons. *Annual Review of Psychology, 60*, 653–670.

Jackson, P. L., Meltzoff, A. N., & Decety, J. (2005). How do we perceive the pain of others? A window into the neural processes involved in empathy. *NeuroImage, 24*(3), 771–779.

Jackson, P. L., Rainville, P., & Decety, J. (2006). To what extent do we share the pain of others? Insight from the neural bases of pain empathy. *Pain, 125*(1–2), 5–9.

Jensen, K. B., Petrovic, P., Kerr, C. E., Kirsch, I., Raicek, J., Cheetham, A., Spaeth, R., Cook, A., Gollub, R. L., Kong, J., & Kaptchuk, T. J. (2014). Sharing pain and relief: neural correlates of physicians during treatment of patients. *Molecular Psychiatry, 19*(3), 392–398.

Jeon, D., Kim, S., Chetana, M., Jo, D., Ruley, H. E., Lin, S. Y., et al. (2010). Observational fear learning involves affective pain system and Cav1 2 Ca2+ channels in ACC. *Nature Neuroscience, 13*(4), 482–488.

Kavaliers, M., Colwell, D. D., & Choleris, E. (2003). Learning to fear and cope with a natural stressor: Individually and socially acquired corticosterone and avoidance responses to biting flies. *Hormones and Behavior, 43*(1), 99–107.

Kawakami, A., & Katahira, K. (2015). Influence of trait empathy on the emotion evoked by sad music and on the preference for it. *Frontiers in Psychology, 6.*

Kelm, Z., Womer, J., Walter, J. K., & Feudtner, C. (2014). Interventions to cultivate physician empathy: A systematic review. *BMC Medical Education, 14*(1), 1.

Knobloch, H. S., & Grinevich, V. (2015). Evolution of oxytocin pathways in the brain of vertebrates. Oxytocin's routes in social behavior: Into the 21st century. *"Precision medicine" approach for oxytocin.* 9.

Knobloch, H. S., Charlet, A., Stoop, R., & Grinevich, V. (2014). Viral vectors for optogenetics of hypothalamic neuropeptides. In *Viral Vector Approaches in Neurobiology and Brain Diseases* (pp. 311–329). Totowa, NJ: Humana Press.

Kong, J., White, N. S., Kwong, K. K., Vangel, M. G., Rosman, I. S., Gracely, R. H., et al. (2006). Using fMRI to dissociate sensory encoding from cognitive evaluation of heat pain intensity. *Human Brain Mapping, 27*, 715–721.

Kosfeld, M., Heinrichs, M., Zak, P. J., Fischbacher, U., & Fehr, E. (2005). Oxytocin increases trust in humans. *Nature, 435*(7042), 673–676.

Kristjansson, K. (2004). Empathy, sympathy, justice and the child. *Journal of Moral Education, 33*, 291–305.

Labuschagne, I., Phan, K. L., Wood, A., Angstadt, M., Chua, P., Heinrichs, M., et al. (2010). Oxytocin attenuates amygdala reactivity to fear in generalized social anxiety disorder. *Neuropsychopharmacology, 35*(12), 2403–2413.

Lamm, C., Decety, J., & Singer, T. (2011). Meta-analytic evidence for common and distinct neural networks associated with directly experienced pain and empathy for pain. *NeuroImage, 54*(3), 2492–2502.

Lancaster, K., Carter, C. S., Pournajafi-Nazarloo, H., Karaoli, T., Lillard, T. S., Jack, A., et al. (2015). Plasma oxytocin explains individual differences in neural substrates of social perception. *Frontiers in Human Neuroscience, 9*, 132.

Langford, D. J., Crager, S. E., Shehzad, Z., Smith, S. B., Sotocinal, S. G., Levenstadt, J. S., et al. (2006). Social modulation of pain as evidence for empathy in mice. *Science, 312*(5782), 1967–1970.

LeDoux, J. E. (2000). Emotion circuits in the brain. *Annual Review of Neuroscience, 23,* 155–184.

Leslie, A. (1987). Pretence and representation: The origins of "theory of mind". *Psychological Review, 94,* 412–426.

Li, W., & Han, S. (2010). Perspective taking modulates event-related potentials to perceived pain. *Neuroscience Letters, 469*(3), 328–332.

Lockwood, P. L., Sebastian, C. L., McCrory, E. J., Hyde, Z. H., Gu, X., De Brito, S. A., et al. (2013). Association of callous traits with reduced neural response to others' pain in children with conduct problems. *Current Biology, 23*(10), 901–905.

Lorenz, K. (1935). Der Kumpan in der Umwelt des Vogels. *Journal of Ornithology, 83,* 137–213.

MacArthur, R., & Wilson, E. (1967). *The theory of biogeography.* Princeton, NJ: Princeton Univ. Press 31–59.

MacLean, P. D. (1990). *The triune brain in evolution: Role in paleocerebral functions.* New York: Plenum Press.

Magnhagen, C. (1992). Parental care and predation risk in fish. *Annales Zoologici Fennici, 29,* 227–232.

Marsh, A. A., Finger, E. C., Fowler, K. A., Adalio, C. J., Jurkowitz, I. T., Schechter, J. C., et al. (2013). Empathic responsiveness in amygdala and anterior cingulate cortex in youths with psychopathic traits. *Journal of Child Psychology and Psychiatry, 54*(8), 900–910.

Martin, G. B., & Clark, R. D. (1982). Distress crying in neonates: Species and peer specificity. *Developmental Psychology, 18*(1), 3–9.

Martin, L. J., Hathaway, G., Isbester, K., Mirali, S., Acland, E. L., Niederstrasser, N., et al. (2015). Reducing social stress elicits emotional contagion of pain in mouse and human strangers. *Current Biology, 25*(3), 326–332.

Masserman, J. H., Wechkin, S., & Terris, W. (1964). "Altruistic" behavior in rhesus monkeys. *The American Journal of Psychiatry, 121*(6), 584–585.

McDiarmid, R. W. (1978). In *Evolution of parental care in frogs in the development of behavior: Comparative and evolutionary aspects* (pp. 127–147). Oxford: Garland STPM Press.

Melchers, M. C., Li, M., Haas, B. W., Reuter, M., Bischoff, L., & Montag, C. (2016). Similar personality patterns are associated with empathy in four different countries. *Frontiers in Psychology, 7,* 290.

Meltzoff, A. N., & Moore, M. K. (1977). Imitation of facial and manual gestures by human neonates. *Science, 198*(4312), 75–78.

Melzack, R., & Casey, K. L. (1968). Sensory, motivational and central control determinants of pain: A new conceptual model. In D. R. Kenshalo (Ed.), *The skin senses.* Kalamazoo, MI: Springfield.

Mier, D., Lis, S., Esslinger, C., Sauer, C., Hagenhoff, M., Ulferts, J., Gallhofer, B., et al. (2012). Neuronal correlates of social cognition in borderline personality disorder. *Social Cognitive and Affective Neuroscience, 8*(5), 531–537.

Milgram, S. (1963). Behavioral study of obedience. *Journal of Abnormal and Social Psychology, 67,* 371–378.

Milgram, S. (1974). *Obedience to authority: An experimental view.* New York, NY: HarperCollins.

Milston, S., Vanman, E., & Cunnington, R. (2013). Cognitive empathy and motor activity during observed actions. *Neuropsychologia, 51*(6), 1103–1108.

Minio-Paluello, I., Baron-Cohen, S., Avenanti, A., Walsh, V., & Aglioti, S. M. (2009). Absence of embodied empathy during pain observation in asperger syndrome. *Biological Psychiatry, 65,* 55–62.

Minzenberg, M. J., Poole, J. H., & Vinogradov, S. (2016). Social-emotion recognition in borderline personality disorder. *Comprehensive Psychiatry, 47,* 468–474.

Mitchell, J. P. (2009). Inferences about mental states. *Philosophical Transactions of the Royal Society B: Biological Sciences, 364*(1521), 1309–1316.

Moore, A., Gorodnitsky, I., & Pineda, J. (2012). EEG mu component responses to viewing emotional faces. *Behavioral Brain Research, 226*(1), 309–316.

Morelli, S. A., & Lieberman, M. D. (2013). The role of automaticity and attention in neural processes underlying empathy for happiness, sadness, and anxiety. *Frontiers in Human Neuroscience, 7*(160), 28–38.

Morelli, S. A., Rameson, L. T., & Lieberman, M. D. (2012). The neural components of empathy: Predicting daily prosocial behavior. *Social Cognitive and Affective Neuroscience, 9*(1), 39–47.

Mu, Y., Fan, Y., Mao, L., & Han, S. (2008). Event-related theta and alpha oscillations mediate empathy for pain. *Brain Research, 1234*, 128–136.

Neufeld, E., Brown, E. C., Lee-Grimm, S. -I., Newen, A., & Brüne, M. (2016). Intentional action processing results from automatic bottom-up attention: An EEG-investigation into the Social Relevance Hypothesis using hypnosis. *Consciousness and Cognition, 42*, 101–112.

Nummenmaa, L., Hirvonen, J., Parkkola, R., & Hietanen, J. K. (2008). Is emotional contagion special? An fMRI study on neural systems for affective and cognitive empathy. *NeuroImage, 43*, 571–580.

Panfile, T. M., & Laible, D. J. (2012). Attachment security and child's empathy: The mediating role of emotion regulation. *Merrill-Palmer Quarterly, 58*(1), 1–21.

Paulhus, D. L., & Williams, K. M. (2002). The dark triad of personality: Narcissism, Machiavellianism, and psychopathy. *Journal of Research in Personality, 36*(6), 556–563.

Perry, A., Troje, N. F., & Bentin, S. (2010). Exploring motor system contributions to the perception of social information: Evidence from EEG activity in the mu/alpha frequency range. *Social Neuroscience, 5*(3), 272–284.

Pineda, J. (2005). The functional significance of mu rhythms: Translating "seeing" and "hearing" into "doing". *Brain Research Reviews, 50*, 57–68.

Preston, S. D., & De Waal, F. B. M. (2002). Empathy: Its ultimate and proximate bases. *The Behavioral and Brain Sciences, 25*(1), 1–20; (discussion 20–71).

Preston, S. D., Hofelich, A. J., & Stansfield, R. B. (2013). The ethology of empathy: A taxonomy of real-world targets of need and their effect on observers. *Frontiers in Human Neuroscience, 7*, 488.

Provine, R. (2005). Yawning. *American Scientist, 93*, 532.

Rameson, L. T., Morelli, S. A., & Lieberman, M. D. (2012). The neural correlates of empathy: Experience, automaticity, and prosocial behavior. *Journal of Cognitive Neuroscience, 24*(1), 235–245.

Rankin, K. P., Kramer, J. H., & Miller, B. L. (2005). Patterns of cognitive and emotional empathy in frontotemporal lobar degeneration. *Cognitive and Behavioral Neurology, 18*, 28–36.

Rhee, S. H., Friedman, N. P., Boeldt, D. L., Corley, R. P., Hewitt, J. K., Knafo, A., et al. (2013). Early concern and disregard for others as predictors of antisocial behavior. *Journal of Child Psychology and Psychiatry, 54*, 157–166.

Ritter, K., Dziobek, I., Preißler, S., Rüter, A., Vater, A., Fydrich, T., et al. (2011). Lack of empathy in patients with narcissistic personality disorder. *Psychiatry Research, 187*(1), 241–247.

Rizzolatti, G., & Craighero, L. (2005). Mirror neuron: A neurological approach to empathy. *Neurobiology of human values*. Berlin-Heidelberg: Springer 107–123.

Rizzolatti, G., Fadiga, L., Gallese, V., & Fogassi, L. (1996). Premotor cortex and the recognition of motor actions. *Cognitive Brain Research, 3*(2), 131–141.

Rochat, P., & Striano, T. (2000). Perceived self in infancy. *Infant Behavior and Development, 23*(3), 513–530.

Saarela, M. V., Hlushchuk, Y., Williams, A. C., Schürmann, M., Kalso, E., & Hari, R. (2007). The compassionate brain: Humans detect intensity of pain from another's face. *Cerebral Cortex, 17*(1), 230–237.

Salmelin, R., & Hari, R. (1994). Spatiotemporal characteristics of sensorimotor neuromagnetic rhythms related to thumb movement. *Neuroscience, 60*, 537–550.

Sargent, R. C., & Gross, M. R. (1985). Parental investment decision rules and the Concorde fallacy. *Behavioral Ecology and Sociobiology, 17*, 43–45.

Schlaffke, L., Lissek, S., Lenz, M., Juckel, G., Schultz, T., Tegenthoff, M., et al. (2015). Shared and nonshared neural networks of cognitive and affective theory-of-mind: A neuroimaging study using cartoon picture stories. *Human Brain Mapping, 36*(1), 29–39.

Shamay-Tsoory, S. G., Tomer, R., Yaniv, S., & Aharon-Peretz, J. (2002). Empathy deficits in Asperger syndrome: A cognitive profile. *Neurocase, 8*, 245–252.

Shamay-Tsoory, S. G., Aharon-Peretz, J., & Perry, D. (2009). Two systems for empathy: A double dissociation between emotional and cognitive empathy in inferior frontal gyrus versus ventromedial prefrontal lesions. *Brain, 132*(Pt 3), 617–627.

Shamay-Tsoory, S. G., Abu-Akel, A., Palgi, S., Sulieman, R., Fischer-Shofty, M., Levkovitz, Y., et al. (2013). Giving peace a chance: Oxytocin increases empathy to pain in the context of the Israeli–Palestinian conflict. *Psychoneuroendocrinology, 38*(12), 3139–3144.

Shahrokh, D. K., Zhang, T. Y., Diorio, J., Gratton, A., & Meaney, M. J. (2010). Oxytocin-dopamine interactions mediate variations in maternal behavior in the rat. *Endocrinology, 151*, 2276–2286.

Shen, L. (2010). On a scale of state empathy during message processing. *Western Journal of Communication, 74*(5), 504–524.

Sigman, M., & Capps, L. (1997). *Children with autism: A developmental perspective.* Harvard: Harvard University Press.

Simner, M. L. (1971). Newborn's response to the cry of another infant. *Developmental Psychology, 5*(1), 136–150.

Singer, T., & Lamm, C. (2009). The social neuroscience of empathy. *Annals of the New York Academy of Sciences, 1156*, 81–96.

Singer, T., Seymour, B., O'Doherty, J., Kaube, H., Dolan, R. J., & Frith, C. D. (2004). Empathy for pain involves the affective but not sensory components of pain. *Science, 303*(5661), 1157–1162.

Smith, A. (2006). Cognitive empathy and emotional empathy in human behavior and evolution. *The Psychological Record, 56*, 3–21.

Smith, A. (2009). The empathy imbalance hypothesis of autism: A theoretical approach to cognitive and emotional empathy in autistic development. *The Psychological Record, 59*, 273–294.

Smith, M. J., Schroeder, M. P., Abram, S. V., Goldman, M. B., Parrish, T. B., Wang, X., et al. (2014). Alterations in brain activation during cognitive empathy are related to social functioning in schizophrenia. *Schizophrenia Bulletin, 41*(1), 211–222.

Spreng, R. N., McKinnon, M. C., Mar, R. A., & Levine, B. (2009). The Toronto Empathy Questionnaire: Scale development and initial validation of a factor-analytic solution to multiple empathy measures. *Journal of Personality Assessment, 91*(1), 62–71.

Stearns, S. C. (1992). *The evolution of life histories* (Vol. 249). Oxford: Oxford University Press.

Sugranyes, G., Kyriakopoulos, M., Corrigall, R., Taylor, E., & Frangou, S. (2011). Autism spectrum disorders and schizophrenia: Meta-analysis of the neural correlates of social cognition. *PLoS ONE, 6*(10), e25322.

Svetlova, M., Nichols, S. R., & Brownell, C. A. (2010). Toddlers' prosocial behavior: From instrumental to empathic to altruistic helping. *Child Development, 81*(6), 1814–1827.

Tams, R. (1998). *Parents' experiences and perceptions of autism: A qualitative study.* Cardiff: University of Wales.

Tomova, L., Majdandžić, J., Hummer, A., Windischberger, C., Heinrichs, M., & Lamm, C. (2016). Increased neural responses to empathy for pain might explain how acute stress increases prosociality. *Social Cognitive and Affective Neuroscience, 12*(3), 401–408.

Treede, R. D., Kenshalo, D. R., Gracely, R. H., & Jones, A. K. (1999). The cortical representation of pain. *Pain, 79*, 105–111.

Trivers, R. L. (1971). The evolution of reciprocal altruism. *The Quarterly Review of Biology, 46*, 35–57.

Tullberg, B. S., Ah-King, M., & Temrin, H. (2002). Phylogenetic reconstruction of parental-care systems in the ancestors of birds. *Philosophical Transactions of the Royal Society of London: Series B, Biological Sciences, 357*, 251–257.

van der Heiden, L., Scherpiet, S., Konicar, L., Birbaumer, N., & Veit, R. (2013). Inter-individual differences in successful perspective taking during pain perception mediates emotional responsiveness in self and others: An fMRI study. *NeuroImage, 65*, 387–394.

Viding, E., McCrory, E., & Seara-Cardoso, A. (2014). Psychopathy. *Current Biology, 24*(18), R871–R874.

Wesolowski, T. (1994). On the origin of parental care and the early evolution of male and female parental roles in birds. *The American Naturalist, 143*, 39–58.

Williams, K. D., Cheung, C. K., & Choi, W. (2000). Cyberostracism: Effects of being ignored over the Internet. *Journal of Personality and Social Psychology, 79*(5), 748.

Williams, J. H., Waiter, G. D., Gilchrist, A., Perrett, D. I., Murray, A. D., & Whiten, A. (2006). Neural mechanisms of imitation and 'mirror neuron' functioning in autistic spectrum disorder. *Neuropsychologia, 44*(4), 610–621.

Wilson, D. S., Near, D. C., & Miller, R. R. (1998). Individual differences in Machiavellianism as a mix of cooperative and exploitative strategies. *Evolution and Human Behavior, 19*, 203–212.

Woodruff, C. C., Martin, T., & Bilyk, N. (2011). Differences in self-and other-induced Mu suppression are correlated with empathic abilities. *Brain Research, 1405*, 69–76.

Woodruff, C. C., Barbera, D., & von Oepen, R. (2016). Task-related dissociation of EEG µ enhancement and suppression. *International Journal of Psychophysiology, 99*, 18–23.

Zahn-Waxler, C., Radke-Yarrow, M., & King, R. A. (1979). Child rearing and children's prosocial initiations toward victims of distress. *Child Development*, 319–330.

Zahn-Waxler, C., Radke-Yarrow, M., Wagner, E., & Chapman, M. (1992). Development of concern for others. *Developmental Psychology, 28*(1), 126.

Zaki, J., Bolger, N., & Ochsner, K. (2008). It takes two: The interpersonal nature of empathic accuracy. *Psychological Science, 19*, 399–401.

Zilles, K. (1987). *Graue und weiße Substanz des Hirnmantels. Anatomie des Menschen.* Stuttgart: InGeorg Thieme Verlag 382-471.

Further Reading

Byrne, R. W. (2002). Emulation in apes: Verdict 'not proven'. *Developmental Science, 5*(1), 20–22.

The Brain that Longs to Care for Others: The Current Neuroscience of Compassion

Larry Stevens*, Jasmine Benjamin**

*Northern Arizona University, Flagstaff, AZ, United States; **University of Arizona, Tucson, AZ, United States

By the time this chapter goes to press, over 500,000 men, women, and children will have been killed as a result of the civil war in Syria, most of them innocent civilians not directly involved in the war effort. Very many of these have been literally shredded and crushed to death in the northern city of Aleppo by relentless air assaults of barrel and bunker-buster bombs, the former barrels, tanks, and cylinders filled with oil, fuel, or gasoline, explosives, and metal fragments and the latter huge bombs designed to level heavily fortified military installations but instead dropped on hospitals and residential apartment buildings reducing towering concrete and steel structures to piles of rubble. As we witnessed this horror each day in news reports, we can't help but to ask ourselves, "How could a compassionate species such as ourselves commit such horrid atrocities upon innocent civilians?" What impels us to suspend our natural tendencies of benevolence, loving-kindness, and compassion toward those we love and to perpetrate such brutality upon others? Before we attempt to answer this question, we would like to present another, perhaps more personal story to which many can relate.

The first author of this chapter was driving to work just recently when he came upon a tragic motor vehicle accident. A semi-tractor trailer rig was positioned perpendicular across all lanes of traffic on a four-lane interstate overpass with a midsized pickup truck wedged under the center of the trailer. The engine and cab of the pickup were completely accordion compressed into a tangled mass of metal against the back of the cab and

The Neuroscience of Empathy, Compassion, and Self-Compassion. http://dx.doi.org/10.1016/B978-0-12-809837-0.00003-9

metal shards were scattered over a good 50 yards of the overpass. Clearly the pickup was traveling at a very high rate of speed and quite clearly the driver could not have survived such an impact and would have been horribly crushed by the blow. As he drove by the wreckage, the author was filled with emotions of profound sadness and regret at the tragic brutality of this accident, and then thoughts about the certain death of the driver (were there passengers?) of the pickup, the loss and pain that his family will suffer, the hope that there wasn't a child in the pickup being taken to school, and the thought of possibly rendering assistance, although there were police cars everywhere around the grizzly scene. He was filled with not uncharacteristic feelings and thoughts of Compassion for the victim(s), thoughts and emotions that the reader of this chapter may well be sharing right now as s/he processes this experience.

As he drove on, on the radio he heard that a young man had *stolen a city vehicle and had run into a tractor trailer rig near the interstate as he fled a police pursuit*. The author, on hearing this report, repeated, "stolen city vehicle" and "police pursuit," and became aware of thoughts of not infrequent reports lately of methamphetamine-related crimes in the city. He felt the feelings of loss and suffering beginning to fade as he drove to work.

What had just transpired in the brain of the author, and perhaps in your brain, as we experience these horrible acts of suffering on the part of another, and how are these experiences modulated by simply hearing a change in the scenario or by our distancing ourselves from the conflict, that the victim(s) had been to blame in some way or responsible for their reckless behavior or their unfortunate deaths. In this chapter, we will explore the neuroscience of this very process and hopefully better understand how the brain processes and modulates the experience of Compassion, how we witness the suffering of others and how, at a neurological level, we cope with such experiences.

COMPASSION

Compassion has been one of the most cherished, acclaimed, practiced, and pursued of human emotions for literally thousands of years, and a foremost part of nearly all organized religions and spiritual quests. Historically, it may be found in the taking of the vow of nonharm in ancient Vedic Upanishads, in the earliest of Buddhist meditations and as the very base of Mahayana Buddhism, in the Islamic recitations of Rahman in the Qur'an, in the Torah ideals of Tzedakah, in Christian prayers, sermons, and Biblical stories, and passed down for hundreds of years in the aural history of Native Peoples across this planet. So commonplace is this trait of compassion that scholars have considered it to be "an emergent, phenotypic property of our minds" and of critical species survival value (Gilbert, 2005). Genetically, it may find its development in enhanced species propagation through (1) its preservation of the welfare of vulnerable offspring, (2) increased perceived desirability in mate selection, and (3) the protective consequences of nonkin cooperative relationships (Decety, Norman, Berntson, & Cacioppo, 2012; Goetz, Keltner, & Simon-Thomas, 2010).

There appears to be considerable consensus as to a definition of *Compassion*. (See Chapter 1 for a discussion of these definitional issues.) Compassion is a sensitivity to the suffering of another and a desire to alleviate that suffering (Batson, 2009; Goetz et al., 2010; Singer & Lamm, 2009). It differs from *Empathy* in that empathy is the general vicarious experiencing or sharing of another person's emotional state, not just their suffering. Empathy lacks the motivational component of compassion (to help), and compassion can involve emotions other than those of the observed (e.g., I might feel anger as well as discomfort at the pain inflicted on another). *Sympathy* is a similar experiencing of another's emotional state but it involves feelings of sorrow for the other and also lacks the intention to help component. Although compassion involves the desire to alleviate another's suffering, that desire is generally considered latent or intentional. The selfless concern for the welfare of others coupled with the actual act of helping the suffering other is called *Altruism* (Goetz et al., 2010; Monroe, 1996; Weng et al., 2013). It thus might be accurate to say that all of these, compassion, sympathy, and altruism, are variations of empathy, for each requires a sharing at some level of another's emotional experience. However, each has its own unique signature.

Compassion is not a "basic emotion" (Ekman, 1992) but involves the experience of several of these affective states within the context of witnessing another's suffering. It also has multiple components: (1) an *affective* component directed at the experiencing of another's suffering, (2) the ability to take perspective on another's suffering and to recognize the *differentiation* of self from other, (3) a regulatory *cognitive* component designed to modulate the affective expression, and (4) a motivational-*intentional* component which is latent, prosocial, and directed at the alleviation of their suffering. Thus, from a neuroscience perspective, one might predict that compassion activates specific emotional, cognitive, self-other differentiation, and intentional motor areas in the brain. Neuroscience research has endeavored to examine these components in the experiencing and behavioral expression of compassion through a number of unique experimental paradigms and utilizing multiple observational strategies.

THE EMOTIONAL EXPERIENCE OF COMPASSION

Time Course: Perhaps the incipient experience of compassion is the emotional response when we first observe the suffering of another. We first *feel* the other's suffering, often at a visceral level, and we rather immediately adopt facial, postural, and verbal characteristics reflective of the other's suffering, followed by a number of interpretative self- and other-statements. Such _somatic prosody_ finds its peripheral source in the parasympathetic ventral vagal system elaborated by Porges (2001, 2003). Studies of this initial affective response have rather clearly identified a more centralized neural network.

The primary positioning of the affective response in the time course described above is suggested indirectly by a scant number of studies on the cognitive reappraisal of sexual arousal (Beauregard, Levesque, & Bourgouin, 2001), sadness (Levesque et al., 2003) and aversive affect (Ochsner et al. 2002) but with direct implications for compassion by two studies that manipulated top-down, higher order processing of the bottom-up, automatic experience of another's negative affect. A review of those studies follows.

In the first of these two studies by Ochsner et al. (2004), 24 female participants were randomly assigned to two conditions: (1) a Self-Focused or personal relevance condition and (2) a Situation-Focused or other relevance condition. Participants in each group were asked to observe a randomly presented series of aversive human images while lying in an fMRI and to increase (up-regulate) or to decrease (down-regulate) their negative emotional responses to the images or, as a baseline, to "respond naturally." fMRI recordings were taken during these cued reappraisals of the negative images and brain regions of interest (ROIs) were analyzed. The authors obtained activation results very similar to those of other researchers reviewed below. Of relevance here to the time-course issue, Ochsner et al. also examined the temporal activation of the amygdala (AMG), an accepted repository of arousal responses and of particularly negative emotions, during the observation and reappraisal of negative images. The researchers observed significantly greater AMG activation during the up-regulation condition and even greater deactivation during the down-regulation condition, both relative to baseline, and an activation time-course that followed the reappraisal directions, with a peak activation during down-regulation, the ostensibly more cognitively demanding exercise, 2 s later than for up-regulation. These results suggest delayed appraisal effects following an initial neural response associated with affectivity (Fig. 3.1).

The second time-course study by Immordino-Yang et al. (2009) examined diffuse fMRI responses to recorded narratives with visual images of pain-related (compassion) and nonpain-related emotional and nonemotional experiences of other people in a repeated-measures design with 13 male and female participants. Specific localization effects are reported below, but the time-course analysis revealed a peaking of activation in the anterior insular (AI) cortex, a part of the affective response network described by Lamm and Singer (2010) and others, approximately 6 s sooner and shorter in duration for the perception of physical pain,

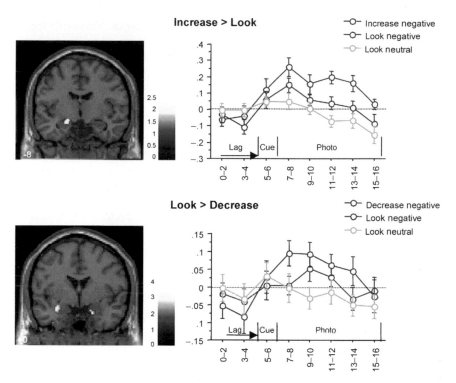

FIGURE 3.1   Left panels show amygdala activation from group contrasts, whereas right panels show percent signal change activation time courses for the left amygdala peak voxel from each contrast. Time courses begin at the onset of a trial. With a 4- to 6-s hemodynamic response lag, and an initial 2-s instruction cue, modulation due to reappraisal may first be observed 6–8 s after trial onset, as shown in the portion of the time course corresponding to the photo presentation period, as indicated in the figure. Top panel shows left amygdala voxels active in the increase > look contrast, and bottom panel shows left and right amygdala voxels active in the look > decrease contrast, which respectively reflect up- and down-regulation of amygdala activity due to reappraisal. Time courses for peak voxels show significant modulation when increasing or decreasing negative emotion 6–8 s after trial onset, which may reflect up- or downregulation of amygdala activity within the first 2 s that participants attempted to reappraise a photo. Activation time course for look trials with neutral photos is shown for comparison. *Source: Reprinted with permission from Ochsner, K. N., Ray, R. D., Cooper, J. C., Robertson, E. R., Chopra, S., Gabrieli, J. D. E., et al. (2004). For better or for worse: Neural systems supporting the cognitive down- and up-regulation of negative emotion. NeuroImage, 23, 483–499.*

an evolutionarily more automatic response, than for the perception of psychological pain, the latter predictably requiring more top-down, higher order processing.

Similar differential timing effects have been observed between earlier bottom-up stimulus recognition and saliency, on the one hand, and later top-down visual search and discrimination, on the other, in implanted electrodes in monkey lateral intraparietal and prefrontal cortices (Buschman & Miller, 2007). Interestingly, this study also found different electrical frequencies in frontal-parietal synchrony consistent with the informational demands of each task. Additionally on an ontogenetic basis, developmental neuroscientists consider affective empathy toward another's suffering to develop earlier in infancy than cognitive, appraisal-based empathic processing occurring much later in childhood and adolescence (Decety & Svetlova, 2012).

Although the studies described above are few in number and certainly need to be replicated, they suggest that the neural affective response (bottom-up) to negative stimuli occurs prior to the cognitive interpretation and appraisal (top-down) of those stimuli. In 1884, William James, one of the founders of modern psychology, argued that we see a bear, experience a physiological response, then interpret that response as fear, and then run away (James, 1890). In the experience of compassion, it appears that James was correct, that we witness suffering in another, rather immediately experience neurological ripples in the current, and subsequently interpret those responses as compassion, or otherwise. As we proceed, we shall see how this appraisal response can be adjusted to modulate the experience of compassion.

Neurological Substrate: A rich and exciting body of research literature has emerged over the past decades investigating the neuroanatomy of emotions in general. Literally hundreds of investigations have been conducted to date to allow at least eight meta-analyses of affective neuroscience research. Initially these meta-analyses took a "locationist approach" either of basic emotions, such as anger, disgust, fear, happiness, sadness, and surprise, or of broader affective dimensions, such as positive and negative affect (Buhle et al., 2014; Costafreda, Brammer, David, & Fu, 2008; Kober et al., 2008; Lindquist, Wager, Kober, Bliss-Moreau, & Barrett, 2012; Murphy, Nimmo-Smith, & Lawrence, 2003; Phan, Wager, Taylor, & Liberzon, 2002; Sergerie, Chochol, & Armony, 2008; Vytal & Hamann, 2010). However, more recently, partly as a result of a failure of many studies to identify regions singularly involved in specific affective states (e.g., the localization of fear, anger, and disgust, all in the AMG), a "psychological constructionist approach" has been offered, in which emotions emerge from more basic psychological operations comprised of diverse sensory inputs and associated contextual perceptual processes. This sensory array is interpreted within the experiential context in a top-down fashion, crosschecked to minimize errors, and then conceptualized and rendered semantically and behaviorally (Kober et al., 2008; Lindquist et al., 2012).

Broadly speaking across these various conceptual and analytical approaches, nine affect-related regions have been identified. The first four of these have been associated with specific affective states, the fifth, sixth, and seventh associated more with the cognitive regulation of emotion, the eighth with behavioral manifestations of emotions, and the ninth with the visual processing and representation of affect. These nine areas are as follows, with their locationist and constructionist representations respectively:

(1) the *AMG* as the repository of fear, uncertainty directed arousal, and motivational salience, (2) the *AI* as the brain site of disgust, somatic and affective representations, and interoception, (3) the *orbitofrontal cortex (OFC)* as the location of anger and the site for integration of interoceptive and exteroceptive information, (4) the *anterior cingulate cortex (ACC) (pregenual and subgenual)* as the brain basis of sadness and as a modulator of somatovisceral status, (5) the *dorsomedial prefrontal cortex (dmPFC), medial temporal lobe, the temporal–parietal junction (TPJ), and retrosplenial cortex/posterior cingulate cortex (PCC)* as the areas involved in Theory of Mind (ToM: see the following section) or self-other differentiation, the self-representation of other's mental states, and the cognitive "mentalizing" of emotions; (6) the *anterior temporal lobe and ventrolateral prefrontal cortex (vlPFC)* as the site of language formation and the linguistic and abstract representation of emotion; (7) the *dorsolateral prefrontal cortex (dlPFC)* as involved in executive attention, working memory, and the cognitive regulation of affect; (8) the *periaqueducal gray* as the site of behavioral adaptations to emotional arousal; and (9) the *visual cortex, both primary and secondary*, involved not only in the visual perception and processing of emotional stimuli but also in the visual representation of affective states and situations. (See Lindquist et al. (2012) for a more complete description of these nine affective regions).

A number of studies have examined the neurological substrate of the emotional response to another's suffering specifically. These investigations have revealed rather consistently an affective compassion network comprised of the AI and ACC, both linked to the AMG. For example, brain imaging studies of the response to one's own and another's pain have implicated the AI, ACC, and diverse other sites, even when simply observing a signal that a loved one in another room was being exposed to a pain that they themselves had recently experienced (Lamm, Decety, & Singer, 2011; Singer et al., 2004). The empathic experience of another's pain would appear to involve only the affective AI/rostral ACC network and not the somatosensory (SS) (posterior insula/secondary SS cortex, sensorimotor cortex, and caudal ACC) components of the pain matrix (Singer et al., 2004). Additionally, Ochsner et al. (2004, 2009) have strongly implicated the AMG in the purer experience of negative affect in general prior to higher order regulation.

In the study mentioned earlier by Immordino-Yang, McColl, Damasio, and Damasio (2009), these researchers pseudorandomly exposed 13 participants to each of five clusters of narratives from the lives of real people while they lay in an fMRI scanner. The narratives were presented orally through recordings and were supplemented with visual images and videos of the protagonist to enhance the reality of each. The stories fell into five categories: Compassion for Physical Pain, Compassion for Social Pain (i.e., difficult psychological situations like social rejection, grief, despair, etc.), Admiration for Skill, Admiration for Virtue, and a nonemotional, neutral control condition. Participants were instructed to "become as emotional as possible" and to rate the magnitude of their emotional experiences. Immordino-Yang et al. found greater activation in the AI, ACC, and hypothalamus during both compassion conditions relative to the nonemotional control condition.

Practitioners of a number of contemplative traditions regularly engage a style of meditation based in compassion and loving-kindness, called Metta Meditation (Analayo, 2015). Metta meditation involves a mental focus on feelings of loving-kindness and a desire to alleviate the suffering of specific others, such as, progressively, a loved one, a family member, an acquaintance, a stranger, an enemy, and common humanity. The ultimate objective of such meditative practice is to create a pure, nonreferential affective envelope of loving kindness around the practitioner. Thought to be the most complete expression of loving-kindness and compassion and a meditation procedure taught by The Dalai Lama, Metta meditation has been the subject of a number of studies by Antoine Lutz, Richard Davidson, and associates at the University of Wisconsin.

In their initial investigation of 8 long-term Buddhist Metta practitioners compared with 10 student volunteers with 1-week of beginning Metta practice, Lutz, Greischar, Rawlings, Ricard, and Davidson (2004) examined electroencephalography (EEG) power spectral frequencies and phase synchrony in frontal, temporal, and parietal ROIs during meditation. Both an initial and an ongoing baseline, the latter across four 90-s rest-meditation blocks, were recorded over 128 surface electrodes. Results revealed significantly enhanced spectral power and phase synchrony in the gamma-band (25–42 Hz) relative to both baseline conditions for the experienced practitioners only in all four ROIs. Although this study was unique among neuroscience studies of compassion in utilizing high density EEG technology with improved temporal resolution over MRIs, the poorer spatial resolution allows for only general inferences regarding localization effects. Nonetheless, observation of the presented brain maps suggests increased gamma-wave power and synchrony over frontal and temporoparietal sites specific to the commonly-observed affective regions reported above and the ToM regions described below. This study also had the distinction of being on the cover of and reported to the public in the March 2005 National Geographic magazine (Shreeve, 2005).

Lutz, Brefczynski-Lewis, Johnstone, and Davidson (2008) then conducted a constructive replication of their earlier study with 15 similarly accomplished Buddhist loving-kindness/compassion meditators compared with 15 age-identical novice volunteers similar to the earlier control group. This study utilized an fMRI of identified ROIs and the random presentation of positive, negative, and neutral digitized sounds during the end of meditation and resting blocks in order to enhance the emotional response of meditators. Similar to outcomes of the studies reported above, Lutz et al. found enhanced activity in AI and SS cortex (SII) in experts compared with novices, during meditation compared to rest, and in response to emotional vocalizations relative to neutral, with increased AI activation as a function of meditation intensity. Particularly, the right insula showed greater activity in response to negative versus positive sounds during meditation for the experts. Additionally, an examination of a main effect of meditative state indicated stronger activation during compassion meditation in the AI and ACC, as well as in the temporal lobes, posterior superior temporal sulcus (pSTS), TPJ, medial prefrontal cortex (mPFC), and PCC/precuneus (Pre). This latter cluster is associated with perspective taking, mentation, and ToM (Fig. 3.2).

Klimecki, Leiberg, Lamm, and Singer (2013) developed a unique variation of the visually elaborated narratives of Immordino-Yang et al. by creating brief silent video sequences drawn from news or documentary presentations of real people in either distressing, emotionally charged scenarios or participating in common, everyday activities. These sequences were shown

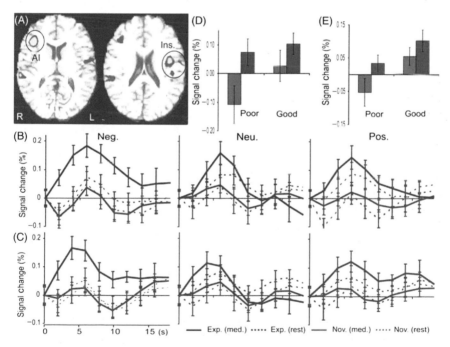

FIGURE 3.2 State by group by valence interaction. (A) (AI) and (Ins.) stand for anterior insula and insula, respectively ($z = 12$ and $z = 19$, 15 experts and 15 novices, color codes: (orange) $p < 5.10^{-2}$, (yellow), $p < 2.10^{-2}$). (B–C) Impulse response from rest to compassion in response to emotional sounds in AI (B) and Ins. (C). (D–E) Responses in AI (D) and Ins. (E) during poor and good blocks of compassion, as verbally reported, for 12 experts (red) and 10 novices (blue). Source: Reprinted with permission from Lutz, A., Brefczynski-Lewis, J., Johnstone, T., & Davidson, R. J. (2008). Regulation of the neural circuitry of emotion by compassion meditation: Effects of meditative expertise. PLoS One, 3(3), 1–10.

during 15-min fMRI scans in randomized, blocked groups to a sample of 28 naïve female participants who had received a 6-h Metta meditation training course followed by 2–12 days of classroom and home practice (for a mean of 5.7 practice hours) and to a group of 30 similar participants who had received a memory-enhancement control training course followed by home practice over the same time period. Empathy and compassion questionnaire and behavioral measures of compassion and fMRI ROIs were examined pre- and post-training. Analysis of results revealed that observing distressing videos mapped to increased activation in the AI and the medial ACC and that compassion training, compared to memory training, was associated with increased activity in the medial orbital frontal cortex, ventral tegmental area/substantia nigra, putamen, and pallidum, all lateralized to the right hemisphere. These observed activations following compassion training have been previously associated with feelings of love, affiliation, and positive affective experiences (Klimecki et al., 2013).

Taken together, these studies support the role of the AI cortex, with its rich network of neural connections to the ACC and the AMG, as paramount in the affective experience of compassion. In reviews of the involvement of the insular cortex in empathy for another's experiences, Singer and colleagues (Lamm & Singer, 2010; Singer, Critchley, & Preuschoff, 2009) have highlighted the role of the AI in social emotions in general and in the neurological representation of ongoing and future feeling states. Furthermore, Lamm and Singer (2010) have suggested that the posterior insula has a primary role in the more direct experience of nociceptive (pain) states while the anterior insula conducts a higher order integrative experience of associated affective states. These authors have also observed that compassion and love appear to activate the more medial portions of the insular cortex bilaterally and that general empathy involves the anterior subdivision of the insula, suggesting somewhat differential functions of this anatomically prominent and complex portion of the cerebral cortex. However, as we shall see, the experience of compassion is much more complex than merely an emotional state and involves an integration of processes across multiple domains, more consistent with the constructionist approach described above.

THE INTENTION TO HELP

From our definition of compassion, we see that compassion also involves a motivational-intentional component, a desire to alleviate the suffering of another. We might therefore expect to see some representation of this intention to help in the brain. Interestingly, within the context of the role of the AI in the affective experience of compassion, Lamm and Singer (2010) have pointed to the dense array of neural connections with cortical motor structures, such as medial and lateral PFC, from the dorsal, more dysgranular portion of the AI in monkeys and primates. Such putative connections in humans may serve as a mechanism for the conversion of affective states into action tendencies or intentions (Weng et al., 2013). Indeed, in the early development of humans, in young rhesus monkeys, and even in adults of less cortically developed species, we see the presence of what de Waal calls "preconcern," or the irresistible impulse to run toward and to physically share in the suffering of another (de Waal, 2009). Ostensibly, this primitive impulse becomes overwhelmed by higher order control mechanisms as the animal ages, but it is likely that a vestige remains and could manifest at a prebehavioral, and perhaps cognitive, level.

Quite likely as a mesial and lateral elaboration of these associated premotor areas, the Mirror Neuron System (MNS) may suggest a network of cortical motor neurons involved in "action understanding" and intentional movement. This exciting "motor empathy" network began its development with the 1992 and 1996 publications by di Pellegrino, Gallese, Rizzolatti, and colleagues in three reports of a ground-breaking discovery in two Macaque monkeys of motor neurons in the rostral ventral portion of the premotor cortex (rvPMC), also known as PMC Field 5 (F5) just caudal to the inferior arm of the arcuate nucleus, that responded not only to actual reach, hand grasp, and placing in the mouth of desired objects, but also to the *observation only* of this same activity in a conspecific Macaque (Gallese, Fadiga, Fogassi, & Rizzolatti, 1996; Gallese & Goldman, 1998; Di Pellegrino, Fadiga, Fogassi, Gallese, & Rizzolatti, 1992; Rizzolatti, Fadiga, Gallese, & Fogassi, 1996). These authors point to the proximal association of F5 in monkeys and primates with Broca's speech area in humans. More recently, Fogassi et al. (2005) and Tkach, Reimer, and Hatsopoulos (2007) have extended such "intention understanding" to the inferior parietal lobe (IPL), a region having rich connections to F5, and to primary motor cortex, suggesting a more diffuse distribution of the MNS (Gallese, 2009; Rizzolatti & Craighero, 2004) (Fig. 3.3).

In an evolutionary extrapolation of these findings, Rizzolatti et al. (1996) have suggested that F5 in monkeys is the "anatomical homologue of human Broca's area," that reaching, grasping, and mouthing objects served as the neurological foundation for the development of speech, and that vocal and semantic refinements occurred through a progressive evolution from basic mammalian laryngeal phonetic vowel and consonant utterances to open-closed lip and mouth alterations that formed the basis of syllable formation (Davis & MacNeilage, 2004; MacNeilage & Davis, 2005). The commonly-observed, virtually automatic association of gestures when speaking in humans is perhaps a telling manifestation of this evolutionary anachronism. The rather widespread cortical MNS may play a role in the more evolutionarily recent semantic representation and processing of affective components of compassion described later in this chapter.

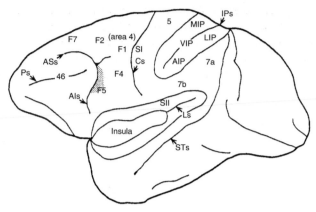

FIGURE 3.3 **Lateral view of the monkey brain. The shaded area shows the anatomical localization of the recorded neurons.** Frontal agranular cortical areas are classified according to Matelli et al. *AIP*, Anterior intraparietal area; *AIs*, inferior arcuate sulcus; *ASs*, superior arcuate sulcus; *Cs*, central sulcus; *IPs*, intraparietal sulcus; *LIP*, lateral intraparietal area; *Ls*, lateral sulcus; *MIP*, medial intraparietal area; *Ps*, principal sulcus; *SI*, primary somatosensory area; *SII*, secondary somatosensory area; *STs*, superior temporal sulcus; *VIP*, ventral intraparietal area. Note that IPs and Ls have beeen opened to show hidden areas. *Source: Reprinted with permission from Rizzolatti, G., Fadiga, L., Gallese, V., & Fogassi, L. (1996). Premotor cortex and the recognition of motor actions. Cognitive Brain Research, 3,131–141.*

While the role of the MNS in intention understanding and action is reviewed in another chapter (Chapter 6) in this book and will not be repeated here, it is important to note that although a number of animal and human analogue studies have been conducted since di Pellegrino et al.'s (1992); seminal investigation, controversy still exists over the actual presence of mirror neurons in humans (Mitchell, 2009; Mitchell et al., 2006). Human MNS existence has only been inferred from putative effects on electrocortical (EEG) mu and beta frequencies and on neuroimaging observations of action and intentions in regions homologous to those of monkey brains (Lamm & Singer, 2010; Woodruff & Maaske, 2010). Otherwise, to our knowledge, no direct investigations of motivational-intentional neurological manifestations of compassion in the human brain have been conducted to date. Only future research utilizing innovative technologies and strategies will clarify if the latent forms of such communicative gestures as described above could reflect a similar homologue of intentional actions during the experience of compassion.

THEORY OF MIND

A Chimp Named "Sarah" and Perspective Taking: Premack and Woodruff formalized the notion of ToM in 1978. Inspired by Kohler's earlier work which demonstrated chimpanzee problem solving, tool use, and object manipulations, Premack and Woodruff sought to understand chimps as "psychologists." They wanted to determine if chimps have a "'theory of mind,' [whether they] impute mental states to [themselves] and to others" (Premack & Woodruff, 1978). These mental states could include purpose or intention, belief, thought, knowledge, guessing, attitudes, or doubt.

In order to experimentally approach this construct of ToM in chimpanzees, Premack and Woodruff examined their problem comprehension rather than problem-solving performance. They showed a chimp videotapes of a human actor in a cage struggling to reach inaccessible bananas. The tape would be shown until a critical moment, then placed on hold. The experimenters would then present a pair of photographs (one of a solution and the other not), and allow the chimp, Sarah, to select from the alternatives. Sarah was remarkably accurate in her choices, selecting correctly 21 of 24 trials ($p < .001$).

Several explanations exist for the success of Sarah at this task. First, she could simply be matching physical elements from the videotape to the photograph. This suggestion was quickly eliminated by a smart design which included every element in every scene. Second, Sarah could be using associationism, or solving problems through familiarity with the sequences involved, a thoroughly plausible explanation based on the problems presented. However, the theory of generalization is weakened by her later success with unfamiliar problems, suggesting choice based on theory and not associations. Much more interestingly, Sarah could be utilizing a ToM to solve problems by "imputing states of mind," namely, intention or purpose and belief or knowledge, to the human actor (Premack & Woodruff, 1978). Alternatively, Sarah could simply be acting out of empathy, choosing the actions she would perform if in the actor's position.

Premack and Woodruff developed experiments to decide among the interpretations of Sarah's success. First, they broadened the problems explored to include those not restricted to physical inaccessibility, including a human actor locked in a cage or shivering with cold near an unlit heater. Again, Sarah was remarkably successful in choosing the correct photograph "solutions," making no errors on a first general alternatives round, and one error in twelve choices on a more discriminating round. Based on the novel problems presented, it became increasingly unlikely that associationism explained her accuracy.

Second, they presented an identical series of problems featuring two actors: one Sarah liked and one she disliked, along with "good" and "bad" problem-solving alternatives. Sarah favored "bad" events for the disliked trainer, indicating that she was not simply choosing the alternative representative of her choice as if she were in the actor's position, but choosing based on the character of the actor.

Lastly, Premack and Woodruff attempted to discover if Sarah would make different choices based on agent-specific knowledge. To assess this, they made two more sets of videotapes featuring a 4-year-old child and an adult attempting to solve problems. Sarah chose the correct, age-specific photograph on 10 out of 12 trials.

Through these experiments with Sarah the chimpanzee, Premack and Woodruff discovered that chimps can impute wants, purposes, or affective attitudes to others, but that they may fail to impose states of knowledge. The chimp has "a theory of mind restricted to purpose... as opposed to a more nearly complete theory that takes into account not only the other's motivation, but his cognition as well" (Premack & Woodruff, 1978). Thus began the nearly 40-year-long study of ToM.

The definition of ToM has been broadened since Premack and Woodruff's initial conceptualizations. ToM is also referred to as mentalizing, mindreading, perspective taking, and cognitive empathy. For many, ToM is considered the cognitive component of many prosocial behaviors, including empathy and compassion.

Certain cognitive and social exposures are necessary for successful ToM to develop in children. Components of a ToM are present shortly after birth, beginning with imitation at 12 months, joint attention and protodeclarative pointing at 18 months, engagement in pretend play which is distinct from reality at 18–24 months, a grasp of desire by 2 years, an elementary understanding of false beliefs by 3–4, an understanding of second order beliefs by 6–10, and an understanding of *faux pas* by 9–11 years (Frith & Frith, 2001; Singer, 2006; Stone, Baron-Cohen, & Knight, 1998). The common litmus test of ToM in children is the *false belief task* such as the Sally-Anne test, developed by Baron-Cohen, Leslie, and Frith in 1985. In this challenge, Sally hides a marble in her basket and leaves the room. While she is away, Anne transfers the marble to her box. Sally then returns, and the child being tested is asked a belief question, "Where will Sally look for her marble?" (Baron-Cohen, Leslie, & Frith, 1985). The child with a developed ToM will be able to take Sally's perspective, even though it is false, and report that Sally will look in the basket.

ToM Theories: Two dominant and oppositional explanations for ToM are known as "Theory Theory" and "Simulation Theory." Theory Theory generally states that ToM is acquired in a process similar to the scientific method; infants begin with a theory, later experience provides infants with information that cannot be accounted for by their present ToM, so they update it. In other words, ToM is based on distinct theoretical knowledge acquired and updated throughout development (Baron-Cohen et al., 1985; Gopnik & Wellman, 1994; Leslie, 1987; Vogeley et al., 2001). Simulation Theory states that instead, individuals use mental modeling to take the perspective of another, simulating how the other would think or feel in order to understand their beliefs, desires, and future actions (Shanton & Goldman, 2010; Vogeley et al., 2001). These two perspectives have been debated rather extensively and no clear consensus appears to have developed (Carruthers & Smith, 1996; Gallagher, 2001). Indeed, this is in part due to the definitional problems alluded to in Chapter 1.

ToM Deficits: ToM deficits are a hallmark of the autism spectrum disorders. One of the ways in which ToM and emotional empathy are dissociated from one another involves the differential selective impairments seen in *autism* versus *psychopathy*. Individuals with autism have deficits in ToM, but not emotional empathy, while those with psychopathy have no problem with ToM, but lack the ability to emotionally empathize (Völlm et al., 2006). Deficits in mentalizing are also seen in *schizophrenia* (Cassetta & Goghari, 2014; Csulky, Polgár, Tombor, Benkovits, & Réthelyi, 2014; Dodell-Feder, Tully, Lincoln, & Hooker, 2014; Konstantakopoulos et al., 2014; Ng, Fish, & Granholm, 2015; Pickup & Frith, 2001; Sprong, Schothorst, Vos, Hox, & Engeland, 2007), *alcoholism* (Bosco, Capozzi, Colle, Marostica, & Tirassa, 2013; Uekermann & Daum, 2008), *major depressive disorder* (Berecz, Tényi, & Herold, 2016; Bora & Berk, 2016; Inoue, Yamada, & Kanba, 2006; Lee, Harkness, Sabbagh, & Jacobson, 2005; Mattern et al., 2015; Wang, Wang, Chen, Zhu, & Wang, 2008; Wolkenstein, Schönenberg, Schirm, & Hautzinger, 2011; Zobel et al., 2010), *bipolar disorder* (Bora, Bartholomeusz, & Pantelis, 2016; Montag et al., 2010), *social anxiety disorder* (Hezel & McNally, 2014), and individuals with a *specific language impairment* (Farrant, Fletcher, & Maybery, 2006; Farrar et al., 2009; Nilsson & de López, 2016).

Neural Correlates of ToM: Virtually every medium from verbal and written stories, to comics, cartoons, and animations, to simulated games has been used to tap the construct of ToM. Potential neural correlates of ToM have been sought across a variety of imaging tools, such as fMRI, PET, SPECT, EEG, and ERP. Given the diversity of definitions, neuroimaging techniques, and tasks used for elicitation, it has been challenging to settle on an agreeable neural mechanism for ToM.

However, a consensus seems to have emerged around the following structures: Mentalizing is strongly associated with the TPJ (Gallagher et al., 2000; Gobbini, Koralek, Bryan, Montgomery, & Haxby, 2007; Kédia, Berthoz, Wessa, Hilton, & Martinot, 2008; Mahy, Moses, & Pfeifer, 2014; McCleery, Surtees, Graham, Richards, & Apperly, 2011; Saxe & Kanwisher, 2003; Saxe, Moran, Scholz, & Gabrieli, 2006; Saxe & Powell, 2006; Schurz, Radua, Aichhorn, Richlan, & Perner, 2014; van Veluw & Chance, 2014; Völlm et al., 2006), ACC (Gallagher & Frith, 2003; Gobbini et al., 2007; Mahy et al., 2014; Rilling, Sanfey, Aronson, Nystrom, & Cohen, 2004; Vogeley et al., 2001), superior temporal sulci (STS) (Gallagher & Frith, 2003; Rilling et al., 2004), mPFC (Frith & Frith, 2005; Gallagher et al., 2000; van Veluw & Chance, 2014; Völlm et al., 2006), precuneus (*Pre*) (Gobbini et al., 2007; Kédia et al., 2008;

Mahy et al., 2014; Saxe et al., 2006; van Veluw & Chance, 2014), the medial frontal gyrus (mFG) (Fletcher et al., 1995; Völlm et al., 2006), and the temporal poles (TP) (Gallagher & Frith, 2003; Völlm et al., 2006) (Fig. 3.4).

With so many, and, in some cases, such anatomically remote sites associated with ToM, as well as neuroimaging and design limitations, it has been difficult to represent the functional contributions of each of these sites to the overall ToM. Rebecca Saxe has spent much of her career in researching ToM, has been a prolific contributor to our understanding of the neuroscience of this complex construct, and more recently has conducted reviews and component analyses of the possible roles of these various sites and their unique contributions (Gweon, Dodell-Feder, Bedny, & Saxe, 2012; Koster-Hale & Saxe, 2013; Saxe, 2006; Schurz et al., 2014). Unfortunately, such analyses have not, to date, yielded a clear functional differentiation of these cortical sites. While by no means comprehensive, detailed examples of some of this supportive research are presented below.

In an earlier investigation of ToM localization, Fletcher et al. (1995) conducted a PET study examining ToM in normal subjects through written comprehension tasks of three types: ToM stories requiring mental state attribution, "Why did the burglar do this?", physical stories (PS) with human presence but no mental state attribution, "Why did the alarm go off?", and groups of unlinked sentences (US), "Did the children take their walk?". In the ToM stories compared to the PS, Fletcher et al. found left mFG and PCC activation; in the ToM stories compared to the US control they found increased activation in the TP, left superior temporal gyrus, PCC, and left mFG. Notably, there was no left mFG activation in the PS or US tasks, suggesting that this region may be uniquely involved in mentalizing (Fletcher et al., 1995).

Gallagher et al. (2000) conducted an fMRI study on normal controls using ToM and non-ToM story tasks culled from the aforementioned Fletcher et al. (1995) study, and cartoon tasks, along with a jumbled word or picture control. ToM stories involved mental state attribution, "Why did the burglar do that?" and ToM cartoons involved attribution of false belief or ignorance of characters. Non-ToM stories and cartoons involved simple factual comprehension, "Why did the Blue army win?". Jumbled word controls contained passages of US, "The new book is about statistics and experimental design, and contains many graphs. The front room contained a little bird in a cage." and the jumbled picture controls contained images of "randomly positioned objects, animals and people". ToM stories elicited greater activation in mPFC, TP, and the TPJ compared to non-ToM stories. ToM cartoons elicited greater activation in the mPFC, TPJ, right mFG, the Pre, and the fusiform gyrus (FG) than did non-ToM cartoons. This common activation of the mPFC and TPJ across modalities suggests their importance in mentalizing (Gallagher et al., 2000).

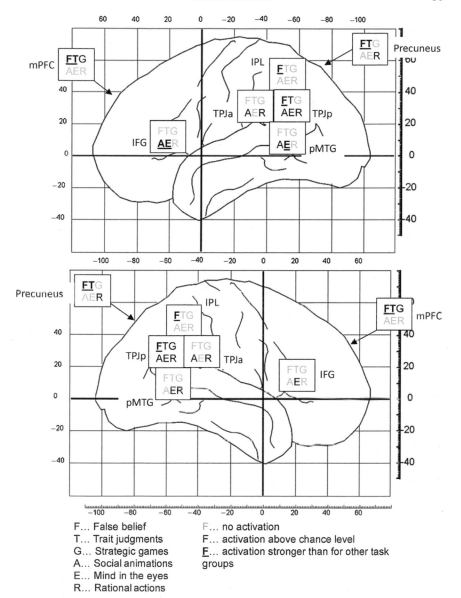

F... False belief
T... Trait judgments
G... Strategic games
A... Social animations
E... Mind in the eyes
R... Rational actions

F... no activation
F... activation above chance level
F... activation stronger than for other task
groups

FIGURE 3.4 **Schematic summary of significant activations in ROIs that are linked to the structural connectivity networks of TPJa and TPJp.** Labels for ROIs are the same as in previous figures. Task groups are abbreviated by capital letters. Black font indicates that mean-analysis shows significant analysis activation for a task group in that ROI ($p < 0.005$ uncorrected, $z > 1$). Underlined letters indicate that linear-contrasts found stronger activation for this task group compared to others in an area ($p < 0.005$, Bonferroni for the number of pairwise comparisons). *Source: Reprinted with permission from Schurz, M., Radua, J., Aichhorn, M., Richlan, F., & Perner, J. (2014). Fractionating theory of mind: A meta-analysis of functional brain imaging studies. Neuroscience and Biobehavioral Reviews, 42, 9–34.*

An fMRI study conducted by Völlm et al. (2006) used a cartoon task with ToM, empathy, physical causality stories with one character, and physical causality stories with two characters in comic strip form to examine the extent of the neural relationship between the related constructs of ToM and emotional empathy. They found that activations in mPFC, TPJ, and middle and inferior temporal gyri including the left TP were increased in both ToM and empathy. Compared with empathy however, ToM revealed increased (primarily right-hemispheric) activations in lateral OFC, middle FG, and STS (Völlm et al., 2006).

Saxe and Kanwisher (2003) examined fMRI neural correlates of ToM using written stories and photographs of common inanimate objects. They found increased activation to false beliefs in the TPJ bilaterally, as well as to human action over nonhuman description stories, and a right TPJ trend toward greater response to photos of people than objects. Then, in a follow-up study these researchers compared BOLD responses to five new sets of stories, finding increased activation in the bilateral TPJ to ToM stimuli versus non-ToM stimuli and to false beliefs compared to false photographs (implying that the inference of mental states causes increased activation) at the TPJ, Pre, right aSTS, and mSTS. Lastly, they found increased BOLD signals in the TPJ and right aSTS during desire stories compared to physical people or nonhuman description stories, indicating that these regions respond selectively to mental state inference.

Saxe and Powell (2006) used fMRI and three types of story stimuli to differentiate brain activity specific for detecting the mere presence of another person, inferring internal states of another person, and understanding another person's thoughts or beliefs. These researchers found that bilateral TPJ and Pre showed significantly greater response to thought stories than to the other stories, and that the mPFC BOLD response was the same for all types of stories. This finding suggests a blanket role for the mPFC in "representing socially or emotionally relevant information about another person," and a strong role for the TPJ, particularly on the right side, for the attribution of thoughts to another, the very skill which "marks the transition from the early- to the late-developing component of [ToM]" (Saxe & Powell, 2006).

And finally, in a study mentioned earlier in this chapter, Immordino-Yang et al. (2009) used a novel stimulus in their fMRI investigation of social emotions. Employing compelling, true stories in four categories of admiration for virtue and for skill and compassion for social/psychological pain and for physical pain, they attempted to evoke real emotions in the MRI scanner. Results indicated differentially greater activation of ToM regions in the inferior/posterior sections of the posteromedial cortices, as well as in the AI, ACC, and hypothalamus, during the Compassion for Social Pain and Admiration for Virtue conditions, suggesting enhanced social processing, mentalizing, and perspective taking on another's psychological state, relative to the Compassion for Physical Pain and Admiration for Skill conditions (Immordino-Yang et al., 2009).

Schaafsma, Pfaff, Spunt, and Adolphs (2015) have recently written one of the most telling critiques of the current study of ToM. They argue that the considerable heterogeneity in neuroimaging methods and behavioral manipulations used to study ToM, combined with the broad reaching and complex definitions of the construct lead to undue confusion. A "way forward" in the study of ToM is proposed by these authors: First, deconstruct this large concept into more basic processes, and then reconstruct our mapping of it using a tool such as Neurosynth, which can create a large scale synthesis of the neuroimaging literature (Schaafsma et al., 2015). Confusion notwithstanding, ToM appears to relate to activation of a cluster of sites involved in mentalizing one's perspective on the motivation and intention, affect, and cognition of others. Seemingly, this ability to understand the other, both through perspective taking and self-other differentiation, can be seen as a prerequisite for Compassion, in which one would potentially act to end another's suffering.

BOTTOM-UP EXPERIENCING VERSUS TOP-DOWN REGULATION

At the beginning of this chapter, two scenarios were presented that hopefully engendered an experience of Compassion in our readers. One was the story of the merciless and tortuous bombings in the Syrian city of Aleppo; the other was a more personal experience of the author in coming upon a grizzly motor vehicle accident. In both scenarios, the "top-down" mentalizing subsequent to the "bottom-up" raw experiencing of sadness, or anger, or regret, or whatever you felt as you read these stories quite likely modulated your experiencing of compassion for the various victims.

The constructs of top-down and bottom-up processing derive from cognitive psychology and relate to the manner in which attention is allocated to the processing of sensory information from the environment (Buschman & Miller, 2007; Phelps, 2006; Sarter, Givens, & Bruno, 2001). Bottom-up processing refers to the acquisition of and attention to the more automatic, sensory, and contextual characteristics of incoming stimuli, whereas top-down processing describes the more volitional, regulatory, and knowledge-driven mechanisms involved in the enhancement of neural processing of such information. Although such distinctions have historically been considered as more functional in nature, recently in monkeys, bottom-up attentional responses to a visual target have been implicated in posteri-or, parietal SS neurons while top-down mechanisms have been localized more to prefrontal, executive control regions, suggesting an anatomical differentiation of these distinct attentional processes (Buschman & Miller, 2007; Sarter et al., 2001).

Research on top-down and bottom-up neurological distinctions in the processing of human emotional states has been only recently developing and has been virtually absent in the context of empathy and compassion. What few investigations have been conducted, however, have been very revealing and have considerably illuminated our understanding of how such basic emotional responses to the suffering of another are processed at a more contemplative, higher order level in the human brain. First as mentioned earlier, the greater number of bottom-up studies has suggested that the AMG plays a prominent role in emotional learning and memory (Phelps, 2006). Fewer studies, however, have examined at a neurological level the higher order structures that modulate basic emotions.

Among this handful of studies, Ochsner and colleagues have examined the up- and down-regulation of negative emotions in humans by directed manipulations of top-down, cognitive appraisal processes. For example, in the study mentioned earlier in the time-course section, Ochsner et al. (2004) presented 24 female participants in an MRI scanner with a random-ly intermixed series of negative and neutral pictures of human events pre-ceded by cued narratives to either increase or to decrease negative affect. Participants were instructed to utilize either of two top-down strategies: (1) a *self-focus strategy*, in which they were guided to increase negative affect by increasing their sense of subjective proximity to the event or to decrease negative affect by increasing their perceived distance from the event, from a "detached, third-person perspective," or they were instruct-ed to employ (2) a *situation-focused strategy*, in which they were instructed to focus on the context of the other person's suffering and to increase or to decrease the negative context of that experience. *Look only (negative & neutral)* (bottom-up) trials were also provided as controls, in which par-ticipants were asked to "respond naturally." ROIs were examined under all conditions and the time-course of BOLD activity was plotted (reported earlier in this chapter). Interestingly, this appraisal strategy imposed an implicit self-other distinction in the participant's perspective-taking (vis-à-vis ToM explored above), but with the use of nonselfimages during the self-appraisal and instructions to decrease negative emotions by "view-ing pictured events from a detached, third-person perspective," thus imposing a blurring of that distinction for the "detached, third-person" decreased negative instructions in the self-focus strategy.

Results revealed significant changes in affective ratings consistent with up- or down-regulation of negative affect relative to look-only trials. In the bottom-up condition of look negative relative to neutral, increased and generally more sudden and less sustained AMG activity was reported, consistent with the putative role of the AMG in the automatic processing of emotion. Such AMG activity was up-regulated toward significance in the increase negative reappraisal and significantly down-regulated in the decrease negative reappraisal conditions. However, across the two top-down reappraisal conditions, relative to the bottom-up, look negative condition, more PFC and other ToM-related regions were involved, including dorsal and ventrolateral PFC, dorsomedial PFC, ACC, bilateral TPJ, medial Temporal Gyrus, the subcortical sites of Caudate and Thalamus, and the Cerebellum. Specific reappraisal valence and self-other effects were reported in subregions of these areas, but are consistent with greater involvement of these top-down PFC and ToM regions during the reappraisal and modulation of more automatic bottom-up AMG and related emotional structures.

Ochsner et al. (2009) later published another part of this study in which 20 female participants viewed either neutral or aversive visual stimuli in an MRI with instructions to either simply view the neutral and negative images (the bottom-up condition) or to view the *neutral* images in negative ways (top-down modulation condition). Although both top-down and bottom-up negative processing resulted in greater negative affective ratings and in enhanced AMG activity relative to the bottom-up neutral condition, the bottom-up negative condition showed greater bilateral AMG, as well as occipito-temporal cortex, right parietal cortex, and PFC, activation than the top-down neutral with negative appraisal condition. This later finding suggests greater AMG involvement in the un-modulated "real" negative event than in a purely "imagined" negative experience, but that the latter can still involve AMG activation. However, the top-down condition also selectively recruited left ventral and dorsolateral PFC, bilateral dorsomedial PFC, ACC, bilateral temporal cortex, and putamen. Ochsner et al. (2009) highlight the engagement of the AMG in both types of negative emotional processing, albeit stronger for the bottom-up stage. But they clarify the role of AMG and associated areas in the bottom-up attention to and encoding of event properties, and the involvement of more prefrontal areas in the top-down, higher order, cognitive interpretations of such events.

Kedia et al. (2008) conducted a fascinating study of moral emotions in which 29 right-handed participants were first screened for their abilities to recognize and to communicate internal affective states, then were reclined in an MRI, and were instructed to read and then to imagine each of 120 brief stories in which an "agent harms a victim." Beginnings and endings of each story were separated according to whether the agent was the self or another and whether the victim was the self or another. In this manner, the researchers were able to present moral dilemmas involving harm inflicted by self to self (Self-Anger), self to other (Self-Other or Guilt), other to self (Other-Anger), and other to other (Other-Other or Compassion). Two emotionally neutral conditions (Self-Self and Other-Other) in which no harm occurred were employed as controls. After reading and imaging each scenario, the participant pressed a button and the MRI scan was recorded.

Results revealed that (1) top-down processing of emotional conditions activated bilaterally the dmPFC, the supplemental motor area, the left insula, the left AMG, and the left TPJ, (2) all other-as-agent conditions (Other-Anger and Compassion) activated the ToM regions of bilateral dmPFC, bilateral precuneus, and left TPJ relative to the self-as-agent conditions, and (3) the Guilt, Other-Anger, and Compassion conditions activated these same ToM regions of dmPFC, precuneus, and TPJ, all bilaterally, relative to the Self-Anger condition. Increased involvement of the emotional network of left insula and AMG were found for all harm conditions involving both self and other. The Guilt, Other-Anger, and Compassion conditions, which each involved another as the agent or victim, did not show differential anatomical effects from each other, suggesting with regard to compassion that the top-down activation effects for the focus of our attention in this chapter may have to do with the self-other differentiation that occurs with ToM mentalizing. In other words, as with empathy, compassion requires the ability to separate self from other and to recognize that the observed suffering is occurring in another and not in oneself (Fig. 3.5).

The paucity of investigations into the higher order processing of observed human suffering notwithstanding, to date nearly 50 studies of the cognitive appraisal of emotional states in general have been conducted. Although these studies have not been specific to compassion, their outcomes as a group do have implications for our understanding of the neuroscience of compassion. In 2014, Buhle et al. conducted a meta-analysis of 48 of these neuroimaging studies concerning the effects of the cognitive reappraisal of emotions, from the first such investigation ever published up to 2012. Buhle et al. (2014) reported that these studies consistently support the role of the dlPFC, the vlPFC, the dmPFC, and posterior parietal cortex in the reappraisal of emotions, with consistent involvement of primarily left posterior temporal cortex (PTC) and with the principle influence of these frontal and temporo-parietal regions on bilateral AMG activity. And, all of these processing regions would appear to be active whether one is up-regulating or down-regulating emotions. Given the rather established roles of dlPFC in selective attention and working memory, of vlPFC in response selection and inhibition, of dmPFC in the monitoring and processing of changing emotional states, of PTC in perceptual and semantic representations of information, and of AMG as the repository of affective states, a model begins to emerge for the processing and regulation of emotions, including those experienced in compassion. Indeed, we begin to understand how these regions could

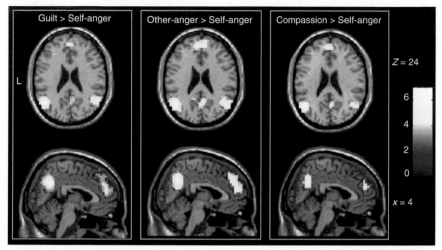

FIGURE 3.5 Comparison of the guilt, other-anger, and compassion conditions to the self-anger condition with height threshold ($p < 0.001$) and extent threshold (25 voxels). Guilt minus self-anger (left). Other-anger minus self-anger (middle). Compassion minus self-anger (right). The three contrasts revealed activity in the bilateral dorsal medial prefrontal cortex, the bilateral precuneus, and the bilateral temporo-parietal junction. The bar shows the range of the Z score. Within the image, L indicates left. *Source: Reprinted with permission from Kédia, G., Berthoz, S., Wessa, M., Hilton, D., & Martinot, J. -L. (2008). An agent harms a victim: A functional magnetic resonance imaging study on specific moral emotions. Journal of Cognitive Neuroscience, 20(10), 1788–1798. http://doi.org/10.1162/jocn.2008.20070*

perform critical attention-driven selections of sensory and cognitive information into working memory (dlPFC), considerations and manipulations of possible response options (vlPFC), the regulation and valuations of such options as a function of affective status and meanings attributions (dmPFC), the involvement of semantic representations of these affective states and manipulations (PTC), and the subsequent modulation of emotional responses to stimuli (AMG). Furthermore, many of these foci overlap conveniently with ToM regions identified earlier.

But before we move on to a presentation of the developing theoretical model for the neuroscience of compassion, let us look at one additional neuroimaging study that directly addresses our question at the beginning of this chapter. In an experiment pivotal to our understanding of this specialized tuning of our affective piano, Fehse et al. (2015) utilized a quite creative design to directly manipulate the ToM neurological cluster and, in so doing, to massage research participants' affect toward or away from the experiencing of compassion. And these researchers did so by simply manipulating imputed blame or responsibility for the discomfort-inducing act. (Sometimes, the most thrilling part of neuroscience research, yay any research, is the creation of a clever experimental design that not only answers perplexing social questions but also does so with such an elegance and simplicity that the reader has to sit up and to take notice. Such was the design of the Fehse, Silveira, Elvers, and Blautzik (2015) study).

Fehse et al. created scenarios that were likely to engender the experience of human suffering, but followed each with one of two cognitive reframes of the experience. Twelve such scenarios were created dealing with common life experiences, with an initial sentence for each describing a life event (e.g., "a man dies in a car accident on the highway") and a second sentence modulating the experience with either a blameworthy statement (e.g., he was "passing carelessly in a curve") or a careworthy, innocence statement (e.g., he was the "father of four children"). Pretesting allowed the selection of scenarios judged to be most compassion-generating. An additional 12 control scenarios were developed utilizing sentences from the experimental scenarios but with a nonsuffering context (e.g., "passing carelessly in a curve, the Formula 1 champion yields win"). A sample of 18 male and female participants reclined in an MRI scanner and observed blocks of pseudo-randomized visual stimuli comprised of the above-described scenarios projected into an overhead mirror. Participants also rated their felt levels of compassion for each scenario. Both whole brain and ROI analyses were conducted.

Behavioral results revealed that the careworthy scenarios indeed generated significantly more compassion than the blameworthy scenes and that both generated significantly more compassion than the control scenarios. MRI analyses of the careworthy relative to the blameworthy scenarios found more activation of right SS cortex, bilateral primary motor cortex (PMC: motivational–intentional?), left FG, left hippocampus and parahippocampal gyrus, left insula (I), mPFC, and ACC, the first five components suggesting more SS, motor, and mnemonic manifestations of the scenarios and the latter three previously implicated in the experience of affective empathy (Decety et al., 2008; Lamm & Singer, 2010; Seth, 2013; Singer et al., 2009; Singer et al., 2004). In examining the blameworthy relative to the careworthy scenarios, greater activation was found in bilateral TPJ, right precuneus, and right dlPFC, regions previously implicated in ToM mentalizing (greater differentiation of other from self?). Fehse et al. (2015) also conducted a connectivity analysis on the right dlPFC ROI. They found that in the blameworthy conditions, right dlPFC activation was associated with *decreased* activation in a mPFC/ACC (particularly subgenual cingulate cortex [SCC]) cluster, left dlPFC, and the left I. These analyses suggest a direct attenuation of behavioral and affective compassion, the latter as manifested in mPFC, SCC, left dlPFC, and left I, by increased activation of right dlPFC and associated ToM regions, these latter regions indicating greater self-other differentiations, following cognitive mediation of responsibility for suffering. In other words, this study suggests a neurological pathway and mechanism for the suppression of compassion by directed cognitions (Fig. 3.6).

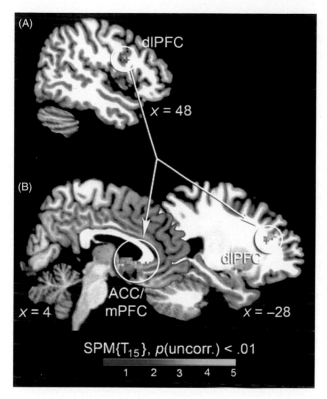

FIGURE 3.6 **Effective connectivity using the right dorsolateral prefrontal cortex (dlPFC) as a seed region.** (A) Anatomical mask for the seed region defined by a group peak voxel (Responsible <Innocent) and a 10 mm sphere; (B) brain areas inversely connected with the right dlPFC activation. *ACC, Anterior cingulate cortex; mPFC, medial prefrontal cortex. Source: Reprinted with permission from Fehse, K., Silveira, S., Elvers, K., & Blautzik, J. (2015). Compassion, guilt and innocence: An fMRI study of responses to victims who are responsible for their fate. Social Neuroscience, 10(3), 243–252.*

AN INTEGRATED THEORY OF THE NEUROSCIENCE OF COMPASSION

And so, a man drives down the street and comes upon a horrible, cruelly fatal accident and is overwhelmed with grief and sadness, but then he hears that the victim was fleeing the police in a stolen vehicle and he suspects that drugs were involved, and the compassion for the victim melts away. And, the leader of a country of over 17 million people hears in his mind the screams and pleas of some 500,000 human beings, many of whom have been shredded to pieces by cluster and bunker-buster bombs and thinks to himself, "they were sympathizers of Al-Qaeda terrorists and merciless insurgents trying to take over my country," steals himself against their suffering, and orders more bombings. Couldn't similar

intellectualizing be ascribed to Hitler's henchmen during the brutal genocide of 6,000,000 Jews, to the democidal purges, expulsions, displace-
ments, imprisonments, manufactured famines, torture, mass murder,
massacres, and war deaths of over 40,000,000 Russian citizens by Joseph
Stalin and his Bolshevic militia, to the mass murders of over 40,000,000
Chinese citizens by Mao Zedong and his Red Army, and to scores of human atrocities committed by despots, dictators, emperors, tribal lords and
their followers over thousands of years? Certainly not to excuse such cruel
atrocities against one's own species, but now, perhaps, we see more clearly
a neurological process for the suppression of what has become through
our evolution a mechanism for preserving our species, for protecting our
progeny, for guarding ourselves against assaults of others, and for joining
with our mates to advance our phylogeny, that mechanism being Compassion for our fellow human beings.

And that process, on the basis of the research reviewed in this chapter,
would appear to be, on witnessing another's suffering, an initial and rather
immediate neurophysiological sharing of, and an impulse to alleviate, that
suffering of another through activation of a cortico-limbic circuit involving
at least the bilateral Anterior Insular Cortex, the Anterior Cingulate Cortex,
and the Amygdaloid Cortex, and perhaps of diffuse mirroring motor structures (MNS) in the PMC and IPL. These bottom-up, ancestral affective pathways, however, become subsequently influenced by slower, higher order,
top-down regulatory circuits that we have acquired much more recently on
an evolutionary timescale. These regulatory circuits involve selective attention to exteroceptive and interoceptive afferents related to our experiencing
and their processing in working memory in the dlPFC, the logical prun-
ing of the response options tree in the vlPFC, the subsequent monitoring
and processing of resultant affective status in the dmPFC, and the perhaps
simultaneous representation of this rather expedient deliberative process
semantically in Posterior Temporal Cortex. And, perhaps to render our response options more personally and socially acceptable and to diminish our
personal distress, we accentuate our self-other differentiation through activation of the ToM circuit of bilateral TPJ, Precuneus, and dmPFC. This model is consistent with the event–feature–emotion complex framework earlier
suggested by Moll et al. (2005) as the neurological foundation of moral cognition. Fehse et al. (2015) further highlight the specialized interactions that
occur between more cognitive control features of lateral and middorsal PFC
in direct contrast to subcortical emotional and motivational pressures chan-
neled through orbital and medial PFC. Through this mechanism, higher
order selective cognitions come to modulate subcortical affective impulses
toward or away from the experience of, in the context of this chapter, Compassion. Perhaps William James, again, had it right in his admonishment,
"The greatest weapon against stress is our ability to choose one thought
over another." Except in the case of Compassion, the only thing that stands

between the suffering of others and our experience of Compassion is "our ability to choose one thought over another."

DIRECTIONS FOR FUTURE RESEARCH

Certainly this connection between our emotional reactions to externally and internally generated stimuli on the one hand and our cognitive appraisals on the other is not a new discovery. Cognitive psychologists and cognitive behavior therapists have been researching and therapeutically utilizing this relationship for decades, and psychodynamically-oriented psychotherapists have been sensitive to the role of "intellectualizing" in controlling human emotions for well over 100 years. However, only recently have the underlying neurological mechanisms of this interaction been more clearly understood. Now, notwithstanding the predilection of our still somewhat primitive reasoning abilities to overly simplify neurological processes that presently may be beyond our comprehension, an initial acceptance of this rather linear and mechanistic stimulus-response chain leads us logically to other questions to clarify our understanding. A number of those questions follows, with suggestions for experimental paradigms to answer them.

If you've read thus far through this chapter, then it will not escape you that the vast majority of neuroscience conducted on the topic of compassion has been fMRI studies. While fMRI offers quite pleasing spatial resolution of the functional anatomical substrates of neurological processes, the nearly exclusive focus on blood flow dynamics gives only a limited perspective on these processes. SPECT and PET scans may offer some improvements but still involve blood flow and metabolic dynamics and have been virtually absent from compassion neuroscience investigations. Additionally, fMRI, SPECT, and PET studies require very expensive recording equipment and are only available in limited laboratories across the country.

EEG offers an examination of changing electrical characteristics of vast assemblies of neurons and while it provides much more precise resolution of the temporal dynamics of primarily cortical regions, and is much less intrusive and expensive than other imaging methods, its spatial resolution is far inferior to that of fMRI and PET. Consequently, only a few of the studies reviewed in this chapter have been EEG studies. More recently however, current source density (CSD) algorithms applied to EEG surface recordings have been developed to allow more precise localizations of brain functions deeper within the cortex and certain subcortical structures. Over the years, these EEG algorithms have been developed to permit spatial resolutions of brain images comparable to those of fMRI, with the advantage of diminished intrusiveness of the neuroimaging technology into the experimental paradigm, greater availability across laboratories, and improved application to complex task challenges such as those utilized in the Fehse et al. (2015), Kedia et al. (2008), and Lutz et al. (2004, 2008) studies. Additionally, EEG event-related potentials (ERP) of neuronal response characteristics to discrete cognitive challenges related to compassion would potentially improve our understanding of this complex cognitive and affective process. As these technologies, particularly CSD analyses, become more widely accepted, more spatially precise, and more comparable, as well as supplemental, to established fMRI strategies, we hope to see their increased application to the study of the neuroscience of empathy, compassion, and self-compassion. Indeed, an initial step in this progression would be a replication of these and other studies utilizing this technology, with the added advantage of an examination of the electrocortical characteristics of the assigned tasks.

Additionally, most of the studies reviewed above as well in the published meta-analyses have examined fMRI ROIs derived from previous investigations. While a fine-tuning of our understanding of the involvement of specific structures in cognitive and affective processes is certainly important, such a narrowed focus may overlook other peripheral structures that play a role in these processes. More recently, and highlighted in several of the studies reviewed above, we have seen connectivity studies which show functional relationships among selected ROIs, as in the Fehse et al. (2015) study. Such analyses of the interactions of more diffuse brain regions, also available with CSD algorithms, vastly clarify our understanding of complex relationships among functional structures and should be conducted.

Given the intention to help as a secondary component of our definition of compassion, and the absence of any directed neurological investigations of this component, it is important that research into motivational-intentional manifestations of compassion be conducted. Of the compassion studies reviewed for this chapter, only one reported activation in primary motor cortex during the experience of compassion (Fehse et al., 2015). Future studies of this motivational-intentional component would include a recording of EEG mu or fMRI BOLD activity, the latter specifically in motor areas, during compassion-eliciting relative to neutral and other scenarios.

Immordino-Yang, Lutz, Klimecki, and Singer and colleagues, in the studies reviewed above, as well as other researchers, have identified an initial and more unfiltered, by higher order processing, affective response circuit involving the AMG, the AI, and the ACC. Lamm and Singer (2010) have further spotlighted the Insular Cortex as a prominent site for the experience of compassion, with differential roles of various subcomponents for the experiencing of empathy, love, compassion, and integrative emotional states. It will be important for future researchers to further refine and to clarify the more specialized and inter-related roles of components and subdivisions of this affective circuit.

And regarding the top-down filtering, the mentalizing, of affective experience, the TPJ, the ACC, the STS, the mPFC, the Pre, the mFG, and the TP have been rather consistently associated with ToM. Somewhat counter-intuitively, and notwithstanding the established neural connectivity among diverse cortical localizations, these sites are not only scattered across anterior and posterior cortical regions but also appear to be somewhat specialized bilaterally. It will be useful to our understanding of more specific ToM functions to conduct additional connectivity studies and component analyses of the operational features of compassion, as well as other affective states. Neuroimaging, electrocortical, and connectivity investigations of the sequential separation of stages involved in the processing of perceived suffering of others, and of one's desire to help alleviate that suffering, will be useful to our further understanding of the role of ToM components and subfunctions in the neurological experience of compassion. The deconstruction and reconstruction recommendations of Schaafsma et al. (2015) are particularly relevant here.

While we are on the intriguing and complex subject of higher order control of bottom-up emotional processes, the neurological representations of and mechanisms for the cognitive (thought) control of affect present a longstanding and philosophically incorrigible challenge for neuroscientists. Quite simply stated, how are our thoughts transmuted into neurological moderators of our emotional experiences? This question has perplexed neuroscientists, as well as philosophers, for generations. Perhaps, an answer to this question is emerging from the discovery of mirror neurons and of their localizations, in part, within the expressive and receptive speech areas in humans. If we consider phonetics, morphetics, and semantics as little more than progressively refined and coordinated motor efferents directly tied to basic survival drives (fighting, fleeing, feeding, and mating) and to raw affective states (that we subsequently label as anger, disgust, fear, happiness, sadness, and surprise), then the role of speech in the expression of affective status is little more than behavioral manifestations of emotions. And standing between these emotions and intended behaviors is an evolutionarily advanced, higher order, top-down modulation of these motor efferents by cognitions. How these thoughts (perhaps we only become aware of them as words "after the fact," following the "Bereitschaftspotential" or "readiness potential") come to modulate our actions and to regulate our compassion will doubtlessly be the course of future cognitive/affective neuroscience research (Holden, 2004; Kornhuber & Deecke, 2016). Perhaps a beginning would be to investigate mirror neuron activity, both spatially, temporally, and sequentially, during the experience of compassion.

The complexity, variations, and external validity of stimulus characteristics in published studies to date have indeed been clever and highly relevant in the recreation of compassionate states of consciousness in notably artificial contexts (i.e., MRI scanners). Moving the neuroscience of compassion out of the laboratory scanner environment and into more real world contexts and designs will be important in future research. Again, EEG technology, while still imposing artificial, yet increasingly comfortable, recording headgear and utilizing miniaturized, wearable, remote-sending–recording units, will allow neuroscience research to move into the more natural social environment. A related concern in the need to increase the external validity of compassion neuroscience research is the undergraduate volunteer bias effect. Demir et al. (2016) have cogently articulated the potential biasing effects of utilizing nearly exclusively undergraduate volunteers in social science research. This concern extends to neuroscience research as well, since nearly all of the studies reviewed in this chapter (with the exception of those few involving seasoned Tibetan meditators) have utilized undergraduate volunteers, most right-handed to control for potential lateralization disparities, if only as control participants. Such an overuse of convenience samples having unique personal, social, and neurological characteristics further limits the generalization of reported outcomes to other (e.g., older, more experienced, more compassionate?) populations. Additionally, we made an effort to present the number of participants in each reviewed study in order to highlight the relatively small Ns used in virtually all neuroscience investigations. Such small Ns are unavoidable in resource-intensive neuroscience research, but this phenomenon certainly necessitates replication.

And finally, before leaving this topic for the time being, how could we close without considering on a more global scale the issue of wars between peoples on this planet. A consideration of this question naturally leads to neuroscience research on how to enhance or to engender compassion in others, particularly on a group or societal stage. Knowing the neurological components and mechanisms involved in the experience of compassion to the extent that we presently do, can we use this knowledge to anticipate research or programs of influence to change compassion? A first step would be to examine existing efforts to enhance compassion and their effects on neurological structures and processes. That effort is the subject of Chapters 8 and 9 in this book. If that examination reveals that indeed we can alter these phenomena in a positive manner, then our next step is to design and to improve such interventions, to demonstrate further their positive impacts both behaviorally and neurologically, and to begin such a program on a larger, more societal scale.

Of particular interest would be the impact on compassion of brief interventions such as the Self-Compassion Metta Meditation described in Chapter 4, directed at strengthening one's immersion into the experience of Common-Humanity. We wonder what the impact of such an intervention would be on an enemy's commitment to their aggressive, war-like pursuits if they were immersed in a similar culturally-sensitive manner in the experience of common-humanity. Could such an intervention be a more effective counter-insurgency tactic than our present use of torture of war criminals? Such a question clearly needs to be examined in strategically designed laboratory settings and then followed up in field studies. Once we begin to take the neuroscience of compassion out of the laboratory and into real-world contexts to address such troubling societal issues as war, torture, and the callous mutilation of our fellow human beings then we will have embarked upon the truly translational purpose of our work, to create a more compassionate world.

References

Abu-Akel, A., & Shamay-Tsoory, S. (2011). Neuroanatomical and neurochemical bases of theory of mind. *Neuropsychologia, 49*, 2971–2984.

Analayo, B. (2015). *Compassion and emptiness in early Buddhist meditation*. Cambridge, UK: Windhorse Publications 6.

Baron-Cohen, S. (1991). Precursors to a theory of mind: Understanding attention in others. In A. Whiten (Ed.), *Natural theories of mind: Evolution, development and simulation of everyday mindreading*. Oxford, UK: Basil Blackwell.

Baron-Cohen, S., Leslie, A. M., & Frith, U. (1985). Does the autistic child have a "theory of mind"? *Cognition, 21*(1), 37–46.

Batson, C. D. (2009). These things called empathy: Eight related but distinct phenomena. In J. Decety, & W. Ickes (Eds.), *The social neuroscience of empathy* (1st ed., pp. 3–15). Cambridge, MA: MIT Press.

Beauregard, M., Levesque, J., & Bourgouin, P. (2001). Neural correlates of conscious self-regulation of emotion. *Journal of Neuroscience, 21*(18), 1–6 RC165.

Berecz, H., Tényi, T., & Herold, R. (2016). Theory of mind in depressive disorders: A review of the literature. *Psychopathology, 49*, 125–134.

Bora, E., & Berk, M. (2016). Theory of mind in major depressive disorder: A meta-analysis. *Journal of Affective Disorders, 191*, 49–55.

Bora, E., Yucel, M., & Pantelis, C. (2009). Theory of mind impairment in schizophrenia: Meta-analysis. *Schizophrenia Research, 109*(1–3), 1–9.

Bora, E., Bartholomeusz, C., & Pantelis, C. (2016). Meta-analysis of Theory of Mind (ToM) impairment in bipolar disorder. *Psychological Medicine, 46*(2), 253–264.

Bosco, F. M., Capozzi, F., Colle, L., Marostica, P., & Tirassa, M. (2013). Theory of mind deficit in subjects with alcohol use disorder: An analysis of mindreading processes. *Alcohol and Alcoholism, 493*, 299–307.

Buhle, J. T., Silvers, J. A., Wager, T. D., Lopez, R., Onyemekwu, C., Kober, H., et al. (2014). Cognitive reappraisal of emotion: A meta-analysis of human neuroimaging studies. *Cerebral Cortex, 24*(November), 2981–2990.

Buschman, T., & Miller, E. K. (2007). Top-down versus bottom-up control of attention in the prefrontal and posterior parietal cortices. *Science, 315*, 1860–1862.

Bzdok, D., Schilbach, L., Vogeley, K., Schneider, K., Laird, A. R., Langner, R., et al. (2012). Parsing the neural correlates of moral cognition: ALE meta-analysis on morality, theory of mind, and empathy. *Brain Structure and Function, 217*(4), 783–796. http://doi.org/10.1007/s00429-012-0380-y.

Call, J., & Tomasello, M. (2008). Does the chimpanzee have a theory of mind? 30 years later. *Trends in Cognitive Sciences, 12*(5), 187–192.

Carruthers, P., & Smith, P. K. (1996). *Theories of theories of mind*. Cambridge: Cambridge University Press.

Cassetta, B., & Goghari, V. (2014). Theory of mind reasoning in schizophrenia patients and non-psychotic relatives. *Psychiatry Research, 218*(1–2), 12–19.

Churchland, P. M. (1991). Folk psychology and the explanation of human behavior. In J. D. Greenwood (Ed.), *The future of folk psychology* (pp. 51–69). Cambridge: Cambridge University Press.

Costafreda, S. G., Brammer, M. J., David, A. S., & Fu, C. H. Y. (2008). Predictors of amygdala activation during the processing of emotional stimuli: A meta-analysis of 385 PET and fMRI studies. *Brain Research Reviews, 58*, 57–70.

Csulky, G., Polgár, P., Tombor, L., Benkovits, J., & Réthelyi, J. (2014). Theory of mind impairments in patients with deficit schizophrenia. *Comprehensive Psychiatry, 55*(2), 349–356.

Davies, M., & Stone, T. (1998). Folk psychology and mental simulation. *Royal Institute of Philosophy Supplement, 43.* http:// doi: 10.1017/S1358246100004306.

Davis, B., & MacNeilage, P. F. (2004). The frame/content theory of speech evolution: From lip smacks to syllables. *Primatologie, 6*, 305–328.

de Waal, F. (2009). *The age of empathy*. New York: Three Rivers Press 6.

Decety, J., & Svetlova, M. (2012). Putting together phylogenetic and ontogenetic perspectives on empathy. *Developmental Cognitive Neuroscience, 2*, 1–24.

Decety, J., Michalska, K., & Akitsuki, Y. (2008). Who caused the pain? An fMRI investigation of empathy and intentionality in children. *Neuropsychologia, 46*, 2607–2614.

Decety, J., Norman, G. J., Berntson, G. G., & Cacioppo, J. T. (2012). A neurobehavioral evolutionary perspective on the mechanisms underlying empathy. *Progress in Neurobiology, 98*, 38–48.

Demir, M., Haynes, A., Orthel-Clark, H., & Ozen, A. (2017). Volunteer bias in research on friendship among emerging adults. *Emerging Adulthood, 5*(1), 53–68.

Di Pellegrino, G., Fadiga, L., Fogassi, L., Gallese, V., & Rizzolatti, G. (1992). Understanding motor events: A neurophysiological study. *Experimental Brain Research, 91*, 176–180.

Dodell-Feder, D., Tully, L. M., Lincoln, S. H., & Hooker, C. I. (2014). The neural basis of theory of mind and its relationship to social functioning and social anhedonia in individuals with schizophrenia. *Neuroimage: Clinical, 4*, 154–163.

Ekman, P. (1992). An argument for basic emotions. *Cognition and Emotion, 6*(3/4), 169–200.

Farrant, B. M., Fletcher, J., & Maybery, M. T. (2006). Specific language impairment, theory of mind, and visual perspective taking: Evidence for simulation theory and the developmental role of language. *Child Development, 77*(6), 1842–1853.

Farrar, M. J., Johnson, B., Tompkins, V., Easters, M., Zilisi-Medus, A., & Benigno, J. P. (2009). Language and theory of mind in preschool children with specific language impairment. *Journal of Communication Disorders, 42*(6), 428–441.

Fehse, K., Silveira, S., Elvers, K., & Blautzik, J. (2015). Compassion, guilt and innocence: An fMRI study of responses to victims who are responsible for their fate. *Social Neuroscience, 10*(3), 243–252.

Fletcher, P. C., Happé, F., Frith, U., Baker, S. C., Dolan, R. J., Frackowiak, R. S. J., et al. (1995). Other minds in the brain: A functional imaging study of "theory of mind" in story comprehension. *Cognition, 57*(2), 109–128. http://doi.org/10.1016/0010-0277(95)00692-R.

Fogassi, L., Ferrari, P. F., Gesierich, S. R., Rozzi, S., Chersi, F., & Rizzolatti, G. (2005). Parietal Lobe: From action organization to intention understanding. *Science, 308*, 662–667.

Frith, U., & Frith, C. D. (2001). The biological basis of social interaction. *Current Directions in Psychological Science, 10*(5), 151–155.

Frith, C. D., & Frith, U. (2005). Theory of mind. *Current Biology, 15*(17), 644–645. http://doi.org/10.1016/j.cub.2005.08.041.

Frith, C. D., & Frith, U. (2006). The neural basis of mentalizing. *Neuron, 50*, 531–534. http://doi.org/10.1016/j.neuron.2006.05.001.

Gallagher, S. (2001). The practice of mind: Theory, simulation, or primary interaction? *Journal of Consciousness Studies, 8*(5–7), 83–108.

Gallagher, H. L., & Frith, C. D. (2003). Functional imaging of "theory of mind". *Trends in Cognitive Sciences, 7*(2), 77–83. http://doi.org/10.1016/S1364-6613(02)00025-6.

Gallagher, H. L., Happé, F., Brunswick, N., Fletcher, P. C., Frith, U., & Frith, C. D. (2000). Reading the mind in cartoons and stories: An fMRI study of "theory of mind" in verbal and non-verbal tasks. *Neuropsychologia, 38*(1), 11–21. http://doi.org/10.1016/S0028-3932(99)00053-6.

Gallese, V. (2009). Motor abstraction: A neuroscientific account of how action goals and intentions are mapped and understood. *Psychological Research, 73,* 486–498.

Gallese, V., & Goldman, A. (1998). Mirror neurons and the simulation theory of mind-reading. *Trends in Cognitive Sciences, 2*(12), 493–500 December.

Gallese, V., Fadiga, L., Fogassi, L., & Rizzolatti, G. (1996). Action recognition in the premotor cortex. *Brain, 119,* 593–609.

Gallese, V., Keysers, C., & Rizzolatti, G. (2004). A unifying view of the basis of social cognition. *Trends in Cognitive Sciences, 8*(9), 396–403. http://doi.org/10.1016/j.tics.2004.07.002.

Gilbert, P. (Ed.). (2005). *Compassion: Conceptualisations, research, and use in psychotherapy* (1st ed.). London: Routledge.

Gobbini, M. I., Koralek, A. C., Bryan, R. E., Montgomery, K. J., & Haxby, J. V. (2007). Two takes on the social brain: a comparison of theory of mind tasks. *Journal of Cognitive Neuroscience, 19*(11), 1803–1814. http://doi.org/10.1162/jocn.2007.19.11.1803.

Goetz, J. L., Keltner, D., & Simon-Thomas, E. (2010). Compassion: An evolutionary analysis and empirical review. *Psychological Bulletin, 136,* 351–374.

Goldman, A. I. (1989). Interpretation psychologized. *Mind and Language, 4,* 161–185.

Goldman, A. I. (1992). In defense of the simulation theory. *Mind Language, 7,* 104–119.

Goldman, A. I. (2006). *Simulating Minds*. Oxford: Oxford University Press.

Gopnik, A., & Wellman, H. M. (1994). The theory theory. In L. Hirschfield, & S. Gelman (Eds.), *Mapping the mind: Domain specificity in cognition and culture* (pp. 257–293). New York: Cambridge University Press.

Gordon, R. M. (1986). Folk psychology as simulation. *Mind and Language, 1*(2), 158–171.

Gweon, H., Dodell-Feder, D., Bedny, M., & Saxe, R. (2012). Theory of mind performance in children correlates with functional specialization of a brain region for thinking about thoughts. *Child Development, 83*(December (6)), 1853–1868.

Hezel, D. M., & McNally, R. J. (2014). Theory of mind impairments in social anxiety disorder. *Behavior Therapy, 45*(4), 530–540.

Hill, S. Y., Kostelnik, B., Holmes, B., Goradia, D., McDermott, M., Diwardkar, V., et al. (2007). fMRI BOLD response to the eyes task in offspring from multiplex alcohol dependence families. *Alcoholism Clinical and Experimental Research, 31*(12), 2028–2035.

Holden, C. (2004). The origin of speech. *Science, 303,* 1316–1319.

Immordino-Yang, M. H., McColl, A., Damasio, H., & Damasio, A. (2009). Neural correlates of admiration and compassion. *Proceedings of the National Academy of Sciences of the United States of America, 106*(19), 8021–8026.

Inoue, Y., Yamada, K., & Kanba, S. (2006). Deficit in theory of mind is a risk for relapse of major depression. *Journal of Affective Disorders, 95*(1–3), 125–127.

James, W. (1890). *The principles of psychology.* New York: Henry Holt and Company 6.

Kédia, G., Berthoz, S., Wessa, M., Hilton, D., & Martinot, J. -L. (2008). An agent harms a victim: A functional magnetic resonance imaging study on specific moral emotions. *Journal of Cognitive Neuroscience, 20*(10), 1788–1798. http://doi.org/10.1162/jocn.2008.20070.

Klimecki, O. M., Leiberg, S., Lamm, C., & Singer, T. (2013). Functional neural plasticity and associated changes in positive affect after compassion training. *Cerebral Cortex, 23*(July), 1552–1561.

Kober, H., Barrett, L. F., Joseph, J., Bliss-Moreau, E., Lindquist, K., & Wager, T. D. (2008). Functional grouping and cortical–subcortical interactions in emotion: A meta-analysis of neuroimaging studies. *NeuroImage, 42,* 998–1031.

Konstantakopoulos, G., Ploumpidis, D., Oulis, P., Patrikelis, P., Nikitopoulou, S., Papadimitriou, G. N., et al. (2014). The relationship between insight and theory of mind in chizophrenia. *Schizophrenia Research, 152*(1), 217–222.

Kornhuber, H. H., & Deecke, L. (2016). Brain potential changes in voluntary and passive movements in humans: Readiness potential and reafferent potentials. *Pflügers Archiv: European Journal of Physiology, 468*(7), 1115–1124.

Koster-Hale, J., & Saxe, R. (2013). Functional neuroimaging of theory of mind. In S. Baron-Cohen, H. Tager-Flusberg, & M. V. Lombardo (Eds.), *Understanding other minds: Perspectives from developmental social neuroscience* (pp. 132–162). Oxford, UK: Oxford University Press.

Lamm, C., & Singer, T. (2010). The role of anterior insular cortex in social emotions. *Brain Structure and Function, 214*, 579–591.

Lamm, C., Decety, J., & Singer, T. (2011). Meta-analytic evidence for common and distinct neural networks associated with directly experienced pain and empathy for pain. *NeuroImage, 54*, 2492–2502.

Lee, L., Harkness, K. L., Sabbagh, M. A., & Jacobson, J. A. (2005). Mental state decoding abilities in clinical depression. *Journal of Affective Disorders, 86*(2–3), 247–258.

Leslie, A. M. (1987). Pretense and representation: The origins of "theory of mind". *Psychological Review, 94*(4), 412–426.

Levesque, J., Eugene, F., Joanette, Y., Paquette, V., Mensour, B., Beaudoin, G., et al. (2003). Neural circuitry underlying voluntary suppression of sadness. *Biological Psychiatry, 53*, 502–510.

Lindquist, K. A., Wager, T. D., Kober, H., Bliss-Moreau, E., & Barrett, L. F. (2012). The brain basis of emotion: A meta-analytic review. *Behavioral and Brain Sciences, 35*(3), 121–143.

Lutz, A., Brefczynski-Lewis, J., Johnstone, T., & Davidson, R. J. (2008). Regulation of the neural circuitry of emotion by compassion meditation: Effects of meditative expertise. *PLoS One, 3*(3), 1–10.

Lutz, A., Greischar, L. L., Perlman, D. M., & Davidson, R. J. (2009). BOLD signal in insula is differentially related to cardiac function during compassion meditation in experts vs novices. *NeuroImage, 47*, 1038–1046.

Lutz, A., Greischar, L. L., Rawlings, N. B., Ricard, M., & Davidson, R. J. (2004). Long-term meditators self-induce high-amplitude gamma synchrony during mental practice. *Proceedings of the National Academy of Sciences of the United States of America, 101*(46), 16369–16373.

MacNeilage, P. F., & Davis, B. L. (2005). The frame/content theory of evolution of speech: A comparison with a gestural-origins alternative. *Interaction Studies, 6*(2), 173–199.

Mahy, C. E. V., Moses, L. J., & Pfeifer, J. H. (2014). How and where: Theory-of-mind in the brain. *Developmental Cognitive Neuroscience, 9*, 68–81. http://doi.org/10.1016/j.dcn.2014.01.002.

Mattern, M., Walter, H., Hentze, C. M., Schramm, E., Drost, S., Schoepf, D., et al. (2015). Behavioral evidence for an impairment of affective theory of mind capabilities in chronic depression. *Psychopathology, 48*(4), 240–250.

McCleery, J. P., Surtees, A. D. R., Graham, K. A., Richards, J. E., & Apperly, I. A. (2011). The neural and cognitive time course of theory of mind. *Journal of Neuroscience, 31*(36), 12849–12854. http://doi.org/10.1523/JNEUROSCI.1392-11.2011.

Mehta, U. M., Bhagyavathi, H. D., Kumar, C. N., Thirthalli, J., & Gangadhar, B. N. (2014). Cognitive deconstruction of parenting in schizophrenia: the role of theory of mind. *The Australian and New Zealand Journal of Psychiatry, 3*(48), 249–258.

Mitchell, J. P. (2009). Inferences about mental states. *Philosophical Transactions of the Royal Society, 364*, 1309–1316.

Mitchell, J. P., Macrae, C. N., & Banaji, M. R. (2006). Dissociable medial prefrontal contributions to judgments of similar and dissimilar others. *Neuron, 50*, 655–663.

Moll, J., Zahn, R., de Oliveira-Souza, R., Krueger, F., & Grafman, J. (2005). The neural basis of human moral cognition. *Nature Reviews Neuroscience, 6*(October), 799–809.

Monroe, K. R. (1996). *The heart of altruism: Perceptions of a common-humanity*. Princeton: Princeton University Press.

Montag, C., Ehrlich, A., Neuhaus, K., Dziobek, I., Heekeren, H. R., Heinz, A., et al. (2010). Theory of mind impairments in euthymic bipolar patients. *Journal of Affective Disorders, 123*(1–3), 264–269.

Murphy, F. C., Nimmo-Smith, I., & Lawrence, A. D. (2003). Functional neuroanatomy of emotions: A meta-analysis. *Cognitive, Affective, and Behavioral Neuroscience, 3*(3), 207–233.

Nandrino, J. L., Gandolphe, M. -C., Alexandre, C., Kmiecik, E., Yguel, J., & Urso, L. (2014). Cognitive and affective theory of mind abilities in alcohol-dependent patients: The role of autobiographical memory. *Drug and Alcohol Dependence, 143,* 65–73.

Ng, R., Fish, S., & Granholm, E. (2015). Insight and theory of mind in schizophrenia. *Psychiatry Research, 225*(1–2), 169–174.

Nilsson, K. K., & de López, K. J. (2016). Theory of mind in children with specific language impairment: A systematic review and meta-analysis. *Child Development, 87,* 143–153.

Ochsner, K. N., Bunge, S. A., Gross, J. J., & Gabrieli, J. D. (2002). Rethinking feelings: An fMRI study of the cognitive regulation of emotion. *Journal of Cognitive Neuroscience, 14*(8), 1215–1229.

Ochsner, K. N., Ray, R. D., Cooper, J. C., Robertson, E. R., Chopra, S., Gabrieli, J. D. E., et al. (2004). For better or for worse: Neural systems supporting the cognitive down- and up-regulation of negative emotion. *NeuroImage, 23,* 483–499.

Ochsner, K. N., Ray, R. R., Hughes, B., McRae, K., Cooper, J. C., Weber, J., et al. (2009). Bottom-up and top-down processes in emotion generation: Common and distinct neural mechanisms. *Psychological Science, 20*(11), 1322–1331.

Pederson, A., Koelkebeck, K., Brandt, M., Wee, M., Kueppers, K. A., Kugel, H., et al. (2012). Theory of mind in patients with schizophrenia: Is mentalizing delayed? *Schizophrenia Research, 137*(1–3), 224–229.

Phan, K. L., Wager, T., Taylor, S. F., & Liberzon, I. (2002). Functional neuroanatomy of emotion: A meta-analysis of emotion activation studies in PET and fMRI. *NeuroImage, 16,* 331–348.

Phelps, F. A. (2006). Emotion and cognition: Insights from studies of the human amygdala. *Annual Review of Psychology, 57,* 27–53.

Pickup, G. J., & Frith, C. D. (2001). Theory of mind impairments in schizophrenia: Symptomatology, severity, and specificity. *Psychological Medicine, 31*(2), 207–220.

Porges, S. W. (2001). The polyvagal theory: Phylogenetic substrates of a social nervous system. *International Journal of Psychophysiology, 42,* 123–146.

Porges, S. W. (2003). The polyvagal theory: Phylogenetic contributions to social behavior. *Physiology and Behavior, 79,* 503–513.

Premack, D., & Woodruff, G. (1978). Does the chimpanzee have a theory of mind? *Behavioral and Brain Sciences, 1*(4), 515–526. http://dx.doi.org/10.1017/S0140525X00076512.

Rilling, J. K., Sanfey, A. G., Aronson, J. A., Nystrom, L. E., & Cohen, J. D. (2004). The neural correlates of theory of mind within interpersonal interactions. *NeuroImage, 22*(4), 1694–1703. http://doi.org/10.1016/j.neuroimage.2004.04.015.

Rizzolatti, G., & Craighero, L. (2004). The mirror-neuron system. *Annual Review of Neuroscience, 27,* 169–192.

Rizzolatti, G., Fadiga, L., Gallese, V., & Fogassi, L. (1996). Premotor cortex and the recognition of motor actions. *Cognitive Brain Research, 3,* 131–141.

Sarter, M., Givens, B., & Bruno, J. P. (2001). The cognitive neuroscience of sustained attention: Where top-down meets bottom-up. *Brain Research Reviews, 35,* 146–160.

Saxe, R. (2006a). Four brain regions for one theory of mind? In J. T. Cacioppo, P. S. Visser, & C. L. Pickett (Eds.), *Social neuroscience: People thinking about thinking people* (pp. 83–101). Cambridge, MA: The MIT Press.

Saxe, R. (2006b). Uniquely human social cognition. *Current Opinion in Neurobiology, 16*(2), 235–239. http://doi.org/10.1016/j.conb.2006.03.001.

Saxe, R., & Kanwisher, N. (2003). People thinking about thinking people: The role of the temporo-parietal junction in "theory of mind ". *NeuroImage, 19*(4), 1835–1842. http://doi.org/10.1016/S1053-8119(03)00230-1.

Saxe, R., & Powell, L. J. (2006). It's the thought that counts: Specific brain regions for one component of theory of mind. *Psychological Science, 17*(8), 692–699. http://doi.org/10.1016/j.tics.2014.11.007.

Saxe, R., Moran, J. M., Scholz, J., & Gabrieli, J. (2006). Overlapping and non-overlapping brain regions for theory of mind and self reflection in individual subjects. *Social Cognitive and Affective Neuroscience, 1*(3), 229–234.

Schaafsma, S. M., Pfaff, D. W., Spunt, R. P., & Adolphs, R. (2015). Deconstructing and reconstructing theory of mind. *Trends in Cognitive Sciences, 19*(2), 65–72. http://doi.org/10.1016/j.tics.2014.11.007.

Schurz, M., Radua, J., Aichhorn, M., Richlan, F., & Perner, J. (2014). Fractionating theory of mind: A meta-analysis of functional brain imaging studies. *Neuroscience and Biobehavioral Reviews, 42*, 9–34.

Sergerie, K., Chochol, C., & Armony, J. L. (2008). The role of the amygdala in emotional processing: A quantitative meta-analysis of functional neuroimaging studies. *Neuroscience and Biobehavioral Reviews, 32*, 811–830.

Seth, A. K. (2013). Interoceptive inference, emotion, and the embodied self. *Trends in Cognitive Sciences, 17*, 565–573.

Shanton, K., & Goldman, A. (2010). Simulation theory. *WIREs Cognitive Science, 1*(4), 527–538.

Shreeve, J. (2005). Beyond the brain. *National Geographic, 207*(3), 2–31.

Siegal, M., & Varley, R. (2002). Neural systems involved in 'theory of mind'. *Nature Reviews Neuroscience, 3*(6), 463–471.

Singer, T. (2006). The neuronal basis and ontogeny of empathy and mind reading: Review of literature and implications for future research. *Neuroscience and Behavioral Reviews, 30*, 855–863.

Singer, T., & Lamm, C. (2009). The social neuroscience of empathy. *Annals of the New York Academy of Sciences, 1156*, 81–96.

Singer, T., Seymour, B., O'Doherty, J., Kaube, H., Dolan, R. J., & Frith, C. D. (2004). Empathy for pain involves the affective but not sensory components for pain. *Science, 303*, 1157–1162.

Singer, T., Critchley, H. D., & Preuschoff, K. (2009). A common role of insula in feelings, empathy and uncertainty. *Trends in cognitive sciences, 13*(8), 334–340.

Sprong, M., Schothorst, P., Vos, E., Hox, J., & Engeland, H. V. (2007). Theory of mind in schizophrenia. *The British Journal of Psychiatry, 191*(1), 5–13.

Stone, V. E., Baron-Cohen, S., & Knight, R. T. (1998). Frontal lobe contributions to theory of mind. *Journal of Cognitive Neuroscience, 10*(5), 640–656. http://doi.org/Thesis_references-Converted #463.

Tkach, D., Reimer, J., & Hatsopoulos, N. G. (2007). Congruent activity during action and action observation in motor cortex. *The Journal of Neuroscience, 27*(48), 13241–13250.

Uekermann, J., & Daum, I. (2008). Social cognition in alcoholism: A link to prefrontal cortex dysfunction? *Addiction, 103*(5), 726–735.

van Veluw, S. J., & Chance, S. A. (2014). Differentiating between self and others: An ALE meta-analysis of fMRI studies of self-recognition and theory of mind. *Brain Imaging and Behavior, 8*(1), 24–38.

Vogeley, K., Bussfeld, P., Newen, A., Herrmann, S., Happé, F., Falkai, P., & Zilles, K. (2001). Mind reading: Neural mechanisms of theory of mind and self-perspective. *NeuroImage, 14*, 170–181. http://doi.org/10.1006/nimg.2001.0789.

Völlm, B. A., Taylor, A. N. W., Richardson, P., Corcoran, R., Stirling, J., McKie, S., et al. (2006). Neuronal correlates of theory of mind and empathy: A functional magnetic resonance imaging study in a nonverbal task. *NeuroImage, 29*(1), 90–98. http://doi.org/10.1016/j.neuroimage.2005.07.022.

Vytal, K., & Hamann, S. (2010). Neuroimaging support for discrete neural correlates of basic emotions: A voxel-based meta-analysis. *Journal of Cognitive Neuroscience, 22*(12), 2864–2885.

Wang, Y. G., Wang, Y. Q., Chen, S. L., Zhu, C. Y., & Wang, K. (2008). Theory of mind disability in major depression with or without psychotic symptoms: A componential view. *Psychiatry Research, 161*(2), 153–161.

Weng, H. Y., Fox, A. S., Shackman, A. J., Stodola, D. E., Caldwell, J. Z. K., Olson, M. C., et al. (2013). Compassion training alters altruism and neural responses to suffering. *Psychological Science, 20*(10), 1–10.

Werden, D., Elikann, L., Linster, H., Dykieriek, P., & Berger, M. (2008). Theory of mind (ToM) and depression—An explorative study including narrative ToM-performances. *Annals of General Psychiatry, 7*(Suppl 1), S214. http://doi.org/10.1186/1744-859X-7-S1-S214.

Westby, C. E. (2014). Social neuroscience and theory of mind. *Folia Phoniatrica et Logopaedica, 66,* 7–17.

Wolkenstein, L., Schönenberg, M., Schirm, E., & Hautzinger, M. (2011). I can see what you feel, but I can't deal with it: Impaired theory of mind in depression. *Journal of Affective Disorders, 132*(1–2), 104–111.

Woodruff, C. C., & Maaske, S. (2010). Action execution engages human mirror neuron system more than action observation. *NeuroReport, 21*(6), 432–435.

Young, L., Cushman, F., Hauser, M., & Saxe, R. (2007). The neural basis of the interaction between theory of mind and moral judgment. *Proceedings of the National Academy of Sciences of the United States of America, 104*(20), 8235–8240. http://doi.org/10.1073/pnas.0701408104.

Zobel, I., Werden, D., Linster, H., Dykierek, P., Drieling, T., Berger, M., et al. (2010). Theory of mind deficits in chronically depressed patients. *Depression and Anxiety, 27*(9), 821–828.

The Brain That Longs to Care for Itself: The Current Neuroscience of Self-Compassion

Larry Stevens, Mark Gauthier-Braham,
Benjamin Bush

Northern Arizona University, Flagstaff, AZ, United States

SELF-COMPASSION

Thus far in our journey into the neuroscience of empathy, compassion, and self-compassion, we have explored much of the phylogenic, cultural, and neurologic roots of empathy and of compassion. In the process, we have defined empathy as a manifestation of our ability to take perspective on the experiences of another, to share their experiences both affectively and cognitively, and in addition to appreciate a critical differentiation of ourselves from the experiencing other. Similarly, we have defined compassion as a recognition of a specific emotional and cognitive discomfort on the part of another, but in this case coupled with a desire to alleviate their suffering and, from a Buddhist elaboration of this witnessing, perhaps to also experience a "sympathetic joy" with this potential relief (Analayo, 2015; Gethin, 1998). In this chapter, we continue our exploration into a similar phylogeny, culture, and neurology of Self-Compassion. Our journey is much like hiking the American Appalachian Trail, with long, rolling, graceful, predictable, and contemplative stretches punctuated by abrupt, precipitous, arduous, seemingly impossible and impassable ascents into obscure, smoky, unpopulated "jump-ups" that seem to endlessly climb straight up onto unexplored pinnacles. Such a metaphor is quite fitting for an exploration of self-compassion, for much of the psychosocial elaboration, assessment, implications, and application of this construct has been gracefully developed to date, with the neurologic underpinnings left essentially undiscovered.

The Neuroscience of Empathy, Compassion, and Self-Compassion. http://dx.doi.org/10.1016/B978-0-12-809837-0.00004-0

THE EVOLUTION OF COMPASSION AND OF SELF-COMPASSION

If we define compassion as a sensitivity to the suffering of another and a desire to do something to alleviate that suffering, then it would follow that self-compassion is a sensitivity to our own suffering and a desire to alleviate that suffering. Such a notion of being compassionate with one's self is not a new one and has followed the evolution of the concept of compassion in Buddhist science of mind. Ancient Buddhist discourses advise a pervasive mental dwelling in four divine abodes, known as *brahmaviharas*. These four ubiquitous mental involvements are *metta* (loving-kindness), *karuna* (compassion), *mudita* (sympathetic joy), and *upek(k)ha* (equanimity) (Analayo, 2015). The loving-kindness abode encourages *metta meditation*, a deep and often prolonged meditation on loving-kindness toward a progression of objects from oneself to common humanity, culminating in a nonreferential, objectless absorption into the pure experience of compassion. The first of these object loving-kindness meditations, however, is one's self, and often this practice can last for months and years as one learns to experience kindness and the pure sense of common humanity with regard to the self (Kornfield, 1993, 2008). Thus we see in these earliest of Buddhist teachings the development of the concepts of loving-kindness and common humanity self-compassion.

However, self-compassion has found more contemporary recognition and appreciation with the writings of Kristin Neff (Neff & Vonk, 2009). Neff (2011) reintroduced self-compassion as an important distinction from the popular interest in self-esteem, which has been recognized as a self-evaluative characteristic based on perceived standards, social comparisons, and the judgments of others. As such, self-esteem is associated with a number of negative consequences, such as social- and self-distortions, narcissism, self-absorption, self-centeredness, diminished concern for others, out-group prejudices, and even misdirected aggression and violence. Self-compassion on the other hand develops directly from one's ability to understand the suffering of another and to desire to lessen that suffering. Consequently, self-compassion embodies many of the characteristics and practices of compassion. Self-compassion involves an understanding of and openness to one's own discomforts, the experience of loving-kindness toward the self, the ability to find balance among the myriad of life's experiences and to not overly attend to one's discomforts or disappointments, and the recognition that we all, as members of the family of personkind, enjoy a multitude of pleasures and excitements in living as well as losses, disappointments, and injuries. Such a combined self- and other-awareness brings us peace, joy, and even greater compassion for ourselves and for others (Neff, 2003a). In fact, we cannot experience true compassion for others without an equally profound compassion toward ourselves (Kornfield, 1993).

In an extensive body of research, Neff has developed and validated an instrument to assess the bipolar components of self-compassion, called the *Self-Compassion Scale (SCS)*. Utilizing this instrument over the past decade, Neff and colleagues have proceeded to examine the relationships among overall self-compassion and its separate constituents on the one hand and a host of mental and bodily health characteristics on the other. This body of research has revealed that self-compassion is significantly negatively correlated with Beck Depression Inventory and Zung Self-Rating Depression Scale depression, Speilberger Trait Anxiety Inventory anxiety, Almost Perfect Scale neurotic perfectionism, Rumination scale thought rumination, and White Bear Thought Suppression Inventory avoidance of unwanted thoughts and ideas and is significantly positively correlated with Satisfaction with Life Scale life satisfaction and with Emotional Coping Scale emotion-focused processing. Furthermore, the SCS significantly and moderately positively correlates with self-esteem, self-acceptance, self-determination, autonomy, competence, and relatedness. Neff, Rude, and Kirkpatrick (2007b) have further shown self-compassion to be significantly and positively associated with happiness and optimism, positive mood, reflective wisdom, personal initiative, curiosity and exploration, agreeableness, extroversion, and conscientiousness and significantly negatively associated with negative mood and neuroticism, and that self-compassion predicts positive psychological health independent of NEO Big Five personality characteristics. Interestingly, women rather consistently show lower self-compassion scores than men, ostensibly due to elevated self-judgment, sense of isolation, and over-identification and diminished mindfulness in women (Neff, 2003b; Yarnell et al., 2015). And, in a study of Buddhist Vipassana, which cultivates compassion, mindfulness, and social interdependence, meditators compared with a naïve undergraduate control group scored significantly higher on positive measures of self-compassion and significantly lower on negative measures (Neff, 2003b). Very similar outcomes to these reported above have been replicated in subsequent studies (Neff, Kirkpatrick, & Rude, 2007b; Neff & Vonk, 2009).

Since 2003, there have been over 1000 published articles relating self-compassion to mental well-being across many different cultural, age, and gender groups. Rather than review each of those studies here, we are fortunate that there have been at least two metaanalyses of the relationships among self-compassion and psychological constructs. MacBeth and Gumley in 2012 examined the associations among self-compassion and various psychopathologies. These researchers reviewed 728 published articles, which were reduced to 14 peer-reviewed publications meeting selection criteria, including objective measures of all psychological constructs. These publications represented 20 participant samples and 32 separate effect sizes. Their analysis obtained a large corrected aggregate effect size of -0.61 indicating higher self-compassion ratings associated with lower depression, anxiety, and stress psychopathologies (MacBeth & Gumley, 2012).

A 2015 metaanalysis of the published relationships between self-compassion and psychological health screened 1433 articles and reduced that number to 65 articles that included quantitative data comparisons and met additional strict inclusion criteria. These 65 articles involved a total of 79 measured samples and 134 effect sizes. Analyses revealed self-compassion and overall well-being effect sizes of +0.47, with statistically significant moderate to large correlations ranging from 0.39 to 0.62 across cognitive, positive, negative, psychological, and other types of well-being. Additionally, a causal analysis of a small subset of controlled intervention studies (5 and 9 with 394 and 650 participants, respectively) yielded statistically significant increases in well-being measures following both state and trait self-compassion manipulations (Zessin, Dickhauser, & Garbade, 2015).

Despite these quite numerous and impressive relationships and intervention effects of self-compassion on mental well-being, fewer studies have examined similar effects on bodily health. Raque-Bogdan, Ericson, Jackson, Martin, and Bryan (2011) examined self-compassion as a mediator in the relationship between attachment and physical health on a sample of 208 college students. In contrast to their predictions, SCS self-compassion failed to emerge as a mediator between attachment avoidance and anxiety on the one hand and functional physical health, as measured by the Medical Outcomes Short Form, on the other. And, there was only a very small and negative, but statistically significant, -0.176 correlation between self-compassion and functional physical health, suggesting to the authors that poorer physical health lead to higher self-compassion in their sample (Raque-Bogdan et al., 2011). Hall, Row, Wuensch, and Godley (2013) conducted correlational and regression analyses of SCS self-compassion subscales (see below for a description of SCS subscales) on Cohen–Hoberman Inventory of Physical Symptom (CHIPS) scores in their sample of 182 upper level psychology college students. These researchers found significant small and positive correlations between CHIPS physical symptoms and SCS Self-Judgment minus Self-Kindness and SCS Over-Identification minus Mindfulness, indicating that higher self-compassion subscores were associated with lower physical symptoms. Their subsequent regression analysis identified SCS self-judgment minus self-kindness as a strong predictor of physical well-being, with SCS isolation minus common humanity as a suppressor variable in their analysis.

Several investigators have examined the effects of trait and state self-compassion on heart rate variability (HRV), reflecting healthy heart functioning and suggested by a growing body of research to be an index of vagally mediated parasympathetic nervous system flexibility and emotional regulation. These studies have in general found greater self-compassion to be associated with higher HRV (Petrocchi, Ottaviani, & Couyoumdijian, 2016; Svendsen et al., 2016). Friis, Johnson,

Cutfield, and Consedine (2015) examined the role of self-compassion in predicting disease-specific distress and blood sugar control in diabetic patients and found that self-compassion moderated the negative metabolic effects of distress on control. These researchers then followed up with an investigation of the effects of an 8-week mindfulness self-compassion intervention, relative to a wait-list control, on depression, diabetes distress, and blood sugar regulation and found increases in self-compassion and clinically- and statistically-significant decreases in depression, distress, and blood sugar for the intervention group only (Friis, Johnson, Cutfield, & Consedine, 2016). And, in a series of studies, two groups of researchers have examined the moderating effects of self-compassion on physiological measures of acute psychosocial stressors, suggesting that trait self-compassion and self-compassion training can positively impact both immune measures of peripheral inflammation and biochemical markers of sympathetic nervous system arousal (Arch, Landy, & Brown, 2016; Breines et al., 2014, 2015). This developing body of research is most encouraging in suggesting a positive relationship between self-compassion and multiple measures of physical well-being.

Unfortunately, there has been a striking paucity of published studies reporting neurological manifestations of Self-Compassion. In lieu of such studies, in this chapter we will consider what we might expect from such neuroimaging investigations of self-compassion. We shall focus our inferential lens by first exploring Neff's subcomponents of self-compassion, then examining existing neuroscience studies of those and related components, building toward reasoned projections of what such a neuroscience of Self-Compassion might yield in the future.

THE COMPONENTS OF SELF-COMPASSION

From a consideration of Buddhist psychology, Neff has conceptualized self-compassion as devisable into three bipolar subcomponents. Subjecting those hypothetical subcomponents to exploratory and confirmatory factor analyses in the development of the SCS, a 6-factor model emerged, anchored by the following terms: *Self-Kindness versus Self-Judgment, Mindfulness versus Over-Identification,* and *Common Humanity versus Isolation* (Neff, 2003b). Although Neff is clear from her analyses that self-compassion is a higher order integration of these three subcomponents, given the virtual absence of a neurology of self-compassion, we will address current neuroscience findings independently for each of these bipolar constructs in hopes that a subsequent integration of these findings will yield predictions for neurological manifestations of the unitary self-compassion construct.

Self-Kindness versus Self-Judgment

Neff (2003a) describes self-kindness, in part, as feeling for oneself the same compassionate love and caring one might feel toward another who is suffering, as well as a desire to alleviate one's own discomfort and suffering. When self-kindness is practiced toward a painful memory, it allows for the softening of that painful memory and the creation of a kind, compassionate, and understanding inner dialogue which leads to a very real sense of compassion for the self. As such, self-kindness is a core component of self-compassion.

(Self-kindness also involves accepting and forgiving one's own mistakes and failings and recognizing one's successes, strengths, and accomplishments on an equivalent basis, without self-evaluation or social comparison. Neff originally conceptualized self-kindness as part of a single bipolar factor, anchored at the opposite end by the more negative construct of self-judgment. However, her confirmatory factor analysis revealed these two constructs to be separate but correlated and nonmutually exclusive components, such that one may be nonjudgmental toward oneself but at the same time be not kind to the self. Therefore, true compassionate self-kindness requires a loving kindness and a diminished judgment toward the self (Neff, 2003b).

There has been very little neuroscience on the construct of self-kindness per se. However, there is a sizable literature on positive and negative self-referential processing, self-criticism, self-enhancement, and even self-judgment which may provide some expectations for what such a neuroscience of self-kindness versus self-judgment might reveal. Typically self-referential neuroimaging studies require the participant to lie in an MRI or PET scanner while considering adjectives or experiences that represent the self versus those that do not. Stimulus domains are characterized as representing the "proto-self," the "minimal self," the "core or mental self," the "autobiographical self," the "narrative self," the "emotional self," the "spatial self," the "facial self," the "verbal or interpreting self," the "social self," or "the experiential self" and all represent stimuli that are experienced as strongly reflecting one's own person, a sense of ownership or "mineness." For example, Kjaer, Nowak, and Lou (2002) asked 7 normal healthy young Danish volunteers to lie in an $H_2^{15}O$ PET scanner while reflecting on each of four counterbalanced sets of considerations: one's own personality traits, one's own physical appearance, the personality traits of the Danish Queen, and the physical appearance of the Danish Queen. Self-referenced personality traits, relative to the Queen nonself control condition, produced significant activations in the precuneus, bilateral temporoparietal cortex, and left orbitofrontal cortex; self-referenced physical traits, relative to the control condition, significantly activated the anterior cingulate gyrus. Subsequent connectivity analyses revealed these regions to be functionally interconnected during self-referential processing (Kjaer, Nowak, & Lou, 2002).

Phan et al. (2004) conducted fMRI scans of 12 young normal volunteers while they viewed 180 positive, neutral, and negative images selected to elicit varying amounts of personal relevance and emotional intensity. Participants subsequently evaluated each image on emotional valence and personal association. A priori, research-based regions of interest (ROIs) and whole brain analyses were examined as a function of these subjective ratings. While evaluation of emotional intensity activated the left amygdala and bilateral insular cortices, self-referential appraisal activated the anterior ventral medial prefrontal cortex (vmPFC) and the bilateral insular cortex. Anterior and posterior vmPFC activations were significantly greater during self-relatedness appraisals than during emotional intensity appraisals, suggesting the specific involvement of mPFC structures during such self-referential processing. Additionally, observation of activation peaks during these appraisals suggested a possible modulation of amygdaloid emotional valence during mPFC appraisal of self-relatedness (Phan et al., 2004). Phan, Wager, Taylor, and Liberzon (2004) suggested from their own two prior metaanalyses of the neuroimaging of human emotions that the mPFC, with its extensive connections to amygdala and insular cortex, plays a primary, top-down role in self-referential processing and regulation of personal affective states (see Chapter 3 in this book for a more extensive review of this literature). The Phan et al. studies are particularly interesting since evaluations of self are most often value-laden and involve a prominent emotional component.

Northoff et al. (2006) conducted a metaanalysis of 27 PET and MRI studies published up to 2004 that investigated the neuroimaging of self-referential processing tasks compared to those nonself-referencing (Fig. 4.1).

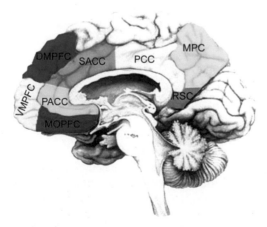

FIGURE 4.1 **Schematic illustration of cortical midline structures.** *Source: Reprinted with permission of Northoff, G., Heinzel, A., de Greck, M., Bermpohl, F., Dobrowolny, H., Panksepp, J. (2006). Self-referential processing in our brain—a meta-analysis of imaging studies on the self. NeuroImage, 31, 440–457.*

This metaanalysis included only whole-brain studies, omitting those that examined only ROIs, and involved self-related tasks across multiple domains. Domain-specific and hierarchical cluster analyses were conducted. Three primary self-referential clusters emerged, comprised of vmPFC/ pre- and subgenual anterior cingulate cortex (pACC), supra-genual anterior cingulate cortex/dorsomedial prefrontal cortex (sACC/dmPFC), and posterior cingulate cortex/precuneus (PCC/precuneus).

Northoff and Bermpohl (2004) had earlier christened these localizations according to their rather centralized anatomical array as "cortical midline structures (CMS)" and consider them to be a supra-modal (across multiple sensory and conceptual domains), interconnected functional system specifically involved in the sense of "Self." Northoff and Bermpohl further specialized these self-referential functions as (1) orbitomedial omPFC involved in the generation of a representational model of the self, (2) supragenual sACC involved in the housekeeping functions of response selection/inhibition, error detection, and performance/conflict monitoring, (3) dmPFC involved in emotional and moral judgments, and (4) PCC and precuneus involved in the integration of self-referential stimuli and autobiographical information toward a unified sense of self. Related to our examination of potential localizations of self-kindness affirmations, verbal and emotional self-referential domain analyses implicated vmPFC, pACC, dmPFC, precuneus, and supplementary motor area for the former and vmPFC, pACC, sACC, and dmPFC for the latter (Northoff et al., 2006).

A further implication of the findings of Northoff et al. (2006) is that the more anterior portions of the CMS may reflect modulation of the affective attributes of a "core" or "mental" self, with posterior CMS, and subcortical midline connections, more involved in pure, "bodily," or "proto" self-references. We will consider the ramifications of this interpretation when we explore the third component of self-compassion and the potential neurological impacts of a tripartite meditation on self-compassion below.

More specific to self-kindness and self-judgment, Longe et al. (2010) examined fMRI ROI localization responses to self-reassurance and self-criticism during exposure to blocks of visually presented generally negative and neutral scenarios, rated on a 1–7 Likert scale afterwards for intensity of self-thoughts. Engagement of self-reassurance (self-kindness) thoughts to scenarios that represented a "threat to self" compared with neutral scenarios and with self-criticism revealed activation of left superior temporal gyrus (left STG) (Brodmann Area 38; left temporal pole) and associated insular cortex (I). Self-criticism relative to neutral scenarios, on the other hand, was associated with a broad cluster of sites in left and right lateral PFC, lateral orbital frontal cortex (lat OFC), and dlPFC; self-criticism relative to self-reassurance was associated with similar activations in dlPFC, dmPFC, left and right vlPFC, left PCC, medial and inferior temporal gyrus (MTG/ITG), cuneus, bilateral lingual gyrus, and bilateral caudate. The authors explain the self-criticism localizations in lateral PFC and OFC and in dlPFC as reflecting error processing, resolution, and inhibitory functions of these frontal regions, but the more distinct left temporal pole and insular activations, the latter with prominent amygdaloid and OFC projections, during self-reassurance suggesting a monitoring of emotional status and related positive self-talk and self-feelings (Longe et al., 2010). These findings are consistent with localization studies of both self-conscious experiences of pride and joy and the experience of compassion for others (Lutz, Brefczynski-Lewis, Johnstone, & Davidson, 2008). Similar findings have also been reported by Beer and Hughes (2011) in the activation of OFC and dACC during protocols designed to engage and to modulate the self-enhancement bias.

Doerig et al. (2014) asked 20 healthy adult volunteers to identify negative, self-critical adjectives that were the most personally relevant out of a group of 52 negative prototypes, compared to nonself-referential negative adjectives and to neutral control adjectives, and to focus on their personal meanings and any emotional reactions while lying in an fMRI scanner. These researchers also administered a German version of Neff's *SCS* and focused particularly on the *Self-Judgment* subscale as a measure of self-critical thinking and the *Mindfulness* subscale as an assessment of cognitive appraisal. These two trait measures, as well as *Big Five Inventory Neuroticism*, were examined as potential moderators of obtained cortical localizations of self-criticism. Whole brain and ROI fMRI analyses yielded (1) anterior insular (AI) and hippocampal-amygdala cluster, (2) medial superior frontal cortex extending to right lateral superior frontal lobe cluster, (3) bilateral inferior frontal, orbital frontal, and middle frontal cluster, (4) right medial temporal gyrus, and (5) left cerebellum (crus II) activation to self-critical adjectives relative to neutral control adjectives. Self-critical compared to negative nonself-referential adjectives resulted in activation of more posterior medial PCC and precuneus. Additionally, neuroticism and cognitive appraisal significantly correlated positively and negatively, respectively, with right superior frontal activation. Taken together, these results indicate activation of, among other regions, CMS similar to those reported by Northoff et al. (2006) and Longe et al. (2010) in response to personalized self-criticism and a potential moderation of these activations by neuroticism and mindfulness cognitive appraisal.

Since the 2006 metaanalysis of Northoff et al., at least five additional meta-analyses of self-reference have been conducted (Denny, Kober, Wager, & Ochsner, 2012; Murray, Schaer, & Debbane, 2012; Qin & Northoff, 2011; Sperduti et al., 2011; van der Meer et al., 2010). Although these reviews examine differing characteristics of the self (self-judgment, self-reflection, self-specificity, self-agency, and self-relatedness), several common and converging observations may be garnered from these analyses that hold implications for a neuroscience of self-kindness. *First*, CMS are decisively involved in the processing of self-related stimulus input, with differential functional specificity for distinct structures. *Second* and related to this specificity, the medial PFC rather consistently emerges as a locus of self-reflective processing. However, van der Meer, Costafreda, Aleman, and David (2010), Murray, Schaer, and Debbane (2012), and Denny, Kober, Wager, and Ochsner (2012) argue for a differentiation of the mPFC into dorsal (dmPFC) and ventral (vmPFC) components having quite distinct functions. dmPFC would appear to be more involved in a top-down, cognitive, directed, and perhaps social/other-comparison appraisal and evaluation of self-related stimulus material, whereas the vmPFC is more involved in the processing and regulation of value-laden, emotional self-referential information. Additionally, Denny et al. (2012) have distinguished a gradient of activations within the mPFC, with progressively more vmPFC activations in self-judgments and progressively more dmPFC activations (as well as bilateral TPJ and cuneus) in other-judgments.

Third, a similar dorsal/ventral distinction may be made for the ACC, with dACC engaging more top-down attentional, monitoring, and conflict-detection functions and vACC, also called the pACC (Qin & Northoff, 2011), facilitating the resolution of emotional conflict for the self (Murray et al., 2012; van der Meer et al., 2010). *Fourth*, the AI cortex, with its intimate connections with the amygdala and prefrontal regions, represents "the embodied self" or "protoself" manifesting the interoceptive bodily state of the organism (Sperduti, Delaveau, Fossati, & Nadel, 2011; van der Meer et al., 2010). *Fifth*, the more posterior CMS regions of PCC and precuneus, along with their projections to the temporal/parietal junction (TPJ)/angular gyrus (ANG), appear to play a role in differentiating self from others (and, as we shall see, in the lack of such a differentiation), in social cognition (vis-à-vis, ToM), and in autobiographical memory retrieval (Qin & Northoff, 2011).

In order to simplify our understanding of these components of self-perception and appraisal, van der Meer et al. (2010) have offered a "Cognitive Neuropsychiatric Self-reflection/Self-appraisal Model" for self-reflection in the brain (Fig. 4.2). This model can be integrated with the above analysis and easily be applied to self-kindness/self-judgment appraisals, as follows: On presentation of a stimulus demanding self-appraisal, the dACC would activate and direct attentional and conflict-monitoring resources to that stimulus. An emotional valence would be attached to this incipient self-processing and would modulate self-relevance assessments as a function of affective tone in the vmPFC, with further involvement of the vACC for emotional conflict resolution. Relevant autobiographical material would be accessed through PCC/precuneus pathways to the hippocampus and somatic affective status would be assessed via AI afferents. This integrative evaluation and

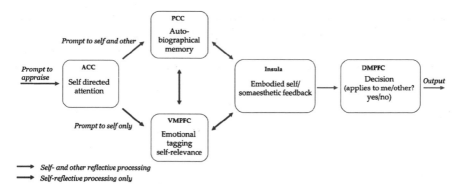

FIGURE 4.2   **A model for self-reflection in the brain.** In *dark gray* (*blue* in the web version) the pathway, that is, followed for both self- and other-reflective processes. In *gray* (*red* in the web version) the pathway, that is, followed for self-reflective processing only. Thus, if the stimulus is tagged for self, both the *gray* (*red* in the web version) and *dark gray* (*blue* in the web version) pathways are followed. *Source: Reprinted by permission of van der Meer, L., Costafreda, S., Aleman, A., & David, A. S. (2010). Self-reflection and the brain: a theoretical review and meta-analysis of neuroimaging studies with implications for schizophrenia. Neuroscience and Biobehavioral Reviews, 34(6), 935–946.*

subsequent decisional valence would elicit progressively greater dmPFC involvement as a function of social relevance and other semantic or motor pathways relative to intrinsic/extrinsic actions to be taken. Although such self-kindness/self-judgment appraisals are described as occurring in a linear fashion, it is understood that each of these components is intimately interconnected, feeds back on each other, and interacts in a dynamic fashion, such that self-referential processing is highly reciprocal, multifactorial, and nonlinear. Additionally, any disturbances in this process, as from anomalous dysfunctions of any component, can produce emotional and mental health disorders, such as depression, autism, borderline personality disorder, and schizophrenia (Murray et al., 2012; van der Meer et al., 2010).

Mindfulness versus Over-Identification

The concept of mindfulness also has its roots in some of the earliest teachings of Buddhism (Brown & Ryan, 2003). However, the concept has changed over the years as it has become increasingly cemented into the contemporary architecture of western culture. The first mention of Mindfulness was perhaps in The Dhammapada over 2000 years ago: "Content with the simplest material requisites, moderate in eating, restrained in their senses, they up their energy, abide in constant *mindfulness* and still the restless waves of thought," and later "The five to be cultivated are the five spiritual faculties: faith, energy, *mindfulness*, concentration, and wisdom" (Buddharakkhita, 1985). Over time, this concept has been given broader definitions by psychologists. For example, Brown and Ryan (2003) define mindfulness as "The state of being attentive to and aware of what is taking place in the present." This notion was further expanded by Kristin Neff as a subtype for Self-Compassion and is defined as being open to, and acknowledging, both the good and bad that happen in life (Neff, 2003a). Neff has also been careful to juxtapose mindfulness to its opposite, "over-identification," or a tendency to become preoccupied with, overwhelmed by, and/or to catastrophize about unpleasant experiences (Neff, 2003b). In her development of the SCS, both mindfulness and over-identification emerged as separate, but highly intercorrelated, factors in her initial normative studies (Neff, 2003b).

To better understand the role of mindfulness in self-compassion, let us examine a practical application. Consider that a student has a midterm exam, spends a great deal of time studying for it, and ends up passing, but gets a much lower grade than expected. Many would immediately have a negative reaction to this outcome, perhaps saying to oneself, "My work wasn't good enough; despite giving it my all, it wasn't good enough for the class. I must not be as smart as the rest." However, if we apply the concept of mindfulness to this example, we would be more equalitarian and nonjudgmental, considering the negative as well as the positive aspects of the experience: "Well, I didn't do as well as I had hoped. That really is disappointing, as I thought I would have done better, but I took the test, I passed, and I learned some things in the process, and isn't that what it's all about anyway. So, I suppose it was a draw. I feel better now, so let me direct my attention to other present experiences." As we can see, the person is not denying that the event is negative, but rather than dwelling on this aspect s/he keeps in mind the positive side as well, and moves on to other thoughts, to balance, and perhaps to "emptiness" and to a sense of being present in the moment (Analayo, 2015; See the discussion below of the concept of "nonduality" for an understanding of "emptiness" in the present context). Thus, we can perceive mindfulness as a useful coping mechanism for negativity and self-denigration. In fact, research has established a direct link between mindfulness and general well-being, as well as lowering levels of neuroticism, anxiety, and depression (Brown & Ryan, 2003). However, as we shall see, the practice of mindfulness has direct, and potentially long lasting, neurological effects as well.

Holzel et al. (2011) have conceptualized the above mindful reconstrual of such life events as involving three interacting components: Increased attentional control, enhanced emotional regulation, and shifts in self-awareness from self-referential processing to greater somatic awareness. While it is beyond the intent and breadth of this brief review to consider this rather large and growing literature in a comprehensive fashion, we shall mention a few representative studies and then summarize this literature with a recent comprehensive review and model for the neuroscience of mindfulness meditation.

Mindfulness and Attentional Control

Holzel et al. (2007) compared 15 experienced Vipassana (mindfulness) meditators with 15 matched nonmeditators in an fMRI study examining cortical ROIs across blocked eyes-closed mindful breathing and eyes-open mental arithmetic conditions. Despite important differences between conditions in terms of participant expertise, direction of focus (internal vs. external), and open versus closed eyes, all of which argue for caution in interpreting outcomes, Holzel et al. found significant condition × group interaction differences, with peak activation for meditators during mindfulness meditation in bilateral rostral ACC and dmPFC sites. Interestingly with regard to the discussions in the self-kindness and the common-humanity meditation sections of this chapter, no group or condition differences were found for posterior precuneus or PCC ROI sites. These obtained activations, in particular those seen in the rostral ACC, as well as self-reports of increased task attention for the meditators, were suggested by these researchers to reflect enhanced attentional control. Increased dmPFC activations were also attributed to increased emotional regulation in the mindfulness meditators. Although this was a cross-sectional investigation, the authors noted that the amount of ACC activation correlated with expertise and experience in the meditative practice.

In one of the few longitudinal active-control investigations conducted to date, Allen et al. (2012) recruited 61 meditation-naïve participants, with 38 remaining following a 38% attrition rate approximately equivalent between conditions, and randomly assigned them to one of two conditions: a 6-week course in mindfulness meditation or a time- and intensity-equivalent 6-week course in shared reading, both with reported home practice. Whole brain fMRI scans were conducted pre- and posttraining during an affective Stroop task that challenged executive processing attention and conflict resolution. Results revealed increased left dlPFC response spreading into rostral PFC over time for the mindfulness training group and significantly greater activation in left posterior insular cortex, left superior spreading to middle frontal gyrus (FG), ACC, and superior medial frontal lobule (FL), and right orbital FG spreading to AI and right superior medial FL for the mindfulness training group relative to the reading group. Additionally, mindfulness training reduced affective Stroop conflict compared with the reading control condition. These improvements in emotional conflict resolution with increased dlPFC and frontal-insular involvement in naïve participants suggest enhancements in top-down working memory processing and in conflict resolution following 6-weeks of mindfulness training (Allen et al., 2012).

Mindfulness and Emotional Regulation

Investigations of the influence of mindfulness meditation on affective control have in general examined prefrontal modulation of amygdalar and insular responses to emotional stimuli following training in mindfulness skills. For example, Lutz et al. (2014) exposed 46 participants to either a brief mindfulness instruction or to a basic attentional control condition and recorded fMRI responses to both the expectation and the presentation of emotional or neutral pictures. ROI results indicated decreased activation of right AMG during *perception* of negative stimuli, preceded by increased activation of left and right dmPFC, left AI, left dlPFC during the *expectation* of negative pictures, for the mindfulness instructions group compared with the basic attentional group. Expecting unknown stimuli resulted in similar outcomes. In whole brain analyses, the perception of negative stimuli was associated with increased activation of neural clusters in left middle FG but decreased activation in right hippocampus and left posterior insular cortex. In these analyses, the expectation of negative stimuli indicated enhanced left PFC (inferior dlPFC, medial and inferior FG, and dmPFC extending into ACC) and medial temporal gyrus activations for the mindfulness group compared with the basic group. Taken together, these outcomes suggest a neurological modulation of emotional reactivity to negative visual images following increased attentional and interoceptive processing as a function of simple instructions to view stimuli with a sense of openness and nonjudgmental attention to present awareness (Lutz et al., 2014).

Earlier, Desbordes et al. (2012) identified a subgroup of 36 research participants from a larger investigation conducted by the Emory University Compassion and Attention Longitudinal Meditation study. These participants were specifically trained in one of three interventions: Mindful Attention Training, Cognitively Based Compassion Training, and an active-control health education program, each including prescribed home practice exercises. fMRI ROI brainscans were recorded during a nonmeditative state 3 weeks before and 3 weeks after 8 weeks of training while participants were shown positive, negative, and neutral images from the same stimulus database as used by Lutz et al. (2014) and many other researchers. These researchers found a significant longitudinal decrease in the activation of the right AMG for the mindfulness training group for both positive and all images, suggesting a lessening of emotional arousal to visual stimuli following mindfulness training. The findings of diminished AMG activity during the nonmeditative state suggest that mindfulness training effects may transfer from repeated practice to a more natural state of everyday awareness (Desbordes et al., 2012).

Mindfulness and Self-Awareness

Much of the mindfulness self-awareness literature investigates the same CMS ROIs as are involved in self-referential processing, discussed in the Self-Kindness section above. The hypotheses of such investigations are generally that mindful practices alter CMS processing from resting and more balanced default mode network (DMN) activations, shifting arousal and connectivity from frontal executive processing regions to more posterior somatic awareness and self-other localizations. In one of the earlier studies, Farb et al. (2007) differentiated *"narrative self-reference,"* or a linking of self-awareness across time, from *"experiential self-reference,"* an in-the-moment or immediate awareness of self, reasoning that the latter is more characteristic of mindfulness states of awareness and that the former is a more "stream of consciousness," DMN state of self-awareness. They hypothesized that narrative self-focus would engage DMN CMS and that experiential self-focus would involve more right-lateralized and more posterior interoceptive insular and exteroceptive somatic cortices. To test this hypothesis, 36 naïve participants were recruited from an 8-week Mindfulness-Based Stress Reduction (MBSR) program and were randomly assigned to either a pre-training wait-list control group or to the posttraining MBSR group. All participants were first carefully trained to differentiate and to engage an experiential and a narrative form of self-focus. Members of each group were then reclined in an fMRI scanner and were asked to read intermixed trait descriptive adjectives successively presented on a viewing screen. Prior to word presentation, a cue was presented prompting either the narrative or the experiential self-focus. Whole brain, ROI, and functional connectivity analyses were conducted for separate self-referential and adjective valence conditions. As predicted, main effects for narrative self-focus relative to pretraining revealed activation of the CMS of rostral and dmPFC, PCC, left language areas of inferolateral PFC and medial temporal gyrus, left hippocampus, right inferior FG, right precentral gyrus, cuneus, left caudate head, and cerebellum. Following mindfulness training, however, an experiential focus compared with narrative focus led to deactivations of anterior CMS, including rostral dmPFC, vmPFC, and, left dorsal AMG, along with activations of right inferolateral and dPFC, insular cortex, and secondary somatosensory area II extending to the ANG. Functional connectivity analyses revealed a strong coupling of right insular cortex with CMS for the novices, but a decoupling of the right insula from vmPFC (emotional regulation) and increased coupling with dlPFC (working memory) for the mindfulness group. Altogether, these outcomes indicate a shift with mindful experiential focus away from CMS and toward right-lateralized, synchronized, and perhaps more ancestral "protoself" posterior viscerosomatic structures (Farb et al., 2007). These rather acute effects of short-term mindfulness training are consistent with observed cortical thickening in right insular, somatosensory, and inferior parietal cortices following more extended meditation practice (Lazar et al., 2005).

Many neuroimaging studies of mindfulness have focused on the awareness of pain and its modulation with mindfulness meditations. Although mindfulness interventions often target chronic pain populations, the neuroscience research in this area has been almost exclusively directed at experimentally induced pain. Bilevicius, Kolesar, and Kornelsen (2016) have conducted a very recent critical review of this literature and although they screened 946 publications up to 2015, only 5 met their strict inclusion criteria, many for a failure to adequately define mindfulness. Among these five studies, remarkable inconsistencies emerged in the relationships of neural activations to the varied pain components. In general, mindfulness-based pain reductions were associated with dlPFC deactivations and rather paradoxical ACC and insular cortex activations, the latter attributed to increased attentional allocations during mindfulness. Although the number of studies selected for this review was unfortunately so few as to render conclusions for the neuroscience of mindfulness pain sensitivity tentative at best, these outcomes are rather consistent with those for mindfulness self-referential processing reported above by Farb et al. (2007).

A General Overview of the Neuroscience of Mindfulness

In a recent critical review of the neuroscience of mindfulness, Tang, Holzel, and Posner (2015) examined cross-sectional and longitudinal experimental designs involving novice and expert meditators and varied control conditions within the conceptual framework of the Holzel et al. (2011) model of mindfulness meditation. Their review suggests the emergence of a pattern of progressive neurological alterations as a result of mindfulness mental regulation. These changes begin with enhanced frontal activations in dlPFC, dmPFC, vlPFC, and ACC during mindful experiential focus for naïve, inexperienced learners. These neurological changes result from increased attentional effort and modulation of affectivity as attention is directed away from salient thoughts and emotions toward balance and equanimity of cognitions and affectivity. With continued practice and developing skill, the aspirant further progresses to a gradual decrease in mPFC activation as more insular and posterior somatosensory components of the CMS and their lateral projections become paramount, enhanced functional connectivity among these posterior components occurs, particularly between precuneus and dlPFC, and prototypical self and body awareness emerges. Continued mindfulness practice toward expertise results in a further progression of these posterior CMS localization and connectivity shifts, decreased self-referential processing in DMN, a blurring of self-other boundaries, and potentially increasingly frequent intrusions of nonduality experiences. From this elaboration of the Holzel et al. (2011) model, a progression from frontal to more posterior CMS activations and synchronizations evolves quite naturally into the third component of Self-Compassion.

Common-Humanity versus Isolation

Neff et al. (2003a,b) conceptualizes the experience of common-humanity as the realization that one is a member of the community of personkind, that we all experience very similar joys, disappointments, successes, and failures, that one's experiences are shared by all at some level. As stated so eloquently by His Holiness The Dalai Lama:

> If I look at you superficially, we are different, and if I put my emphasis on that level, we grow more distant. If I look on you as my own kind, as human beings like myself, with one nose, two eyes, and so forth, then automatically that distance is gone. We are the same human flesh. I want happiness; you also want happiness. From that mutual recognition, we can build respect and real trust for each other. From that can come cooperation and harmony. (The Dalai Lama, 1984)

Just as at an atomic level, our physical nature is truly boundless and overlaps with that of every object on this planet, so are our experiences of living shared by all sentient beings (Kornfield, 1993). Enrico Fermi is credited with calculating that for every breath we take today, there is a 99% probability that we are inhaling a molecule of Julius Caesar's dying *"Et tu Brute?"* breath from over 2000 years ago! Thus, we are all interconnected at multiple levels. This realization of nonseparateness stands in opposition to the feeling of separation and isolation, that one exists apart from others and alone in one's experiences. As with self-kindness and self-judgment and with mindfulness and over-identification, common-humanity and isolation are opposite poles of a two-factor model subscale represented on the SCS (Neff, 2003b). While a supra-ordinate appeal to common-humanity may actually have damaging effects on subgroup identity and collectivist actions, such an over-arching group membership is generally perceived as beneficial to individual psychological well-being (Greenaway, Quinn, & Louis, 2011; Hall et al., 2013).

Philosophically, a perfection of the construct of common-humanity is very similar to the ancient Buddhist concept of "emptiness," a sense of infinite space, of infinite consciousness, of balance in the equanimity of all things (Analayo, 2015). The ultimate entry into such emptiness is a *Metta* experience of a union of self with others toward a sense of nonself and of a universal Self. Ancient discourses refer to such "nothingness" as Nirvana, or profound peace and liberation from suffering. Thus a deep perception of common-humanity may be seen as a vehicle for the experience of nonsuffering through a joining of the self with the universe of personkind, an abiding recognition of a universal oneness of all things, contributing to a recognition of true self-compassion.

Not unexpectedly, neuroscience research has been slow to study the neurological underpinnings of this rather abstract construct of common-humanity, and even of its opposite of isolation. In fact, a search of neuroscience investigations into these constructs reveals no published studies to date. One recent study which examined self-generated feelings of caring, friendship, and love toward and from others instructed 19 participants to recline in an fMRI scanner and to visualize with eyes closed receiving love from close others and with eyes open directing loving kindness toward photographs of neutral strangers. Eyes opened and closed visual conditions of self and strangers in neutral settings and of neutral physical features were also provided as controls. Whole brain and ROI analyses were conducted. The entire social connection task generated activation in an extended cortical region involving the anterior cingulate cortex (ACC) and the dmPFC, with the *receipt* of loving kindness centered on a peak area within the mPFC and with expression of loving kindness *toward others* activating peaks in the ACC (Hutcherson, Seppala, & Gross, 2015). Although these outcomes are consistent with the self-referential literature reviewed above and are somewhat suggestive of what one might expect from feelings of love and caring toward and from others, the prescribed feelings of social connection in this study differ from the experience of nonseparateness from others, of a sharing with or union of our life experiences with those of personkind in general that is suggested by Buddhist's conceptualizations of common-humanity.

Perhaps a closer approximation of what one might expect from a neuroscience of common-humanity could be obtained from neuroimaging and electrocortical studies of a related state called *nonduality*. Nonduality, or nondual "awareness," is a difficult state to describe cognitively, for it is the pure absence of cognition and of verbal, visual, aural, or emotional representation of reality. It is the profound experiencing of a natural, background state of nonawareness which is void of phenomenological content and of fragmentation of reality into its opposing dualities. In a nondual state, there is no good or bad, yes or no, inside or outside, right or wrong, direction or intentionality, or self or other; all is one. In fact, this state is often called "Universal Oneness" from ancient Vedic Samhitas, "Absolute Unitary Being" (d'Aquili & Newberg, 1993), "Pure Consciousness" (Travis & Pearson, 2000), "The Gap" between thoughts (Chopra, 1989), and "Mental Silence" (Manocha, 2011). Many consider nonduality to be the culminating state of all contemplative, meditative practices and a fourth state of consciousness, along with waking, dreaming, and deep sleep, but without content (Analayo, 2015; Baars, 2013; The Dalai Lama, 1984). Within the context of Self-Compassion's component of Common-Humanity, one might consider the ultimate experience of nonseparateness of self from other to be represented by a nondual state of consciousness.

Not surprisingly, for such a broadly referenced and universally pursued state of mind, there is a developing neuroscience research literature on nonduality. Zoran Josipovic and his research group have been the most active proponents of research in this area. Quantification of the nondual awareness (NDA) state, however, is unfortunately problematic, for its identification naturally precludes its presence and returns the practitioner to duality, a rather extreme manifestation of the Observer Effect, also mistakenly known as Heisenberg's Uncertainty Principle. Josipovic and colleagues (Josipovic et al., 2012) attempted to circumvent this problem by recruiting a cohort of 24 experienced (8–33 years of meditation with 4000–37,000 estimated hours of practice) Tibetan Buddhist meditation practitioners, 14 of whom practiced a combination of Focused Attention (FA: focusing attention on an internal object or experience) and NDA meditation, 4 who practiced only NDA meditation, and 4 who practiced only FA meditation. Each meditator was scanned in an fMRI during fixation without meditation, engagement of FA meditation only, and engagement of NDA meditation only. The expectation was that during NDA meditation a unique brain state would develop that would be different from the control fixation condition and the FA condition. Fifteen ROIs were identified on the basis of extrinsic (i.e., externally stimulated, sensory and motor) and intrinsic (i.e., internally stimulated, default mode) processing systems and were analyzed for functional connectivity during the performance of each condition. As hypothesized, Josipovic, Dinstein, Weber, and Heeger (2012) found greater functional connectivity among extrinsic and intrinsic processing areas during NDA than during fixation or FA meditation, which they interpreted as reflecting the presence of a more nondual state of consciousness. However, these authors acknowledged their difficulty in determining the extent to which each meditator was engaging a nondual state during each condition. This concern is particularly noteworthy in that both Josipovic and Baars have described such nondual states as occurring in brief interruptions during stream of consciousness mediations for less experienced meditators, becoming more stabilized, enduring, and predictable for more experienced meditators (Josipovic & Baars, 2015). Clearly, improved strategies need to be developed to better identify the presence of a nondual state during meditations and contemplative activities.

Josipovic (2013) subsequently reported on a follow-up study to the above with NDA meditators during meditation compared to relaxed rest. In this preliminary study, he examined the functional connectivity among the central precuneus and its projections to dlPFC, dmPFC, and ANG. Josipovic's interest in these regions was derived from previous research implicating the precuneus in episodic memory, visuospatial processing, self-referential processing, and states of consciousness, and precuneus projections in, respectively, working memory, top-down self-other appraisals and differentiations, and multisensory representations and integrations, spatial cognition, and future self-representations. Taken together, these areas of what Josipovic termed "the central precuneus network" appear to be involved in reflexive awareness (pure awareness or "awareness being aware of itself," Josipovic, p. 6) and expanded spatial boundaries, defining features of NDA. Results from this study revealed that NDA meditation was associated with *increased* connectivity between the central precuneus and dlPFC (working memory), *decreased* connectivity between the central precuneus and right ANG (spatial self-representations and projections of self into space), decreased connectivity between left and right dlPFC, and *increased* connectivity among right ANG, right dlPFC, and left dmPFC. Josipovic interpreted these preliminary outcomes as suggesting a broadening of awareness and of spatial boundaries during nonduality meditation (Josipovic, 2013).

Of particular interest from these findings and speculations by the Josipovic research team regarding the precuneus network and its involvement in experiences of NDA are the early reports of Wilder Penfield's human brain stimulation studies, and more recently those of Blanke and colleagues, that found a merging of self with God, rapturous experiences in some participants, out-of-body experiences, a loss of self and a sense of oneness, all on stimulation of temporoparietal junction surface sites (Blanke, Ortigue, Landis, & Seeck, 2002; Fenwick, 1996; Penfield, 1959; Penfield & Erickson, 1941; Tong, 2003). Interestingly, d'Aquili and Newberg (1993) have referred to the neighboring posterior superior parietal lobe (PSPL), Brodmann's Area 7, as a part of a God Circuit, and speak of such loss of self as resulting from a deafferentation of, a diminished neurological input to, the PSPL (d'Aquili & Newberg, 1993; Newberg & Waldman, 2009).

Berman and Stevens (2015) have conducted the only EEG study to date of NDA, utilizing a unique methodology for identifying in a nonintrusive manner the presence of the nondual state during meditation. These researchers recruited a large and heterogeneous group of 44 meditators from Sedona, Arizona, the reputed "New Age Capital of the World," and surrounding communities and invited them to come to an EEG laboratory for the continuous recording of a broad range of electrocortical bandwidths during up to 1 h of meditation. Meditation style was varied and included both FA and Open Monitoring (mindfulness-like meditations) styles. Participants had been meditating for 0.5–44 years and had accumulated an estimated 65–21,900 h of practice. Nearly all acknowledged having experienced the occurrence of nondual states during their meditation practice, some only occasionally and briefly and some for the entire meditation. Each was instructed to simply wink their left eye when they experienced coming out of a nondual state during the recorded meditation. A 24-channel

EEG was attached with scalp electrodes and an additional electromyography electrode was attached to the left eye orbicularis oculi muscle and displayed winks clearly on the EEG trace. Pre- and postmeditation eyes-closed nonmeditation baselines were recorded. Participants were allowed to meditate using their preferred style for up to an hour in a sound-attentuated meditation suite, with recording equipment and monitors in the adjoining suite. Forty-eight discreet nonduality events were identified by this methodology, and double verified by independent observers and by participants after the recording session, and the entire meditation session and the 30-s epoch immediately prior to the wink signal were power spectral analyzed across nine frequency bins.

Analysis of these EEG results revealed that the wink methodology was indeed nonintrusive in that postwink 30-s epochs did not differ significantly from prewink epochs; this statistical finding was further verified by participant self-reports. When the 30-s nondual epoch was compared with the meditation session as a whole, as well as with baselines, it was found that high frequency EEG signals (Beta and Gamma) significantly dominated the meditation as a whole (with Gamma having the largest and moderate effect sizes), but that a remarkable and statistically significant shift in this frequency toward very slow wave activity (Delta, Theta, and Alpha) occurred diffusely across the cortex, with largest, and moderate, effect sizes seen in Delta and Alpha frequencies, during the nondual events. The possibility of sleep during these nondual epochs was ruled out by visual inspection of each EEG trace and by self-reports of each meditator. Furthermore, visual observation of the EEG trace during the nondual events indicated highly synchronized slow wave activity across the entire cortex, although a formal coherence connectivity analysis is currently underway to statistically ratify this observation. These outcomes suggest (1) the engagement of hyperfocused (Beta and Gamma) attentional activity during the meditation session which (2) shifted into a diffuse very slow wave, relaxed, alert, readiness state during the nondual events (Berman & Stevens, 2015).

To our knowledge, the studies by Josipovic et al. and by Berman and Stevens are the only published investigations into the altered state of consciousness called "NonDuality." Certainly, the experience of nondual consciousness is quite different from the more superficial, but highly therapeutic recognition of the mutual sharing of everyday human experiences. Perhaps if we extend the construct of common-humanity to a more ultimate experience of nonseparateness, then the findings from these few nonduality studies can suggest what we might find from more directed MRI and EEG studies of common-humanity. To pursue that tentative inferential leap, then we might predict that a deep focus upon, a directed contemplation of, our sharing of our experiences with the community of personkind, of our unity with others, would produce a wave of synchronized low frequency activity radiating across the entire cerebral cortex and muting at the very least all cognitive, higher order self-referential functions and allowing deeper brain background resonant, perhaps even protoself, waveforms to emerge, possibly through the precuneus network and to dominate awareness. With increased contemplative practice in the production of such states of nonseparateness, of nonduality, one would be expected to observe increasing intrusions of brief events building to sustained states of "universal oneness," as reported by Josipovic and Baars (2015).

THE NEUROSCIENCE OF SELF-COMPASSION

At this stage of scientific discovery and from the above review of the neuroscience literature that forms the potential foundation of the experience of self-compassion, we can hypothesize a neurological cascade of activations and deactivations that parallels the manifestation of the underlying components (self-kindness, mindfulness, and common-humanity) of this unifying construct (self-compassion). Our phenomenological journey might well proceed as follows: As one begins to entertain verbal affirmations of positive self-valuation, ... of true self-forgiveness, ... of abiding self-acceptance, ... of a verbal internal recognition of universal membership in and commonality with the family of personkind, ... and thence to a suspension of self-judgment entirely, ... moving to an equanimity and balance of all cognitions and emotions, ... and to a mindful inattention to all intrinsic and extrinsic experiences, ... thence toward an ultimate quieting of self-talk, ... and to periods of lasting inner silence, ... and perhaps ultimately to complete nonseparateness, to universal oneness, ... only realized from a subsequent spark of conscious awareness, ... then does one experience the hopefully awe-inspiring panoply of profound self-compassion. Neurologically, this progression from self-kindness appraisals, through mindful awareness, and toward ultimate union with common-humanity would be expected to activate and deactivate the following cortical structures:

The engagement in working memory of self-kindness judgments, positive self-affirmations, and attendant emotional valuations would be expected to initially activate primarily prefrontal regions of the CMS, including dACC, vACC, vmPFC, and dmPFC, dlPFC, and perhaps inferior FG in implicit speech production, toward the direction of attentional resources, modulation of affective tone, potential conflict resolution, and generation of positive self-talk. The subsequent involvement of AI in somatic affective salience and some PCC and precuneus regions in autobiographical memory and a developing blurring of self-other differentiations would be expected to be seen as well. During this stage of self-compassion contemplation, high-frequency EEG Beta and Gamma electrical activity across these CMS regions would be expected. As self-kindness appraisals evolve into a mindful awareness of present extrinsic and intrinsic events, activation of the CMS and associated structures would be expected to spread posteriorly from frontal ACC/dlPFC into parietal attentional regions, accompanied by diminished AMG affectivity through improved mPFC/ACC/AI modulation, eventually showing decreased activity in this latter network with greater acceptance of and disengagement from affective processing, and eventually producing less activity in the DMN with diminished self-referential processing. Then as mindfulness processes develop further toward enhanced experiences of nonseparateness and of a nondual state, increasing functional connectivity among these frontal structures, central precuneus, and TPJ extensions, along with decreasing connectivity between central precuneus and ANG spatial boundary representations and decreasing prominence of frontal executive functions would be expected to occur. As a blurring of self-other representations, possible out-of-body experiences, and an abiding sense of oneness with common-humanity develops, a spreading, diffuse, and synchronized slow wave resonance would be predicted across the cortex.

Two authors of this chapter have had the pleasure of participating in Dr. Neff's Self-Compassion Training Workshops, with the last author having immersed himself in a full 4-day retreat with Kristin Neff and Christopher Germer. His reflections on that intensive workshop are as follows:

> The interplay of mindfulness, self-kindness, and common humanity is seen in full swing at any one of Kristin Neff's and Christopher Germer's Mindful Self-Compassion intensives. Imagine meditating on the breath - noticing how each of us breathes the same air, how plants, animals and every human on Earth shares this air in one way or another. Notice, how does that realization feel? By this alone we are connected and possibly more than we realize. Moving from this realization, we recall a time when we were more self-critical than normal, or we 'screwed-up' and immediately compared ourselves to the seemingly perfect actions of the rest of the people in the world. From this space of insecurity, self-anger, and fear of loss, we are mindfully prompted to a space where we realize that every single human being on Earth has 'screwed-up' in a way of equal and even greater magnitude. In fact, these times are an aspect of what makes us a card carrying member of the human race. Then we come back to meditating on the common air we share and, in light of our recent realization about 'screwing-up,' we notice how we share another thing too, suffering. Each of us has shared the feeling of suffering which comes upon our perceived 'screw-up', and in that we also realize the common human experience. We continue in this way circulating between a meditation on the common breath and mindfully noticing our common suffering, slowly but surely we begin to find it easier and easier to authentically offer ourselves feelings of self-kindness. This is the easy, creative, and simple way that Kristin Neff and Christopher Germer present a holistic, systematic, and undeniably effective approach to self-compassion.

In this reflection on a mindful self-compassion intensive workshop, we see a prominent teaching of the notion of Common-Humanity woven into directed Self-Kindness with implicit Mindfulness between the lines.)We wonder if during other such workshops there is a structured meditation on the integrated construct of Self-Compassion that perhaps proceeds in a sequential fashion similar to that at the beginning of this section, with a focusing on self-kindness, then a progression through mindful self-awareness, then to a joining with common-humanity, and then further to an experience of nonduality) If such a sequential meditation is taught, then we might expect a neurological sequence as described above to develop as well. Such a sequential progression would appear to emulate, but to possibly abbreviate, Buddhist Metta Meditation, that being a progression from the experience of loving-kindness toward the self, thence toward a close family member, thence toward an acquaintance, then a stranger, then an enemy, thence toward common-humanity at large, ultimately building to the nonreferential pure experiencing of loving-kindness compassion (Gethin, 1998). This Self-Compassion Metta Meditation methodology would abbreviate the more traditional approach to a meditative sequence of Loving-Kindness toward the Self, progressing into Mindfulness, then to Common-Humanity, and in advanced experiences toward NonDuality) At this stage in the neuroscience of Self-Compassion, we can also speculate as to the personal and societal ramifications of such a meditation practiced daily by large segments of personkind.

DIRECTIONS FOR FUTURE RESEARCH

Given the paucity of neuroscience research on the integrated construct of Self-Compassion, and even on the specific components of Self-Kindness and Common-Humanity, the path seems clear and open for the development of a body of research on these constructs. Certainly the established methodology of fMRI neuroimaging applied to the integrated experience of Self-Compassion would be in order. An example of needed studies would be MRI, PET, and EEG neuroimaging before and after established self-compassion workshop training.

However, following the sequential progression from directed Self-Kindness through Mindfulness and into the experience of Common Humanity as described above would be recommended to validate this hypothesized neurological CMS and projections pathway. MRI connectivity studies would be quite informative in our understanding of this process. EEG studies of this progression would be essential to an understanding of the electrocortical changes that occur during such a directed meditation or contemplation. As well, despite Neff's position on Self-Compassion as a supra-ordinate construct integrating the three sub-components of self-kindness, mindfulness, and common-humanity, examining each bipolar component discreetly and targeting the suggested ROIs would be a useful first step. Indeed, each of these three subcomponents is comprised of somewhat poorly understood functions themselves, such as is the case with self-kindness. Self-processing in the brain is poorly understood, not to mention the concept of kindness and its neural instantiation. It follows that future research should address neural markers of these subordinate components with an eye to how the interplay of these markers produces self-compassion.

An expedient test of the proposed progression of CMS and their projections during the Self-Compassion Metta Meditation described above could be conducted before and after a brief (2–3 h) training program in naïve participants, compared with a suitable time- and intensity-balanced control training condition utilizing any of a wide variety of neuroimaging protocols. Such an investigation would necessarily involve time-locked recordings during each phase (Self-Kindness, Mindfulness, and Common Humanity) of the meditation. For this investigation, EEG might be more cost-efficient and least intrusive for a prolonged meditation in naïve participants and would offer the possibility of looking at both temporal and spatial electrocortical effects of the interventions.

While such cross-sectional studies as suggested above can be informative regarding neurological structures and mechanisms involved in self-compassion practice, longitudinal studies would better assess the effects of experience/expertise in the application of outcomes of self-compassion training and regular contemplation/meditation. Comparison with a suitable balanced, active-control experience, as well as a passive control condition, would better examine the specific effects of the self-compassion intervention and the role of motivation and practice.

Quite naturally, neuroscience research on contemplative practices attracts contemplative practitioners as investigators. We are impressed with the observation in reviewing this literature that many of the researchers are themselves longstanding meditation practitioners and even involve consultations from recognized authorities and His Holiness The Dalai Lama himself. We are also impressed that these researchers have taken considerable efforts to render impartial the conduct of analyses and to lessen effects of trainer bias where possible. However, we must point out the increasing concern with "volunteer bias" in psychophysiological research (Demir, Haynes, Orthel-Clark, & Ozen, 2017). The first author recently recruited participants for an investigation of the neuroscience of hypnosis and tested volunteers for hypnotizability. Sixty-five percent of the volunteers were highly hypnotizable and only 13% were low; in the general population, only 10% are highs and 10% are lows. Certainly participants also volunteer for meditation studies because of an interest in, and perhaps a predilection for, meditation and likely have resting neurological signatures that differ from those not so interested. This bias in neuroscience research must be addressed or at least acknowledged and circumvented or controlled wherever possible. Demir et al. (2017) offer suggestions for lessening such a volunteer bias.

Considerable research has accumulated on the subcomponent of Mindfulness. However, as described above, very little research has examined Self-Kindness/Self-Judgment, and virtually none has looked at the experience of Common-Humanity/Isolation. Examining each of these components individually would better clarify localization, activation, and electrocortical characteristics of each and would provide a test of the localization inferences enumerated in this review.

Neuroscience research is by its nature highly resource intensive, requiring lengthy and costly scanning of neurological tissue during individual involvement in a prescribed condition. Furthermore, intervention studies are somewhat limited by the time- and response-cost of the training programs and by availability of experienced practitioners for longitudinal or expertise studies. Hence, such investigations by necessity involve small numbers of participants. These small n's stand in remarkable contrast to the increasing use of online surveys by our colleagues in the social sciences, studies which can easily involve hundreds of thousands of participants, and accordingly less statistical variability and higher power. We have made it a point in this review to cite the size of each study to impress upon the reader this shortcoming in neuroscience research. We urge neuroscience researchers to at least replicate studies from other laboratories, also utilizing alternative (e.g., fMRI, EEG, SPECT, PET, etc.) protocols, as a way of increasing the reliability and validity of outcomes, and to involve larger numbers of participants where possible.

Finally, we can not leave this examination of the neuroscience of Self-Compassion without addressing the need for more translational research in this area. The authors of this chapter believe that the higher purpose of research is to inform society and to advance human understanding and evolution. Toward this objective, the direct application of outcomes of self-compassion neuroscience research in the lessening of personal suffering and in the enhancement of happiness and well-being must be our ultimate quest. Researchers are encouraged to include such "soft" social psychological measures wherever possible toward this objective, and to refine interventions, training programs, and public educational initiatives that not only generate healthy neurological alterations but positive societal changes as well.

References

Allen, M., Dietz, M., Blair, K. S., van Beek, M., Rees, G., Vestergaard-Poulsen, P., et al. (2012). Cognitive-affective neural plasticity following active-controlled mindfulness intervention. *Journal of Neuroscience, 32*(44), 15601–15610.

Analayo (2015). *Compassion and emptiness in early Buddhist meditation*. Cambridge: Windhorse Publications.

Arch, J. J., Brown, K. W., Dean, D. J., Landy, L. N., Brown, K. D., & Laudenslager, M. L. (2014). Self-compassion training modulates alpha-amylase, heart rate variability, and subjective responses to social evaluative threat in women. *Psychoneuroendocrinology, 42,* 49–58.

Arch, J. J., Landy, L. N., & Brown, K. W. (2016). Predictors and moderators of biopsychological social stress responses following brief self-compassion meditation training. *Psychoneuroendocrinology, 69,* 35–40.

Baars, B. J. (2013). A scientific approach to silent consciousness. *Frontiers in Psychology, 4,* 1–3.

Beer, J. S., & Hughes, B. L. (2011). Self-enhancement: A social neuroscience perspective. In D. A. Mark, & S. Constantine (Eds.), *Handbook of self-enhancement and self-protection* (1st ed., pp. 49–65). New York: The Guilford Press.

Berman, A. E., & Stevens, L. (2015). EEG manifestations of nondual experiences in meditators. *Consciousness and Cognition, 31,* 1–11.

Bilevicius, E., Kolesar, T. A., & Kornelsen, J. (2016). Altered neural activity associated with mindfulness during nociception: A systematic review of functional MRI. *Brain Sciences, 6*(14), 1–12.

Blanke, O., Ortigue, S., Landis, T., & Seeck, M. (2002). Stimulating illusory own-body perceptions. *Nature, 419,* 269–270.

Breines, J. G., Thoma, M. V., Gianferante, D., Hanlin, L., Chen, X., & Rohleder, N. (2014). Self-compassion as a predictor of interleukin-6 response to acute psychosocial stress. *Brain, Behavior, and Immunity, 37,* 109–114.

Breines, J. G., McInnis, C. M., Kuras, Y. I., Thoma, M. V., Gianferante, D., Hanlin, L., et al. (2015). Self-compassionate young adults show lower salivary alpha-amylase responses to repeated psychosocial stress. *Self and Identity, 14*(4), 1–13.

Brown, K. W., & Ryan, R. M. (2003). The benefits of being present: Mindfulness and its role in psychological well-being. *Journal of Personality and Social Psychology, 84*(4), 822–848.

Buddharakkhita, A. (1985). *The Dhammapada: The Buddha's path of wisdom (translated from the Pali).* Kandy: Buddhist Publication Society.

Chopra, D. (1989). *Quantum healing: Exploring the frontiers of mind/body medicine.* New York: Bantam.

d'Aquili, E. G., & Newberg, A. B. (1993). Liminality, trance, and unitary states of ritual and meditation. *Studia Liturgica, 23,* 2–34.

Demir, M., Haynes, A., Orthel-Clark, H., & Ozen, A. (2017). Volunteer bias in research on friendship among emerging adults. *Emerging Adulthood, 5*(1), 53–68.

Denny, B. T., Kober, H., Wager, T. D., & Ochsner, K. N. (2012). A meta-analysis of functional neuroimaging studies of self- and other-judgments reveals a spatial gradient for mentalizing in medial prefrontal cortex. *Journal of Cognitive Neuroscience, 24*(8), 1742–1752.

Desbordes, G., Negi, L. T., Pace, T. W. W., Wallace, B. A., Raison, C. L., & Schwartz, E. L. (2012). Effects of mindful-attention and compassion meditation training on amygdala response to emotional stimuli in an ordinary, non-meditative state. *Frontiers in Human Neuroscience, 6,* 1–15.

Doerig, N., Schlumpf, Y., Spinelli, S., Spati, J., Brakowski, J., Quednow, B. B., Seifritz, E., & Holtforth, M. G. (2014). Neural representation and clinically relevant moderators of individualised self-criticism in healthy subjects. *Social, Cognitive, and Affective Neuroscience, 9*(9), 1333–1340.

Farb, N. A. S., Segal, Z. V., Mayberg, H., Bean, J., McKeon, D., Fatima, Z., & Anderson, A. K. (2007). Attending to the present: Mindfulness meditation reveals distinct neural modes of self-reference. *Social, Cognitive, and Affective Neuroscience, 2,* 313–322.

Fenwick, P. (1996). The neurophysiology of religious experiences. In B. Dinesh (Ed.), *Psychiatry and religion* (1st ed., pp. 167–177). London: Routledge.

Friis, A. M., Johnson, M. H., Cutfield, R. G., & Consedine, N. S. (2015). Does kindness matter: Self-compassion buffers the negative impact of diabetes-distress on HbA1c. *Diabetic Medicine, 32,* 1634–1640.

Friis, A. M., Johnson, M. H., Cutfield, R. G., & Consedine, N. S. (2016). Kindness matters: A randomized controlled trial of a mindful self-compassion intervention improves depression, distress, and HbA1c among patients with diabetes. *Diabetic Care, 39*(11), 1963–1971.

Gethin, R. (1998). *The foundations of Buddhism.* Oxford: Oxford University Press.

Greenaway, K. H., Quinn, E. A., & Louis, W. R. (2011). Appealing to common humanity increases forgiveness but reduces collective action among victims of historical atrocities. *European Journal of Social Psychology, 41*, 569–573.

Hall, C. W., Row, K. A., Wuensch, K. L., & Godley, K. R. (2013). The role of self-compassion in physical and psychological well-being. *The Journal of Psychology, 147*(4), 311–323.

Holzel, B. K., Ott, U., Hempel, H., Hackl, A., Wolf, K., Stark, R., et al. (2007). Differential engagement of anterior cingulate and adjacent medial frontal cortex in adept meditators and non-meditators. *Neuroscience Letters, 421*, 16–21.

Holzel, B. K., Lazar, S. W., Gard, T., Schuman-Olivier, Z., Vago, D. R., & Ott, U. (2011). How does mindfulness meditation work? Proposing mechanisms of action from a conceptual and neural perspective. *Perspectives on Psychological Science, 6*(6), 537–559.

Hutcherson, C. A., Seppala, E. M., & Gross, J. J. (2015). The neural correlates of social connection. *Cognitive, Affective, & Behavioral Neuroscience, 15*, 1–14.

Josipovic, Z. (2013). Neural correlates of nondual awareness in meditation. *Annals of the New York Academy of Sciences, 1307*, 1–10.

Josipovic, Z., & Baars, B. J. (2015). Editorial: What can neuroscience learn from contemplative practices? *Frontiers in Psychology, 6*, 1–3.

Josipovic, Z., Dinstein, I., Weber, J., & Heeger, D. J. (2012). Influence of meditation on anti-correlated networks in the brain. *Frontiers in Human Neuroscience, 5*, 1–11.

Kjaer, T. W., Nowak, M., & Lou, H. C. (2002). Reflective self-awareness and conscious states: PET evidence for a common midline parietofrontal core. *NeuroImage, 17*, 1080–1086.

Kornfield, J. (1993). *A path with heart: A guide through the perils and promises of spiritual life.* New York: Bantam Books.

Kornfield, J. (2008). *The wise heart: A guide to the universal teachings of Buddhist psychology.* New York: Bantam Books.

Lazar, S. W., Kerr, C. E., Wasserman, R. H., Gray, J. R., Greve, D. N., Treadway, M. T., et al. (2005). Meditation experience is associated with increased cortical thickness. *NeuroReport, 16*(17), 1893–1897.

Longe, O., Maratos, F. A., Gilbert, P., Evans, G., Volker, F., Rockliff, H., et al. (2010). Having a word with yourself: Neural correlates of self-criticism and self-reassurance. *NeuroImage, 49*, 1849–1856.

Lutz, A., Brefczynski-Lewis, J., Johnstone, T., & Davidson, R. J. (2008). Regulation of the neural circuitry of emotion by compassion meditation: Effects of meditative expertise. *PLoS One, 3*(3), 1–10.

Lutz, J., Herwig, U., Opialla, S., Hittmeyer, A., Jancke, L., Rufer, M., et al. (2014). Mindfulness and emotional regulation—An fMRI study. *Social, Cognitive, and Affective Neuroscience, 9*, 776–785.

MacBeth, A., & Gumley, A. (2012). Exploring compassion: A meta-analysis of the association between self-compassion and psychopathology. *Clinical Psychology Review, 32*, 545–552.

Manocha, R. (2011). Meditation, mindfulness, and mind-emptiness. *Acta Neuropsychiatrica, 23*(1), 46–47.

Murray, R. J., Schaer, M., & Debbane, M. (2012). Degrees of separation: A quantitative neuroimaging meta-analysis investigating self-specificity and shared neural activation between self- and other-reflection. *Neuroscience and Biobehavioral Reviews, 36*, 1043–1059.

Neff, K. (2003a). Self-compassion: An alternative conceptualization of a healthy attitude toward oneself. *Self and Identity, 2*, 85–101.

Neff, K. (2003b). The development and validation of a scale to measure self-compassion. *Self and Identity*, 2, 223–250.

Neff, K. (2011). Self-compassion, self-esteem, and well-being. *Social and Personality Psychology Compass*, 5(1), 1–12.

Neff, K., & Vonk, R. (2009). Self-compassion versus global self-esteem: Two different ways of relating to oneself. *Journal of Personality*, 77(1), 23–50 February.

Neff, K. D., Kirkpatrick, K. L., & Rude, S. S. (2007a). Self-compassion and adaptive psychological functioning. *Journal of Research in Personality*, 41, 139–154.

Neff, K. D., Rude, S. S., & Kirkpatrick, K. L. (2007b). An examination of self-compassion in relation to positive psychological functioning and personality traits. *Journal of Research in Personality*, 41, 908–916.

Newberg, A., & Waldman, M. R. (2009). *How God changes your brain: Breakthrough findings from a leading neuroscientist*. New York: Ballantine.

Northoff, G., & Bermpohl, F. (2004). Cortical midline structures and the self. *Trends in Cognitive Science*, 8(3), 102–107.

Northoff, G., Heinzel, A., de Greck, M., Bermpohl, F., Dobrowolny, H., & Panksepp, J. (2006). Self-referential processing in our brain—A meta-analysis of imaging studies on the self. *NeuroImage*, 31, 440–457.

Penfield, W. (1959). The interpretive cortex. *Science*, 129, 1719–1725.

Penfield, W., & Erickson, T. C. (1941). *Epilepsy and cerebral localization*. England: Charles C. Thomas, Oxford.

Petrocchi, N., Ottaviani, C., & Couyoumdijian, A. (2017). Compassion at the mirror: Exposure to a mirror increases the efficacy of a self-compassion manipulation in enhancing soothing positive affect and heart rate variability. *The Journal of Positive Psychology*, 12(6), 525–536.

Phan, K. L., Taylor, S. F., Welsh, R. C., Ho, S. -H., Britton, J. C., & Liberzon, I. (2004a). Neural correlates of individual ratings of emotional salience: A trial-related fMRI study. *NeuroImage*, 21, 768–780.

Phan, K. L., Wager, T. D., Taylor, S. F., & Liberzon, I. (2004b). Functional neuroimaging studies of human emotions. *CNS Spectrums*, 9(4), 258–266.

Qin, P., & Northoff, G. (2011). How is our self related to midline regions and the default-mode network. *NeuroImage*, 57, 1221–1233.

Raque-Bogdan, T. L., Ericson, S. K., Jackson, J., Martin, H. M., & Bryan, N. A. (2011). Attachment and mental and physical health: Self-compassion and mattering as mediators. *Journal of Counseling Psychology*, 58(2), 272–278.

Sperduti, M., Delaveau, P., Fossati, P., & Nadel, J. (2011). Different brain structures related to self- and external-agency attribution: A brief review and meta-analysis. *Brain Structure and Function*, 216, 151–157.

Svendsen, J. L., Osnes, B., Binder, P. -E., Dundas, I., Visted, E., Nordby, H., et al. (2016). Trait self-compassion reflects emotional flexibility through an association with high vagally mediated heart rate variability. *Mindfulness*, 7(5), 1103–1113.

Takahashi, H., Matsuura, M., Koeda, M., Yahata, N., Suhara, T., Kato, M., et al. (2008). Brain activations during judgments of positive self-conscious emotion and positive basic emotion: Pride and joy. *Cerebral Cortex*, 18, 898–903.

Tang, Y. -Y., Holzel, B., & Posner, M. (2015). The neuroscience of mindfulness meditation. *Nature Reviews Neuroscience*, 16(4), 213–225.

The Dalai Lama (1984). *Kindness, clarity, and insight*. Boston, MA: Snow Lion.

Tong, F. (2003). Out-of-body experiences: From Penfield to present. *Trends in Cognitive Sciences*, 7(3), 104–106.

Travis, F., & Pearson, C. (2000). Pure consciousness: Distinct phenomenological and physiological correlates of 'consciousness itself'. *International Journal of Neuroscience*, 100(1–4), 77–89.

van der Meer, L., Costafreda, S., Aleman, A., & David, A. S. (2010). Self-reflection and the brain: A theoretical review and meta-analysis of neuroimaging studies with implications for schizophrenia. *Neuroscience and Biobehavioral Reviews, 34*(6), 935–946.

Yarnell, L. M., Stafford, R. E., Neff, K. D., Reilly, E. D., Knox, M. C., & Mullarkey, M. (2015). Meta-analysis of gender differences in self-compassion. *Self and Identity, 14*(5), 499–520.

Zessin, U., Dickhauser, O., & Garbade, S. (2015). The relationship between self-compassion and well-being: A meta-analysis. Applied Psychology: Health and well-being, 7(3), 340–364.

Sometimes I Get So Mad I Could …: The Neuroscience of Cruelty

Taylor N. West, Leah Savery, Robert J. Goodman

Northern Arizona University, Flagstaff, AZ, United States

"Our greatest evils flow from ourselves."—Jean-Jacques Rousseau

In 1928, on a warm Monday in New York, a friendly farmer from Farmingdale invited his coworker's 10-year-old daughter, Grace, to accompany him for an afternoon of fun at his niece's birthday party. Grace never returned home. After 6 agonizing years of uncertainty, her parents—Delia and Albert—received the following anonymous letter:

> "On Sunday June the 3—1928 … we had lunch. Grace sat in my lap and kissed me. I made up my mind to eat her, on the pretense of taking her to a party. You said Yes she could go. I took her to an empty house in Westchester I had already picked out. When we got there, I told her to remain outside. She picked wild flowers. I went upstairs and stripped all my clothes off. I knew if I did not I would get her blood on them. When all was ready I went to the window and called her. Then I hid in a closet until she was in the room. When she saw me all naked she began to cry and tried to run down stairs. I grabbed her and she said she would tell her mama. First I stripped her naked. How she did kick—bite and scratch. I choked her to death then cut her in small pieces so I could take my meat to my rooms, cook and eat it. How sweet and tender her little ass was roasted in the oven. It took me 9 days to eat her entire body."

The man who committed this atrocity was Albert Fish, a notorious psychopath who claimed to have raped and/or cannibalized over 100 children. How are some people able to be so calloused to the suffering of others that they take pleasure in atrocity? Are the seeds of cruelty within us all? Previous work in this volume has discussed the neurological processes and underpinnings of empathy and compassion. In contrast, cruelty is in direct opposition to these capacities. As such, a stronger understanding of

The Neuroscience of Empathy, Compassion, and Self-Compassion. http://dx.doi.org/10.1016/B978-0-12-809837-0.00005-2

empathy and compassion can be gleaned from considering circumstances in which these positive qualities are absent. How is it that everyday people can seemingly become immune to the suffering of others and treat them as arbitrary objects? This chapter aims to define cruelty and to discuss what is known about how and why humans become cruel or engage in cruel acts. First, it should be noted that cruelty is not distinctly characteristic of psychopathic or violent criminals, but something viewed as a spectrum on which all humans are capable of falling. The classic social psychology experiments by Milgram (1963) on obedience to authority and Zimbardo's (1972) prison experiment point, quite directly, to the potential for cruelty among everyday people and highlight the power of situational factors to bring about unspeakably cruel behavior among common, good-natured citizens. Because of the complexity of the construct of cruelty and its many and varied manifestations, only representative studies for particular types of cruelty will be described to give a flavor of the research on the topic and to identify common neurological structures involved in its expression among normative samples. Following this review, we will discuss cruelty that emerges as a consequence of psychopathology and the neurological structures and activity involved in psychological disorders that lead to cruel thoughts, feelings, and behaviors.

DEFINING CRUELTY

Put simply, cruelty causes suffering in other people. This unfortunately quite common social behavior has been examined in terms of the motives and intentions of the perpetrator, as well as the consequential suffering of undeserving victims. More specifically, cruelty is defined as unjustified voluntary behavior that causes foreseeable suffering toward an undeserving victim or victims (Taylor, 2009). In everyday cruelty, behavior may be understood as cruel from an outside observer, even when, from the perpetrators' standpoint, the behavior may be rationalized as innocuous. This definition of cruelty places it on a spectrum, on which one end includes *callousness*, in which the perpetrators' intentions are not directly cruel and which aim to achieve a secondary goal that requires someone to suffer as a means to that end. On the other end of the spectrum is *sadistic cruelty*, in which the perpetrator deliberately intends to cause suffering. However, most people who engage in cruelty are not dispositionally cruel or evil people, but often succumb to situational forces that overwhelm them and shape their behavior in ways that promote suffering in others (Darley, 1993; Milgram, 1963; Zimbardo, 1972). As a way to blunt the traditional perspective on cruelty, which suggests cruel behaviors come from evil people, Baron-Cohen (2012) has suggested that cruelty should be understood and assessed in terms of "empathy erosion"—degrees on an empathy spectrum—in which individual differences and situational factors may modulate the degree to which common people experience more or less empathy in response to human suffering. This reframing of the cruelty as empathy erosion has the benefit of minimizing the reactionary, retaliatory otherization of people who commit cruel acts (e.g., as "evil people"), an ironic twist in which empathizing with victims can lead to the rationalization of cruelty against perpetrators.

Causes of Cruelty: Dehumanization and Otherization

How do ordinary people rationalize cruelty? In many cases, the victim is gradually seen as less human and less deserving of empathy in the eyes of the perpetrator. The social and cognitive processes by which this unfolds can be described as *otherization* or moral exclusion, where there is a distinct "us" and "them", in which the person deemed cruel is perceived as crossing a boundary that no longer warrants moral consideration (Opotow, 1990). Once a group or person is "otherized", their traits, characteristics, and behaviors are viewed as possessing unchangeable and undesirable innate qualities (Taylor, 2009). The tendency to otherize has its roots in infancy (Kinzler, Dupoux, & Spelke, 2007), and negative, otherizing behaviors can be elicited in common people by simply categorizing them into groups, even when the categorization criteria are essentially meaningless and random (Tajfel & Turner, 1979). *Deindividuation*, a psychological state in which an individual becomes less self-aware, feels more anonymous, and becomes less likely to experience evaluation apprehension (Diener, Lusk, DeFour, & Flax, 1980), is another psychological process implicated in empathy erosion (Reimann & Zimbardo, 2011; Zimbardo, 1972). Deindividuation typically arises when social atrocities and violence occur among people in crowds. While otherization and deindividuation are typically understood to occur as a consequence of group membership, intergroup bias is not the only source of empathy erosion. On the contrary, people can be, and often are, cruel to those who are closest to them.

Dehumanization is a similar concept to otherization and involves denying the "humanness" of another group or person, often when people feel disgust toward them (Harris & Fiske, 2006). According to Harris and Fiske, there are four categories of emotions people feel toward social groups: *pride, envy, pity,* and *disgust.* The emotion of disgust is central to the dehumanization process. It is tightly intertwined with moral intuitions, and people who are particularly sensitive to disgust are predisposed to endorse particular ideological orientations that are antithetical to empathy, such as social dominance orientation and right-wing authoritarianism (Hodson & Costello, 2007) and prejudice toward a variety of out-groups, including lesbian, gay, bisexual, transgender, queer (LGBTQ) people

(Dasgupta, DeSteno, Williams, & Hunsinger, 2009; Inbar, Pizarro, Knobe, & Bloom, 2009; Terrizzi, Shook, & Ventis, 2010), immigrants (Navarrete & Fessler, 2006), and Muslims (Choma, Hodson, & Costello, 2012). While the disgust response can be elicited by a variety of conditions (e.g., vomit, incest, out-group members), sensitivity to disgust plays a prominent role in the dehumanization of out-group members. For example, disgust can be elicited by seeing someone as incompetent and not warm (or not approachable), which leads to dehumanization of the target. As such, addicts and the homeless are among the most dehumanized out-groups. Based on neuroimaging research, experiencing disgust toward an out-group member is associated with increased AMG and insula (INS) activation. In contrast, the medial prefrontal cortex (mPFC), a region known to be involved in the regulation of negative emotions (Etkin, Egner, & Kalisch, 2011), is least activated by disgust (Harris & Fiske, 2006). According to Harris and Fiske (2011), dehumanized perception involves perceiving another with disgust while failing to consider the mind of that person, which can lead to torture, genocide, and other cruel behaviors.

One theoretical model of dehumanization further distinguishes between two types of dehumanization: *Animalistic dehumanization*, in which uniquely human characteristics are denied (intelligence, culture), and *mechanistic*, in which elements of human nature, such as warmth, are denied and instead, cold and superficial qualities become predominant (Haslam, 2006). The animalistic form of dehumanization expresses itself through disgust and contempt while the mechanistic form comes through as indifference and social distancing (Haslam, 2006). *Infra-humanization* is another closely related concept that refers to a discounting of the human qualities (e.g., emotion, identity, beliefs) of another group or person and is not predicated on intergroup conflict (Haslam, 2006). Infra-humanization would most closely align with animalistic dehumanization.

Once otherization and/or dehumanization have unfolded and the "others" are perceived as evil and less human, it becomes easy to consider them as no longer deserving of empathy (Frankfurter, 2006). This form of cruelty often arises out of indifference as the result of social forces in which moral values and judgments enforce intergroup bias. The person who inflicts suffering may do so actively, in which another is intentionally caused to suffer, or passively, by withholding the means to relieve the other's suffering. It is worth noting that it is not necessarily pleasurable for the perpetrator to cause suffering. However, taking pleasure in cruel acts is typically associated with sadistic psychopathy—as in the case of Albert Fish. While it is true that the more one engages in otherizing processes, the easier it is to become cruel, it is also true that the more empathy one exhibits, the more difficult it is to be cruel (Baron-Cohen, 2012). It follows then, that increased empathy may reduce the tendency to otherize and dehumanize.

Cruelty, as we have discussed, encompasses a wide spectrum of behaviors. On a small scale, this could include gossip, bullying, and verbal abuse. On a larger scale, cruelty results in mass shootings, genocide, and terrorism. Hate-crimes, for example, can range from verbal harassment to violent physical attacks, both of which entail the same processes in varying degrees. Cruel acts are often preceded by moral evaluations and judgments that tend to protect individual or group beliefs and values from perceived outside threat. Theories of moral agency address the psychosocial and cognitive mechanisms that result in moral disengagement leading to moral justification or minimization of inhumane acts of cruelty (Bandura, 2002). Furthermore, the diffusion of responsibility toward dehumanized groups is one mechanism that results in heightened aggression (Bandura, Underwood, & Fromson, 1975). This is apparent during instances of genocide or terrorism, where mass groups of people engage in cruel, inhumane behaviors and are not held accountable or believed to be directly responsible, thus being absolved of feelings of guilt or responsibility.

Neural Markers of Dehumanization and Otherization

Dehumanization and otherization processes develop by the natural tendency for humans to be divided into groups, creating in- and out-groups. Groups can range from family, race and ethnic identification, to national and religious associations. The result of this division is often feelings of competition, primarily stemming from perceptions of differing values and beliefs that are threatening to an individual's or group's identity (Branscombe, Wann, Noel, & Coleman, 1993; Riek, Mania, & Gaertner, 2006). For example, one may respond with empathy to a person in their group who is suffering, but perhaps pleasure at the suffering of an out-group member. In fact, this pleasurable feeling associated with watching the rival suffer may elicit an urge to harm the rival. Cikara, Botvinick, and Fiske (2011) studied this phenomenon with neuroimaging while having zealous fans of the Red Sox and Yankees teams view baseball plays. When the participants witnessed a positive outcome, such as favored team success or rival failure, the ventral striatum (VS) was activated, a region involved in reward processing (O'Doherty, 2004). In addition, viewing these positive outcomes activated the left middle frontal and superior frontal gyrus, left INS, and bilateral caudate. Prior research has indicated that the VS is activated in response to receiving rewards, while the superior frontal gyrus, INS, and caudate regions also activate in response to positive outcomes (Nieuwenhuis, Slagter, Alting von Geusau, Heslenfeld, & Holroyd, 2005).

Moreover, the researchers looked at the likelihood of the participants acting aggressively toward the rival. It was found that those who self-reported a greater likelihood of harming rival fans showed even more VS activation while watching their rival fail, than those with a lower reported likelihood of acting out aggressively, indicating heightened reward activity elicited by the failure of out-group members. On the other hand, while viewing negative outcomes, such as the favored team failing and the rival team succeeding, the anterior cingulate cortex (ACC) and the right INS were activated, brain regions associated with pain perception. Thus, the researchers found a correlation between the ACC activation during negative plays and the participants' self-reported pain (Cikara, Botvinick, & Fiske, 2011). Supporting these findings, Hein, Silani, Preuschoff, Batson, and Singer (2010) demonstrated greater activation of the INS when participants observed painful shocks delivered to a member of their home team soccer club but showed increased nucleus accumbens activation (associated with reward) when they observed a rival team member receiving the same shock. These data are consistent with feeling more empathic pain when an in-group member is the subject but experiencing *schadenfreude*— joy in the suffering of others—when it is an out-group member's pain.

A recent study used neuroimaging to investigate how social exclusion effected prosocial behaviors and considerations of fairness in adolescents and adults (Moor et al., 2012). First, participants played Cyberball, which is a commonly used paradigm where participants play a computer ball-tossing game and are ostracized by other players, to explore effects of social exclusion in various contexts (Williams & Jarvis, 2006). Next, participants played a Dictator game in which they could divide coins between players who had previously included or excluded them in Cyberball. An interaction was found in which the participants divided up the coins quite fairly between themselves and those who included them, and extremely unfairly (eight for themselves, two for the other team) for those who excluded them. When "punishing" excluders with low offers, participants showed activations in the right superior temporal sulcus (STS), the temporoparietal junction (TPJ), and the ventral lateral PFC. The TPJ and STS are involved in social decision-making, perspective-taking, and Theory of Mind (ToM) processes (Decety & Lamm, 2007; Pelphrey, Morris, & Mccarthy, 2004; Rilling & Sanfey, 2011; see section on Social Exclusion and Aggression, as well as Chapter 3 for a detailed presentation of Theory of Mind). Specifically, the STS is involved with social perception, which is the "tendency to take an intentional stance in predicting and interpreting the behaviors of others" (Pelphrey et al., 2004), while the TPJ is involved with understanding the intentions of others. Together, these social decision-making, perspective-taking, and ToM processes allowed for the participants to punish the player that excluded them.

The formation and preferences for in-groups may also develop arbitrarily, by mere random assignment. One study investigated neural substrates associated with intergroup processing when participants were assigned to arbitrary mixed-race groups. Without the role of preexisting beliefs and attitudes, viewing in-group members, as opposed to out-group, was associated with activation in the bilateral fusiform gyri, AMG, orbitofrontal cortex, and the dorsal striatum (Van Bavel, Packer, & Cunningham, 2008). It is important to note that although previous research has indicated that the AMG activates in response to out-group members (negative stimuli), this study found the opposite effect. There were two tasks participants had to complete within this study: a social categorization task (categorizing a person as young or old) and an individuation task. During the social categorization task, the AMG activation in participants was greater in response to racial out-group faces; yet, during the individuation task, AMG activation was greater in response to racial in-group faces. Van Bavel et al. suggest that these findings show how flexible the AMG can be and how it is involved not only in fear but also responds to positive stimuli. Additionally, they suggest that the AMG is involved with the motivational relevance of stimuli. Thus, the activation of the AMG toward both in-group and out-group members may be due to the motivational relevance of the task (Van Bavel et al., 2008).

Many instances of cruelty can originate back to in-group and to out-group distinctions. These distinctions may be based on common beliefs and identities, or be completely arbitrary. Those with whom we feel a common identity, as in the team research studies, we tend to empathize with their pain and with joy at their success. To those we have decided are our "rivals", our empathy is diminished, and we may instead feel joy at their pain. When we feel we have been treated unfairly, we tend to take an opportunity to punish those who have wronged us. When "us" is different from "them", it is easy to exclude moral principles and to rationalize cruel behavior. These processes tend to be automatic responses that have evolved over time.

Why We Are Cruel: The Role of Threat Responses

As previously mentioned, the ability to distinguish between in-group and out-group develops in infancy (Kinzler, Dupoux, & Spelke, 2007). Humans possess several automatic responses to threat, or perceived threat, which primarily include fear, anger, and disgust. For the sake of brevity, we will primarily discuss fear-based responses and the role of disgust. While fear and disgust primarily evolved from environmental and predatory threats, they extend into social domains such that out-group members often trigger fear and disgust responses (Öhman et al., 1985).

The AMG is the central region associated with fear processing and early threat response (predatory and social; Buhle et al., 2014; Costafreda, Brammer, David, & Fu, 2007; Kober, Barrett, Joseph, Bliss-More, Lindquist,

&Wager, 2008; Lindquist, Wager, Kober, Bliss-Moreau, & Barrett, 2012). The AMG is richly interconnected to cortical and subcortical regions, reaching down to the brain stem and having pervasive influences on physiological responses to fear, anger, and threat (Öhman, Carlsson, Lundqvist, & Ingvar, 2007). Perceptual and visual processes are also mediated by the AMG, since it receives input from the primary visual cortex and projects into ventral visual processing streams, suggesting a reciprocal influence of fear and threat responses on perceptual processes (Öhman et al., 2007).

Disgust is an aversive response to potential sources of contamination, such as bodily fluids and rotten food, but the disgust response is also elicited by behaviors we consider immoral, such as bestiality and incest (Rozin, Haidt, & McCauley, 2000). Evolutionary disease avoidance is associated with aversion to out-groups in hunter gatherer societies that could potentially harbor diseases to which in-group members do not have an immunity. As a consequence of these adaptive responses, disgust is associated with out-group derogation and prejudice (Curtis, Aunger, & Rabie, 2004; Taylor, 2007, 2009). Although it appears across all cultures, disgust is strongly influenced by environmental factors. For example, children do not develop disgust responses until about 6 years of age, and a review of feral human cases has noted a lack of the disgust response among feral children (Malson, 1964; Rozin, Fallon, & Augustoni-Ziskind, 1985). The emotion of disgust is also heavily involved in moral judgments and decision-making processes. For example, the orbitofrontal cortex (OFC) tends to be activated in response to moral connotations and violations relating to disgust (Moll et al., 2005).

The AMG is also involved in disgust processing and shows heightened activity when participants view extreme social out-groups such as addicts and the homeless, as previously mentioned (Harris & Fiske, 2009). The mPFC, involved in social cognition, also shows lowered activity during the viewing task. The medial frontal cortex (mFC) is also associated with ToM, and in the context of this chapter, is a central component of empathic processing (Bagozzi et al., 2013). ToM generally refers to cognitive empathy and is the ability to recognize and to represent the mind of another (Blair, 2005). While most acts of cruelty are associated with decreased ToM, there are instances in which there are relatively high levels of ToM, particularly in personality disorders such as Machiavellianism (Bagozzi et al., 2013; see section on personality disorders). ToM is also associated with activation in the TPJ, the STS, the precuneus, and the temporal poles (Bagozzi et al., 2013; Decety & Lamm, 2007; Vogeley et al., 2001), regions associated with a wide variety of tasks, but in this context, with perspective-taking and the experience of agency (Cavanna & Trimble, 2006). Infrahumanization, where others are not perceived as having human qualities (e.g., beliefs, morals), could then be explained as a reduced capacity of ToM for certain out-groups.

As a species, we have evolved to respond to our environment, to react to threat, and to protect ourselves and those with whom we identify. These responses served a purpose to protect from predatory threat, but as they have leaked into the way we perceive others socially, threat responses are often a catalyst for aggression and empathy erosion. The primary region involved with threat and fear processing is the AMG, which can influence and trigger physiological responses to perceived threat. Other, frontal lobe processes react to these threats, such as OFC activation to moral disgust. When people engage in cruel behaviors, there is less mFC activation—a marker of impaired abilities to cognitively empathize with another. This allows humans to commit cruel acts, because we are no longer able to empathize to the same degree and are consequently able to justify cruel behavior.

Morality and Cruelty

Cruelty cannot be discussed without reference to morality and the neural processes by which we make moral judgments, evaluations, and decisions. The ability for people to commit atrocities often begins with moral disengagement of self-regulated agency, followed by moral justification (Bandura, 2002). This basically means that people are able to convince themselves that the typical moral standards no longer apply to a given context and render one feeling less responsible for their actions. Moral function is based on networks involving cortical and subcortical regions, as well as prominent influences by hormones and neurotransmitters. Moral judgment is associated with the ventromedial prefrontal cortex (vmPFC), regions related to emotional processing and appraisal, as well as in the AMG (Greene, Sommerville, Nystrom, Darley, & Cohen, 2001; Heekeren, Wartenburger, Schmidt, Schwintowski, & Villringer, 2003; Rolls, 2000). Dysfunction in the vmPFC and AMG are also associated with psychopathy (Blair, 2007; see section on psychopathy below). The left vmPFC is associated with higher activity in those with a low ability to utilize moral principles in justifications of moral dilemmas. This is because those lower in moral competence relied more heavily on this neural region than those with higher competency, and thus, used more cognitive resources during these tasks (Fumagalli & Priori, 2012; Prehn et al., 2008).

Moral processing is generally associated with the cingulate cortex (Greene et al., 2001), however, other regions have been implicated as well. For example, the insular cortex has been associated with morality, emotional processing, disgust processing, and uncertainty (Fumagalli et al., 2012). The dorsolateral prefrontal cortex has been associated with moral reasoning and is activated during deception or lying (Greene et al., 2001; Greene & Paxton, 2009). The STS, within the temporal lobe, and the angular gyrus, within the parietal lobe, have been implicated in moral judgments, intention of moral action, and moral dilemmas (Fumagalli & Priori, 2012). These areas are also associated with ToM, which is necessary for moral processing as well.

Although multiple brain regions have been associated with morality, this critical prosocial reasoning ability is largely assumed to be a frontal lobe process, with the orbital and ventromedial prefrontal cortices responsible for moral decision-making and the dorsolateral prefrontal cortex serving as a rational measure and filter for moral reasoning (Fumagalli & Priori, 2012). Dysfunction in these regions is associated with psychopathy. It could be argued that moral reasoning and justification are primary reasons that cruelty is perpetrated by typical, even decent, people. To quote T.S. Eliot, "Most of the evil in this world is done by people with good intentions." These acts of everyday cruelty that common people are capable of committing are described in detail below.

EVERYDAY CRUELTY: ANGER, AGGRESSION, AND HATRED

Now that we have an understanding of the values and beliefs that may lead to cruelty, this next section will focus on how particular emotions may lead to cruel behavior in ordinary people. Specifically, this section seeks to understand the associated neurological activity in the instances where the average human tends to display lower levels of empathy. It is important to recognize that all humans, including yourself, are capable of cruelty and that it is not the sole product of a marginalized psychopathic population. To understand how we develop this capability, we will discuss how human emotions (anger, aggression, hatred, jealousy) and experiences (trauma, social rejection) may reduce empathy and result in cruel behavior.

Anger and Aggression

Anger and aggression are distinct constructs in which anger is considered to be an emotion associated with psychological arousal, and aggression is typically defined as a behavior. Aggression has been viewed generally as bodily or verbal action toward another living being with the intention to do harm (Leary et al., 2006). Although anger may lead to aggression, one can behave aggressively without anger (e.g., sports). There have been many definitions, frameworks, and models of aggression used in psychological research (Anderson, Deuser, & DeNeve, 1995; Buss & Perry, 1992; Lindsay & Anderson, 2000), and so, we will briefly discuss basic definitions and neurophysiological processes associated with aggression and anger.

Although there are many types of aggression, Blair (2007) conceptualizes two primary types that people can experience: *reactive aggression* and *instrumental aggression*. Reactive aggression occurs in response to an aggravating event when there is no clear goal in mind. Road rage is an example of reactive aggression in that people become frustrated with other drivers and may yell, honk, or make provocative gestures, but have no clear goal other than expressing anger. Instrumental aggression occurs when there is a clear goal in mind, such as robbing someone (Blair, 2007). Frequent reactive aggression is associated with hyperactivity in the AMG, shown by a functional magnetic resonance imaging (fMRI) experiment in which men with reactive aggressive traits tended to have hyperactivity in the AMG when viewing neutral faces, indicating that otherwise neutral faces are not seen as neutral but as negative and perhaps as threatening (Bobes et al., 2012).

Continuing with this binary distinction of aggressive behaviors, Dorfman, Meyer-Lindenberg, and Buckholtz (2014) reduce aggression even further, comparing human aggression to animal aggression. They split aggression into *functional* and *pathological aggression*, which is how nonhuman animal aggression is often described. Functionally aggressive acts are acts that appear rational given the context. In humans, this type of aggression is seen in sports, such as hockey and football. The players act extremely aggressively toward each other, but given the sports context, such behavior is construed as socially acceptable. Pathological aggression, on the other hand, includes violent acts that are out of place and do not follow any social norms. Within pathological aggression are two subtypes: *reactive-impulsive aggression* and *proactive-instrumental aggression*. These subtypes follow Blair's (2007) nomenclature, but take it a step further, defining reactive-impulsive aggression as defensive and proactive-instrumental as predatory (Dorfman et al., 2014).

Other researchers have looked at aggression as being either general or displaced, with *general aggression* distinguished by "anger and direct retaliation" toward whomever or whatever provoked the anger, and *displaced aggression* highlighted by rumination and acting aggressively to those who did not cause the anger, such as *taking it out* on a partner (Denson, 2009; Denson, Pedersen, Ronquillo, & Nandy, 2009). Relationally, those high in displaced aggression often report more partner abuse and lashing out violently when intoxicated. Rumination, the remembering of and dwelling on a specific event, activates the hippocampus, directly involved in retrieval of episodic memory, or memory for specific events (Tulving, 1983). Moreover, it was observed that rumination was related to increased activity in the cingulate cortex, the mPFC, and lateral prefrontal cortex, as well as the INS. Displaced aggression results in more activation in the mPFC than general aggression does; however, general aggression is associated with more activity in the left dorsal ACC (dACC) than displaced aggression is (Denson, 2009).

Anger and aggression may sound like they are strongly correlated, but researchers have found that is not the case. Giumetti and Markey (2007) had participants complete the anger scale of the Aggression Questionnaire (AQ; Buss & Perry, 1992), play a violent or nonviolent video game, and then complete a task measuring aggression. Their results indicated that anger and aggression are not significantly correlated (r [165] = .12, $p > .05$). Motivated by this surprising result, other researchers examined why anger often leads people to act aggressively (e.g., hitting someone, yelling; Hortensius, Schutter, & Harmon-Jones, 2011). One group used transcranial direct current stimulation (tDCS), "a neuromodulatory intervention" (Nitsche et al., 2008) in which cortical tissue is polarized, across the frontal cortex, coupled with interpersonal provocation. This polarization of the tissue alters both neuronal excitability and activity, thus giving researchers a way to directly manipulate neural activity (Nitsche et al., 2008). The results indicated that when *left* frontal cortical activity was increased, through the use of tDCS, participants became more aggressive compared to the participants with an increase in *right* frontal cortical activity. The authors concluded that anger that leads to aggressive behavior is "likely the result of an increase in left frontal cortical activity and a decrease in right frontal cortical activity" (Hortensius et al., 2011), a pattern of brain activity highly related to increased approach motivation. This study shows that the manipulated increase in left frontal cortical activity resulted in not only an increase in anger but also in a correlation between anger and aggressive behavior.

A different study investigated the effect of ruminating on anger-evoking memories using neuroimaging (Fabiansson, Denson, Moulds, Grisham, & Schira, 2012). Participants were instructed to recall a memory of a time when they were angry and then were told to modulate their anger by engaging one of three strategies: cognitive reappraisal, analytical rumination, and angry rumination. Cognitive reappraisal is characterized by allowing oneself to look back on an emotional experience from the perspective of a neutral third party in order to reduce the negative emotions associated with the memory. Reappraising a negative memory has been widely associated with activation within the dorsal and/or ventral lateral PFC (Fabiansson et al., 2012; Ochsner & Gross, 2008). Analytical rumination is characterized by "focusing on why an event occurred by analyzing the event's causes, consequences, and meaning" (Fabiansson et al., 2012). Angry rumination, as described above, is the remembering of and dwelling on a specific event and focusing on the angry feelings that are associated with that event. Results revealed activation of the inferior frontal gyrus and the AMG during the two rumination conditions, but not during the reappraisal condition. Furthermore, activation of the right putamen was also observed, especially during angry rumination, as this area is active when viewing hated individuals (Zeki & Romaya, 2008).

This study helps clarify the neurological pathways underlying functional and dysfunctional emotion regulation, particularly anger regulation, that lead people to behave aggressively and/or violently, or to reappraise and to channel their anger in socially appropriate ways.

Denson (2009) also looked at the neural correlates of anger and how anger leads to aggressive acts. Interpersonal provocation is one of the most effective ways to induce anger in a laboratory setting, and it was found that anger was positively associated with the left dACC (Denson, 2009). Other research has shown that the left OFC, right ACC, as well as the bilateral anterior temporal poles are activated when healthy men feel anger (Dougherty et al., 1999). Compared to a neutral state, an anger state elicits more activation of the midline septum, right anterior temporal cortex, and right mPFC. Anger and aggression are also both associated with left PFC activity (Harmon-Jones & Sigelman, 2001).

Researchers have examined a neural circuit in primates that is responsible for aggression to see how it affects the primates' behaviors (Mercadillo & Arias, 2010). It was found that a pathway following the periaqueductal grey, anterior hypothalamus, stria terminalis nucleus, AMG, and the OFC are all activated during threatening experiences. This neural circuit leads one to become alert, with a high heart rate and other adaptive physiological responses (Mercadillo & Arias, 2010). The OFC in humans is involved with social cognition and moral reasoning, which suggests that aggression requires prior knowledge and analysis of a situation. In addition to this research, investigators have examined decision-making during decisions to act aggressively and/or violently. Dunn, Dalgleish, and Lawrence (2006) suggest that the *somatic marker hypothesis* explains the execution of decisions. This hypothesis proposes that a specific event elicits a somatic state and such a pattern in the body allows a person to evaluate a situation. This process also allows for people to consider the consequences of their behavior. However, it has been shown that at the cerebral level, people with damage to the PFC are unable to foresee the consequences of their behavior and do not have this somatic marker to guide their decisions. Thus, they act impulsively and can lash out violently at others, being unable to foresee the consequences of their actions.

Due to the neural circuits and brain structures involved in aggressive and violent acts, researchers have studied the brain trauma history of various offenders. A meta-analysis found that in several studies, a majority of offenders had a serious history of head trauma (Fabian, 2010). Specifically, in a study of 62 habitually violent offenders, 61% had a prevalence of head injury; in a different study of 15 convicts on "death row" 67% had a prevalence of head injury; and in a study of 97 admissions to a UK mental institution, 42% had a prevalence of head injury (Fabian, 2010). These findings suggest that a history of brain trauma can have detrimental behavioral impacts, such as impulsive and violent behavior. Moreover, aggressive acts can result from a reduction in right frontal cortical activity, which reduces inhibition (Hortensius et al., 2011).

The inability to control urges can result in extremely socially inappropriate and violent behaviors. Lacking impulse control has been shown to be related to lesions to the frontal lobes, underdeveloped frontal lobes, or frontal brain trauma (Penney, 2012). For example, it has been found that lesions to the frontal lobes can result in dramatic changes in a person's behavior which is seen through heightened tendencies to behave violently and criminally. A classic example is that of Phineas Gage whose behavior and personality changed dramatically, and more aggressively, following traumatic frontal lobe damage, specifically to the vmPFC (Damasio, Grabowski, Frank, Galaburda, & Damasio, 1994; Harlow, 1868).

Yet, why are some people able to control their impulsive motives while others are not? Penney (2012) suggests that there are two pathways in the brain that compete with one another. One is an impulsive track, which includes the AMG and which works to obtain pleasure and to stop pain. The other is the reflective track, which includes the vmPFC and which is responsible for thinking through situations to understand the consequences of one's actions. According to Penney, impulse control issues are a result of an imbalance between the two systems, allowing the AMG to influence people's actions more so than the vmPFC. Individuals with such an imbalance are likely to have their decisions influenced by greater, emotionally driven, amygdalar activation and less by deliberation-related, vmPFC activation.

In summary, anger and aggression may both lead to violent and cruel behavior. Anger and aggression tend to predominately activate left frontal cortical regions, while decreasing right cortical activity, resulting in reduced inhibition. Those with PFC damage, such as many violent offenders, lack the ability to understand and to foresee consequences of aggressive behavior. Aggression is a common experience, especially when one feels that they have been wronged and may be exacerbated by genetic or biological predispositions.

MAOA gene as being linked to aggression: MonoAmine Oxidase A (MAOA) is an enzyme that affects how the neurotransmitters serotonin, dopamine, and norepinephrine are molecularly deactivated in the brain (McDermott, Tingley, Cowden, Frazzetto, & Johnson, 2009). Serotonin has an inhibitory effect on behavior and is important for emotional and behavioral regulation (Seo, Patrick, & Kennealy, 2008). Thus, when a mutation on the MAOA genes, located on the X chromosomes, hinders serotoninergic activity, aggressive behaviors are not regulated nor inhibited, resulting in an increase in violent behaviors and a heightened response to threatening stimuli (Dorfman et al., 2014). Inversely, a depletion of serotonin leads to an increase in dopamine, which also leads to impulsive behavior (Seo et al., 2008). Early studies in mice show even minor variations in the gene are associated with large behavioral implications (Shih, Chen, & Ridd, 1999). However, it has been found that this mutation, known as low activity MAOA (MAOA-L), does not independently predict aggressive behavior. One study found that there is instead an environment x gene interaction, in which participants with MAOA-L reacted more aggressively to people who took 80% of their money than to those who only took 20% (McDermott et al., 2009; see Chapter 7 in this volume). Essentially, this finding suggests that having MAOA-L does not alone predict aggression, but instead it leads to aggression in high provocation scenarios. Further, research has indicated that this MAOA gene x environment interaction is associated with children's mental health (Kim-Cohen et al., 2006). The presence of this gene abnormality along with stressful and traumatic early childhood events is a large and critical predictor of antisocial behavior and violence among adults (Fumagalli & Priori, 2012; McDermott et al., 2009).

Social rejection and aggression: Aggression may also be a result of a threatened sense of belonging or social rejection (Twenge & Campbell, 2003). Further, much research has looked at the role of childhood peer rejection as a predictor of heightened aggression and antisocial or conduct disorder (CD) development (Dodge et al., 2003; Miller-Johnson, Coie, Maumary-Gremaud, & Bierman, 2002). Social rejection is associated with the same neural pathways as bodily pain, in the dACC and the anterior INS (Chester et al., 2013). It is also highly associated with aggression and sadistic retaliatory aggression or revenge (Chester et al., 2013).

Anger and aggression are often a result of perceived threat of rejection, such as in instances of unrequited love, or feeling ignored by others (Leary, Twenge, & Quinlivan, 2006). In relationships, this may arise when a partner feels undervalued, and jealousy may result in domestic violence or crimes of passion (Takahashi et al., 2006). Social rejection has also been the main culprit in a majority of school shootings (Leary, Kowalski, Smith, & Phillips, 2003). Individuals higher in narcissism also report higher anger and are more likely to aggress against others after experiencing social rejection (Twenge & Campbell, 2003).

Hatred

Hatred can be felt for an individual or for a group, such as particular racial or religious groups. Furthermore, we can experience hatred for people we personally know, such as a past romantic partner, or for people we have not met, such as a political figure. Zeki and Romaya (2008) conducted exploratory research to investigate the neural correlates of hatred. These researchers recruited a small sample of people ($N = 17$) based on how strongly the participants self-reported experiencing hatred for someone. Participants provided a profile picture of their hated person as well as three faces of people to whom they felt neutral. Neuroimaging results revealed that when participants viewed images of someone they hated, there was increased activation in the medial frontal gyrus, right putamen, the frontal pole, and bilaterally in both the premotor cortex and the medial INS. In addition, it was found that the more the participant hated the person they were looking at, the more their right INS, right premotor cortex, and right frontomedial gyrus activated. These regions are involved with motor planning premotor cortex (PMC), predicting actions of others (frontal poles), and disgust (putamen and INS), which may combine in preparation for defense or attack (Calder, Keane, Manes, Antoun, & Young, 2000; Frith & Frith, 2006; Zeki & Romaya, 2008). The area of the brain with the most deactivation when viewing hated faces was the superior frontal gyrus, which is generally associated with a variety of cognitive and motor control tasks. This research was exploratory, as there were few neurological studies of hatred as of 2008, but it represents an important contribution to our early understanding of this construct. Zeki and Romaya (2008) describe hatred as "a complex biological sentiment which throughout history has impelled individuals to heroic as well as evil deeds."

In addition to hating other individuals or groups, people can engage in self-loathing behaviors, which can be thought of as cruel in that they are expressed as a lack of compassion and sympathy for the self. If we can be cruel to others with our words, we can certainly be cruel to ourselves. Self-criticism is a form of self-loathing in which people reflect on personal attributes, such as appearance, intellectual ability, or personality characteristics, and evaluate and judge themselves negatively. In fact, people can go as far as making themselves feel "controlled and beaten down" by their own self-criticism (Longe et al., 2010).

Self-criticism has been compared to self-reassurance on the neurological level in order to find where brain regions differ (Longe et al., 2010). An fMRI study was conducted in which participants read both negative and non-emotive scenarios and were asked to picture themselves experiencing each statement. When participants thought negatively, such as "the third job rejection letter in a row arrives in the post" and imagined that experience personally, there was activation in the lateral prefrontal cortex as well as in the dorsal anterior cingulate (Longe et al., 2010). These regions are associated with error processing and behavioral inhibition. Conversely, self-reassurance was aligned with activation in the left temporal pole and the INS, which are areas associated with feeling compassion and empathy. Thus, this study suggests that self-criticism is the result of lacking compassion for oneself.

In summary, the neuroscience of hatred is a recent development in the literature and plays an important role in understanding cruelty and how it manifests. Research thus far indicates that hatred is generally associated with the mPFC and the putamen. The more hatred felt toward someone, the more right INS and right PMC activation, which are associated with disgust and motor planning. Hate may even extend to the self, such as in self-loathing and self-criticism. These concepts may suggest directions for cruelty research, particularly in terms of how cruelty directed at the self may inform or differ from cruelty toward another.

Jealousy

Another factor that drives people to mistreat others and to act aggressively is jealousy. Jealousy occurs when a person feels that an important relationship is under threat (Harmon-Jones, Peterson, & Harris, 2009). Unfortunately, jealousy can make people act in violent ways, such as through spousal abuse or homicide (Harris, 2003). Jealousy is characterized as an approach emotion, meaning it is an emotion that drives behavior. Other emotions, such as fear and disgust are withdrawal emotions, making people avoid situations likely to induce these emotions. These different emotions activate separate areas in the prefrontal cortex, with greater activation in the left PFC being associated with approach and with the right PFC associated with withdrawal (Harmon-Jones et al., 2009).

To examine this frontal asymmetry, participants in a study were asked to play Cyberball, which was programmed to exclude some players and to include others (Harmon-Jones et al., 2009). In order to evoke feelings of an important relationship being under threat, females chose the male players and males chose the females. It was found that the left frontal cortex was more strongly activated in male participants when they were rejected by females, than by females when they were rejected by males. Further, the males' left frontal activation also correlated with anger, another approach emotion. By contrast, females showed more right frontal cortex activation, ostensibly due to the anxiety of being excluded. This study casts an interesting light on how jealousy arises in men and women, and how jealousy, social exclusion, and aggression are related.

Research has indicated that men feel jealous in relationships more than females (Takahashi et al., 2006). The importance of this finding is seen through the domestic violence that can follow intense feelings of jealousy. To better understand why men feel more jealous over infidelities than women, a study was conducted in which men and women read sentences eliciting sexual infidelity (SI), emotional infidelity (EI), or neither (Takahashi et al., 2006). fMRI was used to examine the neurological differences that arose in the male and female participants. It was found that when looking at the SI sentences compared to the neutral sentences, sexual infidelity neutral (SI-N) men showed greater AMG activation than women. For the EI group, emotional infidelity neutral (EI-N) men showed greater activation in the precentral gyrus, INS, cerebellum, hypothalamus, and hippocampus. The AMG and the hypothalamus are associated with the "appraisal of sexual salience" and reproductive behavior (Takahashi et al., 2006). Moreover, the AMG and the INS are involved in the processing of basic negative emotions, such as fear and disgust. Conversely, women exhibited greater activation of the visual cortex and thalamus during the SI-N condition and greater activation of the visual cortex, posterior STS (pSTS), and thalamus in the EI-N condition. The authors point out that the pSTS has been shown in previous studies to be involved with the "detection of intention, deception, and trustworthiness" (see Takahashi et al., 2006 for review). Overall, these findings indicate that men and women experience relational jealousy differently, which may explain why they act on it differently. In men, activation of the AMG and INS might suggest that there is a sense of fear and/or disgust when imagining relational infidelity. For women, with more activation in the visual cortex, it could be argued that they visually imagine the scenario more vividly than men do.

Thus, jealousy is another emotion that may lead to anger, aggression, and cruelty. As an approach motivated emotion, jealousy is associated with the left PFC. This reaction is especially seen in men who have been rejected by females. Men tend to be more jealous in relationships and this emotional response is associated with AMG activation. Jealousy research may help to understand cruelty in the context of people close to us.

Envy and Schadenfreude

Similar to jealousy is envy. Jealousy, as reported above, is most often felt in close relationships. Envy, on the other hand, is not dependent on the presence of a close relationship but is experienced in response to someone else's fortune or from upward social comparison (Jankowski & Takahashi, 2014). Like jealousy though, it is an emotion that can lead people to act with less empathic concern. In contrast, the experience of schadenfreude ("harm-joy" or feelings of happiness at another's suffering) occurs when misfortunes happen to another person, particularly to someone who was once envied. Thus, envy arises when one has negative wishes for someone who has good fortune, and schadenfreude is a pleasant emotion that arises when an envied target has bad fortune.

One study examined the neural correlates of these two emotions (Takahashi et al., 2009). It was found that the stronger the envy people experienced, the more their dACC activated. This finding suggests that envy is a painful feeling, as the ACC is a site involved in the experience of one's and of another's pain (Singer & Lamm, 2009). Further, the dACC is responsible for conflict-monitoring. Envy often occurs when our perceptions of ourselves do not match external stimuli recognized through social comparison, producing internal conflict. Schadenfreude, however, elicited striatal activation when a misfortune happened to someone who was envied, but not when a misfortune happened to someone who was not envied (Takahashi et al., 2009). Because a misfortune is happening to someone who was once envied, the feeling of pain associated with envy is now reduced and pleasure is felt. These outcomes revealed that the more schadenfreude was experienced, the more the VS and orbitofrontal cortex activated. These areas have also been associated with observing an unfair person receiving deserved punishment or pain. This research suggests that envy is felt as a social pain and schadenfreude is felt as a social pleasure, both in the context of low empathy for others.

Schadenfreude may therefore arise in relation to someone who was once envied, but it also may occur in the absence of envy. Regardless, both concepts allow a deeper understanding of how cruelty arises in 'ordinary' people. Envy is associated with dACC activation, while schadenfreude is related to OFC and VS activation, both central to the experience of recognizing social pain.

The many emotions that may drive cruel behavior in ordinary human beings range from joy at a sporting rival's loss to jealousy within romantic relationships. The neural correlates of the emotions reviewed in this section are critical to understanding how they may manifest into cruel behaviors. There seem to be consistent neural associations within each emotion. For example, aggressive behavior, which may arise from many emotions as well, is consistently associated with increased activation of the AMG and is predominantly characterized by increased left frontal cortical activity. Social rejection has widely been indicated as a precursor to aggressive behaviors in a variety of contexts. While still a young area of research, feelings of hatred are associated with mPFC and putamen activity and may be critical emotions in improving our understanding of human cruelty (to the self and others). Research on jealousy and aggression tends to show clear gender differences, particularly in left PFC and AMG activity in men. Experiencing these emotions is central to being human, but at what point does the experience of these emotions lead to aggression and violence? Perhaps by understanding the neural underpinnings of cruel behaviors in the ordinary person and in the pathologically cruel person, the origination of cruelty may emerge.

THE NEUROSCIENCE OF POPULATIONS CHARACTERIZED BY CRUELTY

In order to understand what makes the average person behave cruelly, it may be necessary to also consider the neuroscience of those characterized by their cruel behavior. Cruelty that arises from a disorder typically encompasses more extreme forms of cruelty, such as the behavior of Albert Fish from the opening of the chapter. When cruelty arises from a disorder or neurological deficit, there are often more clear and distinct differences in the neurophysiology and neuroanatomy, compared to the average person. This section will review these differences in people who suffer from personality disorders, such as CD and antisocial personality disorder, as well as those who exemplify the cruelest of behaviors, such as psychopaths and sex offenders.

Cruelty and Personality Disorders

Machiavellianism: Machiavellianism is defined as manipulating others for one's own personal gain (Bagozzi et al., 2013). Much like the spectrum of cruelty, manipulation can be seen as being on a continuum. Everyone is capable of being manipulative, but others are more willing to use manipulation for their own gain at the expense of others (Wilson, Near, & Miller, 1996). This behavior is most often seen in a corporate setting, with a person of high authority, such as CEO, taking advantage of others for his or her own personal benefit. It has been observed that Machiavellians are "unsupportive and inconsiderate" leaders, do not care about their partners and focus only on maximizing their own profits, are more likely than other employees to steal from the company, and are less likely to be helpful (Bagozzi et al., 2013).

Machiavellians compared to non-Machiavellians show reduced activation of the mPFC, TPJ, and precuneus regions of the brain. Interestingly, these areas are underdeveloped in people with autistic spectrum disorders, disorders in which the capacity to understand other people's emotions and experiences are diminished and communication skills are impaired (Bagozzi et al., 2013). These regions are also associated with ToM, as mentioned earlier in this chapter and presented in depth in Chapter 3. However, it was also found that Machiavellians displayed more activation of the pars opercularis and INS regions of the brain, when compared to non-Machiavellians—areas considered essential to emotional perception and sharing. These findings support the theory that Machiavellians are empathic and can perceive people's emotions more so than non-Machiavellians. With this knowledge of someone's feelings and experiences, Machiavellians are able to use others' vulnerabilities against them and to manipulate them more effectively than non-Machiavellians.

Conduct disorder and callous–unemotional traits: The biological and neurological underpinnings of the spectrum from empathy to callousness and cruelty allow for an understanding of moral evaluations and decision-making, as well as the development of psychopathy and antisocial personality disorder (APD) (Shirtcliff, Vitacco, Graf, Gostisha, Merz, & Zahn-Waxler, 2009). Callous–unemotional (CU) traits, often associated with CD and oppositional defiant disorder (ODD) in juveniles, are also highly correlated with adult psychopathy and antisocial disorder (Frick &

White, 2008; Herpers, Rommelse, Bons, Buitelaar, & Scheepers, 2012). CD, a behavioral disorder that affects children, is characterized by a serious pattern of violating rules and social norms through manipulating others, lying, damage to others' property, animal cruelty, aggressive behaviors, and bullying (Decety, Michalska, Akitsuki, & Lahey, 2009). In fact, one-third of children who meet the criteria for CD also meet the criteria for having CU traits (Mills-Koonce et al., 2015), characterized by a lack of empathy for others, a lack of guilt for wrongdoing, as well as the callous use of other people for one's own gain (Frick & White, 2008). This callousness trait is hypothesized to be the result of "blunted empathic response to the suffering of others" (Blair, 2005; Decety et al., 2009).

If indeed this hypothesis is true and callousness is the result of blunted empathic concern, then those with CD should theoretically show less neurological activation to stimuli depicting others in pain. To the contrary, one study revealed that adolescents with particularly aggressive CD did not display blunted empathic responses to images of others in pain, specifically when the pain was accidental rather than when attributable to someone else (Decety et al., 2009). Interestingly, this study revealed that those with CD actually had more activation in the anterior midcingulate cortex, striatum, and left AMG. In addition, they showed more activation in other areas, such as bilateral amygdalae, ventral striatum, and temporal poles (Decety et al., 2009).

On the other hand, a different study found that boys with CD and CU, compared to boys with neither, showed less right AMG activation to pictures of fearful faces (Harmon-Jones et al., 2009). Both the group of boys with CD and CU and the control group had strong bilateral activation in the ACC to the fearful faces more so than the neutral faces that were shown. Cortisol and testosterone are also associated with empathy and callousness, where youths with high CU traits have decreased cortisol levels and high testosterone levels leading to low fearfulness, high reward seeking, and aggressive behaviors (Herpers et al., 2012; Shirtcliff, Vitacco, Graf, Gostisha, Merz, & Zahn-Waxler, 2009). Brain regions such as the AMG, prefrontal cortex, INS, and the ACC influence cortisol levels. Cortisol and testosterone are important for subcortical communication between primarily the AMG and the vmPFC (Herpers et al., 2012). Decreased cortisol levels are associated with lowered fear responses and, in combination with high testosterone, lead to high aggression. CU traits are also associated with MAOA gene variants, suggesting a predisposition for aggressive and violent behavior as well (Fowler et al., 2009).

Adolescents with CD have been found to show abnormalities in grey matter volume within the bilateral anterior INS, left AMG, and the ACC, which are also regions associated with empathic processing. Specifically, INS and AMG volume in CD patients are significantly negatively correlated with empathy, suggesting that aggression and empathy may be regulated by the anterior INS (Sterzer, Stadler, Poustka, & Klein-schmidt, 2007). Empathy and grey matter volume in the ACC are also correlated (Sterzer et al., 2007). The ACC is involved in the mediation of emotional and rational moral reasoning and also activates in response to observing another in emotional or physical pain, in the same way that it is activated during the first-person experience of pain (Sterzer et al. 2007; Decety & Lamm, 2007; Fumagalli & Priori, 2012). Abnormalities in the INS, AMG, and ACC are indicative of disruptions in empathic processing, particularly in adolescents with CD.

Antisocial personality disorder: Individuals with APD meet at least three of the following seven criteria: (1) failure to conform to social norms, (2) failure to plan ahead, (3) lack of responsibility, (4) deceitfulness, (5) recklessness, (6) indifference to the well-being of others, (7) irritability and aggressiveness (National Collaborating Centre for Mental Health UK, 2010; Hare, Hart, & Harper, 1991). APD is also characterized by impulsivity, high negative emotionality, as well as low conscientiousness. High levels of testosterone are prevalent in those with APD and appear to influence facial threat perception, fear, and anger processing and cues (Van Honk & Schutter, 2007). Additionally, abnormalities in the orbitofrontal cortex have been associated with the diagnosis of APD (Braun et al., 2008).

APD can be seen through functional impairments in the frontal lobe, orbitofrontal cortex, dorsolateral prefrontal cortex, temporal lobe, AMG, hippocampus, as well as in the parietal lobe and ACC/PCC (Raine & Yang, 2006). Specifically, reduced prefrontal glucose metabolism in the frontal cortex has been associated with impulsive aggressive behavior (Juhász, Behen, Muzik, Chugani, & Chugani, 2001). Lesions to the orbito-frontal cortex often result in impulsive behavior and a lack of concern for consequences (Rolls, Hornak, Wade, & McGrh, 1994). Moreover, damage to the dorsolateral prefrontal cortex can result in problems with planning and decision-making (Manes et al., 2002). Reductions in the size of the hippocampus have been observed in violent offenders specifically with APD as well as in antisocial alcoholics (Laakso et al., 2001).

"Cavum septum pellucidum" (CSP—referred to historically as cavum septi pellucidi) is a marker for fetal neural maldevelopment. The septum pellucidum is a component of the septum consisting of "a deep, midline, limbic structure made up of two translucent leaves of glia separating the lateral ventricles, forming part of the septohippocampal system" (Raine, Lee, Yang, & Colletti, 2010). The fusion of the CSP begins during gesta-tion and should be complete shortly after birth. When the fusion is inter-rupted, the CSP will persist through adulthood. Research has indicated that the presence of the CSP can predict CD and ODD in children, as well as APD and psychopathy in adults (Raine et al., 2010). Interestingly, the CSP appears associated with the aggressive aspects of APD, but not with the nonaggressive parts, such as deceitfulness or irresponsibleness (Raine et al., 2010). When the CSP fusion is disrupted, bonding and attachment to caregivers is inhibited. A lack of critical bonding and attachment can result in behavior that is affectionless, antisocial, and even psychopathic. Thus, the CSP could be a neurological marker for and source of cruel behavior in APD.

In summary, Machiavellianism, CU, CD, and APD are all disorders linked to cruel behaviors. Machiavellianists tend to have decreased activation in the mPFC, while CD and CU tend to be characterized by decreased AMG and ACC activation. These disorders and regions are associated with empathy and the ability or inability, to recognize another's suffering. In APD, impairments and/or damage have been linked to various areas in the frontal and temporal lobe, leading to the tendency to be impulsive, aggressive, and indifferent to others. Those with APD tend to have higher levels of testosterone and tend to be more sensitive to facial threat cues. The abovementioned disorders appear to stem from a reduced ability to see or to care about another's suffering, making it easier to be cruel to others.

Psychopaths: In its most extreme form, the ability to be profoundly cruel is most highly exemplified by psychopaths. Psychopaths are characterized by antisocial behavior, reactive and instrumental aggression, manipulation, impulsiveness, as well as emotional shallowness and lack of guilt (Blair, 2007; Frick, O'brien, Wootton, & McBurnett, 1994; Hare, Hart, & Harpur, 1991; Harpur et al. 1989). When they commit crimes, they tend to be more violent and impulsive/poorly planned compared to nonpsychopathic criminals (Kiehl & Hoffman, 2011). It is estimated that less than 1% of noninstitutionalized males over the age of 18 are psychopaths and about 93% of psychopaths in the United States are in prison, jail, parole, or probation (Kiehl & Hoffman, 2011).

A recent meta-analysis reviewed 19 fMRI studies of nonclinical populations of adult psychopaths (Seara-Cardoso & Viding, 2015). Generally, high psychopathic traits were associated with lower activity in affective regions (AMG, anterior INS, parts of PFC) when participants were presented with emotionally salient stimuli. Further, atypical neural activity was noted in regions associated with reward processing, cognitive control tasks involving moral processing, and decision-making (vmPFC, posterior temporal cortex, rostral anterior cingulate, inferior frontal gyrus). Another meta-analysis investigated 43 brain-imaging studies examining PFC deficits across populations associated with antisocial and violent behavior. The analysis provided converging evidence for localized impairments in psychopaths in the following regions: right OFC, right ACC, and the left dorsolateral prefrontal cortex (dlPFC) (Yang & Raine, 2009).

Since psychopathic behavior is characteristic of APD, there are large overlaps in similarities in neural function between APD and more severe psychopathy. However, a majority of people with diagnosed severe APD are not criminal or severe psychopaths, although psychopaths are characterized partly by their antisocial personality (Patrick, 2007). There are distinct divergent properties that differentiate between the constructs. One major difference is that psychopaths tend to have low negative emotionality, such as low response to threat or stress-provoking situations. On the other hand, those with APD show greater fear and anxiety (Patrick, Bradley, & Lang, 1993). This observation is supported by fMRI data, where APD is positively associated with AMG activity (threat) and more severe psychopathy is negatively associated (Hyde, Byrd, Votruba-Drzal, Hariri, & Manuck, 2014). Abnormal attention allocation, as studied through event-related potential research, is also characteristic of psychopathy and is a potential measure that may differentiate more severe psychopaths from general antisocial personalities (Brazil et al., 2012).

More severe psychopathy has also been characterized by low activity within the orbitofrontal cortex, the region associated with social cognition, such as moral and emotional decision-making. The impairment of the OFC in psychopaths has been studied at length utilizing the Porteus Maze Task (Porteus, 1965) and the one pack card-playing-task, a reinforcement paradigm that tests the ability to shift attention between goals related to gaining reward or avoiding punishment. In both of these tasks psychopaths performed more poorly than nonpsychopaths, indicating deficits in their ability to accurately assess risk. Reward and loss processing deficits, a long theorized marker of psychopathy, has been associated with higher VS activation, particularly in relation to impulsive behavior (Pujara, Motzkin, Newman, Kiehl, & Koenigs, 2013). Dysfunctions in the AMG and vmPFC, associated with moral reasoning along with reward and punishment in reinforcement-based learning, have also been implicated in psychopathy (Blair, 2007; see the section above on Morality and Cruelty).

Additionally, psychopaths perform poorly at reverse learning tasks, in which individuals must learn a response in order to gain a reward, only for that response to subsequently no longer be rewarded and for a new reward association to be learned. This task is interesting because it is considered to require very little involvement of the AMG and appears to utilize primarily orbitofrontal cortex, suggesting an impairment in that neural region for psychopaths (Blair, 2006). Conversely the dorsolateral prefrontal cortex seems to be unaffected, as psychopaths perform as well as nonpsychopaths on executive decision tasks, such as the Stroop and the Wisconsin Card Sorting tasks (Kandel & Freed, 1989). Although severe psychopathy is suspected to have a strong genetic loading, it appears to be mitigated by IQ and socioeconomic status, suggesting strong executive functioning in these individuals (Blair, 2007; Hackman & Farah, 2009). These observations suggest that psychopaths having more cognitive resources may be able to circumvent their predilections toward antisocial behavior.

An fMRI study examined participants considered low, medium, and high on Hare's Psychopath Checklist Revised (Hare, 1991) on their facial processing of happy, sad, fearful, and painful expressions. Those high in psychopathy showed emotional processing deficits across all four expressions. MRI results suggested that emotional facial processing involved reduced activation in the OFC and vmPFC, aligned with affective neuroscience research on psychopathy (Decety, Skelly, Yoder, & Kiehl, 2014). The study did not find support suggesting a specific emotional dysfunction, particularly for the previously hypothesized fear-specific deficit, but instead pervasive deficits across all emotions (Marsh & Blair, 2008).

In summary, psychopathy is often the pathological condition most associated with cruel behavior. This population is consistently characterized by impulsivity, poor decision-making, aggression, and lack of remorse. Extant neuroscience research indicates that psychopathy is associated with low activity in emotionally affective regions such as the AMG and anterior INS. Additionally, there are impairments in right OFC (social cognition), right ACC (reward), and left dlPFC. Psychopaths compared to APD individuals have lower threat and stress responses (thus, the lower AMG activity). Research on psychopathy has important implications for the study of cruelty, through the latter's link to threat and fear.

Sex Offenders: Of course the violence of severe psychopaths is not the only case of extreme cruel behavior that society has had to endure. Sex offenders, from rapists to exhibitionists, act in remarkably contradictory ways to the norms, values, and morals of civilized society. It appears that while psychopathic brains differ from those of average humans in very subtle and consistent ways, sexual criminal brains may be more broadly dysfunctional. CT scans have shown reduced cerebral blood flow and diminished skull density in sex offenders as compared to control patients (Hendricks et al., 1988). Similarly, pedophiles have been shown to have even less blood flow and less skull densities than rapists (Graber et al., 1982; Hendricks et al., 1988). Pedophile cortical asymmetries typically consist of a smaller left hemisphere, whereas sexual aggressives' symmetries appear to be more evenly balanced.

It has been reported that pedophiles have sustained more physically traumatic events and head injuries before the age of 13 compared to the average population. In a study of 513 sex offenders, 48% had a history of head injuries resulting in unconsciousness and 22.5% sustained significant neurological damage, most often caused by motor vehicle accidents (Fabian, 2010). According to one study, between 50%–60% of pedophiles show brain damage or dysfunction (Fabian, 2010). These findings are consistent with the multiple research investigations linking cruelty to traumatic brain injuries.

Thus, in reviewing more characterological cruelty, we find that examining the neural correlates of such disordered cruelty may be particularly useful in shedding light on the neural underpinnings of "everyday cruelty." In adolescents, those who suffer from CD and CU appear to have increased bilateral ACC activation, while those with just CD also show abnormalities within the bilateral anterior INS and left AMG. Into adulthood, APD and psychopathy are associated with many impairments throughout the brain, such as in the frontal lobe, temporal lobe, and AMG, to name a few. These impairments are linked to the tendency to be impulsive, aggressive, and potentially violent toward others. Sex offenders appear to suffer broader, more diffuse dysfunctions such as cortical asymmetries and reduced cerebral blood flow. They are also much more likely to have had physical and head trauma at a young age. By studying these nuances of neurological activity across the average and disordered, we can hope to gain an understanding of how the ordinary person is capable of being cruel.

SUMMARY OF THE NEUROSCIENCE OF CRUELTY

In our review of the neuroscience of cruelty, we have explored many quite diverse manifestations of this construct. Cruelty among everyday people appears to involve moral-emotional processes, ranging from disgust sensitivity and protection of values and beliefs to rage, jealousy, and hatred. From this perspective, the ability to be cruel would appear to be human nature, just as it is commonplace and of survival value to include ourselves as members of certain in- and out-groups (Kinzler et al., 2007). Further, cruelty for the normal personality often feels rational, justified, and/or fair. Disordered cruelty, on the other hand, can range from CU children to the most extreme psychopaths. Understanding the neural underpinnings of cruelty in their varying neurological presentations is critical to development of interventions and preventive strategies targeted at minimizing the perpetuation of cruel behaviors and atrocities.

One limitation in much of the research covered, particularly in disordered cruelty, is the lack of female participants. Antisocial personality and psychopathy are typically associated with males, and investigations of female cases are underrepresented. Aggression research is also a male-dominated area, although women manifest aggression in different ways than men typically do. Another future direction would be more cross-cultural research, particularly in collectivist cultures, to determine how cruelty may arise differently or similarly to strangers and close others.

In briefly touching on many cruelty-associated neural processes, in healthy or disordered individuals, there appears to be corroborating support for localized processes and related neural activations. The frontal and temporal lobes are central to the many processes associated with cruelty. The medial and ventromedial regions of the prefrontal cortex largely dictate social cognition and moral-emotional processing. The orbitofrontal

TABLE 5.1 Overview of Brain Region Activation as Seen in Every Day Cruelty

Action or Thought	Brain Region
Disgust	Amygdala Insula Putamen Medial prefrontal cortex (low activation)
Morality	Amygdala Superior temporal sulcus Insula Angular gyrus Orbitofrontal cortex Ventromedial prefrontal cortex Dorsolateral prefrontal cortex Cingulate cortex
Anger	Medial prefrontal cortex (right) Anterior cingulate cortex (right) Orbitofrontal cortex (left) Dorsal anterior cingulate cortex Bilateral anterior temporal poles Midline septum
Aggression	Amygdala Medial prefrontal cortex Dorsal anterior cingulate cortex Frontal cortex (left) Frontal cortex (right; low activation) Prefrontal cortex (damage causes low activation)
Rumination	Amygdala Insula Hippocampus Medial prefrontal cortex Cingulate cortex Lateral prefrontal cortex Inferior frontal gyrus Putamen
Rejection, exclusion, and otherization	Frontal cortex Anterior cingulate cortex Anterior insula
Hatred	Insula Premotor cortex
Jealousy	Amygdala Insula
Envy and schadenfreude	Dorsal anterior cingulate cortex Ventral striatum Orbitofrontal cortex

TABLE 5.2   Overview of Brain Region Activation as Seen in Psychopathology

Disorder	Region Activation	
	High	**Low**
Machiavellianism	Insula Pars opercularis	Temporoparietal junction Medial prefrontal cortex Precuneus

Conduct disorder	Amygdala (left)
	Ventral striatum
	Anterior cingulate
	  cortex
	Anterior midcingulate
	  cortex
	Temporal poles
		Amygdala (right)
		Insula (abnormal amounts of
		  grey matter)

Antisocial personality disorder	Amygdala	Anterior cingulate cortex Ventromedial prefrontal cortex Dorsolateral prefrontal cortex
Psychopathy		Amygdala Anterior insula Orbitofrontal cortex Ventromedial prefrontal cortex Dorsolateral prefrontal cortex

cortex also is associated with activation during moral-emotional decision-making and reasoning. Low activations in these areas have been associated with aggression, antisocial personality, psychopathy, Machiavellianism, reactions to extreme out-groups, and disgust. The AMG, within the medial temporal lobes, is central to fear and threat processing. The INS, a close neighbor, is involved in rumination, hate, and self-assurance. Taken together, considerable progress has been made in recent years to identify the neural signatures of cruelty. One picture that emerges is that the neural regions activated as a result of cruelty overlap considerably with those activated during states of empathy and compassion, but in distinct ways. Tables 5.1 and 5.2 summarize the findings of our review.

Cultivating compassion through deliberate training, such as mindfulness or compassion meditation (see Chapter 9 in this volume) is one approach that may reduce the tendency for humans to be cruel (Tirch, 2010). Compassion is antithetical to empathy erosion and is predicated on an understanding of shared common humanity and the desire to alleviate the universal experience of suffering. Although many roots of cruel behavior in the typical personality are central to human nature, mindfulness training or other activities that deliberately train empathic sensitivity, may promote prosocial behavior and mitigate cruelty (Berry et al., 2018). In taking firm steps to build empathic sensitivity, rather than allowing it to erode, we are well-poised to wash away many predominant sources of human suffering.

References

Anderson, C. A., Deuser, W. E., & DeNeve, K. M. (1995). Hot temperatures, hostile affect, hostile cognition, and arousal: Tests of a general model of affective aggression. *Personality and Social Psychology Bulletin*, 21(5), 434–448.

Bagozzi, R. P., Verbeke, W. J., Dietvorst, R. C., Belschak, F. D., van den Berg, W. E., & Rietdijk, W. J. (2013). Theory of mind and empathic explanations of Machiavellianism: A neuroscience perspective. *Journal of Management*, 39(7), 1760–1798.

Bandura, A. (2002). Selective moral disengagement in the exercise of moral agency. *Journal of Moral Education*, 31(2), 101–119.

Bandura, A., Underwood, B., & Fromson, M. E. (1975). Disinhibition of aggression through diffusion of responsibility and dehumanization of victims. *Journal of Research in Personality*, 9(4), 253–269.

Baron-Cohen, S. (2012). *The science of evil: On empathy and the origins of cruelty*. New York: Basic books.

Berry, D. R., Cairo, A. H., Goodman, R. J., Quaglia, J. T., Green, J. D., & Brown, K. W. (2018). Mindfulness increases prosocial responses toward ostracized strangers through empathic concern. *Journal of Experimental Psychology: General*, 147(1), 93.

Blair, R. J. R. (2005). Responding to the emotions of others: dissociating forms of empathy through the study of typical and psychiatric populations. *Consciousness and Cognition*, 14(4), 698–718.

Blair, R. J. R. (2006). The emergence of psychopathy: Implications for the neuropsychological approach to developmental disorders. *Cognition*, 101(2), 414–442.

Blair, R. J. R. (2007). The amygdala and ventromedial prefrontal cortex in morality and psychopathy. *Trends in Cognitive Sciences*, 11(9), 387–392.

Bobes, M. A., Ostrosky, F., Diaz, K., Romero, C., Borja, K., Santos, Y., et al. (2012). Linkage of functional and structural anomalies in the left amygdala of reactive-aggressive men. *Social Cognitive and Affective Neuroscience*, 8(8), 928–936.

Branscombe, N. R., Wann, D. L., Noel, J. G., & Coleman, J. (1993). In-group or out-group extemity: Importance of the threatened social identity. *Personality and Social Psychology Bulletin*, 19(4), 381–388.

Braun, C.M.J., Leveille, C., & Guimond, A. (2008). An orbitofrontostriatopallidal pathway for morality: Evidence from postlesion antisocial and obsessive-compulsive disorder. *Cognitive Neuropsychiatry*, 13(4), 296-337.

Brazil, I. A., Verkes, R. J., Brouns, B. H., Buitelaar, J. K., Bulten, B. H., & de Bruijn, E. R. (2012). Differentiating psychopathy from general antisociality using the P3 as a psychophysiological correlate of attentional allocation. *PloS One*, 7(11), e50339.

Buhle, J. T., Silvers, J. A., Wager, T. D., Lopez, R., Onyemekwu, C., Kober, H., et al. (2014). Cognitive reappraisal of emotion: A meta-analysis of human neuroimaging studies. *Cerebral Cortex*, 24(11), 2981–2990.

Buss, A. H., & Perry, M. (1992). The Aggression Questionnaire. *Journal of Personality and Social Psychology*, 63, 452–459.

Calder, A. J., Keane, J., Manes, F., Antoun, N., & Young, A. W. (2000). Impaired recognition and experience of disgust following brain injury. *Nature Neuroscience*, 3(11), 1077–1078.

Cavanna, A. E., & Trimble, M. R. (2006). The precuneus: A review of its functional anatomy and behavioural correlates. *Brain*, 129(3), 564–583.

Chester, D. S., Eisenberger, N. I., Pond, R. S., Richman, S. B., Bushman, B. J., & DeWall, C. N. (2013). The interactive effect of social pain and executive functioning on aggression: An fMRI experiment. *Social Cognitive and Affective Neuroscience*, 9(5), 699–704.

Choma, B. L., Hodson, G., & Costello, K. (2012). Intergroup disgust sensitivity as a predictor of islamophobia: The modulating effect of fear. *Journal of Experimental Social Psychology*, 48(2), 499–506.

Cikara, M., Botvinick, M. M., & Fiske, S. T. (2011). Us versus them social identity shapes neural responses to intergroup competition and harm. *Psychological Science*, 22(3), 306–313.

Costafreda, S. G., Brammer, M. J., David, A. S., & Fu, C. H. (2007). Predictors of amygdala activation during the processing of emotional stimuli: A meta-analysis of 385 PET and fMRI studies. *Brain Research Reviews, 58*(1), 57–70.

Curtis, V., Aunger, R., & Rabie, T. (2004). Evidence that disgust evolved to protect from risk of disease. *Proceedings of the Royal Society of London B: Biological Sciences, 271(Suppl),* S131–S133.

Damasio, H., Grabowski, T., Frank, R., Galaburda, A. M., & Damasio, A. R. (1994). The return of Phineas Gage: Clues about the brain from the skull of a famous patient. *Science, 264*(5162), 1102–1105.

Darley, J. M. (1993). Possible approaches, actual approaches. *Psychological Science, 4*(6), 353–1353.

Dasgupta, N., DeSteno, D., Williams, L. A., & Hunsinger, M. (2009). Fanning the flames of prejudice: the influence of specific incidental emotions on implicit prejudice. *Emotion, 9*(4), 585.

Decety, J., & Lamm, C. (2007). The role of the right temporoparietal junction in social interaction: How low-level computational processes contribute to meta-cognition. *The Neuroscientist, 13*(6), 580–593.

Decety, J., Michalska, K. J., Akitsuki, Y., & Lahey, B. B. (2009). Atypical empathic responses in adolescents with aggressive conduct disorder: A functional MRI investigation. *Biological Psychology, 80*(2), 203–211.

Decety, J., Skelly, L., Yoder, K. J., & Kiehl, K. A. (2014). Neural processing of dynamic emotional facial expressions in psychopaths. *Social Neuroscience, 9*(1), 36–49.

Denson, T. F. (2009). Angry rumination and the self-regulation of aggression. *Psychology of self-regulation: Cognitive, affective, and motivational processes, 11,* 233–248.

Denson, T. F., Pedersen, W. C., Ronquillo, J., & Nandy, A. S. (2009). The angry brain: Neural correlates of anger, angry rumination, and aggressive personality. *Journal of Cognitive Neuroscience, 21*(4), 734–744.

Diener, E., Lusk, R., DeFour, D., & Flax, R. (1980). Deindividuation: Effects of group size, density, number of observers, and group member similarity on self-consciousness and disinhibited behavior. *Journal of Personality and Social Psychology, 39,* 449–459. doi: 10.1037/0022-3514.39.3.449.

Dodge, K. A., Lansford, J. E., Burks, V. S., Bates, J. E., Pettit, G. S., Fontaine, R., et al. (2003). Peer rejection and social information-processing factors in the development of aggressive behavior problems in children. *Child Development, 74*(2), 374–393.

Dorfman, H. M., Meyer-Lindenberg, A., & Buckholtz, J. W. (2014). Neurobiological mechanisms for impulsive-aggression: The role of MAOA. In *Neuroscience of Aggression* (pp. 297–313). Berlin Heidelberg: Springer.

Dougherty, D. D., Shin, L. M., Alpert, N. M., Pitman, R. K., Orr, S. P., Lasko, M., et al. (1999). Anger in healthy men: A PET study using script-driven imagery. *Biological Psychiatry, 46*(4), 466–472.

Dunn, B. D., Dalgleish, T., & Lawrence, A. D. (2006). The somatic marker hypothesis: A critical evaluation. Neuroscience & Biobehavioral Reviews, 30(2), 239–271.

Etkin, A., Egner, T., and Kalisch, R. (2011). Emotional processing in anterior cingulate and medial prefrontal cortex. Trends Cogn. Sci. 15, 85–93. doi: 10.1016/j.tics.2010.11.004.

Fabian, J. M. (2010). Neuropsychological and neurological correlates in violent and homicidal offenders: A legal and neuroscience perspective. *Aggression and Violent Behavior, 15*(3), 209–223.

Fabiansson, E. C., Denson, T. F., Moulds, M. L., Grisham, J. R., & Schira, M. M. (2012). Don't look back in anger: Neural correlates of reappraisal, analytical rumination, and angry rumination during recall of an anger-inducing autobiographical memory. *Neuro Image, 59*(3), 2974–2981.

Frankfurter, D. (2006). *Evil Incarnate: Rumors of demonic conspiracy and ritual abuse in history.* Princeton University Press. Princeton, New Jersey.

Fowler, T., Langley, K., Rice, F., van den Bree, M. B., Ross, K., Wilkinson, L. S., et al. (2009). Psychopathy trait scores in adolescents with childhood ADHD: The contribution of genotypes affecting MAOA, 5HTT and COMT activity. *Psychiatric Genetics, 19*(6), 312–319.

Frick, P. J., & White, S. F. (2008). Research review: The importance of callous-unemotional traits for developmental models of aggressive and antisocial behavior. *Journal of Child Psychology and Psychiatry, 49*(4), 359–375.

Frick, P. J., O'brien, B. S., Wootton, J. M., & McBurnett, K. (1994). Psychopathy and conduct problems in children. *Journal of Abnormal Psychology, 103*(4), 700.

Frith, C. D., & Frith, U. (2006). The neural basis of mentalizing. *Neuron, 50*(4), 531–534.

Fumagalli, M., & Priori, A. (2012). Functional and clinical neuroanatomy of morality. *Brain, 135*(7), 2006–2021.

Graber, B., Hartmann, K., Coffman, J. A., Huey, C. J., & Golden, C. J. (1982). Brain damage among mentally disordered sex offenders. *Journal of Forensic Science, 27*(1), 125–134.

Greene, J. D., & Paxton, J. M. (2009). Patterns of neural activity associated with honest and dishonest moral decisions. *Proceedings of the National Academy of Sciences, 106*(30), 12506–12511.

Greene, J. D., Sommerville, R. B., Nystrom, L. E., Darley, J. M., & Cohen, J. D. (2001). An fMRI investigation of emotional engagement in moral judgment. *Science, 293*(5537), 2105–2108.

Giumetti, G. W., & Markey, P. M. (2007). Violent video games and anger as predictors of aggression. *Journal of Research in Personality, 41*(6), 1234–1243.

Hackman, D. A., & Farah, M. J. (2009). Socioeconomic status and the developing brain. *Trends in Cognitive Sciences, 13*(2), 65–73.

Hare, R. D. (1991). *The Hare psychopathy checklist-revised(PCL-R)*. Toronto, Ontario: Multi-Health Systems.

Hare, R. D., Hart, S. D., & Harpur, T. J. (1991). Psychopathy and the DSM-IV criteria for antisocial personality disorder. *Journal of Abnormal Psychology, 100*(3), 391.

Harlow, J. M. (1868). Recovery from the passage of an iron bar through the head. *Publications of the Massachusetts Medical Society, 2*(3), 246–327.

Harmon-Jones, E., & Sigelman, J. (2001). State anger and prefrontal brain activity: Evidence that insult-related relative left-prefrontal activation is associated with experienced anger and aggression. *Journal of Personality and Social Psychology, 80*(5), 797.

Harmon-Jones, E., Peterson, C. K., & Harris, C. R. (2009). Jealousy: Novel methods and neural correlates. *Emotion, 9*(1), 113.

Harpur, T. J., Hare, R. D., & Hakstian, A. R. (1989). Two-factor conceptualization of psychopathy: Construct validity and assessment implications. *Psychological Assessment: A Journal of Consulting and Clinical Psychology, 1*(1), 6.

Harris, C. R. (2003). A review of sex differences in sexual jealousy, including self-report data, psychophysiological responses, interpersonal violence, and morbid jealousy. *Personality and Social Psychology Review, 7*(2), 102–128.

Harris, L. T., & Fiske, S. T. (2006). Dehumanizing the lowest of the low neuroimaging responses to extreme out-groups. *Psychological science, 17*(10), 847–853.

Harris, L. T., & Fiske, S. T. (2009). Social neuroscience evidence for dehumanised perception. *European Review of Social Psychology, 20*(1), 192–231.

Harris, L. T., & Fiske, S. T. (2011). Perceiving humanity or not: A social neuroscience approach to dehumanized perception. In *Social Neuroscience: Toward Understanding the Underpinnings of the Social Mind* (pp. 123–134). New York, NY: Oxford University Press.

Haslam, N. (2006). Dehumanization: An integrative review. *Personality and Social Psychology Review, 10*(3), 252–264.

Heekeren, H. R., Wartenburger, I., Schmidt, H., Schwintowski, H. P., & Villringer, A. (2003). An fMRI study of simple ethical decision-making. *NeuroReport, 14*(9), 1215–1219.

Hein, G., Silani, G., Preuschoff, K., Batson, C. D., & Singer, T. (2010). Neural responses to ingroup and outgroup members' suffering predict individual differences in costly helpin. *Neuron, 68*(1), 149–160.

Hendricks, S. E., Fitzpatrick, D. F., Hartmann, K., Quaife, M. A., Stratbucker, R. A., & Graber, B. (1988). Brain structure and function in sexual molesters of children and adolescents. *The Journal of Clinical Psychiatry, 49*(3), 108–112.

Herpers, P. C., Rommelse, N. N., Bons, D. M., Buitelaar, J. K., & Scheepers, F. E. (2012). Callous-unemotional traits as a cross-disorders construct. *Social Psychiatry and Psychiatric Epidemiology, 47*(12), 2045–2064.

Hodson, G., & Costello, K. (2007). Interpersonal disgust, ideological orientations, and dehumanization as predictors of intergroup attitudes. *Psychological Science, 18*(8), 691–698.

Hortensius, R., Schutter, D. J., & Harmon-Jones, E. (2011). When anger leads to aggression: Induction of relative left frontal cortical activity with transcranial direct current stimulation increases the anger–aggression relationship. *Social Cognitive and Affective Neuroscience, 7*(3), 342–347.

Hyde, L. W., Byrd, A. L., Votruba-Drzal, E., Hariri, A. R., & Manuck, S. B. (2014). Amygdala reactivity and negative emotionality: Divergent correlates of antisocial personality and psychopathy traits in a community sample. *Journal of Abnormal Psychology, 123*(1), 214.

Inbar, Y., Pizarro, D. A., Knobe, J., & Bloom, P. (2009). Disgust sensitivity predicts intuitive disapproval of gays. *Emotion, 9*(3), 435.

Jankowski, K. F., & Takahashi, H. (2014). Cognitive neuroscience of social emotions and implications for psychopathology: Examining embarrassment, guilt, envy, and schadenfreude. *Psychiatry and Clinical Neurosciences, 68*(5), 319–336.

Jones, A. P., Laurens, K. R., Herba, C. M., Barker, G. J., & Viding, E. (2009). Amygdala hypoactivity to fearful faces in boys with conduct problems and callous unemotional traits. *American Journal of Psychiatry, 166*(1), 95–102.

Juhász, C., Behen, M. E., Muzik, O., Chugani, D. C., & Chugani, H. T. (2001). Bilateral medial prefrontal and temporal neocortical hypometabolism in children with epilepsy and aggression. *Epilepsia, 42*(8), 991–1001.

Kandel, E., & Freed, D. (1989). Frontal-lobe dysfunction and antisocial behavior: A review. *Journal of Clinical Psychology, 45*(3), 404–413.

Kiehl, K. A., & Hoffman, M. B. (2011). The criminal psychopath: History, neuroscience, treatment, and economics. *Jurimetrics, 51*, 355.

Kim-Cohen, J., Caspi, A., Taylor, A., Williams, B., Newcombe, R., Craig, I. W., et al. (2006). MAOA, maltreatment, and gene–environment interaction predicting children's mental health: New evidence and a meta-analysis. *Molecular Psychiatry, 11*(10), 903–913.

Kinzler, K. D., Dupoux, E., & Spelke, E. S. (2007). The native language of social cognition. *Proceedings of the National Academy of Sciences, 104*(30), 12577–12580.

Kober, H., Barrett, L. F., Joseph, J., Bliss-Moreau, E., Lindquist, K., & Wager, T. D. (2008). Functional grouping and cortical–subcortical interactions in emotion: A meta-analysis of neuroimaging studies. *NeuroImage, 42*(2), 998–1031.

Laakso, M. P., Vaurio, O., Koivisto, E., Savolainen, L., Eronen, M., Aronen, H. J., et al. (2001). Psychopathy and the posterior hippocampus. *Behavioural Brain Research, 118*(2), 187–193.

Leary, M. R., Kowalski, R. M., Smith, L., & Phillips, S. (2003). Teasing, rejection, and violence: Case studies of the school shootings. *Aggressive Behavior, 29*(3), 202–214.

Leary, M. R., Twenge, J. M., & Quinlivan, E. (2006). Interpersonal rejection as a determinant of anger and aggression. *Personality and Social Psychology Review, 10*(2), 111–132.

Lindsay, J. J., & Anderson, C. A. (2000). From antecedent conditions to violent actions: A general affective aggression model. *Personality and Social Psychology Bulletin, 26*(5), 533–547.

Lindquist, K. A., Wager, T. D., Kober, H., Bliss-Moreau, E., & Barrett, L. F. (2012). The brain basis of emotion: A meta-analytic review. *Behavioral and Brain Sciences, 35*(3), 121–143.

Longe, O., Maratos, F. A., Gilbert, P., Evans, G., Volker, F., Rockliff, H., et al. (2010). Having a word with yourself: Neural correlates of self-criticism and self-reassurance. *NeuroImage, 49*(2), 1849–1856.

Malson, L. (1964). *Wolf Children and the Problem of Human Nature*. New York: Monthly Review Press 1972.

Manes, F., Sahakian, B., Clark, L., Rogers, R., Antoun, N., Aitken, M., et al. (2002). Decision-making processes following damage to the prefrontal cortex. *Brain, 125*(3), 624–639.

Marsh, A. A., & Blair, R. J. R. (2008). Deficits in facial affect recognition among antisocial populations: A meta-analysis. *Neuroscience & Biobehavioral Reviews, 32*(3), 454–465.

McDermott, R., Tingley, D., Cowden, J., Frazzetto, G., & Johnson, D. D. (2009). Monoamine oxidase A gene (MAOA) predicts behavioral aggression following provocation. *Proceedings of the National Academy of Sciences, 106*(7), 2118–2123.

Milgram, S. (1963). Behavioral study of obedience. *The Journal of Abnormal and Social Psychology, 67*(4), 371.

Miller-Johnson, S., Coie, J. D., Maumary-Gremaud, A., & Bierman, K. (2002). Peer rejection and aggression and early starter models of conduct disorder. *Journal of Abnormal Child Psychology, 30*(3), 217–230.

Mills-Koonce, W. R., Wagner, N. J., Willoughby, M. T., Stifter, C., Blair, C., & Granger, D. A. (2015). Greater fear reactivity and psychophysiological hyperactivity among infants with later conduct problems and callous-unemotional traits. *Journal of Child Psychology and Psychiatry, 56*(2), 147–154.

Moll, J., de Oliveira-Souza, R., Moll, F. T., Ignácio, F. A., Bramati, I. E., Caparelli-Dáquer, E. M., et al. (2005). The moral affiliations of disgust: A functional MRI study. *Cognitive and Behavioral Neurology, 18*(1), 68–78.

Moor, B. G., Güroğlu, B., de Macks, Z. A. O., Rombouts, S. A., Van der Molen, M. W., & Crone, E. A. (2012). Social exclusion and punishment of excluders: Neural correlates and developmental trajectories. *NeuroImage, 59*(1), 708–717.

National Collaborating Centre for Mental Health (UK) (2010). Antisocial Personality Disorder: Treatment, Management, and Prevention. Leicester (UK): British Psychological Society.

Navarrete, C. D., & Fessler, D. M. (2006). Disease avoidance and ethnocentrism: The effects of disease vulnerability and disgust sensitivity on intergroup attitudes. *Evolution and Human Behavior, 27*(4), 270–282.

Nieuwenhuis, S., Slagter, H. A., Alting von Geusau, N. J., Heslenfeld, D. J., & Holroyd, C. B. (2005). Knowing good from bad: Differential activation of human cortical areas by positive and negative outcomes. *European Journal of Neuroscience, 21*(11), 3161–3168.

Nitsche, M. A., Cohen, L. G., Wassermann, E. M., Priori, A., Lang, N., Antal, A., et al. (2008). Transcranial direct current stimulation: State of the art. *Brain Stimulation, 1*(3), 206–223.

Ochsner, K. N., & Gross, J. J. (2008). Cognitive emotion regulation: Insights from social cognitive and affective neuroscience. *Current Directions in Psychological Science, 17*(2), 153–158.

O'Doherty, J. P. (2004). Reward representations and reward-related learning in the human brain: Insights from neuroimaging. *Current Opinion in Neurobiology, 14*, 769–776.

Öhman, A., Dimberg, U., & Öst, L. G. (1985). Animal and social phobias: Biological constraints on learned fear responses. *Theoretical Issues in Behavior Therapy*, 123–175.

Öhman, A., Carlsson, K., Lundqvist, D., & Ingvar, M. (2007). On the unconscious subcortical origin of human fear. *Physiology & Behavior, 92*(1), 180–185.

Opotow, S. (1990). Moral exclusion and injustice: An introduction. *Journal of Social Issues, 46*(1), 1–20.

Patrick, C. J. (2007). Getting to the heart of psychopathy. *The psychopath: Theory, research, and practice*. Mahwah, NJ: Lawrence Erlbaum Associates 207–252.

Patrick, C. J., Bradley, M. M., & Lang, P. J. (1993). Emotion in the criminal psychopath: Startle reflex modulation. *Journal of Abnormal Psychology, 102*(1), 82–92.

Pelphrey, K. A., Morris, J. P., & Mccarthy, G. (2004). Grasping the intentions of others: The perceived intentionality of an action influences activity in the superior temporal sulcus during social perception. *Journal of Cognitive Neuroscience, 16*(10), 1706–1716.

Penney, S. (2012). Impulse control and criminal responsibility: Lessons from neuroscience. *International Journal of Law and Psychiatry, 35*(2), 99–103.

Porteus, S. D. (1965). *Porteus maze tests: Fifty years' application.* England: Oxford.

Prehn, K., Wartenburger, I., Mériau, K., Scheibe, C., Goodenough, O. R., Villringer, A., et al. (2008). Individual differences in moral judgment competence influence neural correlates of socio-normative judgments. *Social Cognitive and Affective Neuroscience, 3*(1), 33–46.

Pujara, M., Motzkin, J. C., Newman, J. P., Kiehl, K. A., & Koenigs, M. (2013). Neural correlates of reward and loss sensitivity in psychopathy. *Social Cognitive and Affective Neuroscience, 9*(6), 794–801.

Raine, A., & Yang, Y. (2006). Neural foundations to moral reasoning and antisocial behavior. *Social Cognitive and Affective Neuroscience, 1*(3), 203–213.

Raine, A., Lee, L., Yang, Y., & Colletti, P. (2010). Neurodevelopmental marker for limbic maldevelopment in antisocial personality disorder and psychopathy. *The British Journal of Psychiatry, 197*(3), 186–192.

Reimann, M., & Zimbardo, P. G. (2011). The dark side of social encounters: Prospects for a neuroscience of human evil. *Journal of Neuroscience, Psychology, and Economics, 4*(3), 174.

Riek, B. M., Mania, E. W., & Gaertner, S. L. (2006). Intergroup threat and outgroup attitudes: A meta-analytic review. *Personality and Social Psychology Review, 10*(4), 336–353.

Rilling, J. K., & Sanfey, A. G. (2011). The neuroscience of social decision-making. *Annual Review of Psychology, 62*, 23–48.

Rolls, E. T., Hornak, J., Wade, D., & McGrh, J. (1994). Emotion-related learning in patients with social and emotional changes associated with frontal lobe damage. *Journal of Neurology, Neurosurgery & Psychiatry, 57*(12), 1518–1524.

Rolls, E. T. (2000). On the brain and emotion. *Behavioral and Brain Sciences, 23*(2), 219–228.

Rozin, P., Fallon, A., & Augustoni-Ziskind, M. (1985). The child's conception of food: The development of contamination sensitivity to "disgusting" substances. *Developmental Psychology, 21*(6), 1075.

Rozin, P., Haidt, J., & McCauley, C. (2000). Disgust. In M. Lewis, & J. M. Haviland (Eds.), *Handbook of emotions* (2nd ed., pp. 637–653). New York: Guilford Press.

Seo, D., Patrick, C. J., & Kennealy, P. J. (2008). Role of serotonin and dopamine system interactions in the neurobiology of impulsive aggression and its comorbidity with other clinical disorders. *Aggression and Violent Behavior, 13*(5), 383–395.

Shih, J. C., Chen, K., & Ridd, M. J. (1999). Monoamine oxidase: From genes to behavior. *Annual Review of Neuroscience, 22*(1), 197–217.

Shirtcliff, E. A., Vitacco, M. J., Graf, A. R., Gostisha, A. J., Merz, J. L., & Zahn-Waxler, C. (2009). Neurobiology of empathy and callousness: Implications for the development of antisocial behavior. *Behavioral Sciences & the Law, 27*(2), 137–171.

Singer, T., & Lamm, C. (2009). The social neuroscience of empathy. *Annals of the New York Academy of Sciences, 1156*(1), 81–96.

Sterzer, P., Stadler, C., Poustka, F., & Kleinschmidt, A. (2007). A structural neural deficit in adolescents with conduct disorder and its association with lack of empathy. *NeuroImage, 37*(1), 335–342.

Tajfel, H., & Turner, J. C. (1979). An integrative theory of intergroup conflict. *The Social Psychology of Intergroup Relations, 33*(47), 74.

Takahashi, H., Msuura, M., Yaha, N., Koeda, M., Suhara, T., & Okubo, Y. (2006). Men and women show distinct brain activations during imagery of sexual and emotional infidelity. *NeuroImage, 32*(3), 1299–1307.

Takahashi, H., Ko, M., Msuura, M., Mobbs, D., Suhara, T., & Okubo, Y. (2009). When your gain is my pain and your pain is my gain: Neural correlates of envy and schadenfreude. *Science, 323*(5916), 937–939.

Taylor, K. E. (2007). Disgust is a factor in extreme prejudice. *British Journal of Social Psychology*, *46*(3), 597–617.

Taylor, K. E. (2009). *Cruelty: Human evil and the human brain*. USA: Oxford University Press.

Terrizzi, J. A., Shook, N. J., & Ventis, W. L. (2010). Disgust: A predictor of social conservatism and prejudicial attitudes toward homosexuals. *Personality and Individual Differences*, *49*(6), 587–592.

Tirch, D. D. (2010). Mindfulness as a context for the cultivation of compassion. *Internional Journal of Cognitive Therapy*, *3*(2), 113–123.

Tulving, E. (1983). *Elements of episodic memory*. Oxford: Clarendon Press.

Twenge, J. M., & Campbell, W. K. (2003). "Isn't it fun to get the respect that we're going to deserve?" Narcissism, social rejection, and aggression. *Personality and Social Psychology Bulletin*, *29*(2), 261–272.

Van Bavel, J. J., Packer, D. J., & Cunningham, W. A. (2008). The neural substrates of in-group bias: A functional magnetic resonance imaging investigation. *Psychological Science*, *19*(11), 1131–1139.

Van Honk, J., & Schutter, D. (2007). Testosterone reduces conscious detection of signals serving social correction: Implications for antisocial behavior. *Psychological Science*, *18*(8), 663–667.

Vogeley, K., Bussfeld, P., Newen, A., Herrmann, S., Happé, F., Falkai, P., et al. (2001). Mind reading: Neural mechanisms of theory of mind and self-perspective. *NeuroImage*, *14*(1), 170–181.

Wilson, D. S., Near, D., & Miller, R. R. (1996). Machiavellianism: A synthesis of the evolutionary and psychological literatures. *Psychological Bulletin*, *119*(2), 285.

Williams, K. D., & Jarvis, B. (2006). Cyberball: A program for use in research on interpersonal ostracism and acceptance. *Behavior Research Methods*, *38*(1), 174–180.

Yang, Y. & Raine, A. (November 30, 2009). Prefrontal structural and functional brain imaging findings in antisocial, violent, and psychopathic individuals: A meta-analysis. Psychiatry Research: Neuroimaging, 174(2), 81–88.

Zeki, S., & Romaya, J. P. (2008). Neural correlates of hate. *PloS One*, *3*(10), .

Zimbardo, P. G. (1972). Comment: Pathology of imprisonment. *Society*, *9*(6), 4–8.

Further Readings

Baumeister, R. F., Wotman, S. R., & Stillwell, A. M. (1993). Unrequited love: On heartbreak, anger, guilt, scriptlessness, and humiliation. *Journal of Personality and Social Psychology*, *64*(3), 377.

Bechara, A., Damasio, H., & Damasio, A. R. (2000). Emotion, decision making and the orbitofrontal cortex. *Cerebral cortex*, *10*(3), 295–307.

Haxby, J. V., Hoffman, E. A., & Gobbini, M. I. (2000). The distributed human neural system for face perception. *Trends in Cognitive Sciences*, *4*(6), 223–233.

Mercadillo, R. E., & Arias, N. A. (2010). Violence and compassion: A bioethical insight into their cognitive bases and social manifestations. *International Social Science Journal*, *61*(200–201), 221–232.

Seara-Cardoso, A., & Viding, E. (2015). Functional neuroscience of psychopathic personality in adults. *Journal of Personality*, *83*(6), 723–737.

6

Reflections of Others and of Self: The Mirror Neuron System's Relationship to Empathy

C. Chad Woodruff

Northern Arizona University, Flagstaff, AZ, United States

While concisely defining empathy, compassion and self-compassion is difficult, it can be said that at a minimum, they have in common the processing of the relationship between self and other. Since their discovery in 1992, mirror neurons (MNs) have generated much interest as they are neurons that respond both to one's own actions as well as to the observation of others' actions. This sort of self–other (S–O) overlap within individual neurons, MNs, has drawn much interest because they likely represent a neural mechanism that contributes to action understanding—a possible neural basis for the rapid transformation of social information from perceptual to intentional.

In recent years however, much of the enthusiasm over MNs has been tempered by claims that they are not necessarily doing what many have theorized (e.g., Southgate & Hamilton, 2008; Cook, Bird, Catmur, Press, & Heyes, 2014; Catmur, 2015). Add to this the difficulty of noninvasively measuring MNs and we have a recipe for a multitude of claims about MNs with likely insufficient scrutiny of many of them (Dinstein, Thomas, Behrman, & Heeger, 2008; Hobson & Bishop, 2017). For example, there are multiple studies which conclude that MN activity was observed simply because blood oxygen changes occurred in areas believed to contain MNs (e.g., Iacoboni et al., 1999), or oscillations of a particular frequency believed to reflect MNs were modulated (e.g., Woodruff & Maaske, 2010). On the other hand, some papers admonishing caution, warranted as caution may be, seemed to miss some of the evidence suggestive of a degree of correspondence between the relevant brain measures and MN activity (e.g., Hobson & Bishop, 2017).

The Neuroscience of Empathy, Compassion, and Self-Compassion. http://dx.doi.org/10.1016/B978-0-12-809837-0.00006-4

This chapter will provide a brief review of the discovery of MNs, followed by a review of some of the most recent findings about them. We will discuss recent invasive, nonhuman animal research, functional magnetic resonance imaging (fMRI) and electroencephalography (EEG) studies, the role of MNs in action understanding, some theoretical models attempting to explain MNs, and end with suggestions for future directions. Anticipating the main conclusions of this chapter, we will argue that MNs play important roles in processes like empathy and compassion, but that current functional neuroimaging techniques, with perhaps a few methodological exceptions, are unable to isolate with certainty MN activity. We will also conclude that MN activity is not sufficient for action understanding because MNs are unlikely to inherently process S–O distinctions. However, their activity profiles do appear to be modulated by S–O distinctions and as such likely make important contributions to action understanding.

DISCOVERY OF MNS AND ATTEMPTS TO MEASURE THEM

MNs were first discovered in premotor cortex (PMC) (Fig. 6.1), field 5 (F5) of the macaque monkey brain somewhat by accident when an experimenter reached toward the monkey's peripersonal space to exchange target objects. To the researchers' surprise, the recorded neuron fired, albeit less vigorously, even though the monkey remained still with no particular intention to move (di Pellegrino, Fadiga, Fogassi, Gallese, & Rizzolatti, 1992). Eventually, Giacomo Rizzolatti and colleagues coined

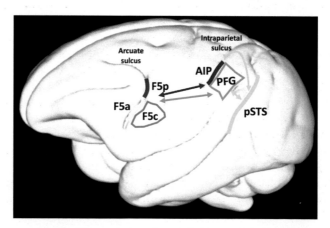

FIGURE 6.1   Regions in the macaque brain believed to be part of the mirror neuron system, as well as the pSTS, believed to provide input to the mirror neuron system.

these neurons MNs, indicating that they not only process one's own actions, but mirror the actions of others as well (Gallese, Fadiga, Fogassi, & Rizzolatti, 1996). As such, MNs are theorized to represent a very rapid mechanism whereby one understands another's intention because observation of the other's action activates that intention in the observer. Arguably, the substantial excitement around the discovery of MNs has contributed to the emergence of social cognitive neuroscience, using functional brain measures to test social-cognitive hypotheses. Such measures range from single-cell and linear multielectrode probes to noninvasive hemodynamic and electromagnetic measures to methods of manipulating MN activity (e.g., transcranial magnetic stimulation [TMS]).

Since the discovery of MNs in macaque monkey area F5, researchers have delineated two particular regions in the monkey brain which contain them: the inferior arcuate sulcus (IAS) and the intraparietal sulcus/inferior parietal lobule (IPL). The mirror properties of these two regions have been studied to a greater extent than some additional regions that have been subsequently identified as potential sites of MNs. These include medial supplementary motor area (SMA) and the hippocampus (in humans). Due to the preponderance of invasive data from macaque monkeys, much more is known about monkey MNs than human. Indeed, Rizzolatti and colleagues have published a recent series of papers describing various new findings related to MN activation profiles, location and interconnectivity between regions containing MNs (Kohler et al., 2002; Fogassi et al., 2005; Caggiano, Fogassi, Rizzolatti, Their, & Casile, 2009; Maeda, Ishida, Nakajima, Inase, & Murata, 2015; Rizzolatti & Fogassi, 2014; Giese & Rizzolatti, 2015). We will begin with MNs in area F5.

Ventral Premotor Cortex (vPMC). Area F5 lies within the banks of the IAS (Fig. 6.1) and contains neurons that appear to encode an animal's intentions (Umiltà et al., 2008; Caggiano et al., 2009; Caggiano et al., 2011). In a recent study using multielectrode linear arrays, Bonini (2014) found that approximately 41% of the neurons they recorded in area F5 were MNs. This region, which is just anterior to the frontal eye fields, has been divided into three subregions: F5a and F5p in the posterior bank of the IAS and F5c in the inferior convexity (Fig. 6.1).

Caggiano et al. (2009) reported newly discovered features of some F5 MNs, noting that about half of them were selective for either peripersonal or extrapersonal space, suggesting that these neurons are sensitive to whether an observed action occurs within the monkey's *actionable* space. Of these space-selective neurons, half of them were either coded in a metric space (Cartesian coordinates) or in an operational space. Caggiano et al. concluded that half were operational due to the fact that their receptive fields were dynamic. Within this class of so-called operational MNs, when presented with an object in peripersonal space, an operational MN with a peripersonal receptive field flipped its receptive field to peripersonal space when a transparent barrier was introduced between the monkey and the action while those neurons that coded peripersonal space stopped responding altogether. The critical point is that the introduced transparent barrier did not change the metric distance between the monkey and the action, but it did change the operational space. An action in peripersonal space that previously did not activate an extrapersonal MN, did activate it when that peripersonal space was rendered nonoperational by the transparent screen. In other words, these neurons seem to be less about precisely how close is the action taking place (metric distance), but is it taking place within an actionable, or operational, distance. This observation lends further support to the idea that some MNs are coding the meanings of actions rather than the simple spatial location of those actions.

Caggiano et al. (2011) reported that one-fourth of MNs from which they recorded in ventral F5 exhibited view-independent activity. In other words, these neurons fired to the observation of conspecifics' actions whether viewed from 0°, 90°, or 180° angles. Given that an animal's point-of-view is irrelevant to the action-goals of the individual he is observing (save, perhaps, cases where the observed is attempting to deceive the observer), neural activity reflecting the intentions of the other should not change with point-of-view. Rozzi and Coudé (2015) suggested that view-independent MNs may represent intentions at a higher-level of understanding whereas view-dependent MNs may be more focused on connecting visual descriptions of actions to motor goals. Following sections of this chapter will discuss the role these regions may play in action understanding and the potential for functional brain measures to reveal MN activity.

IPL. Subsequent to the discovery of MNs in F5, investigations have included a focus on monkey IPL where recordings have been taken in three subdivisions, PF, PFG and PG (Fogassi et al., 2005; Rozzi, Ferrari, Bonini, Rizzolatti, & Fogassi, 2008). Of these three, PFG appears to have been most consistently found to contain MNs. Fogassi et al. reported approximately 75% of recorded MNs in PFG were selective for an intention, responding when executing or observing an act of placing food in the mouth but not when the goal was to place the food in a container mounted on the shoulder, near the mouth. These data represent a double dissociation insofar as neurons that were selective for observing food-to-mouth actions did not respond to place-in-container, while those selective for placing-in-container did not respond to bringing-to-mouth, despite the fact that the arm movements were nearly identical. These results are consistent with the claim that IPL MNs reflect the intention of an observed action.

According to Rozzi et al. (2008), the tight correspondence between PFG MN response preferences for a specific goal to both the executed and observed motor acts lends support to the idea that MNs represent a direct matching between the perception of an actor's actions and the neural representation of those actions in the observer. As will be discussed later, these data are consistent with direct perception (DP) models insofar as it can be argued that perception of an action directly activates the motor plans for that action in the observer. Because PFG receives direct projections from the superior temporal sulcus (STS) (generally construed as a visual region selective to biological motion) and no such direct input to F5 has been found, Rozzi et al. suggested that area PFG may represent the first stage of the MN system.

Another parietal region receiving direct inputs from STS and containing MNs is anterior intraparietal (AIP) sulcus, an area involved in coding other's hand grasps (Rizzolatti & Sinigaglia, 2010). Interestingly, some of AIP's inputs come from a region in the lower bank of the STS that is considered part of the inferior temporal cortex, part of the classic visual ventral, "what" pathway, involved in identifying visual objects (Mishkin & Ungerleider, 1982). As discussed later, debate exists over whether MNs themselves encode the meaning of an action or whether this is done instead by posterior regions believed to process inferred meaning. The fact that AIP receives input from part of the "what" pathway suggests that MN coding of others intentions may be influenced by semantic input from the ventral visual stream. Considering the PFG and AIP findings together, Rizzolatti and Fogassi (2014) suggested that the STS is the source of visual perceptual information into the "MN circuit."

USING NEUROIMAGING TO INFER MN ACTIVATION

Various, relatively noninvasive, techniques have been used to explore correlates of the MN system. These include functional Magnetic Resonance Imaging (fMRI); electroencephalography (EEG); Magnetoencephalography (MEG); Transcranial Magnetic Stimulation (TMS) and transcranial direct current stimulation. The bulk of this work has involved the first two tools, fMRI and EEG, and this is where the focus of this chapter will be aimed. While these tools are indispensable for investigating the human MN system, they are not ideal and have serious limitations. These limitations include the inability to see activity anywhere close to the single-cell level and hence these techniques cannot reveal whether recorded brain signals reflect contributions from individual neurons that fire both during execution and observation of actions. We will discuss the virtues and limitations below as well as current research. We will conclude that these techniques are useful for studying the MN system, but that their limitations warrant great caution and restraint in drawing conclusions about mirror activity.

Extant research strongly suggests that EEG mu suppression, which is known to originate from sensorimotor cortex (Pfurtscheller, Neuper, Andrew, & Edlinger, 1997), is modulated by regions associated with MN's [e.g., vPMC (Pineda, 2005)]. Different labs define mu differently, with some defining it as 8–12/13 Hz, being comprised of the alpha band, while others define it as including alpha as well as 14–30 Hz beta. This latter framework might make sense insofar as mu refers to rhythms coming from the Rolandic fissure (sensorimotor cortex) and is historically associated with both execution and observation of actions. This contrasts with alpha rhythms, which are maximal in occipital electrodes, are *not* modulated by execution/observation, but are modulated by eyes open/eyes closed.

Since rhythms coming from sensorimotor cortex range from 8 to 30 Hz (Pfurtscheller et al., 1997; Hari et al., 1998), it is reasonable to consider both sensorimotor alpha and beta as part of the mu complex (Hari & Salmelin, 1997; Cook et al., 2014). Regardless of nomenclature, significant correlations between 8 and 13 Hz mu and several brain regions traditionally not associated with MNs strongly suggest that mu suppression is nothing like a "pure" measure of MNs (Yin, Liu, & Mingzhou, 2016; Braadbaart, Williams, & Waiter, 2013; Fox et al., 2015). Rather, with potential contributions from as many as seven brain regions, mu suppression could potentially reflect seven, or more, various cognitive and/or emotion processes, thereby creating ambiguity with respect to correlations between mu suppression, behavior and self-report measures. As such, future research should include efforts to resolve this ambiguity. One way might be to "clean" data using methods like Laplacian spatial transformation to potentially distinguish separate contributions to the mu rhythm.

Another useful approach could be to link, to the extent possible, activity in these supposedly MN-unrelated regions to mirroring-unrelated processes. Once identified, holding these mirror-unrelated psychological processes constant in experimental paradigms, we could minimize expected contributions from the MN-unrelated brain regions [e.g., middle frontal gyrus (mFG), cerebellum and thalamus].

Given that Rizzolatti and colleagues discovered MNs in the vPMC of macaque monkeys, it seems reasonable to assume that they exist in human vPMC. Of course, this assumption is nothing more than an untested hypothesis without supporting evidence. However, measures of human MNs (e.g., fMRI, EEG, MEG) in most cases have not allowed the inference that observed effects were specifically related to MNs. In all noninvasive functional brain measures, signals are observed only with a sufficient number of neurons (greater than 10k) synchronously undergoing postsynaptic potentials (Logothetis et al., 2001). Since a MN is defined as *a* neuron that fires both during execution and observation, it requires the ability to see the activity of a particular neuron during both conditions. Any measure, therefore, that requires 10k+ neurons to generate an observable signal could not, strictly speaking, reveal whether a subset (no study has reported greater than 50% of sampled neurons within a given region to be MNs) of those are active at all, let alone whether they are active during both execution and observation.

One particular experimental paradigm, however, offers a possible means of inferring successive activation of a specific population of neurons. *Repetition Suppression* (RS) is a phenomenon observed with noninvasive functional brain measures that occurs when individual neurons are activated by the same stimulus as in the preceding trial. RS is a measure of the magnitude of attenuation of the response of these neurons to the second presentation of the stimulus, relative to the response of the neurons to the initial presentation of the repeated stimulus. The attenuation in RS derives from this reduced, or suppressed, neural response to the second, repeated stimulus. Since the stimuli are identical, it is assumed that the identical neurons are active in response to both the first and the second stimulus presentation and that the suppression results from the identical neurons being less active during the second presentation, rather than from a reduction in the total number of neurons responding (Henson, 2003).

Regarding the measuring of MNs, RS has been used with fMRI and EEG to measure successive activation of the same population of neurons in a crossmodal condition. To understand, consider that motor system activity is reduced for the execution of the second of two identical actions. If a MN is active in response to both execution and observation of the same action, then the second activation of that MN should be suppressed, both when action execution is followed again by execution of that action and also when action execution is followed by *observation* of that action (and vice versa). In the latter, crossmodal condition, only neurons that respond both to execution and observation should be candidates for RS. Such neurons by definition would be MNs as they would be neurons that respond to both execution and observation.

In a clever pair of experiments, Simon and Mukamel (2015a,b) separately used EEG and fMRI to test the hypothesis that MN-related electrical activity and hemodynamic responses, respectively, are dependent on conscious processing. Predicated on the assumption that action understanding requires *conscious* understanding, they asked whether putative measures of MN activity would show sensitivity to whether observed stimuli were perceived consciously. Using the continuous flash suppression paradigm (Tsuchiya & Koch, 2005), they presented to one eye a brief hand movement and to the other a Mondrian display (a seemingly random, geometric display of multiple color swatches), each image flickering on and off in opposite phase of one another, so that, at any given instance, only one eye was being stimulated. With this masking technique, they were able to mask from conscious perception the presentation of some of the hand actions. By comparing putative MN activity elicited by consciously perceived stimuli to that elicited by stimuli not consciously perceived, Simon and Mukamel asked whether these apparent MN measures would be sensitive to this manipulation of conscious perception. We will consider the EEG results, then the fMRI, followed by a discussion of the degree to which the two data sets complement one another.

Simon and Mukamel (2015a) looked at sensorimotor suppression in both the mu (8–13 Hz) and the beta (15–25 Hz) rhythms at central electrode sites C3 and C4, proximal to the central sulcus—the generator of Rolandic mu and beta rhythms (Pineda, 2005). They found sensitivity to conscious perception both in the beta and in a subband of mu (8–10 Hz) whereby suppression was greater for consciously perceived stimuli relative to ones not consciously perceived. As mentioned above, because the frequency band range of occipital alpha rhythms is identical to mu rhythms (8–13 Hz), it is difficult to know to what extent the effects observed in central electrodes in Simon and Mukamel's study may have been driven by alpha, rather than mu, suppression. However, a significant interaction involving electrodes revealed that the pattern of suppression in 8–13 Hz range was different, thereby supporting the claim that the effects in central electrodes could not be due solely to posterior alpha.

The fMRI version of this experiment was very similar in design, though it included an additional opacity manipulation, with half of the observed hand actions being presented with low opacity, and hence being consciously perceived less often. Focusing on the hemodynamic response differences to consciously and not-consciously perceived stimuli, Simon and Mukamel (2015b) found multiple regions believed to contain MNs, including dorsal PMC, primary motor cortex (M1) and somatosensory cortex that were more active when the stimuli were consciously perceived. Two additional and adjacent regions were also preferentially activated by consciously perceived stimuli: (1) The pSTS, a region that is not believed to contain MNs, but is suggested to provide the biological motion detection needed to activate the MN system, and (2) The TPJ, an area not known to contain MNs but commonly believed to be involved in inferential processes associated with so-called *mentalizing* as well as S–O discrimination. Since these five regions were more active during conscious perception, Simon and Mukamel argue that these regions fulfill one necessary condition of action understanding—conscious perception of that action.

There are limitations of course to exactly what conclusions can be drawn from these two studies. To begin with, there is great uncertainty in the degree to which either mu/beta suppression or fMRI activation in classic MN regions reflects the activity of MNs and MNs alone. Concerning mu suppression, we know that it is correlated with activity in PMC, consistent with the claim that mu suppression results from the desynchronizing input of PMC to sensorimotor cortex (Pineda, 2005), but we also know that it is correlated with various other regions, some not obviously part of the MN system. For example, Braadbaart et al. (2013) found that, in addition to regions commonly believed to contain MNs (iFG, PMC, IPL), mu suppression was similarly correlated with activation in the cerebellum, middle temporal lobes, mFG and the thalamus. While the possibility exists that MNs will be discovered in these regions, one must assume the null hypothesis for now—that these areas do not contain MNs. Therefore, it should probably be assumed that any instance of measuring mu suppression likely reflects mirror- and mirror-unrelated activity. Nonetheless, the results of this pair of studies (Simon & Mukamel, 2015a,b) are intriguing in their consistency with the hypothesis that, to the extent that MN activity is associated with action understanding, it is necessarily associated with conscious perception.

Mizuguchi, Nakata, and Kanosue (2016) provided evidence that what they refer to as the action observation network (AON), which includes premotor and inferior parietal regions, is insensitive to inferences about another person's actions while TPJ and pSTS are sensitive. They presented participants with separate videos of two different actors (one small in stature and the other large and muscular) lifting light and heavy dumbbells, with the participants inferring that the smaller stature actor was working harder to lift the heavy weights. This allowed the researchers to analyze fMRI results and to determine that the AON does not respond differentially, whereas TPJ and pSTS do. These results show that the latter brain structures are likely involved in inferencing of the sort characterized by inferring effort while the former appear not to be. Of course, this study represents but only one particular instance of inference (i.e., how much effort is the actor exerting), but it is inferencing specifically about bodily exertion and presumably not about mentalizing. These data suggest that even inferences about motor events may not be happening in the AON; otherwise, one would expect these regions (PMC and IPL) to show differential activation. Of course, absence of evidence is not evidence of absence, so further research should continue to address this question, but the data seem to be in line with claims that MN regions, as constituted by the AON, are not involved in inferential processes, and therefore are unlikely to play a key role in inferring the meaning of an action.

PUTATIVE MEASURES OF MNs AND EMPATHY

MNs are theorized to be involved in empathy and perspective-taking (PT), supported by research from multiple labs that have reported fMRI and EEG measures of putative MN activity that are correlated with PT and empathy. Schülte-Ruther, Markowitsch, Fink, and Piefke (2007) were among the first to report that activations in two different regions, one believed to be in the MN system (left and right inferior frontal) and one believed to be the source of input to MNs, pSTS (Bonini, 2016), were correlated with self-reported empathy.

Complementary to these findings, Zaki, Weber, Bolger, and Ochsner (2009) used fMRI to find brain regions activated by an empathic accuracy (EA) task in which participants gave affective ratings of videos of an actor revealing emotional stories form her/his life. The actor in the stimulus videos had previously given their own ratings of their affect moment by moment and this timecourse of affective ratings was correlated with the actor's own judgments—higher correlations meant higher EA. Zaki et al. found that greater accuracy was associated with greater fMRI activity in PMC, intraparietal sulcus (IPS), superior temporal sulcus (STS), dorsal medial prefrontal cortex (dmPFC), medial prefrontal cortex (mPFC). The PMC and IPL correlations with EA are consistent with the claim that MN function is related to empathy.

Perry, Troje, and Bentin (2010) found significant mu and beta suppression responses to point-light displays of individuals walking. Mu suppression was found to be greatest for a condition that required inferring the intentions of the individual (walking toward or away) as compared to identifying the gender, suggesting that mu suppression reflects activity related to action understanding. Perry et al. were also the first to report a significant correlation between mu suppression and self-reported empathy, as measured by the empathy quotient (EQ; Baron-Cohen & Wheelwright, 2004). Surprisingly, the relationship was negative, such that greater mu suppression was associated with lower EQ scores.

On its own, the negative relationship found by Perry, Troje, and Bentin (2010) could be considered an anomaly. The finding does not stand alone however, as it has been reported by at least two other labs (Woodruff & Klein, 2013; Horan et al., 2014). Woodruff et al. (2011a) initially found a negative relationship between mu suppression and the PT subscale of the interpersonal reactivity index (IRI; Davis, 1983). Although the correlation was nonsignificant after removing an outlier, the negative relationship pointed the researchers to the idea that mu suppression may have a nonlinear relationship to PT, whereby absence of mu suppression (as seen in some studies of individuals with autism (Oberman et al., 2005)), relates to poor PT, while high-levels also work against PT. It may be that, in order to take another's perspective, a moderate amount of mu suppression is ideal. This could be predicted by theories of empathy that emphasize the importance of S–O discrimination (e.g., Batson et al., 1991). This construct is argued to be necessary to keep the social observer from reacting to the intentions of the person he is observing. Because PT implies that the observer recognizes that the intentions he is experiencing belong to the other, not to himself, low S–O discrimination would lead to a focus of attention on the self as though those intentions belonged to the self. Rather, under this model of empathy, PT occurs when the observer's brain is able to distinguish between its own intentions and those of the person he is observing. Consequently, Woodruff et al. (2011a) computed mu suppression difference scores (execution–observation) and found that these difference scores were positively related to PT, consistent with the hypothesis that PT occurs to the extent that the observer's brain is able to sort his own intentions from the ones he is receiving from the observed. A similar finding was subsequently reported by Hoenen, Schain, and Pause (2013).

These experiments show a distinct relationship with empathy and PT, albeit not as straightforward as some would have guessed. The processes reflected by mu suppression appear to subserve empathy, not by enabling the observer to "become" the observed, but to experience some of the observed individual's intentions, however not so much that the observer's brain becomes confused by whose intentions belong to whom.

DOES MU SUPPRESSION REFLECT MNs? YES, AND THEN SOME

A seminal paper on which much of the mu suppression research has been based was published by Pineda (2005) in which he makes a compelling case that suppression of the sensorimotor mu rhythm likely reflects MN input to sensorimotor cortex. Founded on the nearly universal assumption that the EEG signal is generated by postsynaptic potentials, desynchronization of the mu rhythm would be the result of input from PMC, and the MNs within, inducing postsynaptic potentials in sensorimotor neurons. Suppression of oscillatory brain rhythms is believed to reflect the desynchronization of neural oscillations, relative to those oscillations when neural activity is at baseline. This logic can be understood in the example of a 100-member choir: the choir is louder when everyone sings together, compared to say, a solo voice. No matter how loud the soloist sings, she will not have a louder voice than the other 99 members of the choir, even if each choir member is singing at a lower volume than the soloist. This of course is because, when everyone sings together, the sound waves are synchronized and add to one another. Even if everyone is singing quietly, the sound waves of 99 vocalists can add up to a larger number of decibels than a soloist singing at maximum volume.

Therefore, the activation-related desynchronization of the sensorimotor mu rhythm is argued to result from MN input. This section will evaluate evidence relevant to the question of whether mu suppression reflects MN activity. Research will be cited to support the role of MNs in suppressing the EEG mu rhythm, but not exclusively so. The resulting argument will be advanced that, regardless of the extent to which mu suppression does reflect MN and non-MN activity, the signal does appear to be related to empathic processes.

If indeed mu suppression is reflecting MN input, then it should correlate with activation in brain regions believed to contain MNs. Yin et al. (2016) used a combined EEG-fMRI paradigm in which they assessed correlations between mu suppression and BOLD responses. Using Second Order Blind Identification (Tang, Sutherland, & McKinney, 2005) in an attempt to disentangle mu from alpha rhythms, they found correlations in classic MN regions (i.e., the IFG and the IPL) as well as in an area reported to contain MNs in humans (Mukamel, Ekstrom, Kaplan, Iacoboni, & Fried, 2010), namely, the SMA. Not surprisingly, they found that mu suppression also correlated with regions not previously identified as areas containing MNs, including superior frontal, superior parietal cortices, superior, middle and inferior temporal gyri as well as the middle cingulate and precuneus. Those are quite a few areas not traditionally associated with MNs whose potential contributions to mu suppression are concerning points for research using mu suppression as an indicator of MNs.

Hobson and Bishop (2016) report results of a cleverly designed and high powered ($N = 61$) experiment intended to directly evaluate the extent to which mu suppression can be disentangled from posterior alpha and to assess mu suppression's topographic specificity. Using a baseline (moving kaleidoscopic videos) that appears to have drawn participants' attention more than the typical execution and observation conditions, their results indicated that observing this relatively salient baseline condition elicited more alpha blocking in occipital electrodes than did action execution but that this was not the case for central electrodes. If the mu suppression observed by Hobson and Bishop were explained by occipital-derived alpha, one would expect the greater desynchronization seen in occipital alpha to be evident in the central electrodes as well. As the authors note, their results indicate that distinguishing sensorimotor-specific mu rhythms from occipital alpha is possible, at least for action execution. The same pattern was not found however for action observation; Hobson and Bishop (2016) were unable to distinguish mu reactivity from alpha during action observation, suggesting that caution is warranted when attempting to isolate mu suppression during action observation.

Hobson and Bishop (2017) claim that there are few published studies that assessed whether mu suppression can be distinguished from alpha suppression. However, despite citing Woodruff et al. (2011a), they do not mention that this study found a significant interaction between task (execution, observation) and region (central, occipital). Using execution–observation difference scores, Woodruff et al. found that difference scores were all significantly different from null for the central electrodes only. Occipital difference scores were not significantly different from zero and tended toward enhancement rather than suppression (Fig. 6.2). As suggested by Hannah Hobson (personal communique), however, this difference could be explained as occipital alpha, with a contribution from Rolandic mu during execution, but not during observation. It seems

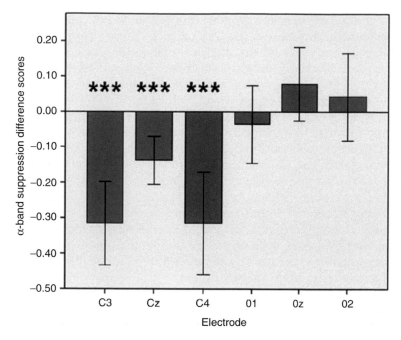

FIGURE 6.2   **Mu suppression self–other difference scores from Woodruff et al. (2011a).** Difference scores were significantly different than zero for the central electrodes (all $p < .001$), but not for occipital electrodes. Furthermore, difference scores related positively to self-reported perspective-taking. Error bars represent 2 SEM.

unlikely however, that this alternative explanation could readily account for why, if central electrode 8–13 Hz suppression reflects Rolandic mu during execution but posterior alpha during observation, execution–observation (S–O) difference scores should correlate with self-reported PT (Woodruff, Martin, & Bilyk, 2011a). Regardless, consideration of this dissociation is important when arguing that mu suppression is not a reliable measure of MN activity.

An important point to consider when comparing the pattern of results from Hobson and Bishop (2016) to most other mu suppression experiments is that they calculated mu desynchronization in a different, though not unprecedented (Muthukumaraswamy & Johnson, 2004a), way. While mu suppression is typically computed as log(task/baseline) (Pineda, 2005), they subtracted task from baseline (task–baseline). This computational difference not only means that their results cannot be directly compared to results utilizing Pineda's convention, but also that their results may be influenced by individual differences in baseline mu suppression. Using ratios normalizes scores so that one is looking at percentage differences rather than absolute differences. For these reasons, caution is warranted in comparing Hobson and Bishop's results to most published mu suppression research.

Fox et al. (2015) performed a meta-analysis on 85 mu suppression studies, testing two hypotheses in particular: (1) If mu suppression reflects MN activity and can be dissociated from posterior alpha, then the meta-analysis should reveal topographical specificity, and (2) if mu suppression reflects MNs, biological, compared to nonbiological, motion stimuli should elicit more mu suppression. With regard to the first hypothesis, topographic specificity was found for mu suppression induced by action execution in that the strongest effect size was in central electrodes with confidence intervals not overlapping with effects in frontal, parietal, and occipital electrodes. This finding indicates that for action execution, the source of mu suppression likely is around the central sulcus, consistent with a sensorimotor source. It should be noted that confirming exactly where the generator of mu suppression is requires a solution to the inverse problem (Jun et al., 2005). Although the central electrodes showed the greatest effect size, without source localization, there is no guarantee that the signal is generated in the sensorimotor cortex. Nonetheless, the data for action execution are encouraging.

The data are less so with regard to such specificity for action observation. The confidence intervals for the effect sizes in all five regions tested (frontal, central, parietal, occipital, temporal) were overlapping, although the authors noted that the n for observation studies was low and that the hypothesis test therefore may have been underpowered. The possibility should be considered that the generator of suppression in the 8–13-Hz range for action observation is distinct from the generator for action execution. As well, it is possible that there are common generators for execution and observation, but that observation-induced suppression may have additional, nonsensorimotor, non-MN generators.

Considering the various findings related to mu suppression as a measure of MN activity, it is likely that mu rhythms do include input from MNs, but also potentially from many other brain regions not believed to contain MNs. Furthermore, not all research measuring mu suppression argues that the signal reflects MNs. As such, future reports of mu suppression research should not attempt to draw strong conclusions about MNs and should focus conclusions instead on mu suppression. Regardless of the actual source of the signal, mu suppression does appear to relate reliably to empathic processes (Hoenen et al., 2013; Perry et al., 2010; Woodruff et al., 2011b; Woodruff & Klein, 2013).

BETA RHYTHMS AND MNs

There is also evidence that oscillations, within the beta frequency (here defined as 14–30 Hz), recorded at central sites, have a similar potential to reflect MN modulation of sensorimotor cortex (Cheng, Tzeng,

Decety, Imada, & Hsieh, 2006; Hari et al., 1998; Muthukumaraswamy & Johnson, 2004b; Pfurtscheller et al., 1997). Like the 8–13 Hz mu rhythms, beta rhythms have been observed to desynchronize in reaction to execution and observation of movements. Given this mirror-like response pattern as well as the high degree of certainty of a sensorimotor generator of the signal, it has been argued that beta rhythms can be taken as a marker of MN activity.

On the other hand, multiple labs have reported beta enhancement rather than suppression, though these have tended to involve static rather than moving stimuli (Güntekin & Başar, 2007; Güntekin & Başar, 2009; Güntekin & Başar, 2010; Woodruff, Daut, Brower, & Bragg, 2011b). Using negative and neutral stimuli from the International Affective Picture Scale (IAPS), both Güntekin and Başar and Woodruff et al., found that a relative synchronization of the beta rhythm was elicited by negative stimuli. Woodruff et al. also administered the IRI and found that greater beta synchronization elicited by negative stimuli was correlated with higher dispositional PD. These findings of synchronization appear contradictory to the desynchronization findings mentioned above (Hari et al., 1998; Muthukumaraswamy & Johnson, 2004a). But, in addition to resulting from static rather than motion stimuli, the stimuli associated with enhancement, IAPS images of highly negative imagery, in some cases grotesque, were highly emotional while the stimuli eliciting beta desynchronization have tended to involve simple hand movements. This observation points to two intriguing alternative possibilities: beta enhancement/suppression represents two states of one system, or it represents two distinct systems, both oscillating in the beta range. The latter possibility implies that the beta oscillations observed at central electrode sites would be a mixture of these two different beta generators. While it might be worthwhile to investigate this question using methods such as blind source separation (e.g., Tang et al., 2005), or inverse modeling (Jun et al., 2005), some extant data offer some interesting details about enhancement/suppression, with one experiment demonstrating, for the first time, both enhancement and suppression within the same experiment.

Our lab recently conducted three different experiments looking at beta enhancement/suppression (Woodruff et al., 2016; Woodruff et al., in prep.). Fig. 6.3 shows the results of three experiments that reveal three distinct patterns of beta enhancement/suppression, divided into two hertz sub bands. Both A and C represent two, as yet unpublished, datasets from two different EA tasks (see Zaki et al., 2009), while B represents data from an emotion discrimination task. While the three tasks differ from one another in important ways, they have in common designs that allow distinguishing self- from other-related beta reactivity. In B, we see a distinct difference between beta elicited by participants' judgments of their own versus others' emotional state. When asked how the

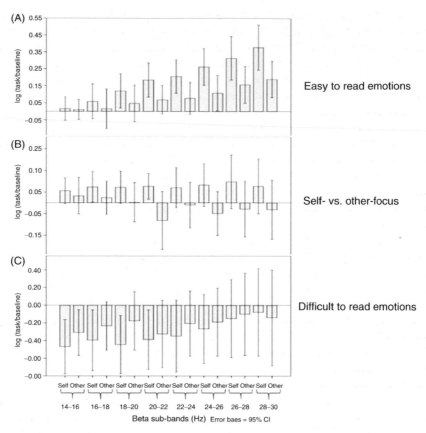

FIGURE 6.3 Beta-band (14–30 Hz; subdivided into 2 Hz bins) suppression/enhancement from central electrodes from three different experiments: Woodruff, Barbera, & Von Oepen, 2016a; Brown et al., in prep.; Woodruff et al., in prep.

person in a photograph felt, beta responses were negative, below zero, indicating suppression. However, when the question for the same photographs asked, "How does the way this person feels make you feel?" beta responses were greater than zero, indicating beta enhancement. These data are the first to demonstrate beta enhancement and suppression within the same task as a function of identity (Woodruff, Goodman & Brown, *in preparation*).

The three datasets taken together indicate a task-related electrophysiological dissociation of beta enhancement/inhibition. These outcomes raise the question of what sociocognitive processes vary across these three experiments that could explain the obtained distinct patterns of data. We suggest an explanation based on the focus of attention to self-relevant compared to other-relevant information. Experiment A involved an EA task of a similar design to experiment C with the difference being that social targets in A were much more emotionally expressive than those in C. As concerns self-focus, because social targets were more expressive, emotion recognition processes were not particularly taxed, leaving attentional resources available for reflection on how the social target's emotions are impacting the self. Indeed, experiment B, in which participants viewed photographs of emotional facial expressions (Ekman & Friesen, 1976), supports this conjecture by showing that participants exhibit beta suppression when asked "How does this person feel?" compared to "How does the way this person feels make you feel?" As can be seen in Fig. 6.3B, focusing on the feelings of individuals in the photographs was associated with suppression throughout much of the beta band range when the question required other-focused attention. In contrast, focusing on one's own emotional reaction to another's feelings was associated primarily with enhancement.

As for experiment C, the task was rather difficult for participants as can be seen by the rather low mean EA correlations for C ($r = .24$) compared to A ($r = .70$). The reason for the difference in task difficulty can be explained by the fact that social targets in C were less emotionally expressive than those in A. It follows that participants in C would need to focus more attentional resources on the target's emotional expressions leaving fewer resources to process the impact on the self. Once again, experiment B supports this claim as it found that other-focused attention related to suppression while self-focused attention related to enhancement. There are then two distinct possibilities as concerns beta enhancement versus suppression: (1) Beta represents one neural process that in some cases synchronizes above baseline (self-focus) and in other cases desynchronizes (other-focus), (2) The generators of the synchronization and desynchronization may represent distinct sets of neurons such that self-focus and other-focus differentially engage these sets. The sociocognitive hypothesis predicts that the scalp distributions of the beta activity will differ significantly between tasks, suggesting that they derive from at least partially nonoverlapping areas of tissue, while the other predicts that, because the neural tissue is assumed to be identical, no difference should obtain. These questions could be addressed by assessing scalp potential distributions (a significant difference would imply two distinct generators) or inverse modeling. Until then, we offer an observation that, in experiment B, it could be argued that the task difficulty is greater for the self-focused condition ("How does the way this person feels make you feel?") as it requires first assessing the emotions of the others and then how that emotion makes the participant feel. The other-focused task by contrast only requires the first of those two processes. Therefore, instead of beta suppression seen with the easier, other-focused task, the task-difficulty hypothesis predicts that, despite being a task focused on others' emotions (experiment C), because it is easier, it should be associated with synchronization rather than desynchronization.

DO MNs CONSTITUTE OR CONTRIBUTE TO ACTION UNDERSTANDING?

This fascinating debate has taken place since at least Hickok's (2009) sharply and concisely titled paper, *Eight Problems for the Mirror Neuron Theory of Action Understanding in Monkeys and Humans*. Perhaps, one of the most productive publications relevant to this debate is one titled *Mirror Neuron Forum* (Gallese, Gernsbacher, Heyes, Hickok, & Iacoboni, 2011) in which leading researchers discussed several issues including the question of MNs' relationship to action understanding. The five contributing authors manage to discuss the question from surprisingly "orthogonal" perspectives ranging from Vittorio Gallese's concept that MNs represent embodied simulation to Cecelia Heyes' evolutionary/developmental account of MNs to Hickok's claim that MN activity does not constitute action understanding. In this section, we will consider some of the philosophical underpinnings of various models, some of the evidence from invasive brain recordings taken to support them, as well as noninvasive recordings (fMRI and EEG), in monkeys and humans. We will conclude that certain questions, such as, "Does action understanding *occur* in MN regions or sensory regions?" conflates levels of analysis. Action understanding should not be considered a property unique to, or fundamentally constitutive of, MN function, nor should it be considered to reside in sensory (Hickok, 2009) systems to the exclusion of mirror mechanisms.

Hickok (2009) makes an argument that combines two observations: (1) the supposed lack of a direct match between the intent of the observed action and the intention encoded by the specific MN, and (2) with the claim that certain actions are ambiguous with respect to their intentions with the same action being associated with multiple possible intentions. For example, if you were in a taxi passing someone looking at the taxi and waiving her hand, it would be difficult to determine whether the person was waving at you or hailing the taxi. Strictly speaking, responding to the sight of an object would be visual processing and should not therefore be part of pure motor processing. On the other hand, there exists in PMC, canonical neurons that respond to the sight of particular objects, apparently as a function of the motor affordances these objects offer. Indeed, how could the activity of the motor system be "about" anything if it did not have a specific relationship to sensory input and to the effects of motor output, as evidenced by sensory feedback? It is likely untenable to view the aboutness of a motor plan as being contained within a specific type of neuron. Equally likely untenable is the claim that the aboutness comes simply from the sensory-evaluated consequences of the motor plan. The aboutness instead is more likely best viewed as the property that arises with highly correlated sensory input, motor output and sensory feedback. By this logic, MNs could not be "where" action understanding occurs—conversely, sensory systems could not be "where" action understanding occurs. Rather, each of these components are subprocesses of action understanding, suggesting future research should concern itself not with any constitutive action understanding theory of MNs but with further characterizing the likely contribution they make to generating emergent action understanding.

Interestingly, a different argument can clearly be made that in such ambiguous situations MNs would on their own be unable to discern between the two possible intentions (hailing a cab vs. waving to a friend). Since MNs by definition respond only to perception of biological motion stimuli, MNs should be ignorant of any nonbiological stimuli, such as the taxi cab [although, inferior temporal cortex input to AIP might suggest otherwise (Nelissen et al., 2011)]. If MN processes cannot on their own process the taxi cab, in motion or not, then they could not on their own understand that the waving is intended to hail the taxi. Because MNs cannot ostensibly process nonbiological stimuli and because in many the meaning of action lies in relationship to a changing world, much of it is nonbiological and therefore inaccessible to MNs.

While it is likely true that action understanding involves the sensory consequences of a motor intention, the claim that action understanding is exclusively a result of processing sensory consequences of a motor intention does not recognize the emergent nature of this construct and it denies a likely important motor contribution. While individual MNs could not possibly be sufficient for action understanding, it would be very surprising indeed if they played no role whatsoever. Rather than action understanding arising simply from MN activity or from purely sensory processing, a likely more progressive approach is to view both sorts of processing as necessary antecedents to action understanding.

Direct-Matching and Inferential Processing Models: Various models of intention understanding have been offered, differentiated primarily by whether they model intention understanding as *what happens* when observation of another's actions activates the corresponding intention in the observer's mirror system or they model it as a more "deliberative" process of inference. Here we will briefly discuss two different models that can be used to explain the MN system's role, or lack thereof, in action understanding. The first of these models is Direct-Matching, or DP, models which hold that MN activation is sufficient for action understanding, claiming that "motor-perception" occurs by virtue of the sensory perception of an action leading to the motor plan for that action (Michael, 2011; Michael & De Bruin, 2015). Inferential processing (IP) models are on the other end of the spectrum of MN involvement in action understanding because they tend to deny a role of MNs in action understanding (Csibra, 2008), and in some cases, claim that MN activation requires action understanding rather than the other way around.

Evidence in favor of DP models includes the observation that F5 neurons coding a grasping goal do not vary as a function of the method used for grasping (left hand, right hand and mouth). Further evidence comes from Umiltà et al. (2008) who found that some F5 neurons responded to the monkey's grasping of an object with a pair of pliers, even when using different pliers engineered to require different hand movements to operate. Traditional pliers require squeezing the handles together to grasp an object. These traditional pliers were used in addition to a pair that required the opposite hand movement—rather than squeezing, these required opening the hand to make the pliers grasp the object. Using this clever manipulation of squeezing versus opening while holding the goal constant for both types of pliers (grasp the object), the researchers were able to isolate neurons that fired to a particular goal regardless of the motor movements used to achieve it. Taken together, these data support the claim that F5 neurons code the intentions of the animal.

Caroline Catmur (2015) offers a more skeptical view, laying out four conditions she believes MN activity profiles must meet in order for that activation to constitute DP of another's intention. First, she suggests that perception of another's actions *should activate only one motor intention in the observer*. This postulate might be an overly simplistic characterization of what actually happens. Instead, understanding may NOT comprise activation of a single intention but graded activation of multiple, highly-related processes, with the intention associated with peak activation corresponding to the observer's best guess about the other's intention. It is certainly the case that a particular intention would come to dominate this graded activation and could be seen as Catmur's "only one intention." Otherwise, the first condition may not be a necessary one.

\Catmur goes on to argue that an additional condition is that the solitary intention activated in the observer must correspond to exactly one intention in the actor. Using the reasoning above, a more realistic view may be that the graded activation of multiple intentions corresponds to a graded activation in the other's brain, with significant overlap between the graded distributions of intentions. While condition two seems reasonable, condition three is not so clear. The third condition suggests that "…this mapping from motor program to intention must be the same in the observer as in the actor…" This condition seems to ignore the central claim of the DP models—that the motor program *is* the intention. Admittedly, as Catmur and others have pointed out, this reasoning may constitute circular logic insofar as proving that MNs code intentions involves showing that MNs are active when the animal activates an intention. But the hypothesis that the motor program simply is the intention is not inherently circular, only the notion that proving the hypothesis involves merely showing that MNs are active when the animal has an intention is circular. In other words, if one assumes the activation of MNs to indicate the activation of an intention, one cannot use as evidence for that assumption, the fact that MNs are active—this is circular. Instead, one must manipulate intentions to determine whether MN activity changes, and indeed it does (e.g., Umiltà et al., 2008). If this is correct, then Catmur's third condition is not really a condition. Rather the mapping required by that condition exists insofar as the motor program just is the intention. This is not a one-to-one mapping, but rather an identity. According to direct-perception models, they are one in the same thing, equivalent to saying that A must map directly onto A.

Condition four seems to similarly confound the issue in that it requires that the activation of a motor plan must automatically lead to the activation of the corresponding intention. These conditions necessarily fail to be met by direct-perception models simply because the conditions deny the fundamental tenet of DP models—that motor programs *are* intentions. And, as Michael (2011) notes, they run the risk of implying dualism because the arguments seem to rest on the assumption that neural activity is not itself the intention, but rather somehow maps *onto* the intention. That is, to say that activating a certain motor plan must activate an intention begs the question of what the intention is. If it's not some set of neural activity, then is it some nonphysical substance? Having said this, it is likely proper not to regard the intention as "in the neurons" but rather as a property that emerges when the activation of these neurons has a specific relationship to the world.

There is still one necessary condition DP models fail to meet but that does not deny the assumption that motor programs *are* intentions. This condition is that activated motor programs distinguish between self and other—understanding another's intention necessitates understanding that the perceived intention belongs not to the observer but to the observed. Despite the fact that MN activation distinguishes self from other, S–O discrimination is unlikely to derive from MN processes themselves but more likely reentrant processing from areas that infer agency. Put differently, if MNs represent intentions, how do they represent *whose* intention? It is unlikely they do. Rather, according to S–O discrimination research, this function seems to have more to do with the temporoparietal junction than classic MN regions.

DP is a compelling idea in many ways, not the least of which is the way it offers a parsimonious neural mechanism for embodied models of social processing. It would seem very efficient for natural selection to have favored understanding others' intentions with the very same brain regions that correspond to understanding our own intentions. To have one's brain and affective states "resonate" with another's would seem to be a relatively quick and relatively low-cost process for experiencing the intentions of others.

However, it is not the case that *experiencing* the intentions of another is equivalent to *understanding* the intentions of another. Suppose that I were to experience your intention to eat ice cream but that I did *not* go through the additional, presumably cognitive (Michael, 2011), inferential, step of recognizing that the intention I was experiencing was not my own but one that I was experiencing because I observed you act on said intention. With the circumvention of this inferential step, I am likely to have the experience of intending to eat the ice cream myself. Surely it is illogical to suppose that I understand *your* intentions if I (erroneously) believe the intention belongs to me. In this case, if asked, I presumably would be unable to answer what was your intention. Rather, I would be able to report only what I falsely perceived as my own intention, at which time I would proceed to wrestle you to the floor for the waffle cone, especially if it were peanut butter and chocolate!

Rather, it is suggested here that strict DP models are nonstarters regarding sufficiency to explain intention understanding. To the extent that they assume that intention understanding occurs without processing the fact that these intentions belong to the other, they deny a necessary condition for intention understanding—agent attribution. It might be argued that MNs themselves code information about intention attribution (Bonini, 2016). Indeed, MNs in the PMC show a variety of preferences, with the preponderance of PMC neurons responding to self-actions more than observation of others' (Rozzi & Coudé, 2015). In other words, most PMC neurons are more active when an animal has the intention to perform an action himself, with significantly fewer neurons activated by observing the actions of others. Additionally, while some projections from PMC (specifically, F5p) do extend directly to the spinal cord, it is to propriospinal and not spinal motor neurons, and therefore not to neurons that synapse with muscles. It is suggested that this is one means by which the observer is able to avoid automatically acting on another person's intentions: PMC MNs do not appear to activate spinal motor neurons, but rather must go through one or more synapses to influence motor output.

An interesting question that emerges here begs whether such apparent S–O discrimination is a *fundamental capacity* of MNs, or is MN activation modulated by *efferent connections* from regions whose job is S–O differentiation (regions like, TPJ). Interestingly, this hypothesis could be tested by exploiting the temporal resolution of EEG to determine the timecourse of S–O differentiation in mu suppression. The *fundamental capacity model* predicts that S–O differentiation should be evident from the onset of mu suppression, whereas the *efferent connections model* predicts no significant difference in mu suppression early in time, only emerging once regions such as the TPJ have settled on a conclusion about whether the action is the observer's or the observed's. Therefore, another test of this hypothesis would involve establishing whether MN regions receive efferent connections from areas like TPJ.

The latter model is consistent with the claim that processes such as action understanding cannot be pointed to in the brain but rather happen as multiple parallel routes of processing increasingly modulate one another over time. Empathic understanding of another's actions might be described as a process that starts with motor simulation of the other's affective state (related to MN activation), followed by subthreshold potentiation of peripheral muscles and resultant changes in skin conductance, facial expression and posture (i.e., the chameleon effect: Chartrand & Bargh, 1999). The process continues with somatic input from the periphery to the somatosensory brain, which sends its interpretation of the signals to TPJ (Matsuhashi et al., 2004). The TPJ assesses the somatosensory evidence for any possibility that the experienced intention belongs to the self. Such evidence could potentially come from the changes in, for example, motor evoked potentials associated with mirroring, with registration of stronger potentials being associated with stronger mirroring. This line of reasoning leads to the, possibly, counter-intuitive idea that increased MN activation leads to increased peripheral stimulation. This effect would result in stronger peripheral input to somatosensory cortex and subsequent delivery of stronger signals to the TPJ which would have a resulting increased likelihood of erroneously modeling the sensory input it is receiving as resulting from the self having executed the action rather than appropriately attributing the action to the observed other.

It seems likely that this binary decision (i.e., either MNs constitute action understanding, or they have nothing to do with it) is but one of many examples of what Dawkins (2004) calls the *tyranny of the discontinuous mind*—the tendency to see continuous phenomena in discrete units. A good example of this would be the emerging conception of gender. Historically, gender has been viewed as binary by many societies, but modern views increasingly regard male and female but two ends of a continuum with the majority of individuals falling somewhere in between those extremes. Similarly, intention understanding is unlikely to be based solely on one or the other of these information processing routes. If DP models are taken to mean that MNs and only MNs generate intention understanding, then such models are nonstarters. As with most psychological processes, intention understanding is unlikely to rely on some modular node in a serial processing assembly line. Rather, any model that incorporates a role of MNs is more likely to succeed by assuming that they contribute an embodied dimension to understanding other's intentions.

Intention understanding implies understanding to whom the attribution should be made. If one experiences an intention but attributes it to no individual, then one does not understand the intention. An intention is such by virtue of it being the strategic cause of a particular person's behavior. If there is no associated behavior then the neural activity we would otherwise call an intention is intention-less. Therefore, intention understanding at a minimum requires agency attribution. Models of agency attribution are generally cognitive and inferential in nature. If agency attribution is an inferential process and a prerequisite for intention understanding, then strict DP models could not be correct. But this of course does not imply that they do not make important *contributions* to action understanding, giving an embodied dimension to one's understanding of another.

While it is difficult to imagine that the agent-attribution necessary for action understanding does not require inference, Michael and De Bruin (2015) discuss the *observability assumption*, which they claim is an assumption made by inferential models that intentions are not perceivable, or observable. By claiming that action understanding cannot be directly perceived, these models are vulnerable to *naïve dualism*, the notion that there are physical causes to some behaviors while others have nonphysical, intentional causes. Of course, dualism is something that does not comport with science since science depends on the assumption that the world is systematic and orderly (e.g., obeys the laws of physics), while any possible nonphysical world, by definition, would be unsystematic and unorderly, not constrained by the laws of physics, and therefore unknowable. Based on this, evaluation of inferential models should include questions about whether the model is dualistic.

SELF–OTHER DISCRIMINATION IN THE MN SYSTEM

Regardless of whether MNs are sufficient for action understanding, if they relate to intentions, then having them activated by other persons poses a problem: How does the brain determine on which intentions to act? In other words, how does the brain discriminate between those intentions derived from one's beliefs, goals and desires and those derived from observing a conspecific acting on said intentions? S–O discrimination therefore is necessary to enable one to act on those intentions directly relevant to his survival. Indeed, it is even necessary for one to have a sense of self-identity—to have a personality. Consider that one's personality is partially determined by the types of intentions he tends to have in specific situations—make fun of his mother, and he'll have the intention to smack you. If one acted not only on his own intentions but also on those of others within his view, the intentions-related part of his personality would be indistinguishable from the personalities of those around him. Given the importance of acting on one's own intentions and not on those of others, what follows is a discussion of what we know about MNs and S–O discrimination.

The original report of the discovery of MNs demonstrated that MNs are more active when the monkey executes, compared to observes, an action (di Pellegrino et al., 1992). A potentially similar pattern has been reported using EEG mu suppression. Woodruff and Maaske (2010) reported reliably more mu suppression to executed, compared to observed actions, with mu suppression in both conditions being significantly greater than zero. Woodruff et al. (2011) found that this S–O difference in mu suppression was positively correlated with self-reported PT as measured by the IRI (Davis, 1983).

Consistent with these findings, Maranesi et al. (2012) found that F5c plays a less direct role in motor movement than other nearby regions of the vPMC. In particular, Maranesi et al. found that electrical stimulation is less effective at exciting F5c neurons than neurons in surrounding areas. Furthermore, while areas like F4 and F5p have relatively direct connections to spinal motor neurons and inactivation of these regions impairs movement, F5c's projections are less direct and inactivation does not seem to suppress movement. These two findings together suggest one possible neural mechanism by which one is able to avoid erroneously acting on the intentions of others as coded by MNs. By "funneling" mirrored actions to a region without direct access to execution stages of the motor hierarchy, risk of other-intended actions being executed is minimized.

Citing evidence that F5 and AIP/PFG (as well as another potential MN region, ventrolateral prefrontal cortex) are interconnected with the putamen, part of the basal ganglia (BG), Bonini (2016) suggests that MNs might even be found there as well. He further posits that motor output is modulated via activation of the indirect or the hyperdirect pathways of the BG. Activation of this cortico-BG circuit constitutes a possible mechanism whereby the activation of the motor system by the observation of others is down-regulated to minimize unwanted imitation. In other words, such an extended network, if it exists, may reflect S–O discrimination and avoid the observer acting on the intentions of others.

As Yoshida et al. (2011) point out, MNs do not themselves process S–O distinctions and a further mechanism to perform this discriminatory process is needed. Similarly, Rozzi and Coudé (2015) rightly point out that the problem posed by MNs is S–O confusion: If observation of another's actions is transformed into an intention in the observer's mind, the observer is at risk of acting as though the intention were his own. Without S–O discrimination, groups of humans might act less like individuals and more like schooling sardines, with one person's action resulting in the rapid transmission of the associated intention throughout the group. Each individual human would simply experience said intention and act on it as though it were his own. Indeed Rozzi and Coudé suggested that S–O discrimination is likely to require multiple areas, some not known to contain MNs. Although Rozzi and Coudé appear favorable to the theory that MNs constitute action understanding, this theory is logically uncon-firmable by virtue of its failure to account for S–O discrimination. While it seems likely that MNs contribute to the emergent process of action under-standing, it does not seem that MN activation on its own could constitute action understanding without S–O discrimination.

However, Rozzi and Coudé (2015) suggest that F5c neurons are particu-larly related to agency. Whereas F5a and F5p neurons respond to obser-vation of videos of actions in minimal contexts (i.e., only the hand and target object were visible), F5c appears to become involved only when the entire person can be seen (Nelissen et al., 2011). Rozzi and Coudé take this finding to imply that F5c activation does not simply reflect actions in gen-eral, but actions as a function of the agent executing them. An interesting hypothesis derives from this finding and the S–O discrimination hypothe-sis mentioned above, which claims that S–O discrimination in MN activity arises only after reentrant input from regions like the TPJ. This hypothesis suggests that initial activity in MNs does not discriminate self from other but only takes on this characteristic later in the timecourse of the neural activity, once TPJ has had sufficient time to perform its computations and to indicate to MNs who is most likely the agent of the action.

CONCLUSIONS AND DIRECTIONS FOR FUTURE RESEARCH

The discovery of MNs has been one of the more exciting developments in the neurosciences, contributing to the growth of the field of social neuro-science. While much of this excitement is warranted, the impulse to over-ascribe functions to MNs should be treated with caution. It is argued here that mirroring a conspecific's actions likely contributes to understanding the intention behind those actions, but that the activation of MNs on their own should not be considered sufficient for action understanding. Future research into the relationship between MNs and action understanding needs to occur on multiple fronts. Theoretically, DP and IP models need to be further developed with DP models addressing the S–O discrimination issue and IP models addressing whether it's reasonable to assume MNs play no role in action understanding.

As discussed here and by others, measuring MNs through noninva-sive methods whose signals sum across tens of thousands of neurons have inherent limitations in their ability to make strong inferences about MN activity since MNs are defined by the characteristics with a single neuron. Since available neuroimaging techniques cannot resolve the activity of a single neuron, they cannot, strictly speaking, unambiguously measure MNs. However, use of RS or fMRI adaptation procedures can yield much greater inferential power as regards MNs. Future research should strive to use such methods where possible. We suggest, however, that methods that do not admit to unequivocal inferences about MNs should not be taken as useless. For one, methods such as Laplacian spatial transformation and Second Order Blind Separation can be used to cleanup mu suppression data, potentially allowing finer spatial resolution of the distribution of rhythms across the scalp, thereby allowing greater confidence that mu rhythms are not unduly influenced by occipital alpha. Similarly, fMRI studies that do not lend themselves to RS could seek to anchor inference of MN activation by systematically modulating specific characteristics of MN function, such as S–O discrimination effects. Given the challenges of measuring MN activity with neuroimaging, it would likely be productive to minimize conclusions about the imaging signal's precise relationship to MNs and focus more on the signal's apparent relationship to the construct of interest (e.g., empathy, action understanding, language, etc.). That is to say, that many interesting conclusions can be drawn about this latter relationship without getting bogged down in controversy about whether the signal specifically reflects MNs.

As for direct measures of MNs, future research should continue to assess the extent to which MNs are necessary and/or sufficient for action understanding. It is our contention that they are not *sufficient*, but may well be *necessary* (or at least very *useful*) to the kind of action understanding that occurs when multiple levels of action representation, from visual descriptions to motor programs, reciprocally interact to yield hypotheses, error predictions and corrections in an ongoing, dynamic process of understanding the actions of others, generating inferences about how those actions relate to self, and selecting appropriate responses.

References

Balconi, M., & Lucchiari, C. (2006). EEG correlates (event-related desynchronization) of emotional face elaboration: A temporal analysis. *Neuroscience Letters, 392*, 118–123.

Baron-Cohen, S., & Wheelwright, S. (2004). The empathy quotient: An investigation of adults with Asperger Syndrome or High Functioning Autism, and normal sex differences. *Journal of Autism and Developmental Disorders, 34*, 163–175.

Başar, E., Özgören, M., Öniz, A., Schmiedt, C., & Başar-Eroglu, C. (2007). The brain oscillations differentiate the picture of the own grandmother. *International Journal of Psychophysiology, 64*, 81–90.

Batson, C. D., Batson, J. G., Slingsby, J. K., Harrell, K. L., Peekna, H. M., & Todd, M. (1991). Empathic joy and the empathy-altruism hypothesis. *Journal of Personality and Social Psychology, 61*, 413–426.

Bonini, L. (2014). The extended mirror neuron network: Anatomy, origin, and functions. *The Neuroscientist, 23*, 1–12.

Bonini, L. (2016). The extended mirror neuron network: Anatomy, origin, and functions. *The Neuroscientist, 23*, 55–67.

Braadbaart, L., Williams, J., & Waiter, G. (2013). Do mirror neuron areas mediate mu rhythm suppression during imitation and action observation? *International Journal of Psychophysiology, 89*, 99–105.

Brown H., Woodruff, C.C., Goodman, A. (in prep.). Effect of familiarity on EEG b-rhythm activity and empathic accuracy.

Caggiano, V., Fogassi, L., Rizzolatti, G., Their, P., & Casile, A. (2009). Mirror neurons differentially encode the peripersonal and extrapersonal space of monkeys. *Science, 324,* 403–406.

Caggiano, V., Fogassi, L., Rizzolatti, G., Pomper, J. K., Their, P., Giese, M. A., et al. (2011). View-based encoding of actions in mirror neurons of area f5 in macaque premotor cortex. *Current Biology, 21,* 144–148.

Catmur, C. (2015). Understanding intentions from actions: Direct perception, inference and the roles of mirror and mentalizing systems. *Consciousness and Cognition, 36,* 426–433.

Chartrand, T. L., & Bargh, J. A. (1999). The chameleon effect: The perception–behavior link and social interaction. *Journal of Personality and Social Psychology, 76,* 893–910.

Cheng, Y., Tzeng, O. J. L., Decety, J., Imada, T., & Hsieh, J. (2006). Gender differences in the human mirror system: A magnetoencephalography study. *Cognitive Neuroscience and Neurophysiology, 17,* 1115–1119.

Cook, R., Bird, G., Catmur, C., Press, C., & Heyes, C. (2014). Mirror neurons: From origin to function. *Behavioral and Brain Sciences, 37,* 177–241.

Csibra, G. (2008). Action mirroring and action understanding: An alternative account. In P. Haggard, Y. Rossetti, & M. Kawato (Eds.), *Sensorimotor foundation of higher cognition: Attention and performance* (pp. 435–458). Oxford: Oxford University Press.

Davis, M. H. (1983). Measuring individual differences in empathy: Evidence for a multidimensional approach. *Journal of Personality and Social Psychology, 44,* 113–126.

Dawkins, R. (2004). *The ancestor's tale: A pilgrimage to the dawn of evolution.* New York, NY: Houghton, Mifflin and Harcourt.

di Pellegrino, G., Fadiga, L., Fogassi, L., Gallese, V., & Rizzolatti, G. (1992). Understanding motor events: A neuropsychological study. *Experimental Brain Research, 91,* 176–180.

Dinstein, I., Thomas, C., Behrman, M., & Heeger, D. J. (2008). A mirror up to nature. *Current Biology, 18,* R13–R18.

Ekman, P., & Friesen, W. V. (1976). *Pictures of facial affect.* Palo Alto, CA: Consulting Psychologists Press.

Fadiga, L., Fogassi, L., Pavesi, G., & Rizzolatti, G. (1995). Motor facilitation during action observation: A magnetic stimulation study. *Journal of Neurophysiology, 73,* 2608–2611.

Fogassi, L., Ferarri, P. F., Gesierich, B., Rozzi, S., Chersi, F., & Rizzolatti, G. (2005). Parietal lobe: from actin organization to intention understanding. *Science, 308,* 662–667.

Fox, N. A., Bakermans-Kranenburg, M. J., Yoo, K. H., Bowman, L. C., Vanderwert, R. E., Ferrari, P. F., et al. (2015). Assessing human mirror activity with EEG mu rhythm: A meta-analysis. *Psychological Bulletin, 142,* 291–313.

Gallese, V. (2005). Embodied simulation: From neurons to phenomenal experience. *Phenomenology and the Cognitive Sciences, 4,* 23–48.

Gallese, V. (2006). Intentional attunement: A neurophysiological perspective on social cognition and its disruption in autism. *Brain Research, 1079,* 15–24.

Gallese, V., Fadiga, L., Fogassi, L., & Rizzolatti, G. (1996). Action recognition in the premotor cortex. *Neurology, 119,* 593–609.

Gallese, V., Gernsbacher, M. A., Heyes, C., Hickok, G., & Iacoboni, M. (2011). Mirror neuron forum. *Perspectives on Psychological Science, 6,* 369–407.

Giese, M. A., & Rizzolatti, G. (2015). Neural and computational mechanisms of action processing: Interaction between visual and motor representations. *Neuron, 88,* 167–180.

Güntekin, B., & Başar, E. (2007). Emotional face expressions are differentiated with brain oscillations. *International Journal of Psychophysiology, 64,* 91–100.

Güntekin, B., & Başar, E. (2009). Facial affect manifested by multiple oscillations. *International Journal of Psychophysiology, 71,* 31–36.

Güntekin, B., & Başar, E. (2010). Event-related β oscillations are affected by emotional eliciting stimuli. *Neuroscience Letters, 483,* 173–178.

Güntekin, B., & Tülay, E. (2014). Event related beta and gamma oscillatory responses during perception of affective pictures. *Brain Research, 1577,* 1–12.

Hari, R. R., Forss, N. N., et al. (1998). Activation of human primary motor cortex during action observation: A neuromagnetic study. *Proceedings of the National Academy of Sciences of the United States of America, 95,* 15061–15065.

Hari, R., & Salmelin, R. (1997). Human cortical oscillations: A neuromagnetic view through the skull. *Trends in Neurosciences, 20,* 44–49.

Heinisch, C., Krüger, M. C., & Brüne, M. (2012). Repetitive transcranial magnetic stimulation over the temporoparietal junction influences distinction of self from famous but not unfamiliar others. *Behavioral Neuroscience, 126,* 792–796.

Henson, R. N. A. (2003). Neuroimaging studies of priming. *Progress in Neurobiology, 70,* 53–81.

Hickok, G. (2009). Eight problems for the mirror neuron theory of action understanding in monkeys and humans. *Journal of Cognitive Neuroscience, 21,* 1229–1243.

Hobson, H. M., & Bishop, D. V. M. (2016). Mu suppression—A good measure of the human mirror neuron system? *Cortex, 82,* 290–310.

Hobson, H. M., & Bishop, D. V. M. (2017). The interpretation of mu suppression as an index of mirror neuron activity: Past, present and future. *Royal Society Open Science, 2,* 1–22.

Hoenen, M., Schain, C., & Pause, B. M. (2013). Down-modulation of mu-activity through empathic top-down processes. *Social Neuroscience, 8,* 515–524.

Horan, W., Pineda, J., Wynn, J., Iacoboni, M., & Green, M. (2014). *Cognitive Affective and Behavioral Neuroscience, 4,* 1049–1060.

Iacoboni, M., Woods, R., Brass, M., Bekkering, H., Mazziotta, J., & Rizzolatti, G. (1999). Cortical mechanisms of human imitation. *Science, 28,* 2526–2528.

Jun, S. C., George, J. S., Paré-Blagoev, J., Plis, S. M., Ranken, D. M., Schmidt, D. M., et al. (2005). Spatiotemporal Bayesian inference dipole analysis for MEG neuroimaging data. *Neuroimage, 28,* 84–98.

Keysers, C., & Gazzola, V. (2009). Expanding the mirror: Vicarious activity for actions, emotions and sensations. *Current Opinion Neurobiology, 19,* 666–671.

Kilner, J. M., Friston, K. J., & Frith, C. D. (2007). The mirror-neuron system: A Bayesian perspective. *NeuroReport, 18,* 619–623.

Kilner, J. M., Neal, A., Weiskopf, N., Friston, K. J., & Frith, C. D. (2009). Evidence of mirror neurons in human inferior frontal gyrus. *Journal of Neuroscience, 29,* 10153–10159.

Kohler, E., Keysers, C., Umiltà, M. A., Fogassi, L., Gallese, V., & Rizzolatti, G. (2002). Hearing sounds, understanding actions: Action representation in mirror neurons. *Science, 297,* 846–848.

Logothetis, N. K., Pauls, J., Augath, M., Trinath, T., & Oeltermann, A. (2001). Neurophysiological investigation of the basis of the fMRI signal. *Nature, 412,* 150–157.

Maeda, K., Ishida, H., Nakajima, K., Inase, M., & Murata, A. (2015). Functional properties of parietal hand manipulation-related neurons and mirror neurons responding to vision of own hand action. *Journal of Cognitive Neuroscience, 27,* 560–572.

Maranesi, M., Roda, F., Bonini, L., Rozzi, S., Ferrari, P. F., Fogassi, L., et al. (2012). Anatomofunctional organization of the ventral primary motor and premotor cortex in the macaque monkey. *European Journal of Neuroscience, 36,* 3376–3387.

Matsuhashi, M., Ikeda, A., Ohara, S., Matsumoto, R., Yamamoto, J., Takayama, M., et al. (2004). Multisensory convergence at human temporo-parietal junction—Epicortical recording of evoked responses. *Clinical Neurophysiology, 115,* 1145–1160.

Michael, J. (2011). Four models of the functional contribution of mirror systems. *Philosophical Explorations, 14,* 185–194.

Michael, J., & De Bruin, L. (2015). How direct is social perception? *Consciousness and Cognition, 36,* 373–375.

Mishkin, M., & Ungerleider, L. G. (1982). Contribution of striate inputs to the visuospatial functions of parieto-preoccipital cortex in monkeys. *Behavioural Brain Research, 6*(1), 57–77.

Mizuguchi, N., Nakata, H., & Kanosue, K. (2016). The right temporoparietal junction encodes efforts of others during action observation. *Scientific Reports, 6*, 1–8.

Mukamel, R., Ekstrom, A. D., Kaplan, J., Iacoboni, M., & Fried, I. (2010). Single-neuron responses in humans during execution and observation of actions. *Current Biology, 20*, 750–756.

Muthukumaraswamy, S. D., & Johnson, B. W. (2004a). Changes in rolandic mu rhythm during observation of a precision grip. *Psychophysiology, 41*, 152–156.

Muthukumaraswamy, S., & Johnson, B. (2004b). Primary motor cortex activation during action observation revealed by wavelet analysis of the EEG. *Clinical Neurophysiology, 115*, 1760–1766.

Nelissen, K., Borra, E., Gerbella, M., Rozzi, S., Luppino, G., Vanduffel, W., et al. (2011). Action observation circuits in the macaque monkey cortex. *Journal of Neuroscience, 31*, 3743–3756.

Oberman, L., Hubbard, E., McCleary, J., Altschuler, E., Ramachandran, V., & Pineda, J. (2005). EEG evidence for mirror neuron dysfunction in autism spectrum disorders. *Cognitive Brain Research, 24*, 190–198.

Peeters, R., Simone, L., Nelissen, K., Fabbri-Destro, M., Vanduffel, W., Rizzolatti, G., et al. (2009). *Journal of Neuroscience, 29*, 11523–11539.

Perry, A., Troje, N. F., & Bentin, S. (2010). Exploring motor system contributions to the perception of social information: Evidence from EEG activity in the mu/alpha frequency range. *Social Neuroscience, 5*, 272–284.

Pfurtscheller, G., Neuper, C., Andrew, C., & Edlinger, G. (1997). Foot and hand area mu rhythms. *International Journal of Psychophysiology, 26*, 121–135.

Pineda, J. A. (2005). The functional significance of μ rhythms: Translating 'seeing' and 'hearing' into 'doing'. *Brain Research Review, 699*, 57–68.

Rozzi, S., & Coudé, G. (2015). Grasping actions and social interaction: Neural bases and anatomical circuitry in the monkey. *Frontiers in Psychology, 6*, 1–19.

Rozzi, S., Ferrari, P. F., Bonini, L., Rizzolatti, G., & Fogassi, L. (2008). Functional organization of inferior parietal lobule convexity in the macaque monkey: Electrophysiological characterization of motor, sensory and mirror responses and their correlation with cytoarchitectonic areas. *European Journal of Neuroscience, 28*, 1569–1588.

Rizzolatti, G., & Fogassi, L. (2014). The Mirror Mechanism: Recent findings and perspectives. *Philosophical Transactions of the Royal Society of London B: Biological Science, 369*, 1–12.

Rizzolatti, G., & Sinigaglia, C. (2010). The functional role of the parieto-frontal mirror circuit: Interpretations and misinterpretations. *Nature Reviews Neuroscience, 11*, 264–274.

Rizzolatti, G., Camarda, R., Fogassi, L., Gentilucci, M., Luppino, G., & Matelli, M. (1988). Functional organization of inferior area 6 in the macaque monkey: II. Area F5 and the control of distal movements. *Experimental Brain Research, 71*, 491–507.

Schülte-Ruther, M., Markowitsch, H., Fink, G., & Piefke, M. (2007). Mirror neuron and theory of mind mechanisms involved in face-to-face interactions: A functional magnetic resonance imaging approach to empathy. *Journal of Cognitive Neuroscience, 19*, 1354–1372.

Simon, S., & Mukamel, R. (2015a). Power modulation of electroencephalogram mu and beta frequency depends on perceived level of observed actions. *Brain and Behavior, 6*, 1–11.

Simon, S., & Mukamel, R. (2015b). Sensitivity to perception level differentiates two subnetworks within the mirror neuron system. *Social Cognitive and Affective Neuroscience, 6*, 1–11.

Southgate, V., & Hamilton, A. F. (2008). Unbroken mirrors: Challenging a theory of Autism. *Trends in Cognitive Science, 12*, 225–229.

Tang, A. C., Sutherland, M. T., & McKinney, C. J. (2005). Validation of SOBI components from high-density EEG. *Neuroimage, 25*, 539–553.

Tsuchiya, N., & Koch, C. (2005). Continuous flash suppression reduces negative afterimages. *Nature Neuroscience, 8*, 1096–1101.

Umiltà, M. A., Escola, L., Intskirveli, I., Grammont, F., Rochat, M., Caruana, F., et al. (2008). When pliers become fingers in the monkey motor system. *Proceedings of the National Academy of Sciences of the United States of America, 105*, 2209–2213.

Woodruff, C. C., & Maaske, S. (2010). Action execution engages human mirror neuron system more than action observation. *NeuroReport, 21,* 432–435.

Woodruff, C. C., Martin, T., & Bilyk, N. (2011a). Differences in self- and other-induced mu suppression are correlated with empathic abilities. *Brain Research, 1405,* 69–76.

Woodruff, C. C., Daut, R., Brower, M., & Bragg, A. (2011b). EEG alpha- and beta-band correlates of perspective-taking and personal distress. *NeuroReport, 22,* 744–748.

Woodruff, C. C., & Klein, S. (2013). Attentional distraction, μ-suppression and empathic perspective-taking. *Exp. Brain Res., 229*(4), 507–515.

Woodruff, C. C., Barbera, D., & Von Oepen, R. (2016). Task-related dissociation of EEG β enhancement and suppression. *International Journal of Psychophysiology, 99,* 18–23.

Woodruff, C.C. Goodman, A., Brown, H. (in prep.). Self–other differences in EEG μ-suppression reflect familiarity and perspective-taking.

Yang, C. -Y., Decety, J., Lee, S., Chen, C., & Cheng, Y. (2009). Gender differences in the mu rhythm during empathy for pain: An electroencephalographic study. *Brain Research, 1251,* 176–184.

Yin, S., Liu, Y., & Mingzhou, D. (2016). Amplitude of sensorimotor mu rhythm is correlated with BOLD from multiple brain regions: A simultaneous EEG-fMRI Study. *Frontiers in Human Neuroscience, 10,* 1–12.

Yoshida, K., Saito, N., Iriki, A., & Isoda, M. (2011). Representation of others' action by neurons in monkey medial frontal cortex. *Current Biology, 21,* 249–253.

Zaki, J., Weber, J., Bolger, N., & Ochsner, K. (2009). The neural bases of empathic accuracy. *Proceedings of the National Academy of Sciences of the United States of America, 106,* 11382–11387.

7

Why Does It Feel So Good to Care for Others and for Myself?

Neuroendocrinology and Prosocial Behavior

Melissa Birkett*, Joni Sasaki**

*Department of Psychological Sciences, Northern Arizona University,
Flagstaff, AZ, United States; **Department of Psychology, University of
Hawaii, Manoa, HI, United States

OVERVIEW AND QUESTIONS

Hormones are an important factor in controlling behavioral and physiological responses to many aspects of the environment, including the social environment. Thinking about the neuroendocrine basis of complex prosocial behaviors raises many fascinating questions. What hormones are involved in caring for the self and others? Do we share the same endocrine basis of caregiving behaviors with other animals? What kinds of research can help us understand the neuroendocrine basis for behaviors such as parental care or trust? Can manipulating hormones change social behavior? This chapter seeks to explore these questions and others as they relate to the neuroendocrinology of caring for the self and others.

Prosocial behaviors are a diverse collection ranging from parental care of young to entrusting a stranger with a loan. This chapter will focus first on the broad category of behaviors that includes caring for others, specifically encompassing questions about the neuroendocrine basis of empathy and compassion. The following section will explore the preliminary research into the neuroendocrine basis of self-compassion. The content of this chapter complements Chapters 2, 3, and 4, focused on the neuroscience of empathy, compassion, and self-compassion.

The Neuroscience of Empathy, Compassion, and Self-Compassion. http://dx.doi.org/10.1016/B978-0-12-809837-0.00007-6

CARING FOR OTHERS: EMPATHY AND COMPASSION

Empathy and compassion are two distinct but related aspects of prosocial experiences and behaviors. For the purposes of this chapter, *empathy* is taken to include multiple aspects of sharing another individual's feelings, including cognitive and affective dimensions of the shared experience (Davis, 1980, 1983; Hoffman, 1985; Lazarus, 1991). In this chapter, we will consider *compassion* to include understanding and responding to another's distress by seeking to alleviate suffering (Lazarus, 1991). Some scholars have suggested that experiencing and exhibiting compassion require a skill set that is more complex than that of basic empathy, including sensitivity to another's needs, stress tolerance, attention, imagery, and nonjudgment (Gilbert, 2009; Gonzalez-Liencres, Shamay-Tsoory, & Brüne, 2013, p. 1539). Further distinguishing it from empathy, compassion results in specific prosocial behaviors without the requirement of a helping individual sharing the identical emotional experience as the individual in distress (Goetz et al., 2010; Gonzalez-Liencres et al., 2013; Singer & Lamm, 2009).

Converging lines of translational evidence suggest that activity in two important endocrine families is critical for prosocial behavior. Arginine vasopressin (AVP or vasopressin) is important in species-typical affiliative behaviors across a number of mammalian species, particularly among males. Emerging clinical research has begun to investigate AVP's role in emotional experience, altruism, aggression, and social interaction in humans. Oxytocin (OT) is involved in several aspects of stress reduction and maternal behavior, as well as pair-bonding and related social behavior. Research is beginning to examine reciprocal interactions and positive OT feedback loops between individuals engaged in social behavior, and in some cases, even among individuals of different species. Additional research has suggested roles for stress hormones in prosocial behavior as well.

Reprinted from Sivaselvachandran, Acland, Abdallah, and Martin (2016), Fig. 7.1 illustrates the diversity of prosocial, empathy-related behaviors that have been documented across species to date. Though the motivations and ultimate functions of prosocial behaviors such as empathy-like and compassion-like behavior remain unclear, the recognition of common underlying neuroendocrine mechanisms has greatly informed our understanding of the systems responsible for human empathy and compassion. From the foundations of preclinical research using animal models, an improved understanding of the neuroendocrine basis of empathy and compassion has begun to emerge.

The remainder of this section seeks to highlight and to summarize important findings from research into the role of two key neuroendocrine systems in prosocial behavior: AVP and OT. This section of the chapter will first explore the role of the AVP system in behaviors related to compassion and empathy, followed by research on the role of OT in

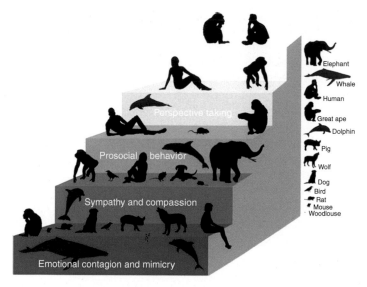

FIGURE 7.1 **The different species that display empathy-related behaviors are repre-sented.** Many instances of empathy have been recorded across numerous species, including (but not limited to) woodlice, mice, rats, canines, dolphins, elephants, nonhuman primates, and humans. The largest land mammal known to demonstrate empathy-like behaviors is the Asian elephant, which has been observed to recognize an upset herd mate and to offer gentle caresses and chirps of sympathy. In animals, empathy-related responding could have an ulterior motive such as survival, the sharing of food, companionship, and pack-oriented mentality. It is difficult to assess an animal's motivation behind an empathically driven response and for some, applying the term empathy to animal behavior is an act of anthropomorphism. This figure only offers a glimpse into the diversity in which empathy-like behaviors have been documented. For instance, we have included the woodlouse as an example of emotional contagion/mimicry in an insect, but honeybees and drosophila are also known to display signs of emotional transference. It should be noted that the animal's used for some of our examples occupy more than one level of the empathy staircase. For example, groups of dolphins will form a body raft to help support an injured or dying dolphin. This one act demonstrates sympathy, prosocial behavior, and possibly perspective taking. Reprinted with permission from Sivaselvachandran, S., Acland, E.L., Abdallah F.S., & Martin, L.J. (2016). Behavioral and mechanistic insight into rodent empathy. Neuroscience & Biobehavioral Reviews. doi:10.1016/j.neubiorev.2016.06.007.

these behaviors. Research on the role of each of these two neuroendocrine systems will be organized into summaries of preclinical and clinical studies. The section draws upon results from research in behavioral neuroendocrinology, behavioral pharmacology, and behavioral genetics. While this section focuses exclusively on the AVP and OT systems, it is important to also note that stress hormones and other neurotransmitters, such as the monoamines, interact with these systems, and serve as important components in the complex milieu responsible for the production of social behavior.

Vasopressin

AVP is a member of the nonapeptide (nine amino acid) family of neuropeptides. Nonapeptides are highly conserved and are found in many invertebrate and vertebrate taxa (Insel, 2010). Vasopressin is synthesized in an androgen-dependent manner in the suprachiasmatic, paraventricular, and supraoptic nuclei of the hypothalamus, the bed nucleus of the stria terminalis, medial amygdala, locus coeruleus, and olfactory bulb (Insel, 2010; Veenema, 2012). Following synthesis, vasopressin is transported to the posterior pituitary, where it is released into circulation. In mammals, vasopressin binds to V1a, V1b, and V2 G-protein coupled receptors in the brain and periphery (Carter, Grippo, Pournajafi-Nazarloo, Ruscio, & Porges, 2008; Insel, 2010). The discovery of the importance of vasopressin in social interaction, particularly in male social behavior, was dependent on an unlikely rodent research model: the vole.

Preclinical Research

Several species of closely related voles differ dramatically in their social behavior, presenting a unique model for comparative study of social behavior in mammals. Nearly identical outward appearances belie fascinating differences in the brains and behaviors of several species of these small, mouse-like creatures. As adults, prairie voles (*Microtus ochrogaster*) and pine voles (*Microtus pinetorum*) pair-bond, form monogamous relationships with their partners and live in extended family units. In contrast, montane voles (*Microtus montanus*) and meadow voles (*Microtus pennsylvanicus*) live in solitary burrows, have promiscuous mating behaviors, and do not engage in extensive pair-bonding (Insel, 2010). Unlike promiscuous species, monogamous vole species exhibit paternal care and pair-bonding. Expression of paternal behavior in prairie voles is dependent on AVP receptors in the lateral septum (De Vries, 2004). AVP is involved in other social behaviors found in monogamous species: territory defense and mate guarding (Carter et al., 2008). Since early research demonstrating the role of AVP in social behavior in pair-bonded male prairie voles (Winslow, Hastings, Carter, Harbaugh, & Insel, 1993), a growing body of research in animal models indicates that vasopressin is critical in male affiliative, pair-bonding, and paternal behavior.

AVP is important in establishing many of the affiliative behaviors observed in monogamous vole species. Administering AVP to adults produces partner preference in both male and female prairie voles, even without mating behavior (which is typically required for induction of partner preference). Over expression of the V1a receptor similarly results in partner preference among both monogamous prairie voles and promiscuous meadow vole males. In contrast, administering an AVP antagonist disrupts partner preference (Gobrogge & Wang, 2016).

Extracellular concentrations of vasopressin and the number of vasopressin-containing cells do not differ between monogamous and promiscuous vole species; however, the expression and distribution of vasopressin receptors *do* vary across species and are likely responsible for differences in behavior between monogamous and promiscuous species (Insel, 2010). Behavior mediated by distributions of vasopressin receptors may have important implications for translational work in humans. For example, changes in social behavior may not be due to extracellular neuropeptide availability but to differences in receptor expression.

Results of comparative research ranging from invertebrates to rodents to nonhuman primates (marmosets) suggest that the AVP system's role in social behavior is important for many different species (Insel, 2010). Unique challenges to studying AVP in human volunteers include difficulty in centrally administering neuropeptides and their ability to cross the blood brain barrier (Insel, 2010). For these reasons, to date, the majority of research investigating AVP and social behavior has been conducted in animal models; however, the number of clinical trials in this area is growing.

Clinical Research

Clinical research examining the role of AVP in social behavior primarily occurs in the realms of behavioral genetics and behavioral pharmacology. Clinical studies have revealed that the AVP 1a receptor is associated with altruism (Israel et al., 2008) and is important for social interaction (see Ebstein et al., 2012 for review). Complementing these findings, behavioral pharmacology studies using AVP intranasal administration, which results in AVP levels detectable inside the blood brain barrier, also suggest an important role for AVP in human social behavior (Born et al., 2002). For example, Thompson, George, Walton, Orr, and Benson (2006) administered intranasal AVP to men and women prior to viewing same-sex facial expressions of emotion. The researchers measured the response of corrugator (associated with threat expressions) and zygomaticus (associated with affiliative expressions) facial muscles in men and women in response to viewing emotional expressions. AVP administration increased corrugator (threat) responses in men viewing emotionally neutral faces. AVP administration in women resulted in reduced corrugator (threat) responses when viewing happy and angry faces and increased zygomaticus (affiliative) responses when viewing neutral faces. The researchers concluded that AVP increased agonistic (threat) responses in men and affiliative responses in women (Thompson et al., 2006).

Rilling et al. (2012) administered intranasal AVP to healthy male participants engaged in the Prisoner's Dilemma game, a model of reciprocal altruism. The researchers used fMRI to assess brain activity in response to the game. AVP administration resulted in increased reciprocal cooperative behavior and activation of the bed nucleus of the stria terminalis, lateral septum, and stria terminalis, areas associated with affiliation that include vasopressin circuitry. With respect to the amygdala, AVP administration reduced activation in regions responsible for initiating autonomic nervous system response and increased functional connectivity in the subgenual anterior cingulate cortex and ventral anterior insula. The authors suggest that this increased activation may contribute to amygdala-facilitated interpretation of somatic signals that can be factors in emotional decision-making. Zink and Meyer-Lindenberg (2012) also used intranasal AVP administration in conjunction with fMRI in healthy male participants to investigate brain regions involved in response to AVP among healthy adults, reporting a *lack* of influence on the amygdala following intranasal AVP administration.

Taken together, results of these animal and human studies suggest that AVP plays several important roles in social behavior. Most research has focused on the effects of AVP in male social behavior; however, some research has revealed effects on female behavior as well. Some studies have produced apparently contradictory results following AVP administration; however, study parameters, social status, or the social environment may influence activity in the AVP system, potentially complicating the interpretation of these results. For more examples of interaction effects, please see the section on OXTR Polymorphisms later in this chapter. Turning our attention from vasopressin, OT, a close chemical relative, is another valuable contributor to the production of prosocial behavior.

Oxytocin

Like vasopressin, oxytocin is a nonapeptide synthesized in the paraventricular and supraoptic nuclei of the hypothalamus. OT and vasopressin differ in only two of their nine constituent amino acids (Carter et al., 2008). OT is released from the posterior pituitary in response to sexual stimulation, uterine dilatation, nursing, stress-related stimuli as well as olfactory, auditory, visual, and physical social stimuli (Nagasawa, Okabe, Mogi, & Kikusui, 2012). While OT has been primarily studied for its role in female social and maternal behavior, it is also implicated in some aspects of male social behavior, including trust and empathy in humans, as well as pain reduction and reactivity to stressors (Carter et al., 2008). Fig. 7.2 (reprinted from Nagasawa et al., 2012) summarizes many of the social stimuli responsible for OT release as well as the corresponding effects of OT on physiology and behavior.

The OT system includes a single receptor (OXTR). OT and vasopressin can be coreleased and interact to influence social behavior (Carter et al., 2008). Due to their similarity in structure, OT and AVP may bind to each other's receptors, facilitating interactions between the two systems (Veenema, 2012).

One unique characteristic of the OT system involves reciprocal interactions and positive feedback loops important in forming bonds between

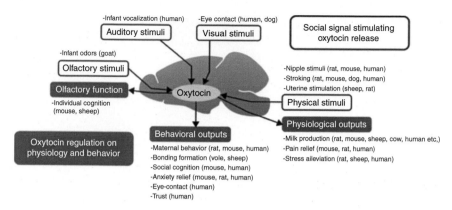

FIGURE 7.2   **Oxytocin release stimulated by social signals and corresponding effects on physiology and behavior.** Central oxytocin release is stimulated by multiple sensory signals, such as olfactory, auditory, visual, and physical inputs. In particular, physiological stimuli are known to induce oxytocin system activation in mammals. When oxytocin release is increased in the central nervous system, many sensory, physiological, and behavioral functions are enhanced. Maternal as well as affiliative behaviors are enhanced by oxytocin. Additionally, negative responses, such as pain, stress endocrine, and anxiety behaviors are diminished by oxytocin. Reprinted with permission from Nagasawa, M., Okabe, S., Mogi, K., & Kikusui, T. (2012). Oxytocin and mutual communicationin mother-infant bonding: Towards a neuroscience of social interaction. Frontiers in Human Neuroscience, 6. doi:10.3389/fnhum.2012.00031.

individuals. For example, physical contact between mothers and infants increased OT among mothers who engaged in affectionate interactions with their infants (Feldman, Gordon, Schneiderman, Weisman, & Zagoory-Sharon, 2010). A similar increase in OT was observed among fathers who engaged in high levels of stimulatory interactions with their infants (Feldman et al., 2010). Reciprocally, increased OT in turn promotes parental behavior (Feldman et al., 2010; Pedersen & Prange, 1979; Weisman, Zagoory-Sharon, & Feldman, 2012) and increases OT in offspring (Weisman et al., 2012). Even more dramatically, parental care can result in life-long changes in the OT system, including increased OXTR binding in adult offspring that experienced high levels of parental care (Francis, Young, Meaney, & Insel, 2002). Reciprocal OT-mediated effects between care provider and recipient may even extend to interspecies relationships, as will be explored in a later section on research on the role of the OT system in interacting with companion animals. Fig. 7.3 illustrates the iterative and overlapping nature of OT positive feedback loops discovered in preclinical rodent research. In this figure depicting murine behavior, not only are short-term effects highlighted, such as immediate increases in maternal behavior in response to offspring, but lifetime and multigenerational nongenetic changes in activity of OT systems can also be seen in the subsequent generation on the right side of the figure.

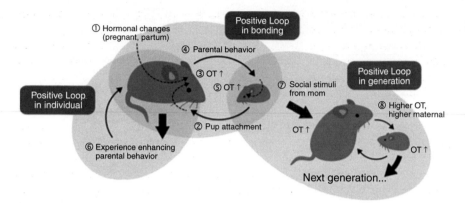

FIGURE 7.3   **A schematic illustrating the positive feedback loop of social bonding controlled by oxytocin.** The mother mouse becomes pregnant and then at partum, certain hormonal changes occur (1). After delivery, new-born infants show attachment behavior toward the mother (2). The hormonal changes related to partum and attachment behavior from the infant stimulate the release of centrally acting oxytocin (OT) (3). OT in the maternal brain facilitates parenting behavior toward the pups (4). This parenting behavior also stimulates infant OT release in the brain (5). Therefore, there is a clear positive loop of OT release in the mother–infant dyad. Once the mother experiences parenting, her maternal behavior is persistently maintained [by the] (6) positive [feedback] loop in individuals. Intensive parenting care stimulates the infants' brain development (7), which in turn brings about higher OT and parenting activities in their adulthood (8). This intensive care is also nongenetically transmitted to the next generation. Reprinted from Nagasawa et al. (2012).

Preclinical Research

Discovery of OT's species-typical social behavioral effects among voles has paralleled research with vasopressin. In general, the results of research with monogamous vole species support the conclusion that administration of OT increases pair-bonding (including associated behaviors, such as partner preference and mate guarding) as well as parental behavior. Administration of an OT antagonist disrupts these behaviors (Lieberwirth & Wang, 2016). OT administration produces several effects, including some that can last a lifetime. For example, administering OT early in development increases pair bonding (Bales & Carter, 2003), affiliative behavior and parental behavior in female prairie voles during adulthood (Bales et al., 2007a). In males, early life exposure to OT results in sexually dimorphic increases in V1a receptors (Bales et al., 2007b). Administering OT in adulthood results in partner preference behavior in both male and female prairie voles, behavior that can be inhibited by OT antagonists (Gobrogge & Wang, 2016).

Some researchers have been careful to point out that the effects of administering OT are likely the result of binding at OT receptors. The pattern and location of OT receptors govern the behavioral response to OT. For example, the distribution of OT receptors differs among vole species.

These patterns correspond to the differences in social behavior between monogamous and promiscuous species (Insel & Shapiro, 1992).

Moving beyond parental and pair-bonding behavior, emerging research has begun to explore the role of OT in situations intended to more closely model empathy-like behavior, helping to bridge the results of preclinical and clinical studies (for review see Keum & Shin, 2016; Meyza, Bartal, Monfils, Panksepp, & Knapska, 2016; Sivaselvachandran et al., 2016). Burkett et al. (2016) describe a novel laboratory protocol to elicit empathy-like, consolation behavior among pair-bonded adult voles. Prairie voles whose partners were exposed to a stressor responded with increased consolation behavior (licking and grooming). When partners were separated but did not experience a stressor, no change in behavior was observed. In response, stressed recipients of consolation behavior demonstrated reduced anxiety-like behavior following the stressor. Unlike their monogamous relatives, promiscuous meadow voles did not engage in consolation behavior following the stress-inducing procedure. The authors of this study suggest that consolation behavior provides social buffering in the monogamous species. They describe evidence of emotional and physiological contagion, important aspects of empathy, in observer animals that responded to their partner's distress with mirrored stress responses, stress-hormone release, and freezing behavior. Engaging in consolation behavior appeared to mitigate these responses in the observing partner. Administering an OT antagonist prevented the expression of consolation behavior, indicating that OT receptor activity is critical for this empathy-like behavior. Gobrogge and Wang (2016) have described OT "as a neurobiological hallmark of prosocial approach behavior in gregarious animals and trust among humans—a necessary prerequisite to social affiliation" (p. 82), summarizing many of these preliminary results of preclinical research in this area.

Clinical Research

Research on OT in humans suggests that OT is implicated in both positive and negative social interactions with others. That is, there is evidence of a link between OT and positive social interactions, such as feeling empathy and compassion and behaving prosocially toward others, but there is also evidence of a link between OT and negative social interactions, such as social withdrawal and intergroup bias.

OXTR Polymorphisms

One very commonly studied gene is the OT receptor gene OXTR, which has a polymorphism (OXTR rs53576) that is localized in a single copy to chromosome 3 of the human genome (Gimpl & Fahrenholz, 2001). Many initial studies examining this specific polymorphism found a link between certain genotypes of OXTR and positive social interactions with others. People who have the G allele (vs. A allele) of OXTR rs53576 tend to be more sensitive to socio-emotional cues in the environment; they show more empathy to others on a variety of measures, including on self-reported traits, behavioral tasks, and physiological and neural measures. For instance, research has shown that people with two copies of the G allele (GG genotype), compared to those with one or two copies of the A allele (AG or AA genotype), report higher levels of empathy as a broad self-identified trait that includes both emotional concern and cognitive perspective-taking components (Rodrigues, Saslow, Garcia, John, & Keltner, 2009; Smith, Porges, Norman, Connelly, & Decety, 2014). Beyond self-report measures, there is also evidence that people with the GG (vs. AG/AA) genotype show greater empathy as indexed by more objective behavioral measures, such as the Reading the Mind in the Eyes Task (Baron-Cohen, Wheelwright, Hill, Raste, & Plumb, 2001b), which requires inferring the mental states of others by viewing only the eye region of various face stimuli (Rodrigues et al., 2009). People with the GG (vs. AG/AA) genotype also show increased sympathetic arousal, as measured by electrodermal activity, while watching a video of a violent physical fight (Smith et al., 2014), and they exhibit greater amygdala activation and connectivity while viewing socio-emotionally relevant stimuli such as facial expressions (Tost et al., 2010), suggesting that people with certain genotypes experience greater empathy when they process emotionally salient information or see others in distress.

Other OT-related genes have been linked to social outcomes as well. Besides OXTR rs53576, another OXTR polymorphism, rs1042778, has been linked to individual differences in socially relevant traits. In particular, people with the GG genotype (vs. GT/TT) of OXTR rs1042778 perceive that they have higher levels of social support available to them and social networks that are larger and more diverse, meaning that they have more varied types of social relationships and frequently interact with them (Creswell et al., 2015). In an investigation of social behaviors and CD38, a gene that plays a key role in regulating the release of OT, Algoe and Way (2014) found that the CD38 rs6449182 polymorphism predicted positive social interactions when interacting with a romantic partner in the lab. Specifically, their results demonstrated that people with the CC (vs. CG/GG) genotype were more likely to perceive that their partner was responsive and felt positive emotions, particularly love, and to behaviorally express gratitude toward their partner during coded lab interactions. This research suggests overall that OT-related genes are relevant for experiencing socially affiliative emotions and ultimately having more positive interactions in social relationships.

Although a good deal of the literature on OT-related genes shows a connection to positive social outcomes, there is also clear evidence that the outcomes are sometimes negative. A study using the commonly studied

OXTR rs53576, for example, had participants engage in a game of Cyberball (Williams, Cheung, & Choi, 2000), a computerized game that reliably induces the experience of social ostracism or rejection. Results of this study found that carriers of the G allele were more likely to experience a sharp decrease in self-esteem and in their meaningful existence, or feeling that their presence in the game mattered (McQuaid, McInnis, Matheson, & Anisman, 2015). People with the GG genotype of OXTR also seem to show greater sympathetic cardiac reactivity in response to stress (Norman et al., 2012) and increased subjective arousal when perceiving that others are in distress (Smith et al., 2014). Thus, people with the G allele of OXTR may be more sensitive to socio-emotional stimuli, even when the potential downstream implications are negative.

In order to unify findings of positive and negative social outcomes, it may be useful to take an interactionist perspective. For many of these studies showing that socially sensitive genotypes of OT-related genes are associated, on the one hand, with socially engaging emotions such as empathy, and on the other hand, with socially disengaging emotions such as feelings of withdrawal, a crucial variable to consider is the nature of the social context. Features of the social context, such as whether experiences are socially supportive or not or whether an interaction partner is an ingroup or outgroup member, may be relevant for understanding systematic variation in the link between genes and an outcome or trait of interest. According to the gene–environment interaction (G × E) framework, the same genetic predisposition may lead to different outcomes depending on the environment, and conversely, the same environment may lead to different outcomes depending on genetic predispositions (e.g., Caspi et al., 2003).

For example, one study found an interaction between OXTR and childhood maltreatment on emotion dysregulation. Although there was no overall association between OXTR genotype and emotion dysregulation, the results showed that among participants with GG genotypes of OXTR rs53576, having a history of childhood maltreatment was linked to emotional dysregulation in adulthood. However, for participants with AG or AA genotypes, there was no association between maltreatment in their childhood and emotion dysregulation as adults (Bradley et al., 2011).

Aspects of the social environment that cannot clearly be classified as beneficial versus harmful, such as the cultural context, can also moderate the association between OXTR and psychological outcomes. Building on gene–environment research, the gene–culture interaction perspective examines how culture shapes the manifestation of genetically influenced traits and behaviors. According to this perspective, people with certain genetic predispositions may be more sensitive to particular features of the environment. Because these environmental features vary systematically across cultural contexts, people with these genetic predispositions may exhibit different behaviors depending on their surrounding culture.

However, people with other genetic predispositions who are less sensitive to those features of the environment may not show these culturally reinforced behaviors as strongly (Kim & Sasaki, 2012, 2014; Sasaki & Kim, 2017).

In a few studies, researchers examined the OXTR genotype in relation to socio-emotional behaviors and psychological outcomes in the United States and Korea. Seeking emotional support openly and explicitly is more strongly encouraged in the United States than in Korea, and interestingly, these different cultural tendencies seemed to manifest in people differently depending on the OXTR genotype. Among Americans, people carrying the G allele of OXTR were more likely to report seeking emotional support when distressed than people without the G allele. However, Koreans did not differ significantly in their willingness to seek emotional support when distressed according to the OXTR genotype (Kim et al., 2010). Restraining emotional expression is more common in Korea, and this cultural tendency is also moderated by OXTR. Kim et al. (2011) found that, in Korea, people with the G allele of OXTR were more likely to suppress emotions than people without the G allele, whereas in the United States, the pattern of results was the opposite: people with the G allele were actually less likely to suppress emotions compared to people without the G allele.

The interaction between genes and culture may also have implications for the extent to which people psychologically benefit from religion. Among Koreans with the GG genotype, being more religious was associated with higher psychological well-being, while for European Americans with the same genotype, religiosity was associated with lower well-being (Sasaki, Kim, & Xu, 2011). Given that religion in collectivist cultural contexts, such as Korea, may provide greater opportunities for connecting with others socially compared to individualistic cultural contexts, such as the United States (Sasaki & Kim, 2011), it is possible that being religious particularly benefits well-being for people who are sensitive to socio-emotional cues in these contexts.

Taken together, this research on OXTR suggests that people with socially sensitive genotypes, such as G carriers of OXTR rs53576, do not express uniformly positive or negative behaviors in social contexts; a clearer interpretation may be that they are more sensitive to socially relevant cues in their environment. In a nonthreatening environment that provides them with opportunities to affiliate with others they feel close to, people with "socially sensitive" genotypes of OT-related genes may express positive emotions and behaviors toward others, such as empathy, compassion, love, and gratitude. Yet, when confronted with a potentially threatening environment that makes them feel that they cannot affiliate meaningfully with others, people with these same genotypes may express emotions and behaviors that are quite negative in valence, showing more social withdrawal. Similarly, research on gene–culture interactions has shown that the broader cultural context may be important for shaping what people with certain genetic predispositions consider a relevant social cue in the first place.

Findings of both positive and negative social outcomes in relation to OT should be taken not as contradicting evidence but as support for a broader conceptualization of how OT plays a role in social behavior. At different levels of biological influence, systematic variations in the social context may be an important part of understanding OT's influence on behavior. Indeed, intranasal OT research has generally mirrored the accumulation of genetic evidence for both positive and negative outcomes.

Intranasal OT Administration Studies

Kosfeld, Heinrichs, Zak, Fischbacher, and Fehr (2005) completed some of the earliest studies investigating the effects of intranasal OT administration. They reported that intranasal OT increased trust behavior in healthy male volunteers playing an investment game with monetary gains and losses. Additional studies demonstrated that OT administration increased financial trust under conditions in which a social benefit could be expected (Mikolajczak et al., 2010). Along with growing interest in OT and trust research, concerns about interpretation and methodology have also been raised (see Nave et al., 2015 for review).

OT administration studies also support a role for OT in determining responses to socio-emotional information. For example, in a study of healthy, young male participants, OT administration increased gaze to eye and mouth regions of faces—areas important in determining emotional/social information (Guastella, Mitchell, & Dadds, 2008). Guastella et al. (2010) suggest that changes in gaze could be one possible mechanism for OT's enhancement of social affiliation in humans. In addition, another study of male participants found that intranasal OT increased levels of empathy in response to both positive and negative emotionally evocative stimuli (Hurlemann et al., 2010). There is also evidence to suggest that OT selectively increases empathy for people with lower baseline levels of social proficiency. For people who score high on the Autism Spectrum Quotient (AQ; Baron-Cohen, Wheelwright, Skinner, Martin, & Clubley, 2011b), intranasal OT increased empathic accuracy compared to a placebo, whereas for people low on AQ, intranasal OT had no significant effect (Bartz et al., 2010).

Intranasal OT studies have also helped establish the role of OT in reducing stress response to social stressors. de Oliveira, Zuardi, Graeff, Queiroz, and Crippa (2012) reported reduced anticipatory anxiety to a psychosocial stressor (public speaking task) among healthy participants administered intranasal OT. Other studies found a positive role for OT in resolving interpersonal conflict. In response to a couple conflict stressor,

OT administration increased positive communication and reduced cortisol (Ditzen et al., 2009) and produced sex-specific effects in couples (Ditzen et al., 2012). OT increases sympathetic activity (measured via salivary alpha amylase) in men and decreases it in women (Ditzen et al., 2012). Intranasal OT administration in conjunction with social support reduced the stress response in men exposed to a psychosocial stressor (Heinrichs, Baumgartner, Kirschbaum, & Ehlert, 2003). Finally, OT administration reduced cortisol response to a psychosocial stressor in people with low emotional regulation ability (Quirin, Kuhl, & Düsing, 2011).

It is worth noting that findings from intranasal OT studies are not always consistent. A recent review found that evidence of the effect of intranasal OT administration on trust in humans is weak (Nave, Camerer, & McCullough, 2015), and other research has shown that the effect of intranasal OT can be negative, eliciting greater ethnocentrism and group-serving dishonesty, for instance (De Dreu, Greer, Van Kleef, Shalvi, & Handgraaf, 2010; Shalvi & De Dreu, 2014). These inconsistencies in the literature point to the need for more contextually attuned theories of how OT impacts behavior in different social environments—a point we discuss in more detail at the end of this section.

OT Release Studies

Complementing the research on OT administration and resulting changes in behavior, studies of OT release have revealed that *behavior* can affect OT release through feedback mechanisms as well, providing further evidence of reciprocal interactions among helpers and recipients. For example, affectionate mother–infant and stimulatory father–infant interactions are related to OT release. Similarly, OT levels increased in highly affectionate mothers and highly stimulatory fathers following parent–infant interactions (Feldman et al., 2010). Morhenn, Beavin, and Zak (2012) reported a significant increase in OT following a 15-min massage in a group of men and women. A control group saw no significant change in OT.

Several studies have even begun to examine the role of OT in relationships with companion animals. In a within-groups design study conducted by Odendaal and Meintjes (2003), a group of male and female participants interacted with dogs or engaged in a reading control. Positive interactions reduced blood pressure in both humans and dogs. Both species also showed increases in OT after the positive interaction. OT increases were significantly greater in the dog interaction condition compared to a reading control condition.

Handlin, Nilsson, Ejdebäck, Hydbring-Sandberg, and Uvnäs-Moberg (2012) investigated psychological characteristics of dog owners that were associated with dog and owner stress hormone (cortisol) and OT levels. Among the results, higher owner-perceived bond and higher frequency of kissing were associated with higher OT levels in dogs. There were significant positive correlations between dog and owner OT levels at various time points during the study, but no correlation between owner and dog cortisol levels. Participants in the study were females with male Labrador retrievers. Similarly, in another small study (10 women, 10 men), women experienced significantly increased OT levels after interacting with their dogs following a stressor (a workday). In this within-subjects design, when participants engaged in a reading control condition, they did not experience OT changes (Miller et al., 2009). Finally, in an interesting study by Nagasawa et al. (2015), domesticated dogs were found to engage in more gaze behavior with humans (compared to hand-raised, but not domesticated, wolves). Longer dog–human gazing behavior resulted in increased human OT and reciprocal dog OT levels. In a second study, administering intranasal OT to dogs increased gaze behavior toward owners in female dogs only. Correspondingly, OT increased only in the owners of female dogs that received intranasal OT. Follow-up analysis revealed that the changes in owner OT were explained by changes in gaze behavior of the female dogs that received intranasal OT. In this second study, participants were instructed not to interact with their dogs, thereby breaking the reciprocal OT cycle. When they did not receive interaction with owners, dogs did not exhibit changes in OT. The authors suggested that domestication resulted in the evolution of dog gaze systems with the ability to activate human OT affiliative systems.

Oxytocin and the Interactionist Perspective

Across different studies of OT in both genetics and pharmacology, it seems clear that OT does not encourage uniformly positive social outcomes. That is, it probably should not be characterized as the "love hormone" or in other ways that largely connote positive influences. Yet, neither does OT encourage uniformly negative social outcomes. Instead, it may be best characterized by socio-emotional sensitivity, which should not necessarily be tied to a clear valence. Bartz, Zaki, Bolger, and Ochsner (2011) have argued that considering features of both the individual and the situation are necessary for understanding the role of OT in prosocial behavior, for instance. Consistent with this argument, research on differential susceptibility suggests that certain genes may predispose people to be sensitive to environmental inputs "for better and for worse" (Belsky, Bakermans-Kranenburg, & van IJzendoorn, 2007), and the gene–culture interaction perspective has shown how cultural tendencies without uniformly positive or negative labels can moderate the link between genes and a variety of psychological outcomes (Kim et al., 2010, 2011; Sasaki et al., 2011). Importantly, these theoretical perspectives are consistent with evidence of epigenetic processes underlying gene–environment effects occurring throughout the course of development (see Meaney, 2010 for review).

CARING FOR THE SELF: SELF-COMPASSION

Complementing definitions of compassion that focus on responding to another's distress, self-compassion encompasses responding to one's own distress. *Self-compassion* includes the desire to alleviate an individual's own suffering through reservation of judgment and consideration of life circumstances as part of a greater lived experience of all people (Neff, 2003a,b). Self-compassion was first suggested as an alternative to previous views of self that were dependent on self-worth and self-esteem. Self-compassion incorporates elements of self-kindness, a sense of common humanity, and mindfulness when considering personal weakness or hardships (Neff, 2003a,b).

The experience of self-compassion is difficult to model in nonhuman animals, and to date, research has focused on the human experience of self-compassion. As yet, there is no research investigating a direct or causal role of the OT or AVP systems in self-compassion. One study reported a change in OT that corresponded with a change in self-compassion but no causal hypotheses have been tested (Lipschitz et al., 2015; described in the next section). Other studies have investigated changes in self-compassion and the resulting changes in stress hormone response (Arch et al., 2014; described in the next section). The following section will explore some preclinical models of self-grooming behavior that may have implications for understanding the roles of AVP and OT in this self-care behavior. The section concludes with summaries of other preliminary clinical research beginning to examine neuroendocrine bases of self-compassion.

Preclinical Research

Animal models of self-compassion remain to be developed, making research into the biological bases of self-compassion challenging. Some preliminary research, however, has examined the role of the OT and AVP systems in self-grooming behavior. As a form of self-directed care, self-grooming may share underlying mechanisms with components of self-compassion.

Qiao et al. (2014) examined the role of the OT and AVP systems in the self-grooming behavior of a monogamous vole species. In general, dominant individuals in this study displayed more social behavior than subordinates. Dominant males and females of the monogamous mandarin vole species exhibited more self-grooming behavior than subordinates. Dominant males had fewer OT-ergic cells in the paraventricular nucleus than did subordinate males. Dominant males had more AVP neurons in several key brain regions, compared to subordinate males. Dominant females had more AVP neurons. These results suggest that in males, self-grooming may be related to reduced OT and increased AVP activity. In females, self-grooming may be related to increased AVP activity only. The results of this research may suggest an interaction among the neuroendocrine systems, stress, and social status.

In a murine model, inactivating the OT receptor produced social deficits but resulted in increased self-grooming behavior compared to wild type mice (Pobbe et al., 2012). However, centrally administering OT increased self-grooming behavior in both wild type and OXTR knockout mice. OT-deficient mice had an enhanced self-grooming response to intracerebroventricular OT administration (Amico et al., 2004). The combined results of these studies suggest that the role of OT in self-grooming varies. Additional research is needed to more clearly understand the biological basis of self-grooming with regard to OT. Improved understanding may have implications for identifying neuroendocrine systems involved in self-compassion.

Clinical Research

Clinical research examining direct roles for OT and AVP in self-compassion is currently needed. However, a small number of studies have begun to explore preliminary relationships between these systems and several aspects of self-compassion. For example, in a sample of cancer survivors with sleep disturbances, a 3-month, mind-body bridging intervention resulted in increased measures of self-compassion and salivary OT (Lipschitz et al., 2015).

In another study, an intervention to increase self-compassion resulted in reduced subjective and cardiovascular stress response, but not cortisol response, to an acute social stressor (Trier Social Stress Test; Arch et al., 2014). While this study did not address OT or AVP, it did demonstrate a relationship between self-compassion and the stress hormone cortisol. This study grew out of the finding that people practicing a compassion meditation intervention had a reduced stress response and self-reported distress in response to the TSST. This change in response was dependent on the degree (length/quantity of time) of compassion meditation engagement (Pace et al., 2009).

Altogether, only limited evidence currently exists linking activity in the OT system with self-compassion. The development of animal models for self-compassion would further this area of research. Looking to clinical studies, increased investigation of genetic polymorphisms associated with self-compassion, AVP or OT administration studies, and the use of selective AVP or OT antagonists coupled with assessment of self-compassion would help reveal potential biological mechanisms underlying caring for the self.

CONCLUSIONS AND DIRECTIONS FOR FUTURE RESEARCH

This chapter sought to explore the neuroendocrine basis of caring for the self and others. The roles of the AVP and OT systems were first examined in relation to empathy and compassion. Preliminary information about the role of these systems in self-compassion was suggested. Much of our current knowledge is derived from the results of important preclinical studies in monogamous and promiscuous vole species. Moving forward, the growth in knowledge regarding prosocial behaviors across species and the development of ligands for AVP and OT receptors provide valuable tools for research in this area.

There are a number of challenges to developing models sensitive to the nuances of compassion and self-compassion. From a basic research perspective, investigating the neuroendocrine underpinnings of prosocial behavior may help researchers to more clearly establish the antecedents of compassion and self-compassion. In addition, human experiences of compassion and self-compassions are influenced by one's social and cultural surroundings, and thus, these experiences are ultimately formed by a combination of biological mechanisms and socially shaped meaning. Future work in this area should rely on careful experimental designs from preclinical research while incorporating aspects of the social context that are relevant for predicting when and why people behave prosocially. In order to make an impact in applied settings, future research may focus on developing targeted interventions to improve prosocial behavior. There is growing interest in the therapeutic potential of OT in particular for enhancing empathy or compassion, attenuating stress-related responses, or mitigating affective or social deficits (Sippel et al., 2017). Chapter 8 of this book addresses several intervention strategies based on basic neuroscience research into empathy, compassion, and self-compassion. Yet, existing investigations of experimental OT administration have also come with varying success (Nave et al., 2015), pointing to the need for more research to understand these effects. Because certain outcomes predicted from animal models may be weak or inconsistent in human samples, future research should continue to investigate differences between species that may explain caring behavior for self versus others.

References

Algoe, S. B., & Way, B. M. (2014). Evidence for a role of the oxytocin system, indexed by genetic variation in CD38, in the social bonding effects of expressed gratitude. Social Cognitive and Affective Neuroscience, 9(12), 1855–1861.

Amico, J. A., Vollmer, R. R., Karam, J. R., Lee, P. R., Li, X., Koenig, J. I., et al. (2004). Centrally administered oxytocin elicits exaggerated grooming in oxytocin null mice. Pharmacology Biochemistry and Behavior, 78(2), 333–339.

Arch, J. J., Brown, K. W., Dean, D. J., Landy, L. N., Brown, K. D., & Laudenslager, M. L. (2014). Self-compassion training modulates alpha-amylase, heart rate variability, and subjective responses to social evaluative threat in women. Psychoneuroendocrinology, 42, 49–58.

Bales, K. L., & Carter, C. S. (2003). Developmental exposure to oxytocin facilitates partner preferences in male prairie voles (*Microtus ochrogaster*). Behavioral Neuroscience, 117, 854–859.

Bales, K. L., van Westerhuyzen, J. A., Lewis-Reese, A. D., Grotte, N. D., Lanter, J. A., & Carter, C. S. (2007a). Oxytocin has dose-dependent developmental effects on pair-bonding and alloparental care in female prairie voles. Hormones and Behavior, 52(2), 274–279.

Bales, K. L., Plotsky, P. M., Young, L. J., Lim, M. M., Grotte, N. D., Ferrer, E., et al. (2007b). Neonatal oxytocin manipulations have long-lasting, sexually dimorphic effects on vasopressin receptors. Neuroscience, 144, 38–45.

Baron-Cohen, S., Wheelwright, S., Hill, J., Raste, Y., & Plumb, I. (2001a). The "Reading the Mind in the Eyes" test revised version: A study with normal adults, and adults with Asperger syndrome or high-functioning autism. Journal of Child Psychology and Psychiatry, 42(2), 241–251.

Baron-Cohen, S., Wheelwright, S., Skinner, R., Martin, J., & Clubley, E. (2001b). The Autism-Spectrum Quotient (AQ): Evidence from Asperger syndrome/high-functioning autism, males and females, scientists and mathematicians. Journal of Autism and Developmental Disorders, 31, 5–17.

Bartz, J. A., Zaki, J., Bolger, N., Hollander, E., Ludwig, N. N., Kolevzon, A., et al. (2010). Oxytocin selectively improves empathic accuracy. Psychological Science, 10, 1426–1428.

Bartz, J. A., Zaki, J., Bolger, N., & Ochsner, K. N. (2011). Social effects of oxytocin in humans: Context and person matter. Trends in Cognitive Sciences, 15(7), 301–309.

Belsky, J., Bakermans-Kranenburg, M. J., & van IJzendoorn, M. H. (2007). For better *and* for worse: Differential susceptibility to environmental influences. Current Directions in Psychological Science, 16, 300–304.

Born, J., Lange, T., Kern, W., McGregor, G. P., Bickel, U., & Fehm, H. L. (2002). Sniffing neuropeptides: A transnasal approach to the human brain. Nature Neuroscience, 5(6), 514–516.

Bradley, B., Westen, D., Mercer, K. B., Binder, E. B., Jovanovic, T., Crain, D., et al. (2011). Association between childhood maltreatment and adult emotional dysregulation in a low-income, urban, African American sample: Moderation by oxytocin receptor gene. Development and Psychopathology, 23(02), 439–452.

Burkett, J. P., Andari, E., Johnson, Z. V., Curry, D. C., de Waal, F. B. M., & Young, L. J. (2016). Oxytocin-dependent consolation behavior in rodents. Science, 351(6271), 375–378.

Carter, C. S., Grippo, A. J., Pournajafi-Nazarloo, H., Ruscio, M. G., & Porges, S. W. (2008). Oxytocin, vasopressin and sociality. Progress in Brain Research, 170, 331–336.

Caspi, A., Sugden, K., Moffitt, T. E., Taylor, A., Craig, I. W., Harrington, H., et al. (2003). Influence of life stress on depression: Moderation by a polymorphism in the 5-HTT gene. Science, 301, 386–389.

Coccaro, E. F., Kavoussi, R. J., Hauger, R. L., Cooper, T. B., & Ferris, C. F. (1998). Cerebrospinal fluid vasopressin levels: Correlates with aggression and serotonin function in personality-disordered subjects. Archives of General Psychiatry, 55(8), 708–714.

Creswell, K. G., Wright, A. G., Troxel, W. M., Ferrell, R. E., Flory, J. D., & Manuck, S. B. (2015). OXTR polymorphism predicts social relationships through its effects on social temperament. Social Cognitive and Affective Neuroscience, 10, 869–876.

Davis, M. H. (1980). A multidimensional approach to individual differences in empathy. JSAS Catalog of Selected Documents in Psychology, 10, 85.

Davis, M. H. (1983). Measuring individual differences in empathy: Evidence for a multidimensional approach. Journal of Personality and Social Psychology, 44(1), 113–126.

De Dreu, C. K. W., Greer, L. L., Van Kleef, G. A., Shalvi, S., & Handgraaf, M. J. J. (2010). Oxytocin promotes human ethnocentrism. Proceedings of the National Academy of Sciences, 108, 1262–1266.

de Oliveira, D. C., Zuardi, A. W., Graeff, F. G., Queiroz, R. H., & Crippa, J. A. (2012). Anxiolytic-like effect of oxytocin in the simulated public speaking test. Journal of Psychopharmacology, 26, 497–504.

De Vries, G. J. (2004). Minireview: Sex differences in adult and developing brains: Compensation, compensation, compensation. Endocrinology, 145(3), 1063–1068.

Ditzen, B., Schaer, M., Gabriel, B., Bodenmann, G., Ehlert, U., & Heinrichs, M. (2009). Intranasal oxytocin increases positive communication and reduces cortisol levels during couple conflict. Biological Psychiatry, 65(9), 728–731.

Ditzen, B., Nater, U. M., Schaer, M., La Marca, R., Bodenmann, G., Ehlert, U., et al. (2012). Sex-specific effects of intranasal oxytocin on autonomic nervous system and emotional responses to couple conflict. Social Cognitive and Affective Neuroscience, 8, 897–902.

Ebstein, R. P., Knafo, A., Mankuta, D., Chew, S. H., & Lai, P. S. (2012). The contributions of oxytocin and vasopressinpathway genes to human behavior. Horm. Behav. 61, 359–379.

Engelmann, M., & Landgraf, R. (1994). Microdialysis administration of vasopressin into the septum improves social recognition in Brattleboro rats. Physiology & Behavior, 55(1), 145–149.

Engert, V., Koester, A. M., Riepenhausen, A., & Singer, T. (2016). Boosting recovery rather than buffering reactivity: Higher stress-induced oxytocin secretion is associated with increased cortisol reactivity and faster vagal recovery after acute psychosocial stress. Psychoneuroendocrinology, 74, 111–120.

Feldman, R., Gordon, I., Schneiderman, I., Weisman, O., & Zagoory-Sharon, O. (2010). Natural variations in maternal and paternal care are associated with systematic changes in oxytocin following parent–infant contact. Psychoneuroendocrinology, 35(8), 1133–1141.

Francis, D. D., Young, L. J., Meaney, M. J., & Insel, T. R. (2002). Naturally occurring differences in maternal care are associated with the expression of oxytocin and vasopressin (V1a) receptors: Gender differences. Journal of Neuroendocrinology, 14(5), 349–353.

Gilbert, P. (2009). Introducing compassion-focused therapy. Adv. Psychiatr. Treat. 15, 199–208.

Gimpl, G., & Fahrenholz, F. (2001). The oxytocin receptor system: Structure, function, and regulation. Physiological Reviews, 81(2), 629–683.

Gobrogge, K., & Wang, Z. (2016). The ties that bond: Neurochemistry of attachment in voles. Current Opinion in Neurobiology, 38, 80–88.

Goetz, J. L., Keltner, D., & Simon-Thomas, E. (2010). Compassion: an evolutionary analysis and empirical review. Psychol. Bull. 136, 351–374.

Gonzalez-Liencres, C., Shamay-Tsoory, S. G., & Brüne, M. (2013). Towards a neuroscience of empathy: Ontogeny, phylogeny, brain mechanisms, context and psychopathology. Neuroscience & Biobehavioral Reviews, 37(8), 1537–1548.

Grippo, A. J., Trahanas, D. M., Zimmerman, R. R., Porges, S. W., & Carter, C. S. (2009). Oxytocin protects against negative behavioral and autonomic consequences of long-term social isolation. Psychoneuroendocrinology, 34(10), 1542–1553.

Grippo, A. J., Pournajafi-Nazarloo, H., Sanzenbacher, L., Trahanas, D. M., McNeal, N., Clarke, D. A., et al. (2012). Peripheral oxytocin administration buffers autonomic but not behavioral responses to environmental stressors in isolated prairie voles. Stress, 15(2), 149–161.

Guastella, A. J., Einfeld, S. L., Gray, K. M., Rinehart, N. J., Tonge, B. J., Lambert, T. J., & Hickie, I. B. (2010). Intranasal oxytocin improves emotion recognition for youth with autism spectrum disorders. Biological psychiatry, 67(7), 692–694.

Guastella, A. J., Mitchell, P. B., & Dadds, M. R. (2008). Oxytocin increases gaze to the eye region of human faces. Biological Psychiatry, 6(3), 3–5.

Handlin, L., Nilsson, A., Ejdebäck, M., Hydbring-Sandberg, E., & Uvnäs-Moberg, K. (2012). Associations between the psychological characteristics of the human–dog relationship and oxytocin and cortisol levels. Anthrozoös, 25(2), 215–228.

Heinrichs, M., Baumgartner, T., Kirschbaum, C., & Ehlert, U. (2003). Social support and oxytocin interact to suppress cortisol and subjective responses to psychosocial stress. Biological Psychiatry, 54(12), 1389–1398.

Hoffman, M. L. (1985). Affect, cognition, and motivation. In E. T. Higgins, & R. M. Sorrentino (Eds.), Handbook of motivation and cognition: Foundations of social behavior. New York: Guilford.

Hurlemann, R., Patin, A., Onur, O. A., Cohen, M. X., Baumgartner, T., et al. (2010). Oxytocin enhances amygdala-dependent, socially reinforced learning and emotional empathy in humans. J. Neurosci. *30*, 4999–5007.

Insel, T. R. (2010). The challenge of translation in social neuroscience: A review of oxytocin, vasopressin, and affiliative behavior. Neuron, *65*(6), 768–779.

Insel, T. R., & Shapiro, L. E. (1992). Oxytocin receptor distribution reflects social organization in monogamous and polygamous voles. Proceedings of the National Academy of Sciences United States of America, *89*, 5981–5985.

Israel, S., Lerer, E., Shalev, I., Uzefovsky, F., Reibold, M., Bachner-Melman, R., ..., & Ebstein, R. P. (2008). Molecular genetic studies of the arginine vasopressin 1a receptor (AVPR1a) and the oxytocin receptor (OXTR) in human behaviour: from autism to altruism with some notes in between. Progress in brain research, *170*, 435–449.

Keum, S., & Shin, H. S. (2016). Rodent models for studying empathy. Neurobiology of Learning and Memory, *135*, 22–26.

Kim, H. S., & Sasaki, J. Y. (2012). Emotion regulation: The interplay of culture and genes. Social and Personality Psychology Compass, *6*, 865–877.

Kim, H. S., & Sasaki, J. Y. (2014). Cultural neuroscience: Biology of the mind in cultural contexts. Annual Review of Psychology, *65*, 24.1–24.28.

Kim, H. S., Sherman, D. K., Sasaki, J. Y., Xu, J., Chu, T. Q., Ryu, C., et al. (2010). Culture, distress, and oxytocin receptor polymorphism (OXTR) interact to influence emotional support seeking. Proceedings of the National Academy of Sciences, *107*(36), 15717–15721.

Kim, H. S., Sherman, D. K., Mojaverian, T., Sasaki, J. Y., Park, J., Suh, E. M., et al. (2011). Gene–culture interaction: Oxytocin receptor polymorphism (OXTR) and emotion regulation. Social Psychological and Personality Science, *2*(6), 665–672.

Kosfeld, M., Heinrichs, M., Zak, P. J., Fischbacher, U., & Fehr, E. (2005). Oxytocin increases trust in humans. Nature, *435*, 673–676.

Lazarus, R. S. (1991). Progress on a cognitive–motivational–relational theory of emotion. American Psychologist, *46*(8), 819.

Lieberwirth, C., & Wang, Z. (2016). The neurobiology of pair bond formation, bond disruption, and social buffering. Current Opinion in Neurobiology, *40*, 8–13.

Lipschitz, D. L., Kuhn, R., Kinney, A. Y., Grewen, K., Donaldson, G. W., & Nakamura, Y. (2015). An exploratory study of the effects of mind–body interventions targeting sleep on salivary oxytocin levels in cancer survivors. Integrative Cancer Therapies, *14*(4), 366–380.

MacDonald, K., & MacDonald, T. M. (2010). The peptide that binds: A systematic review of oxytocin and its prosocial effects in humans. Harvard Review of Psychiatry, *18*(1), 1–21.

McQuaid, R. J., McInnis, O. A., Matheson, K., & Anisman, H. (2015). Distress of ostracism: Oxytocin receptor gene polymorphism confers sensitivity to social exclusion. Social Cognitive and Affective Neuroscience, nsu166.

Meaney, M. J. (2010). Epigenetics and the biological definition of gene/environment interactions. Child Development, *81*, 41–79.

Meyza, K. Z., Bartal, I. B. A., Monfils, M. H., Panksepp, J. B., & Knapska, E. (2016). The roots of empathy: Through the lens of rodent models. Neuroscience & Biobehavioral Reviews, *76*, 216–234.

Mikolajczak, M., Gross, J. J., Lane, A., Corneille, O., De Timary, P., & Luminet, O. (2010). Oxytocin makes people trusting, not gullible. Psychol. Sci. *21*, 1072–1074.

Miller, S. C., Kennedy, C. C., DeVoe, D. C., Hickey, M., Nelson, T., & Kogan, L. (2009). An examination of changes in oxytocin levels in men and women before and after interaction with a bonded dog. Anthrozoös, *22*(1), 31–42.

Morhenn, V., Beavin, L. E., & Zak, P. J. (2012). Massage increases oxytocin and reduces adrenocorticotropin hormone in humans. Alternative Therapies in Health and Medicine, *18*(6), 11.

Nagasawa, M., Okabe, S., Mogi, K., & Kikusui, T. (2012). Oxytocin and mutual communication in mother-infant bonding: Towards a neuroscience of social interaction. Frontiers in Human Neuroscience, 6. https://doi.org/10.3389/fnhum.2012.00031.

Nagasawa, M., Mitsui, S., En, S., Ohtani, N., Ohta, M., Sakuma, Y., et al. (2015). Oxytocin-gaze positive loop and the coevolution of human–dog bonds. Science, 348(6232), 333–336.

Nave, G., Camerer, C., & McCullough, M. (2015). Does oxytocin increase trust in humans? A critical review of research. Perspectives on Psychological Science, 10, 772–789.

Neff, K. D. (2003a). The development and validation of a scale to measure self-compassion. Self and Identity, 2, 223–250.

Neff, K. D. (2003b). Self-compassion: An alternative conceptualization of a healthy attitude toward oneself. Self and Identity, 2, 85–102.

Norman, G. J., Hawkley, L., Luhmann, M., Ball, A. B., Cole, S. W., Berntson, G. G., et al. (2012). Variation in the oxytocin receptor gene influences neurocardiac reactivity to social stress and HPA function: A population based study. Hormones and Behavior, 61, 134–139.

Odendaal, J. S., & Meintjes, R. A. (2003). Neurophysiological correlates of affiliative behaviour between humans and dogs. The Veterinary Journal, 165(3), 296–301.

Pace, T. W., Negi, L. T., Adame, D. D., Cole, S. P., Sivilli, T. I., Brown, T. D., et al. (2009). Effect of compassion meditation on neuroendocrine, innate immune and behavioral responses to psychosocial stress. Psychoneuroendocrinology, 34(1), 87–98.

Pedersen, C. A., & Prange, A. J., Jr. (1979). Induction of maternal behavior in virgin rats after intracerebroventricular administration of oxytocin. Proceedings of the National Academy of Science USA, 76, 6661–6665.

Pitman, R. K., Orr, S. P., & Lasko, N. B. (1993). Effects of intranasal vasopressin and oxytocin on physiologic responding during personal combat imagery in Vietnam veterans with posttraumatic stress disorder. Psychiatry Research, 48(2), 107–117.

Pobbe, R. L., Pearson, B. L., Defensor, E. B., Bolivar, V. J., Young, W. S., Lee, H. J., et al. (2012). Oxytocin receptor knockout mice display deficits in the expression of autism-related behaviors. Hormones and Behavior, 61(3), 436–444.

Qiao, X., Yan, Y., Wu, R., Tai, F., Hao, P., Cao, Y., et al. (2014). Sociality and oxytocin and vasopressin in the brain of male and female dominant and subordinate mandarin voles. Journal of Comparative Physiology A, 200(2), 149–159.

Quirin, M., Kuhl, J., & Düsing, R. (2011). Oxytocin buffers cortisol responses to stress in individuals with impaired emotion regulation abilities. Psychoneuroendocrinology, 36(6), 898–904.

Rilling, J. K., DeMarco, A. C., Hackett, P. D., Thompson, R., Ditzen, B., Patel, R., et al. (2012). Effects of intranasal oxytocin and vasopressin on cooperative behavior and associated brain activity in men. Psychoneuroendocrinology, 37(4), 447–461.

Rodrigues, S. M., Saslow, L. R., Garcia, N., John, O. P., & Keltner, D. (2009). Oxytocin receptor genetic variation relates to empathy and stress reactivity in humans. Proceedings of the National Academy of Sciences, 106(50), 21437–21441.

Sasaki, J. Y., & Kim, H. S. (2011). At the intersection of culture and religion: A cultural analysis of religion's implications for secondary control and social affiliation. Journal of Personality and Social Psychology, 101, 401–414.

Sasaki, J. Y., & Kim, H. S. (2017). Nature, nurture, and their interplay: A review of cultural neuroscience. Journal of Cross-Cultural Psychology, 48, 4–22.

Sasaki, J. Y., Kim, H. S., & Xu, J. (2011). Religion and well-being: The moderating role of culture and the oxytocin receptor (OXTR) gene. Journal of Cross-Cultural Psychology, 42, 1394–1405.

Singer, T., & Lamm, C. (2009). The social neuroscience of empathy. Ann. N. Y. Acad. Sci. 1156, 81–96.

Sippel, L. M., Allington, C. E., Pietrzak, R. H., Harpaz-Rotem, I., Mayes, L. C., & Olff, M. (2017). Oxytocin and Stress-related Disorders: Neurobiological Mechanisms and Treatment Opportunities. Chronic Stress, 1, 1–15. 2470547016687996.

Sivaselvachandran, S., Acland, E. L., Abdallah F.S., & Martin, L. J. (2016). Behavioral and mechanistic insight into rodent empathy. Neuroscience & Biobehavioral Reviews https://doi.org/10.1016/j.neubiorev.2016.06.007, (in press).

Shalvi, S., & De Dreu, C. K. W. (2014). Oxytocin promotes group-serving dishonesty. Proceedings of the National Academy of Sciences, 111, 5503–5507.

Smith, K. E., Porges, E. C., Norman, G. J., Connelly, J. J., & Decety, J. (2014). Oxytocin receptor gene variation predicts empathic concern and autonomic arousal while perceiving harm to others. Social Neuroscience, 9(1), 1–9.

Thompson, R. R., George, K., Walton, J. C., Orr, S. P., & Benson, J. (2006). Sex-specific influences of vasopressin on human social communication. Proceedings of the National Academy of Sciences, 103(20), 7889–7894.

Tost, H., Kolachana, B., Hakimi, S., Lemaitre, H., Verchinski, B. A., Mattay, V. S., et al. (2010). A common allele in the oxytocin receptor gene (OXTR) impacts prosocial temperament and human hypothalamic-limbic structure and function. Proceedings of the National Academy of Sciences, 107(31), 13936–13941.

Veenema, A. H. (2012). Toward understanding how early-life social experiences alter oxytocin-and vasopressin-regulated social behaviors. Hormones and Behavior, 61(3), 304–312.

Weisman, O., Zagoory-Sharon, O., & Feldman, R. (2012). Oxytocin administration to parent enhances infant physiological and behavioral readiness for social engagement. Biological Psychiatry, 72(12), 982–989.

Williams, K. D., Cheung, C. K., & Choi, W. (2000). Cyberostracism: Effects of being ignored over the Internet. Journal of Personality and Social Psychology, 79(5), 748.

Winslow, J. T., Hastings, N., Carter, C. S., Harbaugh, C. R., & Insel, T. R. (1993). A role for central vasopressin in pair bonding in monogamous prairie voles. Nature, 365, 545–548.

Zink, C. F., & Meyer-Lindenberg, A. (2012). Human neuroimaging of oxytocin and vasopressin in social cognition. Hormones and Behavior, 61(3), 400–409.

Can We Change Our Mind About Caring for Others? The Neuroscience of Systematic Compassion Training

Adam Calderon, Todd Ahern, Thomas Pruzinsky

Quinnipiac University, Hamden, CT, United States

INTRODUCTION AND SCOPE OF THE REVIEW

The emerging field of applied contemplative science (Desbordes & Negi, 2013; Farb, 2014; Giorgino, 2015; Wallace, 2007, 2012) is in large measure concerned with empirically investigating how specific mental states and traits can be made stronger, more consistent, and resilient. In this chapter, we present a review of the scientific literature on the changes in brain activation associated with systematic training in compassion, including the seminal work of Richard Davidson and colleagues on the neurobiological correlates of long-term systematic compassion training in highly experienced contemplative practitioners. We also review the programs of research conducted at Stanford and Emory Universities, both of which have developed and evaluated the efficacy of their manualized and secularized compassion training programs. Additionally, we describe the work of Tania Singer and her colleagues at the Max Planck Institute as well as the new intervention (PEACE) developed at Northern Arizona University.

Finally, we also provide an integrative summary of the current neuroscientific findings on systematic compassion training. The summary and synthesis of these complex findings is presented in a series of figures, including two particularly detailed brain maps, which allow for the graphic condensation of current research findings in a clear and compelling way while simultaneously maintaining a respect for the complexity

The Neuroscience of Empathy, Compassion, and Self-Compassion. http://dx.doi.org/10.1016/B978-0-12-809837-0.00008-8

of these outcomes. These brain maps graphically capture the principal findings of our review—that research outcomes investigating compassion training consistently show correlations with activity in a matrix of brain areas that extend from the frontal/prefrontal area posteriorly to the temporoparietal junction (TPJ) and that incorporate multiple cortical (e.g., dorsolateral prefrontal cortex (dlPFC), inferior frontal gyrus (IFG), medial orbital frontal cortex (mOFC), temporal gyrus, superior temporal sulcus (STS), and TPJ), embedded (e.g., insula and amygdala [Amyg]), subcortical (e.g., nucleus accumbens [NAcc], striatum, and ventral tegmental area [VTA]), and midline (e.g., medial anterior cingulate cortex [mACC], pregenualanterior cingulate cortex [pACC], and dorsomedial prefrontal cortex [dmPFC]) structures in a pattern that is visible in both EEG and fMRI studies.

Questions to Consider

Evaluation of compassion training efficacy must consider the questions below, offered here as a heuristic framework for this compelling and rapidly burgeoning body of research. They are very similar to the types of questions that have very effectively guided the multi-decade research on psychotherapy processes and outcomes. At this stage in the development of research on compassion training, many of the following questions remain unanswered:

- Can systematic compassion training reliably result in specific neurobiological changes?
- Is it reasonable to assume that these neurobiological changes reliably associate with predictable changes in cognition, emotion, behavior, and/or perception?
- To what degree might these neurobiological and/or psychological changes be influenced by the specific technique employed, by the length and intensity of the practice (i.e., the "dosage" of the training), by specific characteristics of individuals undertaking compassion training (e.g., devoted long-term Buddhist practitioners as compared to novices with no particular interest in Buddhism, religion, or spirituality), and/or by the experience and skillfulness of the compassion training teacher?
- Is it reasonable to assume that any neurobiological and/or psychological changes are the direct result of the putative "active ingredients" (e.g., the cultivation of self-compassion) of the compassion training technique? Or, might the neurobiological correlates/sequelae be the result of more general "non-specific" factors such as belief in the efficacy of the technique, general learning, and/or changes in attentional focus?

- Are there distinct neurobiological sequelae/correlates of specific components of training (e.g., does training in empathy vs. training in compassion have different effects)?
- Of what specific practical/clinical/training value is there to knowing the neurobiological correlates/sequelae to compassion training and/ or the specific and putatively unique components of compassion training?

Answers to these questions ideally can be addressed through a "transdisciplinary study of contemplative practices" (Dunne, 2016). Development of the CBCT and CCT models of secular compassion training provide excellent vehicles for such an approach. The training manuals for each of these programs were developed and written by geshes. A *geshe* holds a doctoral degree in Tibetan Buddhism and requires approximately 20 years to complete. There is a great deal of complexity involved in understanding the very significant differences in compassion training techniques and how these differences might affect the psychological and/or neurobiological (as well as spiritual) outcomes. Each of these programs of research also integrates varied levels of neuroscience expertise. Similarly, the research conducted by Richard Davidson as well as Tania Singer and collaborators has been done in conjunction with experts in contemplative practice as well as those with neuroscience expertise. In preparing this chapter, we have attempted to emulate this approach by bringing together a neuroscience teacher and researcher (Ahern), a clinical psychologist with approximately 20 years of intensive study and practice of a range of contemplative techniques (Pruzinsky), and an advanced student in Behavioral Neuroscience who has conducted research in this area as well (Calderon).

Compassion Training Techniques Reviewed

Table 8.1 provides an overview of the compassion training techniques discussed in this chapter. To more clearly address the question "Does compassion training reliably result in psychological and/or neurobiological changes?" it is essential to understand distinctions among the training programs. The table encapsulates many of the key similarities and differences among contemporary compassion training strategies.

For example, the highly experienced meditators described in the papers by Lutz et al. (2004, 2008, 2009) and Weng et al. (2013) utilized a form of compassion training that is embedded in the Tibetan Buddhist tradition. For many, if not most, highly experienced meditators, the religious/spiritual context is central to the compassion training process and directly influences the motivation to devote tens of thousands of hours to compassion meditation practice. In contrast, CBCT and CCT

TABLE 8.1 Compassion Meditation Techniques

Type of Training	Origins and Development of the Technique	Training Protocol Brief Description	Standard Amount of Training ("Dose")	Representative Publications
Highly Experienced Meditators (HEMs)	For HEMs, training is highly individualized and part of an ongoing teacher–student relationship. HEMs are committed to the tradition and also subscribe to Tibetan Buddhist worldview and values	HEMs trained by highly accomplished teachers including training in 'wisdom-based' practices (e.g., a deeply practiced form of mindfulness) intended to reduce the probability of being personally distressed by negative emotions associated with compassion training (see Lutz et al., 2008a, b)	Highly intensive training ranging from 10,000–50,000 h of meditative experience in the context of long-term study and/or meditation retreat contexts	Lutz et al. (2004, 2008 a,b, 2009 a,b); Weng et al. (2013)
Cognitively-Based Compassion Training (CBCT)	Developed at Emory University by Geshe Negi Lobsang and colleagues based on the Tibetan Buddhist Lojong (Mind Training) tradition	CBCT is taught in a sequence of 6 weeks addressing specific components which are described in Pace et al. (2009)	6 weeks of training, twice weekly for 1 h with at-home meditation practice	Mascaro et al. (2012, 2013, 2016); Pace et al. (2009, 2010, 2013); Reddy et al. (2013)
Compassion Cultivation Training (CCT)	Developed at Stanford University by Geshe Thupten Jinpa based on the Tibetan Buddhist Lojong (Mind Training) tradition	CCT is taught in a sequence of 8 weeks addressing specific components described in Jazaieri et al. (2013)	8 weeks of training, once weekly 2 h class with daily compassion-focused meditation practice	Jazaieri et al. (2013, 2014, 2015); Chapin et al. (2014)
Project for Empathy and Compassion Education (PEACE)	Developed by Lisa Doskocil at Northern Arizona University in order to engender compassion for others and for oneself, particularly for use in the public school system	PEACE is presented over 6 weeks in which participants are taught compassion, empathy, and self-compassion through lectures and guided practices	Participants meet once a week for 2 h for 6 weeks with daily homework	This is a new compassion training program implemented and tested over a 5-year period with outcome data collected but not yet published

are completely secularized, despite having been directly derived from the same _Lojong_ (Mind Training) tradition of Tibetan Buddhism, and these protocols have been developed for individuals with no background and/or interest in Tibetan Buddhist epistemology, cosmology, ontology, or psychology.

COMPASSION TRAINING PROGRAMS

Cognitively-Based Compassion Training (CBCT)

CBCT was created by Geshe Lobsang Tenzin Negi and colleagues at Emory University. The CBCT definition of compassion includes five separate and distinct components: (1) _cognitive_ (recognizing suffering in oneself or another); (2) _affective_ (a sense of concern or affection for the other); (3) _aspirational or motivational_ (the wish to relieve the suffering of the other); (4) _attentional_ (the degree of immersion and focus); and (5) _behavioral_ (the compassionate response; an action that stems from compassion) (Dodson-Lavelle, Ozawa-de Silva, Negi, & Raison, 2015). As noted above, while CBCT is based on the Lojong (Mind Training) tradition of Tibetan Buddhism, it is entirely secular in its presentation.

The initial studies of CBCT focused on whether or not CBCT would improve psychosocial functioning among adolescents in foster care (Reddy et al., 2013). These researchers found that CBCT, despite the lack of significant between-groups differences, was helpful to some of the adolescents in this pilot study. For instance, CBCT practice sessions were correlated with reduced C-reactive protein (an immune marker associated with stress) (Pace et al., 2013). In addition, CBCT has also been found to decrease loneliness and depression when compared to a control condition (Mascaro, Kelley, Darcher, Negi, Worthman, Miller, & Raison, 2016).

Pace et al. (2009, 2010) observed significant correlations between amount of meditation practice and immune and behavioral responses to psychosocial stress for adults who engaged in CBCT but not for normal controls. The study showed that compassion meditation is an effective method to learn how to cope with social stress and the individuals who practiced this specific type of meditation had lower cortisol levels.

Compassion Cultivation Training (CCT)

Geshe Thupten Jinpa, in collaboration with researchers at Stanford University and the Center for Compassion and Altruism Research and Education (CCARE), has created a compassion intervention program called CCT. Similar to CBCT, CCT is a manualized and secularized approach to compassion training that derives from the Tibetan Buddhist

Lojong (Mind Training) tradition. CCT follows a structured protocol that consists of a 2-h introductory orientation, 9 (once-weekly) 2-h classes, and daily compassion-focused meditation practice. Each class includes: (1) pedagogical instruction with active group discussion, (2) a guided group meditation, (3) interactive practical exercises related to the specific step of the week, and (4) exercises designed to prime feelings of openheartedness or connection to others, either through reading poetry or through reflecting on inspiring stories (Jazaieri et al., 2013).

The first published study evaluating the efficacy of CCT in a randomized-control trial found that compassion training led to increases in compassion felt for others, compassion offered from others, and compassion for the self, and that the amount of meditation practice was related to increased compassion for others (i.e., a dose–response effect) (Jazaieri et al., 2013). Another paper by Jazaieri et al. (2014), using the same sample as the 2013 study, reported increases in mindfulness and well-being in addition to improvements in mood (e.g., worry) and emotional suppression. Experienced meditators had significantly better outcomes than inexperienced meditators on measures of worry and emotional suppression (Jazaieri et al., 2014). Furthermore, a third clinical study also found that individuals had a reduction in pain severity and anger and increased pain acceptance after participating in CCT (Chapin et al., 2014).

Project for Empathy and Compassion Education (PEACE)

In 2012, a new compassion training program called "Project for Empathy and Compassion Education (PEACE)" was developed by Lisa Doskocil at Northern Arizona University. The goal of PEACE is to create educational opportunities for communities to learn about compassion and empathy and to intentionally foster and strengthen compassionate interactions in our daily lives, particularly in the public schools. PEACE is a 6-week course on compassion during which participants meet for training once-a-week for 2 h where they attend lectures and discussions on compassion, empathy, and positive psychology. Toward the end of each session, the instructor leads guided compassion-related practices (30–60 min) which vary from week to week. These activities include yoga, compassionate role-playing, Metta meditation, mindfulness meditation, and compassionate communicating. Outside of class, participants complete a community volunteer assignment and weekly homework tasks, including readings from the scholarly literature on compassion and empathy as well as applying meditation and behavioral practices to one's life (e.g., Tonglen meditation, Vipassana meditation, exploring Non-Violent Communication, doing one positive thing for oneself each day, and engaging in one mindful daily routine). Psychosocial and neuroscience investigations of the effects of PEACE are underway and are anticipated to be published over the coming year.

Highly Experienced Meditators

Highly experienced meditators represent a unique research cohort for neuroscience investigations as they offer quasi-experimental longitudinal investigations of the effects of long-term meditation practice, sometimes relative to no-treatment or brief-practice controls. From a contemplative science perspective, the kinds of meditation that these highly experienced meditators engage in require: (1) highly focused attention; (2) sustained over long periods of time; (3) the steady deepening of concentration over time; (4) mindful development of metacognitive awareness; and (5) an acute awareness of the suffering of all living beings. These meditation techniques also often involve quite elaborate visualization practices, further adding to the complexity of the cognitive processing which is occurring. Convenience samples of such long-term meditators have been made available through the benevolence and scientific interest of His Holiness, The Dalai Lama, as well as through unique community samples. Results of those studies are reviewed below.

THE NEUROSCIENCE OF SYSTEMATIC COMPASSION TRAINING

Highly Experienced Meditators Exhibit Distinct Patterns of Brain Activity

In a 128-channel EEG investigation, Lutz et al. (2004) found that highly trained Buddhist monks (with 10,000–50,000 h of meditation practice) were able to induce synchronized, high frequency and relatively high-amplitude gamma band oscillations (25–42 Hz) during meditation. These differences were most pronounced in the frontal and parietal/temporal lobe regions of the brain (Fig. 8.1). Gamma activity has been shown to be associated with hyperfocused attention and "neural binding", that is, the rapid integration of information across multiple sensory domains (Opitz, 2010). Historically, gamma wave band oscillations have often been overlooked due to their similarity to high-frequency muscle activity. However, their presentation in the Lutz et al., study following careful editing and control of muscle artifacts in these seasoned meditators, suggests hyperattention during the integration of complex, multisensory information, perhaps similar to an elevated information processing state.

While Lutz and colleagues' EEG studies revealed distinct gamma activity in medial and lateral frontoparietal electrodes for expert meditators

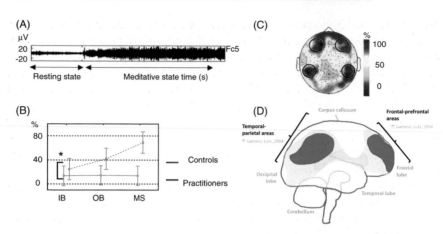

FIGURE 8.1   Adapted from Lutz et al. (2004): (A) depicts the change in EEG brain wave activity of a meditator who has had over 10,000 h of compassion meditation training as he moves from a rest state to a meditative state. The fast, higher-amplitude brain waves are Gamma oscillations. (B) Illustrates that highly experienced meditation practitioners have greater Gamma wave activity at baseline (IB), but they also significantly increase their Gamma activity as they move into a meditative state, whereas novice (Control) meditators do not. (C) With the nose pointing toward the top of the page, this figure shows the approximate locations of the EEG electrodes and areas that showed high levels of Gamma activity in experienced practitioners. (D) This is a graphic depiction of the lateral perspective of the right hemisphere with Red and Orange areas representing the high Gamma wave activity. Note that frontal and temporal-parietal areas show the greatest increase in Gamma wave activity.

(Lutz, Greischar, Rawlings, Ricard, & Davidson, 2004), they did not look for activation of more specific brain areas. In 2010, Engstrom and Soderfelt used fMRI to investigate the neural correlates of compassion meditation in a single experienced meditator and found activity in left medial prefrontal cortex (mPFC) extending to the anterior cingulate gyrus (ACC) (Engström & Söderfeldt, 2010).

Additional studies have added to the constellation of brain areas related to expert meditation and meditation training. For example, one investigation used fMRI to examine how experienced meditators react to emotional stimuli while meditating (Lutz, Brefczynski-Lewis, Johnstone, & Davidson, 2008a). The stimuli were emotionally valenced sounds of human vocalizations, such as a woman screaming or a baby crying. The results showed that experienced meditators exhibited higher Amyg, right TPJ, and right posterior STS (pSTS) activation compared to novices. Furthermore, experts had greater activation in the insula in response to negative sounds than to positive or neutral sounds in comparison to novice meditators. The implication of these outcomes was that, when compared to novice meditators, experts experience more empathy, and empathic arousal, when observing or hearing suffering. The same research group also examined which fMRI-measured brain activity changes were also associated with heart rate (Lutz et al., 2009 a,b). Under compassion meditation conditions, expert meditators exhibited increased heart rates compared to novice meditators and showed increased activity in the Insula and ACC. These outcomes are somewhat paradoxical to the notion that expert meditators would show lower heart rates, decreased activation of midline structures, and less empathic distress when exposed to suffering. However, the authors suggest that, unlike novice meditators, experts have attained through training unique regulatory capabilities (e.g., cultivating equanimity) to allow a deeper experiencing of compassion without undue personal or empathic distress.

In summary, examining the responses of highly experienced meditators reveals several important neuroscientific findings. Prefrontal cortex (PFC) and TPJ cortical regions appear to show enhanced EEG gamma binding activity and increased fMRI blood oxygen-level dependent (BOLD) responses in expert meditators compared to novice meditators when both are engaged in compassion meditation, particularly in response to distressing stimuli (Lutz, Greischar, Perlman, & Davidson, 2009a). fMRI studies have also revealed that a number of midline (e.g., ACC), embedded (e.g., Insula), and subcortical structures (e.g., Amyg) are also activated differentially by experts and novices, and that some of this activity (Insula and ACC) is closely coupled to changes in peripheral state (e.g., heart rate) in response to compassion-inducing stimuli. See Fig. 8.2.

Brief Compassion Training and Neurobiology

Given that the neuroscientific study of meditation is in its infancy, relatively few studies have assessed how experimental manipulation of compassion meditation can alter brain activity. Further, current studies rarely compare different types of training. Taken together, however, the extant literature does reveal a putative network of brain areas and electrophysiological changes affected by compassion training. The use of EEG and fMRI to study expert meditators described above has revealed important changes in the brain wave activity of PFC and TPJ regions as well as increased fMRI BOLD signals in pSTS, ACC, Insula, and Amyg when engaged in compassion meditation in response to distressing stimuli when compared to novices. Many of these same areas have shown altered activity in a number of subsequent studies of much less experienced meditators.

For example, two studies (Desbordes et al., 2012; Mascaro et al., 2013) found that compassion training in novices can apparently induce changes in some of these previously identified brain areas. In the Desbordes et al. (2012) study, participants randomly assigned to Mindful Attention Training (MAT) after 8 weeks of training exhibited significantly decreased Amyg BOLD activity in response to emotional images, even though

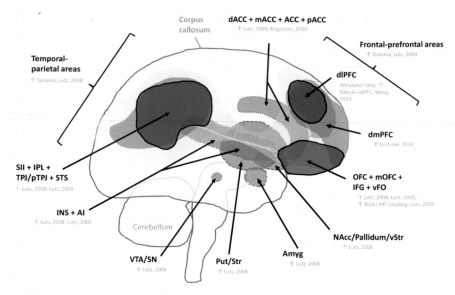

FIGURE 8.2 A graphic depiction/brain map illustrating the approximate location of increased EEG gamma activity in expert practitioners of compassion meditation (*red* and *orange* shading with no lines; compare to Fig. 1D), as well as specific brain areas that show increases in fMRI BOLD signals in expert meditators when compared to baseline or novice trainees. Note the overlap in peak Gamma activity and several cortical (—) areas. Embedded (— · · —), subcortical (− − −), and midline cortical (······) structures also showed increases in fMRI BOLD activity in experts, and the dlPFC and NAcc showed greater coupling (↔). Some changes in brain activity occurred bilaterally, but the most prominent changes occurred in right hemisphere, which are illustrated above. Each area is accompanied by articles that investigated changes in brain activity: First author and year. **Abbreviations:** *ACC*, anterior cingulate cortex; *AI*, anterior insula; *mACC*, medial anterior cingulate cortex; *Amyg*, amygdala; *dACC*, dorsal ACC; *dlPFC*, dorsolateral prefrontal cortex; *dmPFC*, dorsomedial PFC; *IFG*, inferior frontal cortex; *IPL*, inferior parietal lobule; *INS*, Insula; *mOFC*, medial orbitofrontal cortex; *NAcc*, nucleus accumbens; *OFC*, orbitofrontal cortex; *pACC*, pregenual ACC; *pSTS*, posterior superior temporal sulcus; *pTPJ*, posterior temporal parietal junction; *SII*, postcentral somatosensory gyrus (Brodman 40); *SN*, substantia nigra; *TPJ*, temporal parietal junction; *VFO*, ventral frontal operculum; *VTA*, ventral tegmental area.

participants were in a non-meditative rest state during the MRI procedure. This decrease was not observed in either the control group or the group engaged in CBCT training. Interestingly, these researchers also saw a trend toward increased Amyg activation in the CBCT group, suggesting that this CBCT tended to increase Amyg activity in response to distressing images. There was also a trend toward a relationship between these Amyg increases and general affective state (i.e., depression score). However, the sample size was small and not gender matched. Therefore, these apparent CBCT-related changes must be interpreted very cautiously.

Similarly, the second study also used fMRI but in this study they assessed how CBCT might alter both empathic accuracy and BOLD signals.

This study too had a small sample size with gender imbalances (N = 21; CBCT = 7 females, 6 males; Control group = 2 females, 6 males), still the results indicated that CBCT could enhance empathic accuracy as well as alter brain function. In particular, CBCT training significantly increased IFG, STS, dmPFC, and anterior paracingulate cortex activity, and these changes correlated with empathic accuracy (Mascaro, Riling, Negi, & Raison, 2013).

There are also data suggesting that the dlPFC, right inferior parietal cortex (IPC), and the NAcc are affected by compassion-related meditation training. Since compassion training encourages meditators to take the perspective of the sufferer, Weng et al. (2013) hypothesized that compassion training would result in increased altruistic behavior along with changes in brain activity. Using a money-distribution game, participants witnessed one player providing an unfair distribution of money to another player. The participant then had a chance to correct the apparent wrong by contributing a sum that had to be matched by the first player. The more money the participant gave, the higher the altruism score. The group that received compassion training was then compared with a control group that had undergone reappraisal training. Not only did the compassion group redistribute more money (greater altruistic behavior) than the reappraisal group but also the compassion-trained participants exhibited greater fMRI BOLD activity in the right IPC and right dlPFC. Moreover, the degree of signal change was significantly correlated with the level of altruistic redistribution.

Two other findings from this study are important to note. First, the authors reported greater "coupling" between the right dlPFC and NAcc. That is, as the activity of one region increased there was a corresponding increase in the other. The degree of coupling was also associated with altruistic behavior. In short, Weng et al. (2013) observed that compassion training appeared to influence an interconnected network of brain areas simultaneously rather than independently.

Second, the reappraisal training altered the BOLD signals and dlPFC-NAcc coupling in the opposite way. Instead of a positive correlation between brain activity and redistribution behavior, there was a negative correlation. This finding suggests that, while the same brain areas might be affected by cognitive/meditative engagement, the type of training significantly influenced the direction of change.

Compassion training seems to induce greater levels of positive affect and approach behavior. Klimecki et al. (2013) investigated the affective and neurobiological consequences of short-term compassion training. Based on the nature of the training and prior research, they predicted that they would see increased activation in the anterior insula and mACC in comparison to baseline and that by empathizing more with individuals in distressing situations, pain network activity would be enhanced, especially in response to high distress stimuli. Given the focus on compassion, they also predicted that brain areas associated with approach, affiliation, and positive affect would show greater activation (Klimecki, Leiberg, Lamm, & Singer, 2013). These researchers found that short-term compassion training induced increased activity in the mOFC, VTA/SN (ventral tegmental/substantia nigra area, both major sources of dopamine), putamen, and pallidum. Interestingly, the most pronounced changes occurred in the right hemisphere, consistent with the above-cited research, where the increases for the novice trainees paralleled those of expert meditators engaging in compassion (Klimecki et al., 2013).

The goals of empathy and compassion training are similar in some ways but distinct in others. Despite their similarity as social emotions, they tend to activate different, and in some important ways, opposing affective and cognitive process. Specifically, empathy training increases empathic concern, perspective taking, and a sharing in the emotions of another (Singer & Lamm, 2009). However, when witnessing another's suffering, participants can experience empathic (personal) distress, marked by negative affect, avoidance behavior, and burnout, particularly if there is insufficient differentiation between the self and the other (Klimecki et al., 2014). Compassion training, on the other hand, involves a sensitivity to the suffering of another but not necessarily a sharing of their emotional experience. Individuals who undergo compassion training may exhibit greater empathy and negative affect, but compassion is also accompanied by positive affect in the anticipation of the alleviation of suffering, as well as approach and helping behaviors (Klimecki, Leiberg, Ricard, & Singer, 2014). This difference between empathy and compassion suggested to Klimecki, Singer, and colleagues that perhaps these different types of training could lead to different patterns of brain activity.

By directly comparing empathy training with compassion training, Klimecki et al. (2014) aimed to tease apart which patterns of brain activity were associated with which type of training. Such distinct patterns of neurological activation might help explain the affective and behavioral outcomes associated with each type of training. On the neural level, short-term empathy training increased fMRI BOLD signals in the Insula (specifically, AI) and Cingulate Cortex (specifically, medial ACC) compared to compassion training and a control group (i.e., participants who received memory training). They also found increased activity in the temporal gyrus, dlPFC, operculum, and parts of basal ganglia (posterior putamen and head of the caudate). Klimecki et al. (2014) noted that this constellation of structures comprises the pain matrix, which becomes activated when experiencing pain or witnessing other people in pain. The increased activity of the dlPFC and middle temporal gyrus may be related to distress management, as both regions are important for emotion and pain regulation. Compassion training, however, resulted in increased fMRI BOLD activity in the mOFC, pregenual ACC (pACC), and striatum, including the ventral striatum-NAcc. As Klimecki et al. noted, these areas have consistently been linked to positive affect, reward, and pleasure, as might be expected to occur from compassion training (Klimecki et al., 2013, 2014). Given that, when compared directly to empathy training, compassion training resulted in less activation of the mACC and Insula and more activation of the mOFC, pACC, and NAcc, the results suggest that different types of meditation training have distinct effects on how the brain responds to distressing stimuli.

Overlapping but Distinct Systems

The survey of how empathy and compassion training relate to brain activity above suggests a number of important conclusions. First, as discussed at the beginning of this chapter, studying experts who have over 10,000 h of compassion training is a valuable approach for identifying brain systems that might show different activity after training (e.g., Lutz et al., 2004). Given the inherently correlational nature of those studies and the inability to test a specific kind of compassion training as an intervention limits the conclusions we can draw. Nonetheless, the painstaking efforts to conduct these studies with Tibetan monks are indeed laudatory and clearly have advanced the field.

Second, to effectively compare different types of meditation treatments, it is essential that they be compared within the same experimental framework—same training duration, similar training protocols, same measurement techniques, etc. Without such an approach, researchers will continue to see what has been described above, overlapping but not directly comparable measures of brain activation. In the absence of direct comparisons, it will be difficult to identify whether the differences are due to the type of training or simply to an artifact of experimental design.

Understanding these caveats leads us to the third conclusion: many brain areas seem to be affected by training, but identification of specific effects can be daunting. Fig. 8.3 provides an image that is based on the current cutting edge of empathy and compassion training research discussed in this chapter. By no means is it exhaustive, but we believe that it illustrates the pattern of empirical findings related to research on the neuroscience of compassion training. This current mapping suggests a sequence of brain areas that extends from the frontal/prefrontal area posteriorly to the temporo-parietal junction and incorporates multiple cortical (e.g., dlPFC, IFG, mOFC, temporal gyrus, STS, and TPJ), embedded (e.g., Insula and Amyg), subcortical (e.g., NAcc, Striatum, and VTA), and midline (e.g., mACC, pACC, and dmPFC) structures in a pattern that is represented by both EEG and fMRI studies.

The complexity of this system can be reduced to some degree by grouping brain areas based on the networks, affective states, and behaviors to

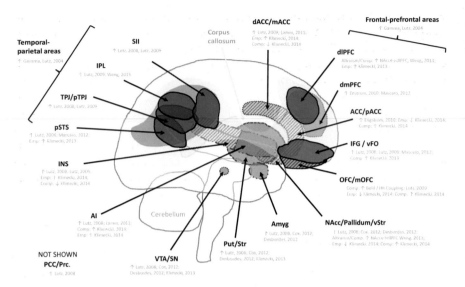

FIGURE 8.3 This graphic depiction adds more detail than presented in Figs. 1D and 2, and provides a more comprehensive map of all of the empathy and compassion findings detailed in this chapter. The graphic clearly demonstrates that there is substantial overlap between studies of the relationship between empathy/compassion meditation and changes in brain activity. There are cortical (—), embedded (— · · —), subcortical (− − −), and midline cortical (······) structures. Most regions show increases in brain activity (↑), some showed decreases (↓), and two areas showed greater coupling/connectivity (↔), depending on whether the study was assessing empathy (Emp) or compassion (Comp) training. Areas illustrated in Blue/Red hashing show increased activation (*Red*) in response to one training regime and less activation (*Blue*) under a different training protocol. Abbreviations: *ACC*, anterior cingulate cortex; *AI*, anterior insula; *mACC*, medial anterior cingulate cortex; *Amyg*, amygdala; *dACC*, dorsal ACC; *dlPFC*, dorsolateral prefrontal cortex; *dmPFC*, dorsomedial PFC; *IFG*, inferior frontal cortex; *IPL*, inferior parietal lobule; *INS*, Insula; *mOFC*, medial orbitofrontal cortex; *NAcc*, nucleus accumbens; *OFC*, orbitofrontal cortex; *pACC*, pregenual ACC; *pSTS*, posterior superior temporal sulcus; *pTPJ*, posterior temporal parietal junction; *SII*, postcentral somatosensory gyrus (Brodman 40); *Put*, putamen; *SN*, substantia nigra; *Str*, striatum; *TPJ*, temporal parietal junction; *VFO*, ventral frontal operculum; *vStr*, ventral striatum; *VTA*, ventral tegmental area.

which they typically contribute. For example, the Insula and mACC are part of the network that underlies pain perception and management, while mOFC, pACC, VTA, and NAcc are part of the network that regulates reward, pleasure, and positive affect. Likewise, the dmPFC and TPJ have been associated with mentalizing or thinking about the mental states of others, also called Theory of Mind (ToM: see Chapter 3 for a more comprehensive presentation of ToM) (Mascaro, Rilling, Negi, & Raison, 2013; Weng et al., 2013).

Such anatomical and functional linkages are essential for making sense of how different types of training might differentially influence brain activity and in turn alter affect, cognition, and behavior. The linkages also provide a basis for future hypotheses or for making predictions about how the training "treatments" that are being developed might enhance one type of brain pattern or another. Klimecki (2015) and Mascaro, Darcher, Negi, and Raison (2015) have both reviewed the distinct patterns of brain activity associated with empathy versus compassion training with Klimecki proposing that the type of training in which participants engage shapes the functioning of two antagonistic systems. Empathy training tips the balance toward one system, while compassion training tips the balance in favor of the antagonistic system. It is proposed that these changes underlie the measured differences in emotional state and behavioral responses. Fig. 8.4A and B illustrate these findings.

DIRECTIONS FOR FUTURE RESEARCH

As impressive as many of the studies we have reviewed are, they are also a good reminder that we are only beginning to probe the questions outlined at the start of the chapter. To outline our view of what to explore next, it is worth looking at a few of the limitations of the current literature. These will provide a foundation for the future studies we propose in the second section.

Understanding the Current Limitations

Techniques like EEG and fMRI are remarkable investigative tools. Moreover, given the overlap between so many studies, it is reasonable to currently conclude that meditation, empathy, compassion, and other cognitive and affective changes really are associated with changes in brain activity. But we must also be appropriately cautious. For example, fMRI requires sophisticated technology, corrections for artifacts (e.g., motion, individual differences in brain morphology, slice acquisition asynchrony, etc.), and the correct choice of statistical methods, any of which has the potential to introduce errors or unknown biases into the data. For example, a recent report by Eklund and colleagues indicated that approximately one in 10 published fMRI studies may be flawed due to processing errors, particularly spatial autocorrelation functions (Eklund, Nichols, & Knutsson, 2016). Thus, we recommend being cautious about taking the results of any single study as irrefutable evidence for a particular outcome.

Additionally, fMRI is an indirect measure of brain activity, recording BOLD blood flow responses associated with an experience. While reflecting metabolic demands of neurons and, by inference, increased activation, fMRI does not directly measure neuronal activity. The same concern can be levied at single-photon emission computed tomography and positron-emission tomography studies. Interestingly, although not yet generating high-resolution neuroimages of neural tissue, EEG is actually a more direct and temporally precise measurement of the activation of large neural networks. With the development of improved cortical and subcortical current source density (CSD) algorithms directly associated with surface EEG potentials, particularly with denser arrays, EEG has the potential to offer more direct measures of electrocortical activity (compared to relatively indirect hemodynamic measures) as well as reliable and valid localization methods.

There is also the concept of neuroplasticity to consider. Such physical brain changes in response to experience comprise some of the most exciting discoveries of contemporary neuroscience. These changes occur throughout life, have been demonstrated at molecular, neuronal, circuit, system, and whole-brain levels, and seem to be the basis of most, if not all, learning and behavioral change (Sweatt, 2016). Though not discussed here, in the compassion literature, as in much neuroscience research, there are many references to neural plasticity. It is important to note, however, that not a single study in this review directly measured neural alterations; such changes are inferred from blood flow or electrocortical modifications. This inference is well-considered in that changes in level of activity following training are likely due to changes in strength of neural connections (e.g., Hebb's Rule, Long-Term Potentiation, Long-Term Depression, etc.; see Sweatt, 2016 for a review). Notwithstanding the challenges in directly measuring in human studies specific alterations in neural networks associated with interventions, it is hoped that technological advances on the horizon will someday allow such measures in a nonintrusive manner.

It is also important to point out that even for studies in which there was an experimental manipulation (e.g., empathy training vs. compassion training vs. memory training; e.g., Klimecki et al., 2014), the relationship between brain measures (e.g., mOFC activity) and the cognitive and affective states are only correlational. None of the studies have shown directly that artificially inducing increased activity in the mOFC, pACC, and ventral striatum, while simultaneously decreasing the activity of the left and right insula and anterior medial cingulate cortex will induce a state of compassion that is accompanied by positive affect and decreased negative affect. A correlational relationship has been shown which suggests that this effect might be possible, but the causal relationship between distinct profiles of brain activity and distinct cognitive and affective states has not been directly demonstrated, as concerns empathy and compassion research. Advancements in transcranial magnetic stimulation (TMS) and deep brain stimulation (de Weijer et al., 2014; Kahan et al., 2014) may soon allow us to perform the types of experiments we propose below to make causal inferences, but as yet, they have not been conducted.

Finally, it is important to note that all of the studies referenced above have limitations with regard to external validity (e.g., the generalizability of the findings). As Davidson's group notes in multiple papers: "novices and experts differ in many respects other than simply the extent of meditative training (such as culture of origin and first language)," as well as belief systems, teachers and their expertise, an assumed prerequisite training of highly experienced meditators (HEMS), etc. (Lutz, Brefczynski-Lewis, Johnstone, & Davidson, 2008a). In addition to culture of origin and first language differences between novices and HEMS, there may also be self-selecting biases when recruiting study participants. Some may self-select for meditative training. Cautions with regard to such volunteer biases are important for consideration in future research (Demir, Haynes, Orthel-Clark, & Ozen, 2016).

Equally important is the fact that several early experimental training studies utilized groups that were not gender matched (i.e., different ratios of males and females in the training vs. control groups [Desbordes et al., 2012; Mascaro et al., 2013]) or studied only female participants (Klimecki et al., 2013, 2014). In practice, recruiting sufficiently large groups of both genders is a challenge and focusing on only one (e.g., females who are more empathetic) enhances homogeneity and provides greater control. However, many of the expert studies, which were based on predominantly male experts, also make generalizing across genders more difficult. Future research needs to address these imbalances in order to clarify our understanding of brain function as it pertains to empathy and compassion (Sacher, Neumann, Okon-Singer, Gotowiec, & Villringer, 2013).

Future Studies

As research advances on compassion training, the field could benefit by focusing on three directions, by conducting studies that are more: (1) descriptive; (2) experimental; as well as (3) deeply collaborative.

Descriptive: Being more descriptive here suggests that researchers compare and contrast different types of training (e.g., CBCT, CCT, PEACE). Specific questions that can be addressed include: Is one type of compassion training more effective than another? Is there a sequence of training components (e.g., the specific components of CBCT, CCT, PEACE) that is more efficacious (e.g., the CBCT training program emphasizes cultivation of equanimity as foundational to compassion training, whereas CCT places somewhat less emphasis on this particular component)? Is there a way to match the specific type of training to the specific individual characteristics (e.g., some individuals might benefit from practicing self-compassion earlier in the training, whereas others may not)?

An increase in the overall specificity in describing the neurobiological effects of compassion training would also be helpful. For example, utilizing more fine-grained analyses of EEG data (e.g., using CSD) as well as comparing, contrasting, and combining EEG assessment with fMRI data could help describe cortical and subcortical brain activation differences between training regimens and during segmented time periods to establish if there are specific changes from baseline measures. Additionally, it would be informative to increase the amount and type of neurophenomenological forms of assessment conducted. If we could make only one suggestion for future research on compassion training, it would be to further develop and to refine a range of phenomenological/qualitative/first-person methodologies (Englander & Folkesson, 2014; Lutz, Slagter, Dunne, & Davidson, 2008b; Lutz & Thompson, 2003; Petitmengin, 2006) in order to link subjective and objective EEG (van Lutterveld et al., 2016) and fMRI data (Garrison et al., 2013). Such an approach could potentially provide unique information regarding how to enhance the efficacy of the training. For example, when some individuals engage in cultivating gratitude and/or self-compassion in the context of compassion training, if not applied correctly, participants can be harshly judgmental of themselves which can be quite a negative subjective experience that may not be captured by current psychometric measures. Additionally, being able to "map" this type of experience onto the neurobiological assessment may help to clarify the neuroimaging conducted thus far.

Experimental: A compelling experimental question is whether there is a "critical period" of development during which one can potentially maximize the efficacy of compassion training. For example, in terms of adult developmental outcomes, would it be more beneficial to provide developmentally appropriate forms of compassion training for young adolescents when compared with older adolescents? Since adolescent brains are more "plastic," it is reasonable to posit that compassion training may have more positive psychosocial and neurobiological effects if started earlier in life. The PEACE program described earlier was developed expressly for this purpose and we await publication of neuroscience outcomes to clarify the differential developmental effects suggested above.

A potentially illuminating experimental approach to enhancing compassion could include using targeted noninvasive stimulation techniques such as TMS (e.g., de Weijer et al., 2014) and Transcranial Direct Current Stimulation (e.g., Zheng, Alsop, & Schlaug, 2011) to selectively activate or deactivate specific brain areas in the compassion/empathy networks. Such strategies could evaluate whether these interventions directly cause a change in the *experience* of compassion/empathy feelings, cognitions, or behaviors and perhaps, even more intriguing, could determine if such interventions bring about neurobiological changes that have putatively arisen from compassion training. Ideally, since fMRI data show the importance of multiple brain areas (networks) changing activity together rather than individually, it would be exciting to extend such a study further to directly manipulate multiple areas simultaneously. In short, could one electromagnetically induce the effects noted in Fig. 8.4A versus B without the need for systematic compassion training?

Deeply Collaborative: To make valid, reliable, and practical progress toward the goal of maximizing the efficacy of compassion training, we believe that researchers involved in this work must have expertise in three separate and distinct disciplines: neuroscience, contemplative practice, and clinical psychology. It is rare that any single individual will have true expertise in two of these three areas and exceptionally rare for any single individual to be expert in all three areas. Therefore, it is imperative when using neuroscience data to evaluate the efficacy of compassion training that an expert perspective from these three disciplines be included in order to maximize our understanding and cultivation of the benefits of such training and to prevent the occurrence of any potential psychological distress that might occur as a result of intensive compassion training (i.e., *primum non nocere*).

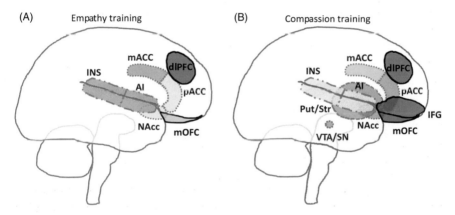

FIGURE 8.4 Distinct brain activity patterns post-empathy training (A) and post-compassion training (B) (Klimecki et al., 2013, 2014). There are cortical (—), embedded (— · · —), subcortical (− − −), and midline cortical (······) structures. In response to each type of training, areas colored *Red* represent increases in activation when the participant is confronted with distressing video clips, whereas areas colored *Blue* represent less or decreased activation in response to the same stimuli. Klimecki et al. (2014) have noted that empathy training (A) increases activation of a pain relevant network, while compassion training (B) increases the activity of pleasure and reward areas associated with approach behavior. Abbreviations: *ACC*, anterior cingulate cortex; *AI*, anterior insula; *mACC*, medial anterior cingulate cortex; *Amyg*, amygdala; *dACC*, dorsal ACC; *dlPFC*, dorsolateral prefrontal cortex; *dmPFC*, dorsomedial PFC; *IFG*, inferior frontal gyrus; *IPL*, inferior parietal lobule; *INS*, insula; *mOFC*, medial orbitofrontal cortex; *NAcc*, nucleus accumbens; *OFC*, orbitofrontal cortex; *pACC*, pregenual ACC; *pSTS*, posterior superior temporal sulcus; *pTPJ*, posterior temporal parietal junction; *SII*, postcentral somatosensory gyrus (Brodman 40); *SN*, substantia nigra; *TPJ*, temporal parietal junction; *VFO*, ventral frontal operculum; *VTA*, ventral tegmental area.

References

Chapin, H. L., Darnall, B. D., Seppala, E. M., Doty, J. R., Hah, J. M., & Mackey, S. C. (2014). Pilot study of a compassion meditation intervention in chronic pain. *Journal of Compassionate Health Care, 1*, 4. doi: 10.1186/s40639-014-0004-x.

Demir, M., Haynes, A., Orthel-Clark, H., & Ozen, A. (2016). Volunteer bias in research on friendship among emerging adults. *Emerging Adulthood, 5*, 53–68. doi: 10.1177/2167696816641542.

Desbordes, G., & Negi, L. T. (2013). A new era for mind studies: training investigators in both scientific and contemplative methods of inquiry. *Frontiers in Human Neuroscience, 7*, 741. doi: 10.3389/fnhum.2013.00741.

Desbordes, G., Negi, L. T., Pace, T. W., Wallace, B., Raison, C. L., & Schwartz, E. L. (2012). Effects of mindful-attention and compassion meditation training on amygdala response to emotional stimuli in an ordinary, non-meditative state. *Frontiers in Human Neuroscience, 6*, 292. doi: 10.3389/fnhum.2012.0029.

Desbordes, G., Gard, T., Hoge, E. A., Hölzel, B. K., Kerr, C., Lazar, S. W., et al. (2014). Moving beyond mindfulness: Defining equanimity as an outcome measure in meditation and contemplative research. *Mindfulness, 6*(2), 356–372. doi: 10.1007/s12671-013-0269-8.

de Weijer, A. D., Sommer, I. E. C., Bakker, E. J., Bloemendaal, M., Bakker, C. J. G., Klomp, D. W. J., et al. (2014). A setup for administering TMS to medial and lateral cortical areas during whole-brain FMRI recording. *J Clin Neurophysiol, 31*, 474–487. doi: 10.1097/WNP.0000000000000075.

Dodson-Lavelle, B., Ozawa-de Silva, B., Negi, G. T., & Raison, C. L. (2015). Cognitively based compassion training for adolescents. In V. M. Follette, J. Briere, D. Rozelle, J. W. Hopper, D. I. Rome, V. M. Follette, & D. I. Rome (Eds.), *Mindfulness-oriented interventions for trauma: Integrating contemplative practices* (pp. 343–358). New York, NY: US: Guilford Press.

Dunne, J. (2016). The transdisciplinary study of contemplative practices. *Challenges and Opportunities* November, Invited Address: Mind and Life Institute, San Diego, CA.

Eklund, A., Nichols, T. E., & Knutsson, H. (2016). Cluster failure: Why fMRI inferences for spatial extent have inflated false-positive rates. *Proceedings of the National Academy of sciences, 113*(28), 7900–7905. doi: 10.1073/pnas.1602413113.

Engen, H. G., & Singer, T. (2015). Compassion-based emotion regulation up-regulates experienced positive affect and associated neural networks. *Social Cognitive and Affective Neuroscience, 10*(9), 1291–1301. doi: 10.1093/scan/nsv008.

Englander, M., & Folkesson, A. (2014). Evaluating the phenomenological approach to empathy training. *Journal of Humanistic Psychology, 54*(3), 294–313. doi: 10.1177/0022167813493351.

Engström, M., & Söderfeldt, B. (2010). Brain activation during compassion meditation: A case study. *J. Altern Complement Med, 16*(5), 597–599. doi: 10.1089/acm.2009.0309.

Farb, N. S. (2014). Can contemplative science bring meditation to (Western) life? In S. Schmidt, H. Walach, S. Schmidt, & H. Walach (Eds.), *Meditation—Neuroscientific approaches and philosophical implications* (pp. 243–259). Cham, Switzerland: Springer International Publishing doi: 10.1007/978-3-319-01634-4_14.

Garrison, K., Santoyo, J., Davis, J., Thornhill, T., Kerr, C., & Brewer, J. (2013). Effortless awareness: Using real time neurofeedback to investigate correlates of posterior cingulate cortex activity in meditators' self-report. *Front Hum Neurosci, 7*, 440. doi: 10.3389/fnhum.2013.00440.

Giorgino, V. B. (2015). Contemplative methods meet social sciences: Back to human experience as it is. *Journal for the Theory of Social Behaviour, 45*(4), 461–483. doi: 10.1111/jtsb.12078.

Jazaieri, H., Jinpa, G., McGonigal, K., Rosenberg, E. L., Finkelstein, J., Simon-Thomas, E., et al. (2013). Enhancing compassion: A randomized controlled trial of a compassion cultivation training program. *Journal of Happiness Studies, 14*(4), 1113–1126. doi: 10.1007/s10902-012-9373-z.

Jazaieri, H., McGonigal, K., Jinpa, T., Doty, J. R., Gross, J. J., & Goldin, P. R. (2014). A randomized controlled trial of compassion cultivation training: Effects on mindfulness, affect, and emotion regulation. *Motivation and Emotion, 38*(1), 23–35. doi: 10.1007/s11031-013-9368-z.

Jazaieri, H., Lee, I. A., McGonigal, K., Jinpa, T., Doty, J. R., Gross, J. J., et al. (2015). A wandering mind is a less caring mind: Daily experience sampling during compassion meditation training. *The Journal of Positive Psychology, 11*(1), 37–50. doi: 10.1080/17439760.2015.1025418.

Kahan, J., Urner, M., Moran, R., Flandin, G., Marreiros, A., Mancini, L., et al. (2014). Resting state functional MRI in Parkinson's disease: The impact of deep brain stimulation on 'effective' connectivity. *Brain, 137*, 1130–1144. doi: 10.1093/brain/awu027.

Klimecki, O. M. (2015). The plasticity of social emotions. *Social Neuroscience, 10*(5), 466–473. doi: 10.1080/17470919.2015.1087427.

Klimecki, O. M., Leiberg, S., Lamm, C., & Singer, T. (2013). Functional neural plasticity and associated changes in positive affect after compassion training. *Cerebral Cortex, 23*, 1552–1561. doi: 10.1093/cercor/bhs142.

Klimecki, O. M., Leiberg, S., Ricard, M., & Singer, T. (2014). Differential pattern of functional brain plasticity after compassion and empathy training. *Social Cognitive and Affective Neuroscience, 9*, 873–879. doi: 10.1093/scan/nst060.

Lamm, C., Decety, J., & Singer, T. (2011). Meta-analytic evidence for common and distinct neural networks associated with directly experienced pain and empathy for pain. *NeuroImage, 54*(3), 2492–2502. doi: 10.1016/j.neuroimage.2010.10.014.

Lutz, A., & Thompson, E. (2003). Neurophenomenology: Integrating subjective experience and brain dynamics in the neuroscience of consciousness. *J Conscious Stud, 9*(10), 31–52.

Lutz, A., Greischar, L. L., Rawlings, N. B., Ricard, M., & Davidson, R. J. (2004). Long-term meditators self-induced high-amplitude gamma synchrony during mental practice. *Proceedings of the National Academy of Sciences, 101*, 16369–16373. doi: 10.1073/pnas.0407401101.

Lutz, A., Brefczynski-Lewis, J., Johnstone, T., & Davidson, R. (2008a). Regulation of the neural circuitry of emotion by compassion meditation: Effects of meditative expertise. *PLoS One, 3*, e1897. doi: 10.1371/journal.pone.00018972004.

Lutz, A., Slagter, H. A., Dunne, J. D., & Davidson, R. J. (2008b). Attention regulation and monitoring in meditation. *Trends in Cognitive Science, 12*(4), 163–169. doi: 10.1016/j.tics.2008.01.005.

Lutz, A., Greischar, L. L., Perlman, D. M., & Davidson, R. J. (2009a). BOLD signal in insula is differentially related to cardiac function during compassion meditation in experts vs. novices. *NeuroImage, 47*(3), 1038–1046. doi: 10.1016/j.neuroimage.2009.04.081.

Lutz, A., Slagter, H. A., Rawlings, N. B., Francis, A. D., Greischar, L. L., & Davidson, R. J. (2009b). Mental training enhances attentional stability: Neural and behavioral evidence. *The Journal of Neuroscience, 29*(42), 13418–13427. doi: 10.1523/JNEUROSCI.1614-09.2009.

Mascaro, J. S., Rilling, J. K., Negi, L. T., & Raison, C. L. (2012). Compassion meditation enhances empathic accuracy and related neural activity. *Social Cognitive and Affective Neuroscience, 8*(1), 48–55. doi: 10.1093/scan/nss095.

Mascaro, J. S., Rilling, J. K., Negi, L. T., & Raison, C. L. (2013). Pre-existing brain function predicts subsequent practice of mindfulness and compassion meditation. *NeuroImage, 69*, 6935–6942. doi: 10.1016/j.neuroimage.2012.12.021.

Mascaro, J. S., Darcher, A., Negi, L. T., & Raison, C. (2015). The neural mediators of kindness-based meditation: A theoretical model. *Front Psychol, 6*, 109. doi: 10.3389/fpsyg.2015.00109.

Mascaro, J. S., Kelley, S., Darcher, A., Negi, L. T., Worthman, C., Miller, C., et al. (2016). Meditation buffers medical student compassion from the deleterious effects of depression. *The Journal of Positive Psychology, 13*(2), 133–142. doi: 10.1080/17439760.2016.1233348.

Opitz, B. (2010). Neural binding mechanisms in learning and memory. *Neuroscience and Biobehavioral Reviews, 34*, 1036–1046. doi: 10.1016/j.neubiorev.2009.11.001.

Pace, T. W., Negi, L. T., Adame, D. D., Cole, S. P., Sivilli, T. I., Brown, T. D., et al. (2009). Effect of compassion meditation on neuroendocrine, innate immune and behavioral responses to psychosocial stress. *Psychoneuroendocrinology, 34*(1), 87–98. doi: 10.1016/j. psyneuen.2008.08.011.

Pace, T. W., Negi, L. T., Sivilli, T. I., Issa, M. J., Cole, S. P., Adame, D. D., et al. (2010). Innate immune, neuroendocrine and behavioral responses to psychosocial stress do not predict subsequent compassion meditation practice time. *Psychoneuroendocrinology, 35*(2), 310–315. doi: 10.1016/j.psyneuen.2009.06.008.

Pace, T. W., Negi, L. T., Dodson-Lavelle, B., Ozawa-de Silva, B., Reddy, S. D., Cole, S. P., et al. (2013). Engagement with cognitively-based compassion training is associated with reduced salivary C-reactive protein from before to after training in foster care program adolescents. *Psychoneuroendocrinology, 38*(2), 294–299. doi: 10.1016/j.psyneuen.2012.05.019.

Petitmengin, C. (2006). Describing one's subjective experience in the second person: An interview method for the science of consciousness. *Phenomenology and the Cognitive Sciences, 5*, 229–269 10.1007s11097-006-9022-2.

Reddy, S. D., Negi, L. T., Dodson-Lavelle, B., Ozawa-de Silva, B., Pace, T. W., Cole, S. P., et al. (2013). Cognitive-based compassion training: A promising prevention strategy for at-risk adolescents. *Journal of Child and Family Studies, 22*(2), 219–230. doi: 10.1007/s10826-012-9571-7.

Sacher, J., Neumann, J., Okon-Singer, H., Gotowiec, S., & Villringer, A. (2013). Sexual dimorphism in the human brain: Evidence from neuroimaging. *Magnetic Resonance Imaging, 31*(3), 366–375. doi: 10.1016/j.rmi.2012.06.007.

Singer, T., & Lamm, C. (2009). The social neuroscience of empathy. *Annals of the New York Academy of Sciences, 1156*, 81–96. doi: 10.1111/j.1749-6632.2009.04418.x.

Sweatt, J. D. (2016). Neural plasticity and behavior: Sixty years of conceptual advances. *Journal of Neurochemistry, 139*(2), 179–199. doi: 10.1111/jnc.13580.

van Lutterveld, R., Houlihan, S. D., Pal, P., Sacchet, M. D., McFarlane-Blake, C., & Brewer, J. D. (2016). Source-space EEG neurofeedback links subjective experience with brain activity during effortless awareness meditation. *NeuroImage, 151*, 117–127. doi: 10.1016/j. neuroimage.2016.02.047.

Wallace, B. A. (2007). *Contemplative science: Where Buddhism and neuroscience converge*. New York, NY, USA: Columbia University Press.

Wallace, B. A. (2012). *Meditations of a Buddhist skeptic: A manifesto for the mind sciences and contemplative practice*. New York, NY, USA: Columbia University Press.

Weng, H. Y., Fox, A. S., Shackman, A. J., Stodola, D. E., Caldwell, J. Z. K., Olson, M., et al. (2013). Compassion training alters altruism and neural responses to suffering. *Psychological Science, 24*, 1171–1180. doi: 10.1177/0956797612469537.

Zheng, X., Alsop, D. C., & Schlaug, G. (2011). Effects of transcranial direct current stimulation (tDCS) on human regional cerebral blood flow. *NeuroImage, 58*, 26–33. doi: 10.1016/j. neuroimage.2011.06.018.

Compassion Training from an Early Buddhist Perspective: The Neurological Concomitants of the *Brahmavihāras*

Robert J. Goodman, Paul E. Plonski, Leah Savery

Northern Arizona University, Flagstaff, AZ, United States

> Like a mother with four sons, namely a child, an invalid, one in the flush of youth, and one busy with his own affairs; for she wants the child to grow up, wants the invalid to get well, wants the one in the flush of youth to enjoy for long the benefits of youth, and is not at all bothered about the one who is busy with his own affairs.
> —Visuddhimagga IX, 108, trans. Ñāṇamoli, The Path of Purification

The deliberate exercise of compassion (Pāli: *karunā*) has been practiced for over 2500 years alongside loving-kindness (*mettā*), sympathetic joy (*muditā*), and equanimity (*upekkhā*), which together represent the four *brahmavihāras*, also known as the divine or immeasurable abodes. While outcomes associated with the deliberate cultivation of compassion are the primary aim of the present chapter, a first step in understanding the construct is to contextualize it alongside the other *brahmavihāras* described in Early Buddhist soteriology, as well as to highlight the similarities and differences among each of the *brahmavihāras*, and other contemplative proficiencies they depend on, such as sustained attention (*samatha*) and open monitoring (*vipassanā*). An exploration of the overlapping theoretical components of the *brahmavihāras* may shed light on conceptual/psychological similarities and differences among them, but more important to the present chapter, may also illuminate distinctions in neural networks that are exercised during their deliberate training in contemplative practice.

The Neuroscience of Empathy, Compassion, and Self-Compassion. http://dx.doi.org/10.1016/B978-0-12-809837-0.00009-X

THE *BRAHMAVIHĀRAS* IN EARLY BUDDHIST SOTERIOLOGY

Much like the meditation exercises of concentrative absorption (*jhāna*), *brahmavihāra* practices predated the historical Buddha and were a common discussion topic among Early Buddhist monastics, members of Vedic or orthodox Brahminical traditions, and their contemporaries (Anālayo, 2015; Gombrich, 2009). While discussion of the *brahmavihāras* occurs across multiple canonical texts, the most widely known source is the *Tevijja Sutta* (DN 13 in Walshe, 1995), in which the Buddha reinterprets how directed contemplation of these four boundless qualities liberates the mind and leads to companionship with Brahma, the supreme goal of life as taught in the Vedas.

The four *brahmavihāras* are characterized by a sustained sense of mental spaciousness in which a practitioner pervades the mind with one of the four abodes and radiates it in all directions, indiscriminately, without a particular object or person. In doing so, *brahmavihāra* practice culminates in the ability to dwell in a "boundless" state that radiates each respective *brahmavihāra* for all beings (Anālayo, 2015). While Early Buddhist canonical texts do not emphasize application of the *brahmavihāras* to a particular being or object, the later commentarial tradition as recorded in Buddhaghosa's *Visuddhimagga* describe approaches in which a practitioner gradually cultivates each state by bringing to mind friends, strangers, and enemies before extending the target object to a depersonalized, objectless experience of mental freedom (Anālayo, 2003; Ñāṇamoli, 1991). To more clearly articulate the nature of the *brahmavihāras*, the commentarial tradition preserved in the *Visuddhimagga* (Ñāṇamoli, 1991) describes each alongside their respective "far enemies"—qualities that are directly opposed to each *brahmavihāra* and promote future suffering—and "near enemies"—qualities that are in subtle opposition but resemble and could be easily mistaken for each (see Table 9.1).

TABLE 9.1   The Near and Far Enemies of the Four *Brahmavihāras*

Brahmāvihara	English Translation	Near Enemy	Far Enemy
Mettā	Loving-kindness; benevolence	Greed; selfish affection	Ill will; hostility
Karunā	Compassion	Grief; sadness	Cruelty
Muditā	Empathic joy; gladness	Merriment; exuberance	Envy; jealousy; schadenfreude
Upekkhā	Equanimity; equipoise	Unknowing indifference	Agitation

Loving-Kindness (Mettā): The first, as well as most frequently mentioned *brahmavihāra* in Early Buddhist literature, is loving-kindness or benevolence (*mettā*), which represents an attitude of friendliness and cordiality in relation to others, and the general wish for another's welfare irrespective of external conditions or personal circumstances (Singer & Klimecki, 2014). Loving-kindness is considered the forerunner of the other three *brahmavihāras* that establishes the foundation to exercise them. Likewise, it is described as the "water" that nourishes the seed of what, with proper cultivation, will become the tree of compassion (Anālayo, 2015). The far enemy, or opposing quality, of loving-kindness is hostility or ill will (*vyāpāda*). Indeed, the cultivation of loving-kindness is thought to weaken the propensity for ill will to arise and pervade the mind (SN 46.51 in Bodhi, 2000). It is considered impossible to experience loving-kindness when angry, and loving-kindness is considered fully established when the causes and conditions that give rise to ill will have been completely eradicated (Anālayo, 2015; Ñāṇamoli, 1991). The near enemy that masquerades as loving-kindness which should be carefully protected against is greed, which, much like loving-kindness, is characterized by affection toward another being but is marred by an unwholesome craving (*taṇhā*), a sense of dissatisfaction with experience that results from perceived lacking or wanting (Analayo, 2012). Put another way, greed is considered an unwholesome state because it is characterized by a self-centered wanting, which implicitly points to an underlying sense of dissatisfaction with the way things are. The picture that emerges from comparing loving kindness to its enemies is a state of benevolence that is empty of self-concern regarding personal benefit, that is central to establishing cordiality in interpersonal relationships, and which reduces the propensity to experience feelings of anger and hostility.

Compassion (Karunā and Anukampā): Compassion (*karunā*) is the second of the four *brahmavihāras* and represents a positive, often joyful state of active concern for others to experience freedom from their suffering and affliction. The deliberate cultivation of compassion is thought to restructure experience such that one is less likely to become overwhelmed by cruelty, compassion's far enemy (Anālayo, 2015). Grief (Ñāṇamoli, 1991), sadness (Anālayo, 2015), or pity (Kornfield, 1993) are commonly described as near enemies of compassion because they share in their confrontation with the suffering of others, but are distinct in that they elicit personal suffering (*dukkha*) in the practitioner. From an Early Buddhist perspective, suffering is a conditioned phenomenon that arises due to a specific cause: craving for the present to be different than it is, which is manifested as wanting or aversion. From this perspective, one see's *the* suffering, rather than *my* or *their* suffering. It is through one's insight into the impersonal nature of suffering, its causes, and the path to its eradication (i.e., understanding the four noble truths) that compassion grows.

From this perspective, compassion can be understood as a natural outgrowth of developing insight into the impersonal nature of suffering and our fundamental interconnectedness with others; and these insights result from making progress on one's personal path toward the cessation of suffering (Salzberg, 2017). From this perspective, compassion is quite distinct from empathic sensitivity, in which one vicariously experiences another person's suffering. Rather, compassion involves developing a new perspective of and relationship with suffering that comes in the wake of one's personal progression toward the cessation of suffering. As one realizes that one's own suffering is impermanent and changing, a compassionate person does not experience the suffering of others, but instead, they experience the bliss of knowing that others can be free from their suffering. This compassionate response to others is thought to flower naturally from the practitioner's direct experience and insight into the impersonal nature of suffering and the realization of the cessation of suffering in their own experience.

Additionally, Early Buddhist canonical texts clearly distinguish between *karunā*—the meditative exercise of compassion—and *anukampā*—merciful, prosocial motivation to act compassionately. *Anukampā* is exemplified in how a parent might selflessly act out to help a child, or in the way a teacher may help a struggling student. Indeed, accounts of the historical Buddha describe how he chose to teach others "out of compassion", and regularly ended sermons by emphasizing that he taught out of compassion for the welfare of his students. Thus, *karunā* and *anukampā* represent two complementary aspects of compassion in Early Buddhism, with the former being a state of boundless compassion one might radiate during directed compassion meditation, and the latter as the motivation to act compassionately and actively reduce the suffering of others, often by teaching (Anālayo, 2015). In sum, compassion represents a positive state in which the experience of wishing others to realize freedom from affliction becomes the object of meditative cultivation.

Sympathetic Joy (*Muditā*): Sympathetic Joy (*muditā*), the third *brahmavihāra*, is characterized by rejoicing in the successes of others. It is described as naturally being brought about by living harmoniously with others in a context of mutual appreciation and concern for their well-being. It stands in direct contrast to the experience of envy, which involves wanting the successes of another for oneself, and schadenfreude, in which one takes pleasure in the misfortunes of others. As a state of positive affect elicited by another's positive emotions, *muditā* could be considered as a type of empathy since it requires understanding of another's mental and affective states. The experience of sympathetic joy is said to eradicate personal discontent (Anālayo, 2015) and strengthens the predisposition to experience personal happiness through sharing in the good fortune of others. However, states of sympathetic joy are not to be confused with merriment or exuberance, a manic type of joy that arises from craving (*taṇhā*). At first blush, merriment and exuberance may seem to be positive states, yet in this context, they represent an uncontrolled and compulsive seeking for happiness that is driven by the experience of craving (lacking or wanting). The near enemy of sympathetic joy involves an egoistic seeking of joy through indulgence in pleasures that serve to temporarily conceal underlying dissatisfaction, much like the hollow excitement and pleasure experienced by the addict who finds temporary relief from the pangs of withdrawal. Similar to the other *brahmavihāras*, sympathetic joy represents a positive, tranquil state that arises from the welfare of others, rather than a pleasure that arises from self-focused craving.

Equanimity (*Upekkhā*): The fourth *brahmavihāra* is equanimity (*upekkhā*), which represents a sense of mental equipoise or balance in the face of positive or negative affect, emotions, and thoughts. It is marked by a sense of psychological distance when attending to the changing flux of agreeable and disagreeable experiences that "rounds off a systematic opening of the heart" (Anālayo, 2012, pp. 165). Similar to the construct of "decentering" (Bishop, 2002), equanimity can be conceived of as the detachment of personal desire (wanting or not wanting) from the positive, negative, and neutral affective tones (*vedanā*) of experience (Desbordes et al., 2015; Hadash et al., 2016). It is through equanimity that a practitioner is capable of retaining clear awareness and presence of mind when confronted with particularly pleasant or unpleasant experiences. Canonical sources attribute equanimity to the capacity to recognize the agreeable in the disagreeable and the disagreeable in the agreeable, such that equanimity represents an approach toward experience that is not enchanted by pleasure or resistant to pain, but instead takes a calm, balanced, middle way through both extremes. In this way, equanimity decouples our well-being from external circumstances by reducing the desire for experience to conform to our likes and dislikes. Thus, when one dwells in the abode of equanimity, experiences are less influenced and reactive to the vicissitudes of changing experience. Agitated reactivity toward experience represents the far enemy of equanimity, an orientation in which our satisfaction is largely contingent on external circumstances matching our personal preferences. The near enemy of equanimity is a dull, uncaring indifference or neutrality toward experience. While loving-kindness, compassion, and sympathetic joy are each the result of reaching out to other people, equanimity complements the other three *brahmavihāras* as a selfless and impartial joy that arises without an active target (Anālayo, 2015).

The *Brahmavihāras* in Context: On the basis of this brief overview, a thread that runs through Early Buddhist accounts of the four *brahmavihāras* can be understood by examining their enemies. The far enemies of the *brahmavihāras* depict negative affective responses to others that are laced with malice and harmful intentions. Moreover, the near enemies represent affective responses to others that, while positive, are tarnished by a sense of self-concern or indifference. While each near enemy involves some type of self-referential appraisal, the *brahmavihāras* themselves clearly represent positive, other-oriented emotional responses that do not involve cognitively elaborating on, filtering the meaning of, or weighing the value of such emotions in relation to self-set desires and goals. Rather, the *brahmavihāras* occur in a context that is empty of self-concern (Anālayo, 2015), and it is from this state that one is in position to deliberately strengthen the ability to feel positively *for* others, irrespective of their emotional state (suffering, joy, etc.), or whether there is a concrete target. From this, it appears that Early Buddhist conceptualizations of the *brahmavihāras* are established on a foundation of minimized self-concerns (e.g., craving) and the active cultivation of pleasant other-oriented emotions and prosocial intentions. However, the ability to proficiently minimize self-concerns and to regulate other-oriented emotions is not simply second nature. These skills are interrelated with and built upon antecedent contemplative proficiencies, a topic to which we will now turn.

ATTENTIONAL FOUNDATIONS OF CONTEMPLATIVE PRACTICE

Alongside living an ethical lifestyle, proficiency in sustained attention and open awareness are commonly emphasized as prerequisite contemplative skills that are trained before progressing to directed *brahmavihāra* practice in Early Buddhist (Pandita, 1992) and contemporary Western approaches (Jazaieri et al., 2013; Mascaro et al., 2012; Mascaro, Darcher, Negi, & Raison, 2015; Ozawa-de Silva & Dodson-Lavelle, 2011). For example, contemporary 8-week training programs designed to cultivate loving-kindness and compassion, such as Compassion Cultivation Training (Jinpa & Weiss, 2013) and Cognitively-Based Compassion Training (CBCT; Negi, 2013; Ozawa-de Silva & Dodson-Lavelle, 2011) begin by training foundational attentional capacities (sustained attention and open awareness) before progressing into compassion training. Empirical evidence is beginning to emerge that supports the advantages of developing foundational attention capacities before *brahmavihāra* practices. Evidence from a large-scale 9-month modularized contemplative training program known as the ReSource Project (Singer et al., 2016) recently demonstrated that people self-report stronger compassionate feelings in response to neutral and negative emotional videos when participants receive attention-based contemplative training (sustained attention to breath and body) before affect-based contemplative training (loving-kindness and compassion), relative to when they receive affect-based contemplative training alone (Trautwein, Kanske, Böckler-Raettig, & Singer, unpublished manuscript).

A burgeoning body of research has examined the adaptive effects of focused attention and open monitoring, as well as training to enhance it, to improve changes in neural networks involved in attention and emotion regulation. These changes are aligned with a variety of positive mental health outcomes, such as improved social relationships, behavior regulation, and other domains of adaptive functioning. While a full review of the literature on sustained attention and open monitoring is beyond the scope of the present chapter, it is important to highlight evidence that demonstrates the neural mechanisms through which attention-based contemplative training may augment cultivation of the *brahmavihāras*. Such a review will allow us to distinguish the neural processes deliberately exercised during *brahmavihāra* training from neural processes influenced by the attention-based contemplative practices that precede them during training.

Early Buddhist perspectives on sustained attention and open monitoring: Two distinct but interrelated systems of practice form the basis of Buddhist meditation (Ñāṇamoli et al., 1995). The first, called *samatha*, exercises sustained attention and reduced mental distraction, which leads to serenity and mental calm (*samādhi*). The second, known as *vipassanā* or insight, is characterized by anchoring attention to the present while opening or broadening it to encompass the rising and passing away of moment-to-moment experiences. The purpose of *vipassanā* meditation is to openly monitor moment-to-moment experience with the purpose of gaining insight into three key characteristics of existence (*tilakkhaṇa*). The first is that all things are perpetually changing and impermanent (*anicca*): anything that arises will eventually fade away. Second, that because all things are constantly changing, there is nothing lasting that can be called a self (or soul). That is, existence is impersonal (*anuttā*). Third, not seeing existence as an impersonal changing process leads people to crave for experience to be different than it is, which leads to dissatisfaction and suffering (*dukkha*). In sum, *samatha* practices train one to focus and sustain attention on one particular object with the purpose of experiencing seclusion and tranquility, while *vipassanā* practices train one to be receptive to changing moment-to-moment experience with the purpose of gaining insight into the nature of existence.

While enhancing the quality of attention is foundational to both practices, they are unique in the way attention is engaged and exercised. In the following section we outline these characteristics in more detail, how they are interrelated in practice, and briefly review their influence on neural markers of attention.

Samatha belongs to a larger body of meditation practices that foster *samādhi*, or concentration. *Samādhi* is literally translated as "to put together" or "to collect" and entails allowing the mind to rest and come to focus on a single point (Anālayo, 2003; Shankman, 2008). This is often called one-pointedness because the mind is firmly and exclusively fixed on its object (i.e., such as the breath or an image) for an extended period of time. During intense periods of *samādhi*, attention becomes so focused on a single object that all other internal and external phenomenon are excluded from awareness, such that noises are not heard and sensations are not felt. Without practice, however, attention is less disciplined and has a tendency to become scattered and habitually wander moment-by-moment from one mental experience to another, and to proliferate thoughts about experience (*papañca*) rather than engaging present-moment experience directly (Ñānananda, 1971; Ñāṇamoli et al., 1995). Thus, for a state of *samādhi* to be sustained, one must recognize when distractions arise and have the skill to gently redirect attention back to the object of concentration without getting conceptually entangled in distractions (Dunn et al., 1999; Lutz et al., 2006; Ñānananda, 1971; Shankman, 2008). In this way, *samatha* practice primarily strengthens the capacity to sustain a stable, alert, and concentrated, yet tranquil state. In addition, *samatha* practice trains one to disengage and reorient attention back to a focal object without losing the sense of focus and calm (Lutz et al., 2006).

The purpose of *vipassanā*, or open monitoring meditation, on the other hand, is to develop insight into the phenomenal nature of experience by broadening the focus of awareness to encompass the entirety of occurrences in the present moment (Anālayo, 2003; Brown & Cordon, 2009; Brown, Ryan, & Creswell, 2007). While attention is stable and maintained on the present during *vipassanā* practice, it is not focused toward a solitary target with such intensity that all other experiences are excluded from awareness. Instead, it involves a fanning out, or opening of awareness to accommodate the whole flux of internal and external experiences as they arise and pass away in the present. It is the broad meta-awareness exercised in *vipassanā* practice that actually monitors the mental state and detects distraction (Lutz, Dunne, & Davidson, 2006).

Vipassanā is typically associated with cultivating mindfulness (*sati*)—an open and receptive awareness of present moment events and experiences (Brown & Ryan, 2003). The literal translation of *sati* is "to remember", yet attention, not memory, is the more proximate process that serves the faculty of mindfulness. As a state of ongoing clarity of the present moment, the subtle contours of experiences are more clearly witnessed and easily remembered when mindful (Anālayo, 2003; Wallace & Bodhi, 2006). The ability to remember present experiences and recall past experiences is facilitated when aware, rather than when distracted and forgetful (Wallace & Bodhi, 2006). By anchoring attention to the flux of present moment experience, the ability to remember experiences is enhanced. This influence of mindfulness may facilitate optimal working and episodic memory function (Atkinson & Shiffrin, 1968; Brown et al., 2016; Van Vugt, 2015). Thus, *sati* is a characteristic that influences both memory and awareness, where, in contrast to narrowing focus of *samādhi*, the attentional spotlight is not focused on a particular object, but broadened to capture the wholeness of present-moment experience with enhanced clarity (Dunn, Hartigan, & Mikulas, 1999). A primary purpose of vipassanā practice is to gradually infuse the ability to clearly comprehend the present and to apply it to daily activities to bring about wisdom into the nature of existence (Nyanaponika, 1965). Thus, while *samatha* practice is exercised to anchor the mind on a solitary stable object, *vipassanā* functions to broaden awareness of present-moment experience, which, in turn, sets the stage for a more clear observation of phenomenological experience and downstream insight into the ever-changing and impersonal nature of psychological suffering.

While clear distinctions exist between *samatha* and *vipassanā*, they are interdependent in application and both types of attention are needed to sustain each other. The functional difference between them lies in the degree to which each attentional capacity is exercised (Lutz et al., 2006). For example, when practicing *samatha*, the most salient effort involves sustaining a one-pointed stable focus, yet a degree of mindful awareness is required to monitor the mind and detect when attention has drifted away from its object. Similarly, the paramount feature of *vipassanā* practice consists of broadening and clarifying awareness, but clarity quickly dithers without concentration fixing the mind on the present moment. While traditions have diverse opinions regarding the relative importance of each technique, virtually all schools of Buddhism emphasize the need for both in varying degrees (Shankman, 2008).

Due to their interdependent nature, developing a sense of balance between these attentional capacities is seen as crucial to progress in meditation (Lutz et al., 2006). Because sustaining a fixed focus on the present is a necessity for practicing *vipassanā*, novice meditators are typically advised to begin practicing *samatha* until the attention can be sustained on its object (usually the breath) with a degree of stability. As stability increases, *vipassanā* practice is engaged to bring about clarity and to enhance precision in detecting and dealing with distraction. Likewise, steps to improve stability are taken to sustain intense levels of clarity. This balancing act is emphasized across sessions of practice, such that a specific skill is exercised more frequently over time, and within a single session based on the demands of a specific meditative state (i.e., emphasizing *vipassanā* when barraged with mental distractions during *samatha* practice).

Interestingly, Buddhist thinking has distinguished between types of attention in ways similar to modern science. For example, the capacity that steers the mind toward an object (*manasikāra*; Wallace & Bodhi, 2006) is considered distinct from *samatha and sati*. The Buddhist scholarship that underlies these meditation techniques clearly indicates an understanding of capacities involved in monitoring the stability of attention, detecting distraction, disengaging attention when it has become distracted, and re-orienting it back to its target object (Lutz et al., 2008b). These scholars have also recognized the connections between the monitoring aspects of attention, memory function, and emotion (Anālayo, 2003).

Neural subsystems of attention: Empirical studies have suggested three functionally distinct but related subsystems of attention with unique patterns of brain activation (Fan, McCandliss, Fossella, Flombaum, & Posner, 2005; Fan et al., 2002; Posner & Petersen, 1990). The first, an alerting system, is responsible for bringing about and sustaining an alert state and is related to the speed and accuracy of attention in response to a stimulus. Alerting attention is associated with increased brain activity in the frontal and parietal regions. This type of attention is also related to levels of norepinephrine in the cortex (Fan, McCandliss, Sommer, Raz, & Posner, 2002; Posner & Petersen, 1990).

The second attentional subsystem functions to orient attention, and is involved in disengagement and reallocation of attention to new perceptual cues. This orienting function has been associated with areas of the parietal and frontal lobes (Posner & Petersen, 1990). When a cue is presented the superior parietal lobe is activated. However, when cues are not provided and one anticipates that attention will be redirected, attention is disengaged prior to the presentation of a stimulus. This disengagement process is associated with increased activity in the temporal-parietal junction (Fan et al., 2002).

The third subsystem of attention, which involves monitoring and resolving conflicts between stimulus sources, is called executive control or conflict monitoring. The executive control system of attention is engaged when a target stimulus must be distinguished and selected from a wide range of competing stimuli. Activation of this system is associated with increased neural activity in the dorsal anterior cingulate and the lateral prefrontal cortices.

In sum, attentional capacities are composed of three orthogonal subsystems associated with distinct anatomical signatures in the brain: The alerting subsystem is involved in maintaining an alert state and is associated with neural activation in the frontal and parietal regions; the orienting subsystem is responsible for disengaging and reallocating attention to new cues and is associated with activation in the frontal and parietal lobes and the temporal-parietal junction; and the executive control subsystem is involved in detecting and monitoring conflicts between competing stimuli, and is associated with activity in the dorsal anterior cingulate and the lateral prefrontal cortices. Deficits in executive control have been linked to individual differences in memory function as well (Redick & Engle, 2006).

The neuroscience of sustained attention and open monitoring: Given the distinct ways these meditation systems are proposed to engage attention, it seems plausible that they would invoke distinct neural subsystems of attention. While *samatha* and *vipassanā* practices are expected to increase activation in neural regions associated with all three subsystems of attention, they should certainly highlight distinct types of attention more than others. Specifically, *samatha* practice should be associated with alerting and reorienting attention because it is characterized by sustaining intense focus on a solitary target, and redirecting attention back to its focal object after distraction. Therefore, *samatha* practice should be associated with increased frontoparietal cortical activity, left-sided anterior intraparietal, inferior parietal and frontal activation, and right-sided temporal parietal junction activity. Meta-awareness and ability to detect distraction associated with skill in *vipassanā* meditation may facilitate the executive control attentional network responsible for conflict monitoring and resolution evidenced by dorsal anterior cingulate and dorsolateral prefrontal cortex (DLPFC) activation.

Several studies have used neuroimaging techniques to assess alterations in brain function during meditative states. In a study using functional magnetic resonance imaging (fMRI), Baerentsen, Hartvig, Stødkilde-Jørgensen, and Mammen, 2001 found increases in DLPFC and the anterior cingulate cortex among mindfulness practitioners. Another study found that *vipassanā* meditation was associated with activity in the frontal and parietal cortices and the dorsal cingulate cortex (Lazar et al., 2003). A third study found mindfulness training to be associated with greater activity in dorsolateral and posterior parietal cortices with greater increases in the left hemisphere (Farb et al., 2007). Thus, each of these studies associate *vipassanā*/mindfulness meditation with increases in neural regions primarily associated with the executive control of attention, with one study also finding increases in regions associated with alerting attention.

Evidence from studies using the Attention Network Task (Fan et al., 2002) to examine differences in attention network function due to meditation practice is just beginning to emerge. One such study found that participation in a mindfulness-based stress reduction retreat had significantly enhanced the conflict monitoring component of attention (Jha, Krompinger, & Baime, 2007). Another study found that 5 days of integrative body–mind training, a form of meditation associated with heightened awareness of breathing, led to significant increases in conflict monitoring (Tang et al., 2007).

Considerably less research has been conducted using neuroimaging techniques to examine *samatha* practice. One recent study conducted by Brefczynski-Lewis et al. (2007) found that Tibetan monks with an average of 19,000 lifetime-hours of meditation had more left-sided activity in the superior frontal gyrus and middle frontal gyrus during focused attention meditation than novices.

Open monitoring and emotion regulation: While changes in attention networks are a central outcome of directed practices to enhance sustained attention and open monitoring, a robust body of contemplative neuroscience literature highlights additional benefits that result from mindfulness training that are relevant and that may help set the stage for the cultivation of the *brahmavihāras* (Desbordes et al., 2015; Tang et al., 2015). More specifically, mindfulness appears to influence how people engage, sustain, and regulate emotional experiences.

Mindfulness has been shown to increase markers of positive affective style and well-being (Barnhofer, Chittka, Nightingale, Visser, & Crane, 2010; Moyer et al., 2011; Urry et al., 2004), as well as to dampened neural activity associated with emotional reactivity, such as reduced amygdala volume (Taren et al., 2013), grey matter density (Hölzel et al., 2011), and amygdala activation (Farb et al., 2007, 2010; Goldin & Gross, 2010; Modinos et al., 2010; Way et al., 2010). Neuroimaging studies have shown that mindfulness training increases neural activation in regions of the prefrontal cortex (PFC) involved in emotion regulation and the top down inhibition of the amygdala (Quirk & Beer, 2006), such as the orbitofrontal cortex (OFC; Hölzel et al., 2007; Way, Creswell, Eisenberger, & Lieberman, 2010; Zeidan et al., 2011, 2015) the dorsomedial prefrontal cortex (Farb et al., 2010; Frewen et al., 2010), and the right DLPFC (Creswell, Way, Eisenberger, & Lieberman, 2007). Convergent evidence across multiple operationalizations of mindfulness (e.g., dispositional, induced, brief and long-term training, experienced practitioners) point to the benefits of mindfulness for reducing emotional reactivity (or increasing equanimity; see Desbordes et al., 2015) and promoting healthy emotional functioning.

In summary, the tendency for mindfulness to strengthen neural networks involved in emotion regulation underscores its position as a foundational skill that may enhance the deliberate cultivation of positive, unfocused emotions as exercised in *brahmavihāra* practices. This is particularly true for compassion, since some degree of emotion regulation will likely be needed to modulate the early negative affect experienced by perceiving the suffering of another person (feeling *as* the other) and transforming it into an affectively pleasant, compassionate response (feeling *for* the other).

Open monitoring and self-referential processing: In addition to the benefits of open monitoring practices on emotion regulation, another growing body of evidence points to the value of these practices for modulating neural activity involved in self-referential processing. Self-referential or narrative processing involves experiencing and cognitively elaborating on mental events as they are related to one's own identity (e.g., as "mine" or "for me"), and devoting attentional resources to evaluating them in more value-laden, emotionally charged ways based on the strength of their relationship to the reflective self (Northoff et al., 2006). This is in contrast to a more experiential mode of processing, in which cognitive elaboration on any one event is minimized in favor of experiencing the ongoing flow of conscious experience in each moment. Put another way, self-referential processing involves identifying *with* experiences while a more experiential mode of processing simply involves recognition of the experiences as they occur (Brewer et al., 2011). The ability to discern when one is self-identifying with experience, and to detach from that identification process in favor of a more experiential mode of conscious experience, is a hallmark skill developed in both sustained attention and open monitoring training. Importantly, the skill gained in downregulating self-referential processing during the training of attention may have important implications when transitioning to the cultivation of affect-based practices like the *brahmavihāras*.

Sustained attention and open monitoring practices have been shown to consistently reduce default mode network (DMN) activity—a key neural network involved in self-referential processing and mind wandering (Brewer, Garrison, & Whitfield-Gabrieli, 2013; Northoff et al., 2006; Whitfield-Gabrieli et al., 2011). The DMN primarily consists of hubs in the precuneus/posterior cingulate cortex (PCC), the medial prefrontal cortex (mPFC), and the temporoparietal junction (Buckner, Andrews-Hanna, & Schacter, 2008; Andrews-Hanna, Reidler, Sepulcre, Poulin, & Buckner, 2010). Past research demonstrates that increased functional connectivity between a key node of the DMN (the PCC) and brain regions involved in top-down executive control, working memory, and conflict monitoring, such as the dorsal prefrontal cortex and dorsal anterior cingulate cortex (dACC), are related to reduced negative affect (Goldin, McRae, Ramel, & Gross, 2008), stress (Cisler et al., 2013), and the experience of pain (Wager et al., 2004). This increased functional connectivity between the PCC and PFC may be a neural basis through which sustained attention and open-monitoring meditation modulate self-referential processing and mind wandering.

Cross-sectional studies comparing experienced meditators and novices have discovered increased functional connectivity between the PCC and regions of the PFC (mPFC, ventrolateral prefrontal cortex (vlPFC), ventromedial prefrontal cortex (vmPFC), dmPFC) and dACC during states of rest (Hasenkamp & Barsalou, 2012; Panda et al., 2016) and during states of contemplative practice (Brewer et al., 2011; Garrison et al., 2013; Pagoni, Cekic, & Guo, 2008; Panda et al., 2016) among experienced meditators. Analogous effects have also emerged as a result of focused attention and open awareness training across a variety of training durations and styles, including 8-week programs such as Mindfulness-Based Stress Reduction (Goldin, Ramel, & Gross, 2009) and Mindfulness Based Exposure Therapy (King et al., 2016), 2-week programs (Doll, Hölzel, Boucard, Wohlschläger, & Sorg, 2015), 3-day programs (Creswell et al., 2016), and more brief exposure to contemplative training (Farb et al., 2007). Widely used psychometric measures of mindfulness, such as the Mindful

Attention Awareness Scale (MAAS; Brown & Ryan, 2003) have significantly predicted the degree of functional connectivity between the same DMN regions (Doll, Hölzel, Boucard, Wohlschläger, & Sorg, 2015).

Leveraging the temporal specificity of electroencephalography (EEG) alongside fMRI, Panda et al. (2016) recently extended these findings and demonstrated that experienced meditators self-induced microstates of DMN connectivity more frequently and for a longer average duration than did healthy controls. Moreover, the average duration of the DMN microstate among experienced meditators was predicted by their years of meditation experience. Additional EEG evidence has found that mindfulness meditation practitioners show less gamma activity over frontal and midline regions, an electrocortical correlate of reduced DMN activity (Berkovich-Ohana, Glicksohn, & Goldstein, 2011).

Together, these findings demonstrate that sustained attention and open monitoring practices may modulate self-referential processing by reducing activation in the PCC, a primary hub of the DMN, via increased resting and intrinsic functional connectivity between the PCC and prefrontal regions involved in executive control and working memory. Neuroscientific studies of empathy—the capacity to vicariously experience other people's emotions—have highlighted the importance of self-other discrimination as a mechanism that distinguishes empathic distress, an aversive, self-oriented response to the suffering of others (Batson et al., 1981; Klimecki et al., 2013; Woodruff, Martin & Bilyk, 2011), from empathic concern, a more adaptive response to the suffering of others that is characterized by positive emotions associated with warmth toward others and concern for their well-being (Klimecki et al., 2013). The changes in self-referential processing that result from sustained attention and open monitoring practices may play a key role in setting the stage for positive emotional responses to suffering that are experienced and exercised in a more focused manner during *brahmavihāra* training.

In summary, training in focused attention and open monitoring practices have been shown to influence a variety of intertwined cognitive and emotional processes (for a more thorough review, see van Vugt et al., 2015). The strengthening of neural networks involved in executive control seems to improve not only the modulation of attention but also the regulation of limbic structures involved in emotional processing and control, and cortical structures in the DMN involved in self-referential processing. Improvements in the control of attention, emotion, and self-referential processing that result from focused attention and open-monitoring training (Tang, Hölzel, & Posner, 2015) may lay the groundwork for downstream training with the *brahmavihāras*, which, in theory, should improve the ability to actively sustain states of positive other-oriented emotional concern (*mettā, karunā, muditā*) and prosocial motivation (*anukampā*). In the sections that follow, we describe how directed *brahmavihāra* practices may uniquely influence neural processes over and above those built upon during these antecedent practices.

THE NEURAL CONCOMITANTS OF *BRAHMAVIHĀRA* PRACTICES

Changes in neural structure and function that result from focused attention and open-monitoring training are likely to have considerable overlap with those found in *brahmavihāra* training. And indeed, training in loving-kindness—the first step in training subsequent *brahmavihāras*—has been shown to decrease blood oxygenation level dependent (BOLD) activity and intrinsic connectivity in the PCC/precuneus, a major hub of the DMN associated with self-referential processing (Garrison, Scheinost, Constable, & Brewer, 2014; Garrison, Zeffiro, Scheinost, Constable, & Brewer, 2015). Deactivation of the amygdala has also been observed during loving-kindness meditation (Brewer et al., 2011), a finding that is consistently replicated in studies that examine focused attention and open-monitoring effects (Creswell et al., 2007; Farb et al., 2010; Frewen et al., 2010; Hölzel et al., 2007; Way et al., 2010; Zeidan et al., 2011, 2015). But what neural circuitry would we expect to be exercised during brahmavihara practice over and above those shared with focused attention and open monitoring?

A variety of neural systems would be strengthened as a result of deliberate *brahmavihāra* training. To date, we are not aware of any cross-sectional or experimental research that has investigated the neural outcomes that follow from expertise or directed training in sympathetic joy or equanimity. While theory and research on equanimity is beginning to emerge (Hadash, Segev, Tanay, Goldstein, & Bernstein, 2016), these nascent studies examine equanimity as a faculty that is developed through mindfulness training, which is distinct from the direct cultivation of equanimity as a *brahmavihāra*. In a similar way, mindfulness training may increase empathic concern and prosocial behavior toward the suffering of other people (Berry et al., 2018), but it is quite distinct from the deliberate exercise of compassion as a *brahmavihāra*.

In contrast, neuroscientific research on the directed cultivation of loving-kindness and compassion is beginning to pepper the contemplative science literature at an accelerated rate. On the basis of our conceptual review of the *brahmavihāras*, we would expect loving-kindness and compassion to modulate the structure or function of brain regions implicated in: (1) receptivity to others' emotions, (2) positive affect and reward processing, and (3) motivation for prosocial connection, including increased motivation to approach others in states of distress. In the following sections we will review fresh scientific literature on loving-kindness and compassion with an ear for what the human brain tells us about the neurological signatures of the *brahmavihāras*.

Receptivity to others' emotions: The deliberate training of the *brahmavihāras* would likely exercise neural processes that permit receptivity to the emotions of others. Certainly, the reduced self-referential processing brought about by proficiencies in sustained attention, open monitoring, loving-kindness, and compassion training would set the stage for more engagement in the emotions of others, but compassion training may uniquely modulate activity in limbic structures and regions in the putative mirror neuron system (see Chapter 6 in this volume), that allow for a heightened receptivity to and experience of others' emotions.

Amygdalae: A key structure involved in the perception of social information and emotional processing are the amygdalae (Mosher, Zimmerman, & Gothard, 2014; Pessoa & Adolphs, 2010). Heightened activity in the amygdalae have been associated with detecting the emotional significance of facial expressions (Sato et al., 2004) and more accurate appraisals of facial expressions during social interaction, including judgments of trustworthiness and attractiveness (Bzdok et al., 2011). Thus, changes in the structure and function of the amygdalae may be involved in facilitating receptivity toward other people's emotions during *brahmavihāra* practice.

Evidence is beginning to emerge that demonstrates increases in amygdala activity in response to other's distress among experienced compassion meditators. Lutz et al., 2008a discovered that, relative to novices who received 1-week of at-home meditation instruction, expert loving-kindness and compassion practitioners displayed increased activity in the amygdala while inducing states of compassion as they listened to distressing emotional sounds of other people. The authors suggest that this effect may represent increased receptivity of expert meditators to the distress of other people during states of compassion. Congruent with this evidence, Desbordes et al. (2012) randomized novices to receive 8 weeks of Mindful Attention Training (MAT), Cognitively-Based Compassion Meditation Training (CBCT), or an active control intervention and after training, measured their neural activity while evoking compassion in response to unpleasant images of human suffering. Results indicated that MAT led to significant decreases in right amygdala activation, a finding that is consistent with past research on open monitoring and focused attention meditation. However, people who received CBCT and reported high hours of practice time demonstrated the opposite effect: a marginal *increase* in right amygdala activity. This increased activation of the amygdala in response to images of human suffering predicted decreases in self-reported depression, which suggests that the activation of the amygdala in response to human suffering during compassion may have downstream benefits for psychosocial health.

A third study compared *Theravada* Buddhist practitioners with 5 years of experience in loving-kindness meditation with people unexperienced in meditation. They discovered increased positive functional coupling between the left amygdala and cortical regions involved in emotion regulation, including the dorsal anterior cingulate and the primary somatosensory cortex while viewing images of happy, relative to neutral people (Leung et al., 2015). This functional connectivity did not emerge for images of sad people, which is consistent with the idea that expertise in loving-kindness meditation would elicit changes in responsiveness to the positive emotions of others. While past studies have found increased functional connectivity between the amygdala and the ACC in response to negative emotional stimuli among sustained attention and open monitoring practitioners, this is traditionally understood to involve the downregulation of negative emotions (e.g., reduced emotional reactivity). In contrast, the positive coupling between the left amygdala and dACC found by Leung et al. (2015) may represent the upregulation or enhancement of positive affect in response to the emotions of other people. Together, these findings suggest that expertise or training in loving-kindness may increase receptivity to the emotions of others by increasing activation of the amygdala, and/or its functional connectivity to regions of the cortex involved in regulating amygdala activity.

While the aforementioned three studies clearly show theoretically relevant distinctions in the activation of the amygdala during loving-kindness and compassion, as compared to foundational attention practices, it is rare for evidence to be so clear cut in such early stages of scientific investigation. Other studies have shown decreased amygdala activation during compassion and loving-kindness meditation. For example, Leung et al., (2017) found that 6 weeks of Awareness-Based Compassion Meditation, which consisted of training novices in focused attention, loving-kindness, and compassion, led to significant decreases in right amygdala activity in response to negative emotional images during non-meditative states, relative to progressive muscle relaxation and guided imagery active control conditions. This evidence of decreased amygdala activity as a result of *brahmavihāra* practice is corroborated by Brewer et al (2011), who found decreased activation of the amygdala among meditation experts who self-induced states of loving-kindness in the absence of any.

However, there are key differences in the tasks being performed in both studies that have demonstrated decreased amygdala activation. For example, participants in the study by Leung et al., (2017) were not actively inducing states of compassion toward the suffering of others. Likewise, the meditation experts in the study by Brewer et al. (2011) were not inducing states of loving-kindness while being exposed to the emotional states of other people. Given the role of the amygdala in detecting and appraising the significance of others' emotions, it is not surprising that this study found decreased amygdala activation because the practitioners were not actively engaging with the emotions of others. In short, we would expect amygdala activity to be increased only when states of loving-kindness or compassion are induced in response to emotionally significant social stimuli.

As reviewed earlier, decreased amygdala volume/activation and increased functional connectivity between the amygdala and regions of the ACC and PFC have been widely associated with lower emotional reactivity and improved emotion regulation (respectively) among sustained attention and open-monitoring practices (Creswell et al., 2007; Farb et al., 2007, 2010; Goldin & Gross, 2010; Hölzel et al., 2007; Modinos, Ormel, & Aleman, 2010; Quirk & Beer, 2006; Taren, Creswell, & Gianaros, 2013; Way et al., 2010; Zeidan et al., 2011, 2015). This convergent body of evidence highlights how foundational attention-based contemplative practices may act on regions involved in the downregulation of negative emotion. Yet there is mixed neurological evidence regarding the influence of *brahmavihāra* practices on the amygdala activation, and future cross-sectional research comparing expert loving-kindness and compassion meditators is needed to tease apart the conditions under which amygdala activity is increased or decreased. To address this question, neurophenomenological approaches, which combine neuroscience measures with descriptions of first-person experiences (phenomenology), may be of particular value, not only to better understand the neural signatures of the *brahmavihāras* but also the complexities of human emotion processing in general (Lutz & Thompson, 2003; Varela, 1996).

Mirror neuron system: Another set of areas that could be implicated in enhanced receptivity to the emotions of others is in the putative mirror neuron system (Di Pellegrino, Fadiga, Fogassi, Gallese, & Rizzolatti, 1992), which is theorized to play a role in motor mimicry, action imitation, self-awareness, and the ability to understand the emotions and intentions of others (Iacoboni & Dapretto, 2006). The mirror neuron system consists of the inferior parietal lobe and the inferior frontal cortex and the anterior insula, and numerous studies have linked brain activation in these areas with the vicarious experience of emotions in other people (Botvinick et al., 2005; Lamm, Batson, & Decety, 2007). A central area of the mirror neuron system that research has shown is influenced by *brahmavihāra* practices is the inferior frontal gyrus, which may play a role in the endogenous generation of emotions (Engen et al., 2017) and the regulation of emotional responses (Phillips et al., 2003).

One study of loving-kindness meditation experts discovered increased activity in the right inferior frontal gyrus (IFG) (and ventral ACC) while viewing pictures of happy people during meditation, relative to novices (Lee et al., 2012). This increase in IFG activation among loving-kindness experts may suggest an increased ability to share in the emotions of others.

Another study that links compassion training with the putative mirror neuron system found that participants who practiced compassion meditation for 30 min per day for 2 weeks demonstrated greater activation in the right inferior parietal cortex (IPC) when eliciting compassion toward images of human suffering (Weng et al., 2013). Moreover, this increased IPC activation among compassion trainees predicted increased altruistic behavior in a financial redistribution task. Given the role of the IPC in the human mirror neuron system, this finding may suggest that compassion training enhances brain activity involved in the simulation and experience of others' distress (but, see Chapter 6 for discussion of difficulties when inferring mirror neuron activity from brain imaging data).

Additionally, Mascaro, Rilling, Negi, and Raison (2012) found that novice participants who completed 8 weeks of CBCT training, relative to a health education control group, performed significantly better on the Reading the Mind in the Eyes Test (RMET), a validated measure of empathic accuracy. Of particular importance, CBCT trainees demonstrated increased activation of the IFG when viewing the emotions of others, and changes in IFG activity explained significant variability in RMET performance. Previous experiments have demonstrated improvements on the RMET by intranasal administration of oxytocin (Domes, Heinrichs, Michel, Berger, & Herpertz, 2007; Guastella et al., 2010)—a hormone involved in social bonding, attachment, maternal behavior, pair bonding, and interpersonal trust (Yang, Wang, Han, & Wang, 2013)—but, CBCT is the first behavioral intervention to yield such an effect on empathic accuracy.

In summary, evidence is accumulating from cross-sectional and intervention-based studies of loving-kindness and compassion training indicating the modulation of activity in regions of the brain involved in experiencing the emotional states of others. These regions include the amygdala, which is involved in detecting the emotional significance of facial expressions (Sato, Yoshikawa, Kochiyama, & Matsumura, 2004), and the human mirror neuron system, which plays a role in the ability to understand the emotions and intentions of others (Iacoboni & Dapretto, 2006).

Positive affect and reward processing: At the heart of the *brahmavihāras* is an increased ability to experience positive emotions in response to others, irrespective of their emotional state. In contrast to empathic sensitivity, which involves feeling *as* others, loving-kindness, compassion, and sympathetic joy each involve the endogenous generation of positive emotions *for* others. Indeed, a recent meta-analysis of 24 studies found that loving-kindness meditation is successful at increasing positive emotional states, as well as more positive emotions in daily life (Zeng, Chiu, Wang, Oei, & Leung, 2015). Therefore, one would expect structural or functional modulation in brain regions that are involved in pleasant emotion and reward, the OFC and the striatum (which includes the nucleus accumbens[NAcc], the caudate nucleus [CN], the ventral tegmental area [VTA], globus pallidus [GP], and the putamen).

Several empirical studies have demonstrated that training or expertise in loving-kindness and compassion meditation can influence areas of the striatum. Increased activation of dorsal striatal structures, which include the CN, GP, and putamen, have been associated with positive emotional states in approximately 70% of published studies (see Phan, Wager, Taylor, & Liberzon, 2002 for a meta-analytic review), including the experience of maternal love (Bartels & Zeki, 2004). Other striatal structures, such as the NAcc and the VTA, play a key role in the detection of reward and the experience of pleasure elicited under a variety of conditions, including sex (Karama et al., 2002), drugs (Breiter & Rosen, 1999; Filbey et al., 2008), classical music (Menon & Levitin, 2005), chocolate (Small, Zatorre, Dagher, Evans, & Jones-Gotman, 2001), monetary rewards (Elliott et al., 2003), romantic love (Aron et al., 2005), affiliation (Bartels & Zeki, 2004), and prosocial behavior (Harbaugh, Mayr, & Burghart, 2007).

Early studies with nonexperienced meditation practitioners have provided initial evidence of the modulation of striatal activity during states similar to loving-kindness and compassion. For example, meditation-naïve participants who were asked to elicit feelings of unconditional love while viewing pictures of people with disabilities were found to have increased activation in many striatal structures, including the right GP, the right CN, and the left VTA (Beauregard, Courtemanche, Paquette, & St-Pierre, 2009). Moreover, an experiment by Kim et al. (2009) found similar effects among participants without proficiency in meditation. Meditation-naïve participants who were asked to elicit states of compassion in response to images of human suffering showed greater activation in the VTA than participants who maintained a passive attitude (Kim et al., 2009). Activation of the VTA during states of compassion to the suffering of others is likely related to the reward processing engaged during the endogenous generation of pleasant emotions (Beauregard et al., 2009). Together, these findings suggest that people untrained in the *brahmavihāras* demonstrate the activation of the mesolimbic dopamine system (the VTA and ventral striatum) when inducing positive emotions in response to other people.

Research on compassion training has uncovered comparable neural influences among novice compassion meditation trainees. For example, Klimecki et al., (2013) found that 1 day of compassion training led to increased activity in the NAcc, putamen, and VTA while viewing videos of human suffering, relative to control training (memory enhancement). Compassion training also led to greater subjective reports of positive emotion in response to the distressing videos (Klimecki, Leiberg, Lamm, & Singer, 2013). A second study replicated these results using the same video task among a sample of females who underwent empathy training before compassion training (Klimecki et al., 2014). Following empathy training, participants self-reported increased negative affect and increased activation in brain regions involved in the experience of pain and negative affect [insula and anterior mid-cingulate cortex (aMCC)], relative to controls, a finding consistent with research on empathic distress. However, after compassion training, these same participants were able to counteract this empathic distress and reported experiencing more positive affect in response to videos of human suffering. These subjective reports were correlated with heightened activity in the ventral striatum and VTA, indicating increased activation of reward-related activity. However, there was no evidence that compassion training reduced the experience of negative affect. After compassion training, participants still not only experienced negative emotions but also experienced significantly more positive ones.

Studies involving expert practitioners have found consistent influences on activity in striatal structures. In one study, experts in compassion meditation were instructed to engage in reappraisal or compassion in response to videos of human distress. In contrast to reappraising the emotional content of the videos, evoking a state of compassion induced increases in positive emotional experiences, and heightened activation in ventral striatum, NAcc, and GP (Engen & Singer, 2015).

While this research on loving-kindness and compassion demonstrate activation of reward centers in a way that is theoretically consistent with the positive emotional experience that, in theory, would result from concern for the welfare of others and insight into the nature of suffering, other psychological states could conceivably be at play. For example, schadenfreude—a state of pleasure or enjoyment in response to the suffering of others (see Chapter 5) —appears to be quite similar to compassion in that it also activates striatal reward structures in response to the suffering of others. Care should be taken to distinguish compassion from schadenfreude in subsequent studies, and one potential avenue to do so would be to measure states of envy. Prior research has indicated that schadenfreude is increased by self-focused states, such as envy toward the target (Takahashi et al., 2009). On the theoretical basis that the *brahmavihāra* should occur as a consequence of reduced self-concern, envy is likely to be minimized during states of loving-kindness and compassion and may be a variable of particular importance to measure. Future research on loving-kindness and compassion should measure envy among *brahmavihāra* practitioners to ensure that the pleasure experienced in response to others is not due to self-focused pleasure that results from observing someone they have negative feelings for who is suffering, but rather a subtle pleasure that results from the insight that others can become more free from suffering.

Motivation for prosocial connection: Central to *brahmavihāra* practice is an increased motivation to connect with other people in prosocial ways, whether that is taking joy in the experiences of other, as in loving-kindness and sympathetic joy, or seeking to help others in states of distress, as in compassion. Recent evidence suggests that contemplative training with the *brahmavihāras* can increase altruism and prosocial behavior (Leiberg, Klimecki, & Singer, 2011; Weng et al., 2013), but what are the neural substrates of this increased propensity for prosocial connection?

The DLPFC and mesolimbic dopamine system: Previous research has highlighted how negative emotions can overwhelm the capacity to help others in distress (Cameron & Payne, 2011). This finding suggests that it may be necessary to regulate these emotions to sustain the motivation to approach others in distress and help, and on the basis of past research, negative affect is not decreased during states of compassion (Klimecki, Leiberg, Ricard, & Singer, 2014). Thus, brain regions involved in the regulation of cognitive and emotional control, such as the DLPFC, may play a role in promoting helping behavior in response to human suffering (Ochsner & Gross, 2005) by either downregulating negative affect or increasing the perceived value of helping.

One study has provided evidence for this link between brain markers of cognitive control and increased helping behavior among compassion trainees (Weng et al., 2013). Participants who received 2 weeks of at-home compassion training (relative to a cognitive reappraisal active control) demonstrated increased activity in the inferior parietal lobe and the DLPFC (a region involved in the putative mirror neuron system) in response to pictures of people in distress. Further, functional connectivity between the DLPFC and the NAcc, a striatal structure involved in reward, predicted greater altruistic behavior in a monetary redistribution game. This outcome may indicate that increased communication between regions involved in cognitive control and reward may increase motivation to help others in distress by upregulating the perceived value and pleasant feelings involved in helping others.

Septal Area and Periaqueductal Gray: Neural systems involved in the formation and maintenance of social bonds may also be influenced by *brahmavihāra* practice. Such systems likely would include activation of brain regions engaged in the formation of social bonds and parental care, such as the periaqueductal gray and the septal area, which support the motivation to nurture offspring (Bartels & Zeki, 2004; Beauregard et al., 2009; Noriuchi, Kikuchi, & Senoo, 2008; Rilling, 2013). These regions are highly sensitive to oxytocin, a hormone known to promote social bonding and maternal nurturing behaviors in human and nonhuman animals (Rilling, 2013) and are known to activate reward systems in the mesolimbic dopamine system (described in the previous section and in Chapter 7).

A study by Morelli, Rameson, and Lieberman, 2012 found that participants who observed others experiencing happy, anxious, or painful events demonstrated increased activation in the septal area in all conditions. This increased activation in the septal area predicted actual helping behavior during daily living across 2 weeks of ecological momentary assessment, a technique in which participants respond to self-report questions about their behavior/experience at random periods throughout the day. This finding provides strong evidence that activation in brain regions involved in maternal care may play a critical role in motivating prosocial connections with others. A second study provides additional evidence for the link between the *brahmavihāras* and the activation of oxytocin-rich brain regions involved in maternal care. Beauregard et al. (2009) found that meditation-naive participants who were asked to elicit feelings of unconditional love while viewing pictures of people with disabilities were found to have increased activation in the periaqueductal gray matter. And a third study corroborated this evidence among meditation-naïve participants who elicited states of compassion in response to images of human suffering. Compassionate participants showed increased activation in the septal nuclei and the periaqueductal gray in response to pictures of sad faces (Kim et al., 2009).

Together, these studies provide compelling evidence that *brahmavihāra* practice may lead to increased activation of areas involved in the motivation and reward of maternal caregiving, particularly to others who are vulnerable or distressed. This is quite an interesting finding that aligns beautifully with Buddhist descriptions of the *brahmavihāras* dating back to the 5th century (Ñāṇamoli, 1991) and particularly the epigraph at the beginning of this chapter. Future research on compassion would do well to closely investigate the influence of *brahmavihāra* training on regions of the brain involved in maternal care, and more specifically, the link between these regions and the active pursuit of prosocial connections with others.

CONCLUSIONS AND DIRECTIONS FOR FUTURE RESEARCH

On the basis of our review of Early Buddhist conceptualizations of the four *brahmavihāras*, as well as the attention-based contemplative practices that serve as their foundation, we set out to establish the unique psychological skills that would be exercised through contemplative training, as well as their likely neurological signatures. Over and above the effects of focused attention and open monitoring, we suggested that training in the *brahmavihāras* would uniquely influence regions of the brain that promote (1) receptivity to the emotions of other people, (2) activation of reward systems and positive affect, and (3) motivation for social connection.

Despite the nascence of this area of contemplative neuroscience, empirical evidence was described—from cross-sectional studies using meditation experts, a range of *brahmavihāra* training programs that varied in both style and duration, and states induced by novice or meditation-naïve participants—that converge in their demonstration that directed contemplative practice of the *brahmavihāras* influences key areas of the brain consistent with what one expect from their conceptual descriptions. More specifically, loving-kindness and compassion training were shown to modulate activity in the amygdala, a key limbic structure involved in the detection and appraisal of others' emotions (Bzdok et al., 2011; Sato et al., 2004). Activation in major hubs of the mirror neuron system were also discovered that play a role in the generation of emotions and the regulation of emotional responses to others (Engen et al, 2017; Phillips, Drevets, Rauch, & Lane, 2003). Loving-kindness and compassion meditation practices were found to activate the mesolimbic dopamine system, a key reward system in the brain that may underscore the universally pleasant experience of the *brahmavihāras*. Finally, compassion training was found to modulate activity in regions of the brain involved in cognitive and emotional control, such as increased functional connectivity between the DLP-FC and the mesolimbic dopamine system. Interestingly, compassion also activates the septal area and the midbrain periaqueductal gray, which are implicated in maternal care of offspring (Bartels & Zeki, 2004; Beauregard et al., 2009; Noriuchi et al., 2008; Rilling, 2013). In short, contemplative neuroscience is beginning to paint a picture of the neural signatures of the *brahmavihāras* in a way that is consistent with descriptions provided by a lineage of Buddhist practitioners that extends back 2500 years.

While it is tempting to draw strong conclusions from the research described in the present chapter, we would be remiss not to acknowledge that this nascent body of work should be interpreted with caution and healthy skepticism. The scientific explorations of directed *brahmavihāra* practices are still in their infancy, and there will likely be considerable growing pains involved in delineating them from their proposed near enemies. Future research would be wise to measure or experimentally manipulate states of greed and self-oriented processing among practitioners of loving-kindness. Studies of compassion should take care to measure states of grief, sadness, and schadenfreude. And forthcoming studies on equanimity should ensure that practitioners are fully engaged with, rather than merely uncaring and indifferent toward, the emotions of others. By measuring or experimentally manipulating the near enemies of the *brahmavihāras* and incorporating them in their statistical models, future studies could paint a much clearer picture of the factors that promote or hinder these states and their neurological correlates.

While more empirical studies are clearly needed, the research described in this chapter calls for increased incorporation of neurophenomenological approaches to studying the *brahmavihāras*. Researchers should leverage the benefits of introspective accuracy brought about by contemplative practices by directly assessing first-person phenomenological perspectives alongside the methods of modern neuroscience (Fox et al., 2012). Such approaches underscore the mutual benefits obtained by the collaboration between contemplative practitioners and neuroscientists. It is in sharing unique areas of expertise with each other that we are more fully able to meet a primary goal of both contemplative practice and scientific inquiry: to more clearly understand the way things are.

References

Anālayo, B. (2003). *Satipaṭṭhāna: The direct path to realization*. Cambridge, UK: Windhorse Publications.

Anālayo, B. (2012). *Excursions into the Thought-World of the Pāli discourses*. Onalaska, WA: Pariyatti Publishing.

Anālayo, B. (2015). *Compassion and emptiness in early Buddhist meditation*. Cambridge, UK: Windhorse Publications.

Andrews-Hanna, J. R., Reidler, J. S., Sepulcre, J., Poulin, R., & Buckner, R. L. (2010). Functional-anatomic fractionation of the brain's default network. *Neuron, 65*, 550–562. doi: 10.1016/j.neuron.2010.02.005.

Aron, A., Fisher, H., Mashek, D. J., Strong, G., Li, H., & Brown, L. L. (2005). Reward, motivation, and emotion systems associated with early-stage intense romantic love. *Journal of Neurophysiology, 94*(1), 327–337. doi: 10.1152/jn.00838.2004.

Atkinson, R. C., & Shiffrin, R. M. (1968). Human memory: A proposed system and its control processes. *Psychology of Learning and Motivation, 2*, 89–195.

Baerentsen, K. B., Hartvig, N. V., Stødkilde-Jørgensen, H., & Mammen, J. (2001). Onset of meditation explored with fMRI. *NeuroImage, 13*(6), 297.

Barnhofer, T., Chittka, T., Nightingale, H., Visser, C., & Crane, C. (2010). State effects of two forms of meditation on prefrontal EEG asymmetry in previously depressed individuals. *Mindfulness, 1*, 21–27.

Bartels, A., & Zeki, S. (2004). The neural correlates of maternal and romantic love. *NeuroImage, 21*(3), 1155–1166. doi: 10.1016/j.neuroimage.2003.11.003.

Batson, C. D., Duncan, B. D., Ackerman, P., Buckley, T., Li, H., & Birch, K. (1981). Is empathic emotion a source of altruistic motivation? Journal of personality and Social Psychology. *Journal of Neurophysiology, 40*(2), 290.

Berry, D. R., Cairo, A. H., Goodman, R. J., Quaglia, J. T., Green, J. D., & Brown, K. W. (2018). Mindfulness increases prosocial responses toward ostracized strangers through empathic concern. *Journal of Experimental Psychology: General, 147*, 93.

Beauregard, M., Courtemanche, J., Paquette, V., & St-Pierre, É. L. (2009). The neural basis of unconditional love. *Psychiatry Research: Neuroimaging, 172*(2), 93–98.

Berkovich-Ohana, A., Glicksohn, J., & Goldstein, A. (2011). Temporal cognition changes following mindfulness, but not transcendental meditation practice. *Proceedings of Fechner Day, 27*(1), 245–250.

Bishop, S. R. (2002). What do we really know about mindfulness-based stress reduction? *Psychosomatic Medicine, 64*(1), 71–83.

Bodhi, B. (2000). *The connected discourses of the Buddha*. Somerville, MA: Wisdom Publications.

Botvinick, M., Jha, A. P., Bylsma, L. M., Fabian, S. A., Solomon, P. E., & Prkachin, K. M. (2005). Viewing facial expressions of pain engages cortical areas involved in the direct experience of pain. *NeuroImage, 25*(1), 312–319. doi: 10.1016/j.neuroimage.2004.11.043.

Brefczynski-Lewis, J. A., Lutz, A., Schaefer, H. S., Levinson, D. B., & Davidson, R. J. (2007). Neural correlates of attentional expertise in long-term meditation practitioners. *Proceedings of the National Academy of Sciences, 104*(27), 11483–11488.

Breiter, H. C., & Rosen, B. R. (1999). Functional magnetic resonance imaging of brain reward circuitry in the human. *Annals of the New York Academy of Sciences, 877*(1), 523–547. doi: 10.1111/j.1749-6632.1999.tb09287.x.

Brewer, J. A., Worhunsky, P. D., Gray, J. R., Tang, Y. Y., Weber, J., & Kober, H. (2011). Meditation experience is associated with differences in default mode network activity and connectivity. *Proceedings of the National Academy of Sciences, 108*(50), 20254–20259.

Brewer, J. A., Garrison, K. A., & Whitfield-Gabrieli, S. (2013). What about the "self" is processed in the posterior cingulate cortex? *Frontiers in Human Neuroscience, 7*, 1–7. doi: 10.3389/fnhum.2013.00647.

Brown, K. W., & Cordon, S. L. (2009). Toward a phenomenology of mindfulness: Subjective experience and emotional correlates. In F. Didonna (Ed.), *Clinical handbook of mindfulness* (pp. 59–81). New York: Springer.

Brown, K. W., & Ryan, R. M. (2003). The benefits of being present: Mindfulness and its role in psychological well-being. *Journal of Personality and Social Psychology, 84*(4), 822.

Brown, K. W., Ryan, R. M., & Creswell, J. D. (2007). Mindfulness: Theoretical foundations and evidence for its salutary effects. *Psychological Inquiry, 18*(4), 211–237.

Brown, K. W., Goodman, R. J., Ryan, R. M., & Anālayo, B. (2016). Mindfulness enhances episodic memory performance: Evidence from a multimethod investigation. *PloS One, 11*(4), e0153309.

Buckner, R. L., Andrews-Hanna, J. R., & Schacter, D. L. (2008). The brain's default network: Anatomy, function, and relevance to disease. *Annals of the New York Academy of Sciences, 1124*, 1–38.

Bzdok, D., Langner, R., Hoffstaedter, F., Turetsky, B. I., Zilles, K., & Eickhoff, S. B. (2011). The modular neuroarchitecture of social judgments on faces. *Cerebral Cortex, 22*(4), 951–961.

Cameron, C. D., & Payne, B. K. (2011). Escaping affect: How motivated emotion regulation creates insensitivity to mass suffering. *Journal of Personality and Social Psychology, 100*(1), 1–15.

Cisler, J. M., James, G. A., Tripathi, S., Mletzko, T., Heim, C., Hu, X. P., et al. (2013). Differential functional connectivity within an emotion regulation neural network among individuals resilient and susceptible to the depressogenic effects of early life stress. *Psychological Medicine, 43*(3), 507–518.

Creswell, J. D., Way, B. M., Eisenberger, N. I., & Lieberman, M. D. (2007). Neural correlates of dispositional mindfulness during affect labeling. *Psychosomatic Medicine, 69*(6), 560–565.

Creswell, J. D., Taren, A., Lindsay, E., Greco, C., Gianaros, P., Fairgrieve, A., et al. (2016). Alterations in resting state functional connectivity link mindfulness meditation training with reduced interleukin-6: A randomized controlled trial. *Biological Psychiatry, 80*, 53–61. doi: 10.1016/j.biopsych.2016.01.008.

Desbordes, G., Negi, L. T., Pace, T. W., Wallace, B. A., Raison, C. L., & Schwartz, E. L. (2012). Effects of mindful-attention and compassion meditation training on amygdala response to emotional stimuli in an ordinary, non-meditative state. *Frontiers in Human Neuroscience, 6*, 1–15. doi: 10.3389/fnhum.2012.00292.

Desbordes, G., Gard, T., Hoge, E. A., Hölzel, B. K., Kerr, C., Lazar, S. W., et al. (2015). Moving beyond mindfulness: Defining equanimity as an outcome measure in meditation and contemplative research. *Mindfulness, 6*(2), 356–372.

Di Pellegrino, G., Fadiga, L., Fogassi, L., Gallese, V., & Rizzolatti, G. (1992). Understanding motor events: A neurophysiological study. *Experimental Brain Research, 91*(1), 176–180. doi: 10.1007/bf00230027.

Doll, A., Hölzel, B. K., Boucard, C. C., Wohlschläger, A. M., & Sorg, C. (2015). Mindfulness is associated with intrinsic functional connectivity between default mode and salience networks. *Frontiers in Human Neuroscience, 9*, 1–11. doi: 10.3389/fnhum.2015.00461.

Domes, G., Heinrichs, M., Michel, A., Berger, C., & Herpertz, S. C. (2007). Oxytocin improves "mind-reading" in humans. *Biological Psychiatry, 61*(6), 731–733. doi: 10.1016/j.biopsych.2006.07.015.

Dunn, B. R., Hartigan, J. A., & Mikulas, W. L. (1999). Concentration and mindfulness meditations: Unique forms of consciousness? *Applied Psychophysiology and Biofeedback, 24*(3), 147–165.

Engen, H. G., & Singer, T. (2015). Compassion-based emotion regulation up-regulates experienced positive affect and associated neural networks. *Social Cognitive and Affective Neuroscience, 10*(9), 1291–1301.

Engen, H., Kanske, P., & Singer, T. (2018). *Endogenous emotion generation ability is associated with capacity to form multimodal internal representations Scientific Reports, 8, 1953.* doi: 10.1038/s41598-018-20380-7.

Elliott, R., Newman, J. L., Longe, O. A., & Deakin, J. W. (2003). Differential response patterns in the striatum and orbitofrontal cortex to financial reward in humans: A parametric functional magnetic resonance imaging study. *Journal of Neuroscience, 23*(1), 303–307.

Fan, J., McCandliss, B. D., Sommer, T., Raz, A., & Posner, M. I. (2002). Testing the efficiency and independence of attentional networks. *Journal of Cognitive Neuroscience, 14*(3), 340–347.

Fan, J., McCandliss, B. D., Fossella, J., Flombaum, J. I., & Posner, M. I. (2005). The activation of attentional networks. *NeuroImage, 26*(2), 471–479.

Farb, N. A., Segal, Z. V., Mayberg, H., Bean, J., McKeon, D., Fatima, Z., et al. (2007). Attending to the present: Mindfulness meditation reveals distinct neural modes of self-reference. *Social Cognitive and Affective Neuroscience, 2*(4), 313–322.

Farb, N. A., Anderson, A. K., Mayberg, H., Bean, J., McKeon, D., & Segal, Z. V. (2010). Minding one's emotions: Mindfulness training alters the neural expression of sadness. *Emotion, 10*(1), 25.

Filbey, F. M., Claus, E., Audette, A. R., Niculescu, M., Banich, M. T., Tanabe, J., et al. (2008). Exposure to the taste of alcohol elicits activation of the mesocorticolimbic neurocircuitry. *Neuropsychopharmacology, 33*(6), 1391. doi: 10.1038/sj.npp.1301513.

Fox, K. C., Zakarauskas, P., Dixon, M., Ellamil, M., Thompson, E., & Christoff, K. (2012). Meditation experience predicts introspective accuracy. *PloS One, 7*(9), e45370.

Frewen, P. A., Dozois, D. J., Neufeld, R. W., Lane, R. D., Densmore, M., Stevens, T. K., et al. (2010). Individual differences in trait mindfulness predict dorsomedial prefrontal and amygdala response during emotional imagery: An fMRI study. *Personality and Individual Differences, 49*(5), 479–484.

Garrison, K. A., Scheinost, D., Worhunsky, P. D., Elwafi, H. M., Thornhill I.V., T. A., & Brewer, J. A. (2013). Real-time fMRI links subjective experience with brain activity during focused attention. *NeuroImage, 81*, 110–118. doi: 10.1016/j.neuroimage.2013.05.030.

Garrison, K. A., Scheinost, D., Constable, R. T., & Brewer, J. A. (2014). BOLD signal and functional connectivity associated with loving kindness meditation. *Brain and Behavior, 4*(3), 337–347.

Garrison, K. A., Zeffiro, T. A., Scheinost, D., Constable, R. T., & Brewer, J. A. (2015). Meditation leads to reduced default mode network activity beyond an active task. *Cognitive, Affective, & Behavioral Neuroscience, 15*(3), 712–720.

Goldin, P., & Gross, J. (2010). Effect of mindfulness meditation training on the neural bases of emotion regulation in social anxiety disorder. *Emotion, 10*(1), 83–84.

Goldin, P. R., McRae, K., Ramel, W., & Gross, J. J. (2008). The neural bases of emotion regulation: Reappraisal and suppression of negative emotion. *Biological Psychiatry: Stress, Anxiety, and Post-Traumatic Stress Disorder, 63*, 577–586.

Goldin, P., Ramel, W., & Gross J. (2009). Mindfulness meditation training and self-referential processing in social anxiety disorder: Behavioral and neural effects. *Journal of Cognitive Psychotherapy, 23*, 242–257.

Gombrich, R. F. (2009). *What the Buddha thought.* Bristol, CT: Equinox.

Guastella, A. J., Einfeld, S. L., Gray, K. M., Rinehart, N. J., Tonge, B. J., Lambert, T. J., et al. (2010). Intranasal oxytocin improves emotion recognition for youth with autism spectrum disorders. *Biological Psychiatry, 67*(7), 692–694. doi: 10.1016/j.biopsych.2009.09.020.

Hadash, Y., Segev, N., Tanay, G., Goldstein, P., & Bernstein, A. (2016). The decoupling model of equanimity: Theory, measurement, and test in a mindfulness intervention. *Mindfulness*, 7(5), 1214–1226.

Harbaugh, W. T., Mayr, U., & Burghart, D. R. (2007). Neural responses to taxation and voluntary giving reveal motives for charitable donations. *Science*, 316(5831), 1622–1625. doi: 10.1126/science.1140738.

Hasenkamp, W., & Barsalou, L. W. (2012). Effects of meditation experience on functional connectivity of distributed brain networks. *Frontiers in Human Neuroscience*, 6, 1–14. doi: 10.3389/fnhum.2012.00038.

Hölzel, B. K., Carmody, J., Vangel, M., Congleton, C., Yerramsetti, S. M., Gard, T., et al. (2011). Mindfulness practice leads to increases in regional brain gray matter density. *Psychiatry Research: Neuroimaging*, 191(1), 36–43.

Hölzel, B. K., Ott, U., Gard, T., Hempel, H., Weygandt, M., Morgen, K., et al. (2007). Investigation of mindfulness meditation practitioners with voxel-based morphometry. *Social Cognitive and Affective Neuroscience*, 3(1), 55–61.

Iacoboni, M., & Dapretto, M. (2006). The mirror neuron system and the consequences of its dysfunction. *Nature Reviews Neuroscience*, 7(12), 942–951.

Jazaieri, H., Jinpa, T. L., McGonigal, K., Rosenberg, E., Finkelstein, J., & Simon-Thomas, E. (2013). Enhancing compassion: A randomized controlled trial of a compassion cultivation training program. *Journal of Happiness Studies*, 14, 1113–1126. doi: 10.1007/s10902-012-9373-z.

Jha, A. P., Krompinger, J., & Baime, M. J. (2007). Mindfulness training modifies subsystems of attention. *Cognitive, Affective, & Behavioral Neuroscience*, 7(2), 109–119.

Jinpa, T. L., & Weiss, L. (2013). Compassion cultivation training (CCT). In T. Singer, & M. Boltz (Eds.), *Compassion: Bridging practice and science*. Leipzig: Max Planck Institute for Human Cognitive and Brain Sciences.

Karama, S., Lecours, A. R., Leroux, J. M., Bourgouin, P., Beaudoin, G., Joubert, S., et al. (2002). Areas of brain activation in males and females during viewing of erotic film excerpts. *Human Brain Mapping*, 16(1), 1–13. doi: 10.1002/hbm.10014.

Kim, J. W., Kim, S. E., Kim, J. J., Jeong, B., Park, C. H., Son, A. R., et al. (2009). Compassionate attitude towards others' suffering activates the mesolimbic neural system. *Neuropsychologia*, 47(10), 2073–2081.

King, A. P., Block, S. R., Sripada, R. K., Rauch, S., Giardino, N., Favorite, T., et al. (2016). Altered default mode network (DMN) resting state functional connectivity following a mindfulness-based exposure therapy for post-traumatic stress disorder (PTSD) in combat veterans of Afghanistan and Iraq. *Depression and Anxiety*, 33(4), 289–299.

Klimecki, O. M., Leiberg, S., Lamm, C., & Singer, T. (2013). Functional neural plasticity and associated changes in positive affect after compassion training. *Cerebral Cortex*, 23(7), 1552–1561.

Klimecki, O. M., Leiberg, S., Ricard, M., & Singer, T. (2014). Differential pattern of functional brain plasticity after compassion and empathy training. *Social Cognitive and Affective Neuroscience*, 9(6), 873–879.

Kornfield, J. (1993). *A path with heart: A guide through the perils and promises of spiritual life*. New York, NY: Bantam Books.

Lamm, C., Batson, C. D., & Decety, J. (2007). The neural substrate of human empathy: Effects of perspective-taking and cognitive appraisal. *Journal of Cognitive Neuroscience*, 19(1), 42–58. doi: 10.1162/jocn.2007.19.1.42.

Lazar, S. W., Rosman, I. S., Vangel, M., Rao, V., Dusek, H., Benson, H., et al. (2003). *Functional brain imaging of mindfulness and mantra-based meditation*. New Orleans, LA: Society for Neuroscience.

Lee, T. M., Leung, M. K., Hou, W. K., Tang, J. C., Yin, J., So, K. F., et al. (2012). Distinct neural activity associated with focused-attention meditation and loving-kindness meditation. *PLoS One*, 7(8), e40054. doi: 10.1371/journal.pone.0040054.

Leiberg, S., Klimecki, O., & Singer, T. (2011). Short-term compassion training increases proso-cial behavior in a newly developed prosocial game. *PloS One, 6*(3), e17798.

Leung, M. K., Chan, C. C., Yin, J., Lee, C. F., So, K. F., & Lee, T. M. (2015). Enhanced amyg-dala–cortical functional connectivity in meditators. *Neuroscience Letters, 590*, 106–110.

Leung, M. K., Lau, W. K., Chan, C. C., Wong, S. S., Fung, A. L., & Lee, T. M. (2017). Medi-tation-induced neuroplastic changes in amygdala activity during negative affective pro-cessing. *Social Neuroscience*, 1–12. https://doi.org/10.1080/17470919.2017.1311939.

Lutz, A., & Thompson, E. (2003). Neurophenomenology integrating subjective experience and brain dynamics in the neuroscience of consciousness. *Journal of Consciousness Studies, 10*(9–10), 31–52.

Lutz, A., Dunne, J. D., & Davidson, R. J. (2006). Meditation and the neuroscience of con-sciousness. In P. Zelazo, M. Moscovitch, & E. Thompson (Eds.), *The Cambridge handbook of consciousness* (pp. 499–555). Cambridge University Press.

Lutz, A., Brefczynski-Lewis, J., Johnstone, T., & Davidson, R. J. (2008a). Regulation of the neural circuitry of emotion by compassion meditation: Effects of meditative expertise. *PloS One, 3*(3), e1897.

Lutz, A., Slagter, H. A., Dunne, J. D., & Davidson, R. J. (2008b). Attention regulation and monitoring in meditation. *Trends in Cognitive Sciences, 12*(4), 163–169.

Mascaro, J. S., Rilling, J. K., Negi, L. T., & Raison, C. L. (2012). Compassion meditation en-hances empathic accuracy and related neural activity. *Social Cognitive and Affective Neu-roscience, 8*(1), 48–55.

Mascaro, J. S., Darcher, A., Negi, L. T., & Raison, C. L. (2015). The neural mediators of kind-ness-based meditation: A theoretical model. *Frontiers in Psychology, 6*(109), 1–12. doi: 10.3389/fpsyg.2015.00109.

Menon, V., & Levitin, D. J. (2005). The rewards of music listening: Response and physiologi-cal connectivity of the mesolimbic system. *NeuroImage, 28*(1), 175–184. doi: 10.1016/j.neu-roimage.2005.05.053.

Modinos, G., Ormel, J., & Aleman, A. (2010). Individual differences in dispositional mindful-ness and brain activity involved in reappraisal of emotion. *Social Cognitive and Affective Neuroscience, 5*(4), 369–377.

Morelli, S. A., Rameson, L. T., & Lieberman, M. D. (2012). The neural components of empa-thy: Predicting daily prosocial behavior. *Social Cognitive and Affective Neuroscience, 9*(1), 39–47.

Mosher, C. P., Zimmerman, P. E., & Gothard, K. M. (2014). Neurons in the monkey amygdala detect eye contact during naturalistic social interactions. *Current Biology, 24*(20), 2459–2464.

Moyer, C. A., Donnelly, M. P., Anderson, J. C., Valek, K. C., Huckaby, S. J., Wiederholt, D. A., et al. (2011). Frontal electroencephalographic asymmetry associated with positive emo-tion is produced by very brief meditation training. *Psychological Science, 22*(10), 1277–1279.

Ñāṇamoli, B. (1991). *The path of purification: Visuddhimagga*. Kandy, Sri Lanka: Buddhist Pub-lication Society.

Ñāṇamoli, B., & Bodhi, B. (1995). *The middle length discourses of the Buddha. A translation of the Majjhima Nikaya*. Somerville, MA: Wisdom Publications.

Ñānananda, B. (1971). *Concept and reality in early Buddhist thought: An essay on 'Papañca' and 'Papañca-Saññā-Saṅkhā'*. Kandy, Sri Lanka: Buddhist Publication Society.

Negi, L. T. (2013). *Emory compassion meditation protocol: Cognitively-based compassion training manual*. Atlanta, GA: Emory University.

Noriuchi, M., Kikuchi, Y., & Senoo, A. (2008). The functional neuroanatomy of maternal love: Mother's response to infant's attachment behaviors. *Biological Psychiatry, 63*(4), 415–423.

Northoff, G., Heinzel, A., De Greck, M., Bermpohl, F., Dobrowolny, H., & Panksepp, J. (2006). Self-referential processing in our brain: A meta-analysis of imaging studies on the self. *NeuroImage, 31*(1), 440–457.

Nyanaponika, T. (1965). *The heart of Buddhist meditation*. San Francisco, CA: Weiser.

Ochsner, K. N., & Gross, J. J. (2005). The cognitive control of emotion. *Trends in Cognitive Sciences, 9*(5), 242–249.

Ozawa-de Silva, B., & Dodson-Lavelle, B. (2011). An education of heart and mind: Practical and theoretical issues in teaching cognitively based compassion training to children. *Practical Matters, 4*, 1–28.

Pagani, G., Cekic, M., & Guo, Y. (2008). Thinking about not thinking:" Neural correlates of conceptual processing during Zen meditation. *PLoS One, 3*(9), e3083.

Panda, R., Bharath, R. D., Upadhyay, N., Mangalore, S., Chennu, S., & Rao, S. L. (2016). Temporal dynamics of the default mode network characterize meditation-induced alterations in consciousness. *Frontiers in Human Neuroscience, 10*, 1–12. doi: 10.3389/fnhum.2016.00372.

Pandita, S. U. (1992). *In this very life*. Boston: Wisdom Publications.

Pessoa, L., & Adolphs, R. (2010). Emotion processing and the amygdala: From a "low road" to "many roads" of evaluating biological significance. *Nature Reviews. Neuroscience, 11*(11), 773–783. doi: 10.1038/nrn2920.

Phan, K. L., Wager, T., Taylor, S. F., & Liberzon, I. (2002). Functional neuroanatomy of emotion: A meta-analysis of emotion activation studies in PET and fMRI. *NeuroImage, 16*(2), 331–348. doi: 10.1006/nimg.2002.1087.

Phillips, M. L., Drevets, W. C., Rauch, S. L., & Lane, R. (2003). Neurobiology of emotion perception I: The neural basis of normal emotion perception. *Biological Psychiatry, 54*, 504–514. doi: 10.1016/S0006-3223(03)00168-9.

Posner, M. I., & Petersen, S. E. (1990). The attention system of the human brain. *Annual Review of Neuroscience, 13*(1), 25–42.

Quirk, G. J., & Beer, J. S. (2006). Prefrontal involvement in the regulation of emotion: Convergence of rat and human studies. *Current Opinion in Neurobiology, 16*(6), 723–727.

Redick, T. S., & Engle, R. W. (2006). Working memory capacity and attention network test performance. *Applied Cognitive Psychology, 20*(5), 713–721.

Rilling, J. K. (2013). The neural and hormonal bases of human parental care. *Neuropsychologia, 51*(4), 731–747.

Salzberg, S. (2017). *Real love: The art of mindful connection*. New York, NY: Flatiron Books.

Sato, W., Yoshikawa, S., Kochiyama, T., & Matsumura, M. (2004). The amygdala processes the emotional significance of facial expressions: An fMRI investigation using the interaction between expression and face direction. *NeuroImage, 22*(2), 1006–1013. doi: 10.1016/j.neuroimage.2004.02.030.

Shankman, R. (2008). *The experience of Samadhi: An in-depth exploration of Buddhist meditation*. Boston, MA: Shambhala Publications.

Singer, T., & Klimecki, O. M. (2014). Empathy and compassion. *Current Biology, 24*(18), 875–878.

Singer, T., Kok, B. E., Bornemann, B., Zurborg, S., Bolz, M., & Bochow, C. (2016). *The ReSource Project: Background, design, samples, and measurements* (2nd ed.). Leipzig: Max Planck Institute for Human Cognitive and Brain Sciences.

Small, D. M., Zatorre, R. J., Dagher, A., Evans, A. C., & Jones-Gotman, M. (2001). Changes in brain activity related to eating chocolate: From pleasure to aversion. *Brain, 124*(9), 1720–1733. doi: 10.1093/brain/124.9.1720.

Takahashi, H., Kato, M., Matsuura, M., Mobbs, D., Suhara, T., & Okubo, Y. (2009). When your gain is my pain and your pain is my gain: Neural correlates of envy and schadenfreude. *Science, 323*(5916), 937–939.

Tang, Y. Y., Ma, Y., Wang, J., Fan, Y., Feng, S., Lu, Q., et al. (2007). Short-term meditation training improves attention and self-regulation. *Proceedings of the National Academy of Sciences, 104*(43), 17152–17156.

Tang, Y. Y., Hölzel, B. K., & Posner, M. I. (2015). The neuroscience of mindfulness meditation. *Nature Reviews Neuroscience, 16*(4), 213.

Taren, A. A., Creswell, J. D., & Gianaros, P. J. (2013). Dispositional mindfulness co-varies with smaller amygdala and caudate volumes in community adults. *PLoS One, 8*(5), e64574.

Trautwein, F., Kanske, P., Bockler-Raettig, A., & Singer, T. (unpublished manuscript). (2017). *Differential benefits of mental training types for attention, compassion, and theory of mind.* Max Planck Institute for Human Cognitive and Brain Sciences. psyarxiv.com/k5dqb.

Urry, H. L., Nitschke, J. B., Dolski, I., Jackson, D. C., Dalton, K. M., Mueller, C. J., et al. (2004). Making a life worth living: Neural correlates of well-being. *Psychological Science, 15*(6), 367–372.

Van Vugt, M. K. (2015). Cognitive benefits of mindfulness meditation. In K. W. Brown, J. D. Creswell, & R. M. Ryan (Eds.), *Handbook of mindfulness: Theory, research, and practice* (pp. 190–207). New York: Guilford.

Varela, F. J. (1996). Neurophenomenology: A methodological remedy to the hard problem. *Journal of Consciousness Studies, 3*(4), 330–350.

Wager, T. D., Rilling, J. K., Smith, E. E., Sokolik, A., Casey, K. L., & Davidson, R. J. (2004). Placebo-induced changes in fMRI in the anticipation and experience of pain. *Science, 303,* 1162–1167.

Wallace, A., & Bodhi, B. (2006). The nature of mindfulness and its role in Buddhist meditation. *A correspondence between B. Alan Wallace and Bhikkhu Bodhi* Unpublished Manuscript.

Walshe, M. (1995). *The long discourses of the Buddha: A translation of the Digha Nikaya.* Somerville, MA: Wisdom Publications.

Way, B. M., Creswell, J. D., Eisenberger, N. I., & Lieberman, M. D. (2010). Dispositional mindfulness and depressive symptomatology: Correlations with limbic and self-referential neural activity during rest. *Emotion, 10*(1), 12.

Weng, H. Y., Fox, A. S., Shackman, A. J., Stodola, D. E., Caldwell, J. Z., Olson, M. C., et al. (2013). Compassion training alters altruism and neural responses to suffering. *Psychological Science, 24*(7), 1171–1180.

Whitfield-Gabrieli, S., Moran, J. M., Nieto-Castan, A., Triantafyllou, C., Saxe, R., & Gabrieli, J. D. E. (2011). Associations and dissociations between default and self-reference networks in the human brain. *NeuroImage, 55,* 225–232.

Woodruff, C. C., Martin, T., & Bilyk, N. (2011). Differences in self-and other-induced Mu suppression are correlated with empathic abilities. *Brain research, 1405,* 69–76.

Yang, H. P., Wang, L., Han, L., & Wang, S. C. (2013). Nonsocial functions of hypothalamic oxytocin. *International Scholarly Research Notices Neuroscience,* 1–13. doi: 10.1155/2013/179272.

Zeidan, F., Martucci, K. T., Kraft, R. A., Gordon, N. S., McHaffie, J. G., & Coghill, R. C. (2011). Brain mechanisms supporting the modulation of pain by mindfulness meditation. *Journal of Neuroscience, 31*(14), 5540–5548.

Zeidan, F., Emerson, N. M., Farris, S. R., Ray, J. N, Jung, Y., McHaffie, J. G., & Coghill, R. C. (2015). Mindfulness meditation-based pain relief employs different neural mechanisms than placebo and sham mindfulness meditation-induced analgesia. *Journal of Neuroscience, 35*(46), 15307–15325.

Zeng, X., Chiu, C. P., Wang, R., Oei, T. P., & Leung, F. Y. (2015). The effect of loving-kindness meditation on positive emotions: A meta-analytic review. *Frontiers in Psychology, 6*doi: 10.3389/fpsyg.2015.01693.

Further Readings

Anālayo, B. (2016). *Mindfully facing disease and death: Compassionate advice from early Buddhist texts.* Windhorse Publications.

Berkovich-Ohana, A., Glicksohn, J., & Goldstein, A. (2014). Studying the default mode and its mindfulness-induced changes using EEG functional connectivity. *Social Cognitive and Affective Neuroscience, 9,* 1616–1624. doi: 10.1093/scan/nst153.

Gard, T., Hölzel, B. K., Sack, A. T., Hempel, H., Lazar, S. W., Vaitl, D., et al. (2011). Pain attenuation through mindfulness is associated with decreased cognitive control and increased sensory processing in the brain. *Cerebral Cortex, 22*(11), 2692–2702.

Grant, J. A., Courtemanche, J., & Rainville, P. (2011). A non-elaborative mental stance and decoupling of executive and pain-related cortices predicts low pain sensitivity in Zen meditators. *Pain, 152*(1), 150–156.

Leung, M. K., Chan, C. C., Yin, J., Lee, C. F., So, K. F., & Lee, T. M. (2012). Increased gray matter volume in the right angular and posterior parahippocampal gyri in loving-kindness meditators. *Social Cognitive and Affective Neuroscience, 8*(1), 34–39.

Pagnoni, G., Cekic, M., & Guo, Y. (2008). Thinking about not-thinking: Neural correlates of conceptual processing during Zen meditation. *PLoS One, 3*(9), 1–10. doi: 10.1371/journal.pone.0003083.

The Language and Structure of Social Cognition: An Integrative Process of Becoming the Other

Jaime A. Pineda, Fiza Singh, Kristina Chepak

University of California, San Diego, CA, United States

INTRODUCTION

The focus of this chapter is on the language and structure of social cognition and on integrative aspects, including common features, inherent drives, and mechanisms that play a role in such behavior. There are at least two major drives motivating organizational behavior (Lawrence & Lorsch, 1967) that have affected the phylogenesis and ontogenesis of human and animal evolution: differentiation and integration. From a biological perspective, differentiation is built on the need for separation, individuation, recognition of self as distinct from others—a process grounded in self-protection, identity building, adaptability, and the creation of many forms from one original. Integration is the opposing drive—grounded in a recognition that at some level there is a unity and commonality and hence a need to functionally rediscover, reconnect, and reconcile with that original source. These drives are in perfect opposition and express themselves at all levels of central nervous system (CNS) function—from molecular to cellular to behavioral levels.

In his 2003 review of the cognitive neuroscience of human social behavior, Ralph Adolphs offered the following (Adolphs, 2003a):

"...neuroscience might offer a reconciliation between biological and psychological approaches to social behaviour in the realization that its neural regulation reflects both innate, automatic and **cognitively impenetrable** mechanisms, as well as acquired, contextual and volitional aspects that include **self-regulation**."

The Neuroscience of Empathy, Compassion, and Self-Compassion. http://dx.doi.org/10.1016/B978-0-12-809837-0.00010-6

The ideas expressed by Adolphs and others, that social cognition is a complicated topic encompassing the regulation of both simple and very complex functions, but one that can be reconciled or integrated in its neural and psychological expressions, are the primary topics of this chapter. Furthermore, interspecies expressions of social cognition can also be part of such an integration. It is our contention that although the taxonomy of social cognition is not yet universally agreed upon, humans share with many species what might be described as semi-independent information processing processes, functions and systems that can be variously recruited depending on circumstances to respond to social demands. We agree with (Adolphs, 2003b) that characterizing those processes, functions and systems, the circumstances under which they are engaged, their interactivity, and coordination to regulate social behavior adaptively, is a major challenge facing 21st century cognitive neuroscience.

One of the goals of this chapter is to propose principles for a rational organization and clarification of the apparent uncertainty and confusion in the human literature with respect to the language and structure of social cognition. A second goal is to narrow the gap between human and animal conceptualizations of what social cognition is. Part of the challenge in determining the structure of social cognition and the factors that may be involved in its expression is that there is little research to support a single unifying scheme. Nonetheless, we believe that sufficient evidence exists to propose a basic set of organizing principles. We present supportive evidence from psychological, sociological, and neuroscientific studies, consistent with previous attempts, to claim that social cognition is a deeply grounded and embodied process of integration, of "becoming" the other. Such a process serves as a primary means of connecting, interacting and understanding conspecifics, but also in terms of creating bonds among social groups that benefit their survival. Taking an evolutionary perspective, we conceptualize social cognitive mechanisms as both hierarchically and heterarchically organized, interdependent, and interpenetrating, with the most sophisticated aspects localized in higher order structures in the frontal cortex, but modulated and influenced by lower level representations. That suggests that the uniqueness of any functional state in the social cognition lexicon, such as empathy, is the result of differential engagement and variability in the means and systems activated at different levels of the CNS during this integrative process.

We also take the perspective that there are few, if any, specialized activities for social cognition (Brothers, 1996). Instead, we see social cognition arising out of a set of domain-general primitive functions (Heyes, 2012; Heyes & Pearce, 2015) that aggregate to produce increasingly complex ones. These new, more complex functions can become more and more adapted to solving "social" problems. We further contend that social cognition components can be conceptualized logically as being organized in an inverted pyramid fashion, in a manner similar to (Dietrich's, 2003) conceptualization of consciousness (see Fig. 10.1). Indeed, the entire set of functions associated with social cognition is conceived as structurally hierarchical but heterarchically embedded (see Bruni & Giorgi, 2015), where activity is dynamically and contextually dependent. In this hierarchy–heterarchy (or what we refer to as the H–H model; see Fig.10.1), higher order structures perform increasingly integrative functions and contribute more sophisticated and domain-specific content. A heterarchical organization means that the functional flow of information allows for the possibility of self-referentiality or recursiveness, reentrance, coordination of qualitatively different domains, and second-order-emergence (Bruni & Giorgi, 2015). For example, as opposed to standard feedback, neural reentry does not depend on fixed error-correcting functions or paths, but involves systems dynamically acquired through experience, which are not prespecified or determined a priori (Edelman & Gally, 2013).

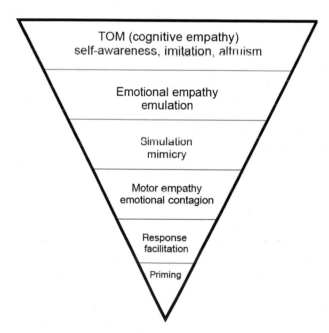

FIGURE 10.1   **The hierarchy–heterarchy (H–H) model of social cognition.** Primitive and domain-general functions are re-represented at higher levels of organization leading to more domain-specific, highly flexible, and complex functions. These levels are interdependent and interpenetrable (i.e., heterarchically embedded). No single neural structure is necessary and sufficient for social cognition and not all areas of the brain contribute equally to it. Damage to any layer will result in an alteration in our ability to relate and understand others, such that the lower the level of malfunctioning, the more fundamental the alteration. Full-fledged processes such as theory of mind require the engagement of higher order structures like the dorsolateral prefrontal cortex.

There is cognitive flexibility inherent in this H–H type of organization, and the more complex functions are associated with the highest levels of neocortical activity and with the most flexibility. We assume that almost every brain process is likely employed in the service of social cognition—from primitive functions, such as priming and response facilitation, to more complex ones such as empathy and theory of mind. These various functions are recruited in the service of responding appropriately to social challenges. Additionally, vision, language, hearing, attention, memory, reward, and other such mechanisms are also recruited for social cognitive processing but are not unique to it (Happé, Cook, & Bird, 2017). This is consonant with the view expounded by (Beer and Ochsner 2006) who argue that to the extent that a social cognitive brain system exists, it may involve neural areas and processes recruited to perform general cognitive processes when the context is social in nature (i.e., relevant to self, other, or interpersonal phenomena).

Finally, there is learning associated with this type of organization. Learning occurs at different levels, from priming to classical and operant conditioning to imitation, and involves manipulations of stored internal representations flowing along hierarchically organized networks that exhibit high degrees of interconnectivity. (Byrne and Russon 1998) have argued that hierarchical organizations of control "are easier than linear ones to repair when they fail, allow the economy of multiple access to common subroutines, and combine efficient local action at low hierarchical levels while maintaining the guidance of an overall structure." We assume that representations and re-representations of function occur at all levels of this information hierarchy, producing a gradient of functions varying in complexity. Hence, we associate priming with the simplest form of learning, and processes such as stimulus enhancement, response facilitation, emotional contagion, mimicry, simulation, emulation, imitation, empathy, and theory of mind as aggregations of simpler functions into progressively more complex ones. These functions reflect the range of means for manipulating the representations of information at different levels of this hierarchy (Byrne & Russon, 1998), where each functional level is integrated with lower levels, but do not necessarily replace nor control them.

To provide some level of support for this conceptualization, we need to first define what social cognition is. Clearly, it is not an exaggeration to say that there is significant disagreement in terms of the language, taxonomy, and structure of social cognition within the human research literature, and those differences are magnified when compared to the animal literature. At least two major problems immediately present themselves when all this is considered. One is to develop a standard taxonomy and vocabulary of socio-cognitive processes and the second is to develop organizing principles to arrange these processes and inter-relatedness in some logical and rational manner. Our aim is to address the second problem, with the hope that the type of unifying principles proposed can help bridge differences and in turn facilitate the development of a more standard taxonomy and language. We start by describing the challenges inherent in developing an agreed-upon language and taxonomy.

THE TAXONOMY OF SOCIAL COGNITION

To begin, we use the term cognition to refer to the level of explanation that lies between neural processes and the physical expression of their outcome, that is, behavior, and which includes emotion (Morton & Frith, 1995). With those assumptions in mind, we define social cognition as a broad set of functions that concern the interaction with and understanding of conspecifics as well as others with whom we must deal socially (Frith & Singer, 2008; Sebanz, Bekkering, & Knoblich, 2006). Understanding the other in a social context requires a pragmatic ability to act appropriately in a particular situation, and to adapt when circumstances change. This naturally entails the proficiency to form and maintain relations, as well as the understanding to act together (De Jaegher, Di Paolo, & Gallagher, 2010). However, social cognition is more than simply recognizing the equivalency between actions perceived and the body's own felt movements. It is more than mimicking, imitating, or simulating. We propose that it is a deep and embodied "becoming" that with whom we wish to interact and whom we wish to know. As such, it is an adaptive, integrative, and dynamical process that must occur at every level of the CNS.

(Seyfarth and Cheney 2015) have suggested that the core building blocks of social cognition in nonhuman animals comprise functions such as individual recognition, knowledge of others' relationships (e.g., dominance), and theory of mind (i.e., understanding of others' mental states). This conceptualization of social cognition in animals has an external focus, namely the other, and appears to be somewhat distinct from a more inner-directed focus in humans. Thus, (Beer and Ochsner 2006), for example, claim that human social cognition is defined as the perception of others, the perception of self, and interpersonal knowledge. Both perspectives argue that an initial step must include functions to perceive and recognize conspecifics, which likely involves multimodal inputs and multiple stages of processing. After this initial assessment, more information must be extracted from both inner and outer sources gathered in the immediate context, as well as stored information derived from previous experience with the context. As these processes unfold, motivational and emotional biases may alter them. In sum, the apparent initial differences in human and animal social cognition end up being different only in terms of what is emphasized by the investigator.

This is not to say that taxonomic differences do not exist. (Fiske and Taylor 2013) identified 14 domains of human social cognition, ranging from basic concepts such as social attention, encoding of social stimuli, and social memory representations, to higher order processes such as social decision making, social inference, attitudes, stereotyping, and prejudice. (Happe & Frith 2014) and (Happé, Cook & Bird 2017) have proposed at least 10 separable functions (affiliation/social motivation, agent identification, emotion recognition, empathy, individuals' information store, mental state attribution/theory of mind, self-processing, social hierarchy mapping, social attention/policing/learning, and in-group/out-group categorization). In a review of findings from the fields of social cognition and social neuroscience to identify social processes impaired in schizophrenia, (Green, Horan, & Lee 2015) argued for at least four critical functions, including perception of social cues, experience sharing, mentalizing, and experiencing and regulating emotion. Finally, the National Institute of Mental Health's research domain criteria (RDoC) initiative currently places the domain of social processes into four constructs as well: affiliation and attachment, social communication, perception and understanding of self, and perception and understanding of others.

From a nonhuman animal perspective, comparative studies that take an anthropocentric approach, as well as more ethologically oriented perspective, suggest that animals exhibit behaviors functionally comparable to those of humans. These behaviors include recognition and categorization of conspecifics and their emotions, the development and management of social relationships such as attachment, friendship, the acquisition of novel skills by interacting with conspecifics (social learning), the manipulation of others by means of communicative signals, the competence to perform joint cooperative actions and the question of "mind-reading" skills, as well as behavioral flexibility across many social situations that involve communication and social learning (Hauser & Nelson, 1991; Miklósi, 1999; Miklósi, Topál, & Csányi, 2004). Impressive as this list is, (Stoesz, Hare, & Snow, 2013) reminds us that there are also many differences, for example, in affiliative behaviors within species (e.g., diurnal lemur [Propithecus diadema]), and even within a single social group (e.g., Japanese macaques [Macaca fuscata]).

Similarities and differences within and across species can reflect ways in which the various functions inherent in social cognition are labeled and may be related (Happé, Cook, & Bird, 2017). For one, there may be different labels for the same function (e.g., motor resonance and mirroring). It is also possible that one function may constitute an essential subcomponent of another (e.g., motor resonance and mirroring), or that functions may rely on at least one common process but also have distinct elements. To note, it is generally assumed that normal human social interactions require a distinction in processing self from other. That is, we need to know and understand the self in order to understand the other (Fiske & Taylor, 2013). It is also the case that functions may have a direct causal link or may be developmentally associated to yet a third factor common to both. Finally, something that has received less attention is the knowledge base individuals bring to their social interactions. (Beer and Ochsner 2006) argue that contextual knowledge is a final and necessary component of social cognition (Wood, 2003). In summary, all these issues reflect the taxonomy problem of social cognition writ large, and point toward the need for more research before further progress can be made on this front.

THE ROLE OF EMPATHY IN THE SOCIAL COGNITION LEXICON

As a means to simplify the present argument, we take a closer look at empathy as a canonical example of the complex architecture of social cognition. Many attempts at defining empathy have put emphasis on behavioral and/or affective responses. For example, it has been thought of as "an affective response more appropriate to someone else's situation than to one's own" (Hoffman, 1984), or "a sense of similarity between the feelings one experiences and those expressed by others" (Decety & Jackson, 2004), or "a complex form of psychological inference in which observation, memory, knowledge, and reasoning are combined to yield insights into the thoughts and feelings of others" (Ickes, 1997). More recently, (Decety and Cowell 2015) have argued that empathy reflects the natural ability to perceive and be sensitive to the emotional states of others, coupled with a motivation to care for their well-being. Although the construct of "empathy" has been difficult to define in the past, the discovery of systems that provide a potential neural substrate has allowed for some progress to be made by suggesting a plausible unifying mechanism for inferring and experiencing what another feels, namely, by simulating it through a shared self-other representation.

Thus, current definitions of empathy grounded in neurobiology make the construct more tractable and testable. A strong trend in this regard has been toward viewing empathy as a uniform response involving higher order cognition. In a review of the literature, (Blair 2005) argued that this might be a misleading perspective and that empathy should be viewed "not as a unitary system but rather as a loose collection of partially dissociable neurocognitive systems." Blair makes the argument for the existence of at least three such systems, namely cognitive empathy, motor empathy, and emotional empathy. This is an argument based primarily on dysfunctions experienced by two groups of individuals—namely those diagnosed with autism and those with psychopathy. It differs from accounts from fields such as social psychology and comparative ethology that offer a more nuanced and fractured view. For example, Preston and de Waal see empathy as "a super-ordinate category that includes all sub-classes of phenomena that share the same mechanism and includes emotional contagion, sympathy, cognitive empathy, helping behavior, etc." (Preston & de Waal, 2002). (Decety and Svetlova 2012) point out that empathy subsumes a variety of neurobiological systems and partially dissociable social, emotional, and cognitive subsystems that operate in parallel fashion and that have a unique evolutionary history.

The preservation of empathy-like responses can be observed across a variety of species (e.g., rats, dogs, nonhuman primates) (Langford, 2006; Panksepp & Panksepp, 2013; Preston & de Waal, 2002). Indeed, all mammalian brains appear capable of experiencing the raw feelings of emotion, ranging from rage, fear, lust, care, and panic, to play. Basic emotions appear to provide the basis for higher level empathic responses, and empathy for the pain of others appears mediated by brain regions aroused by an animal's own learned experience of pain. Despite the fact that empathy in humans is refined and encompasses a multitude of cognitive functional abilities, the phylogenetic continuity of empathy across species is remarkably evident.

Likewise, in cognitive-developmental psychology, it has been recognized for some time that complex behavior is constructed by combining and coordinating low-level components (e.g., mental, perceptual, or motor schemes) into novel sequences. For de Waal and for us, empathy, just like many of the other components of social cognition, comes in many forms rather than an all-or-nothing phenomenon. This more fractured, complex, and dynamical view is quite compatible with the H–H model we are now proposing (Fig. 10.1). Similarly, (Panksepp and Panksepp 2013) proposed a system of nested hierarchies in the brain to explain empathy across species that is also compatible with our model. They divide their system into three progressions: primary, secondary, and tertiary. Primary processes are deeply subcortical functions that are seemingly homologous in all mammals and are involved in basic affective states, including such things as sensory affect, bodily homeostatic affect, and emotional affect. An example of a primary form of empathy is "emotional contagion," specifically pain, which mice display while observing a familiar conspecific in pain (Langford, 2006). Likewise, human infants in nurseries have a strong tendency to start crying after hearing another cry. Finally, and perhaps the paramount example of primary-process empathy is the emotional intelligence and attachment that mothers feel towards their infants. The raw affective feeling of "care" enables parental figures to understand the emotional feelings of their distraught infants leading them to try to pacify them. This may be an essential precursor for the development of other forms of empathy in the tertiary mode

(Panksepp & Panksepp, 2013). Thus, primary processes provide a foundation for the more complex secondary processes of empathy. At that intermediary level, learning and memory take place in humans and animals alike. Learning and memory both intensify affective feelings at an unconscious level. Through fear conditioning, for example, both animals and humans develop responses to specific situations as a function of previous experiences—that are themselves critical for more complex forms of empathy. Tertiary processes are the highest forms of brain activity represented in the neocortex and easier to study in humans because they can verbally describe their experiences. Hence, a multitiered, hierarchical approach allows us to view empathy as a bottom-up, emotional, and developmental brain process that makes phylogenetic continuity from animal to human logically consistent.

What is Compassion?

Although beyond the scope of our chapter, we would argue that compassion for the other and for oneself may reflect motivational and affective dimensions aggregated and engendered when we become aware of entering a state of empathy. Compassion means "to suffer with" or "to suffer together" and is an emotional response of empathy and sympathy, that is, an ability to take the perspective of and feel the emotions of another person. But compassion mechanisms aggregate these cognitive-emotive responses with the motivation and desire to act, even though such action may or may not take place. We see compassion as the full expression of this integrative drive and full embodiment of cognition-emotion-action resources brought to bear on momentary circumstances. Research shows that this unique function is associated with increased heart rate variability as the heart rate slows, increased release of oxytocin, lower levels of stress hormones, as well as increased activity in brain regions linked to pleasure and empathy while showing reduced activity in the default mode network (Bartz, Zaki, Bolger, Hollander, Ludwig, Kolevzon, & Ochsner, 2010; Decety & Jackson, 2004; Happé, Cook, & Bird, 2017). We go further and suggest that there is a unique state associated with compassion. The state is characterized by a temporary decrement or dissolution of self-other distinctions, such that one no longer can see a difference between who one is and who the other is. As such, during this state we act neither to satisfy selfish motives nor for the sake of others—it is simply an act that is required. Additionally, compassion is characterized by an intuitive sense and confidence that the actions taken are appropriate to the circumstance. Finally, there may linger a sense of satisfaction associated with the outcome, which from the outside could be considered positive, such as providing food to a hungry person or negative, such as withholding money from a homeless person.

UNIFYING PRINCIPLES: BECOMING/KNOWING THE OTHER

The Principle of Phylogenetic Continuity

One clue that may provide a link and serve as an organizational principle among the various components of social cognition, such as empathy, theory of mind, imitation, mimicry, and related processes is their phylogenetically continuous characteristic (Adolphs, 2003a). Frans de Waal and Stephanie Preston have argued persuasively that the roots of empathy can be traced to our closest living relatives, the chimpanzees. Indeed, a number of studies have now shown that humans and other mammals (mice, dogs, birds, monkeys) respond empathically to a conspecific they have encountered previously, and thus to the perceived overlap (e.g., familiarity or similarity) between self and other (Preston & de Waal, 2002; Silva, Bessa, & de Sousa, 2012). (Jones and Josephs 2006) found that dogs react to their owner's stress with an increase in negative emotional arousal. Similarly, (Plotnik and de Waal 2014) showed that following a distressing event, elephants affiliated significantly more with other conspecifics through directed physical contact and vocal communication.

It can be argued that successful integration into a social group requires the need for not only effective but also affective communication, something that characterizes a variety of animals (Preston & de Waal, 2002). In environments with ever increasing social complexity, as seen in many large primate groups, it becomes important to be able to communicate information as well as the emotional context of that information with other members of the group. Empathy appears to enhance social function by tuning our response to the emotions of another. Hence, knowing the emotional state of the other, and making decisions based on that understanding, facilitates the most advantageous response to the situation even when fleeing or joining in a fight.

The more fundamental abilities from which empathy might have arisen include social contagion, response facilitation, and emulation. All of these are considered categories of social learning—from observational to active learning. Some of the most salient emotional responses are acquired through observing the behaviors of others, especially those involved in avoidance and withdrawal, such as taste aversion and predator fear (Tomasello, Carpenter, Call, Behne, & Moll, 2005). Thus, from an evolutionary perspective, empathy has survival value in that it helps individuals gather and hunt for food, detect predators, enhance courtship, and ensure reproductive success. It can be considered one of the most important social skills in humans because it not only provides for strong relationships but also affects social learning as well. The problem with making such an evolutionary argument, however, is that it is difficult to see how natural selection works at the level of superordinate categories, such as empathy. It is more logical to suggest that it is the more primitive functions that are selected and that those in turn are combined to produce complex responses. But, just what are these constitutive components of empathy?

To a large degree, our worldview is consistent with that of (Decety and Jackson 2004), who argue that the basic macro components of empathy are mediated by specific neural systems. Furthermore, they have suggested that these include shared neural representations, self-awareness, mental flexibility, and emotion regulation. We agree that mirroring processes, for example, by which we also mean the shared neural representation of information about self and other, along multiple levels and across multiple modalities of the CNS, are critical components. We believe that natural selection for these processes produced the abilities to mimic and imitate, which in turn generated the ability to learn through such mechanisms. Learning may have facilitated the evolution of the abilities to resonate and respond to the emotions of others (empathy) as well as to represent the beliefs and intentions in other minds (a theory of mind). Empathy and theory of mind, plus the underlying functional infrastructure, likely allowed for social learning and the faithful transmission of culture (Gintis, 2003; McElreath, 2003).

Within the context of the H–H model, certain social cognitive skills—notably the ability to represent another conspecific's mind or theory of mind—distinguish humans and perhaps apes from other animals. The implication is that the elaboration of social cognition in different animals (e.g., nonhuman primates, dogs, rodents) may depend on neural resources, with larger brains and larger memory capacities allowing for the development of more complex processes. It is widely agreed that compared to other species, humans exhibit more advanced and flexible forms of social behaviors, including empathy, self-awareness, and perspective-taking (Decety & Svetlova, 2012).

The Principle of Ontogenetic Continuity

Just like phylogenetic continuity can help place the micro- and macrocomponents of social cognition in a rational and meaningful scheme, the development of these components during the lifetime of an organism, that is their ontogenesis, can provide additional information to organize them logically. (Decety and Svetlova 2012) argue that it is essential to consider components, such as empathy, within a neurodevelopmental framework that recognizes both the continuities and changes in socioemotional understanding from infancy to adulthood.

Physiological processes in the brain are inherently embedded in an integrated multilevel neurophysiological hierarchy. One hallmark of the human brain is its adaptability or neural plasticity to dynamically respond to changes in its internal and external environment in an immediate, short- and long-term fashion. Adaptability refers to an outer and inner accommodation to circumstances, a reshaping of structure and function to respond appropriately to circumstances. It has been shown that such adaptability involves epigenetic mechanisms that affect gene expression (McClung & Nestler, 2008; Nelson & Monteggia, 2011). Therefore, we view neuroplasticity as an integral feature of the social "becoming" process. But, adaptation may connote a superficial change, whereas in the context of becoming there is a deeper, interpenetrating change.

Human and animal studies have shown the importance of social connections and context on experience-dependent changes in brain and behavior (Cacioppo, Capitanio, & Cacioppo, 2014). Recently, (Moeller et al. 2016) showed that social interactions among individual chimpanzees creates a set of microbiomes with considerable similarity in bacterial species. Similarly, other studies have shown that social environments can upregulate neurotrophic factors, increase rate of neurogenesis in hippocampus, upregulate CREB and IGF-1, and upregulate genes involved in synaptic transmission and postsynaptic signal transduction (Adlard, Perreau, & Cotman, 2005; Vazquez-Sanroman et al., 2013). These data strengthen one of our main points, that the process of becoming the other is an immediate and long-term process requiring molecular, synaptic, and system-level changes.

(Noë 2006) has proposed that cooperation and social interactions can be classified along different dimensions of form, outcome, and temporal extent. However, to avoid problems of misclassification due to focusing on only one of these dimensions, (Völter, Rossano, & Call 2016) fine-tuned the argument that nonhuman primate social cognition can be best mapped onto two primary axes. On the one hand, they posit the existence of a cognitive axis ranging from social to nonsocial behaviors that involves flexibility/sociality and includes such functions as technical problem solving, social tool-use, and communication. This is complemented by a motivational axis that includes antisocial to other-regarding behavior and involves motivational/prosociality including spite, exploitation, cooperation, and helping behaviors. Since motivation is not the same as emotion, we would suggest that a broader emotional axis is needed. We base this on evidence that most neural structures shown to be important in processing emotions turn out to be important for social and nonsocial behavior as well, including cortical regions such as the left prefrontal, right parietal, anterior and posterior cingulate cortices, as well as regions in orbitofrontal cortex, higher order sensory cortices, amygdala, and ventral striatum (Adolphs, 2003b). Indeed, the most common brain regions associated with social cognition besides the frontal lobes are the temporal lobes (both cortical and subcortical regions) (Adolphs, 2003a,b).

CONSTRAINTS

Folk theories of social cognition tend to emphasize the positive aspects of social interactions and of knowing the other. The deep "becoming" we have argued for in this chapter would likewise tend to suggest that the default mode in social cognition is an inner drive to reach some state of identity with the other. It is, therefore, important to consider why such a state of identity is a rare occurrence, and to highlight processes that limit and constrain this social drive.

It has been suggested that sociocognitive processes reflect three kinds of levels of processing: what, how, and why (Thioux, Gazzola, & Keysers, 2008). (Aragon et al. 2014) have suggested that the modulation in social connectedness may occur at any of the three levels of processing. The neural substrates engaged at these various levels of processing are assumed to work together and integrate their activity to enable capabilities such as empathy, theory of mind, and imitation. However, it is also reasonable to suggest that while in many instances we must connect with others, we at times need to disconnect. For example, it would be completely unproductive to empathize with a child's pain to the point of being unable to do something about it. Hence, in many instances assimilative behavior must give way to complementary behavior and emotional orientation. This hints at the existence of mechanisms that can modulate, change, or alter the "becoming" process.

Another way to conceptualize this issue is to characterize to what extent social cognition functions are engaged automatically and how and when do they come under intentional control? Undoubtedly issues such as the limitation of cognitive resources, experience-dependent training, and the capacity for metarepresentation would provide constraints on social functions. At a behavioral level, issues of predictability (Tricomi, Delgado, McCandliss, McClelland, & Fiez, 2006), affiliation (Aragon, Sharer, Bargh, & Pineda, 2014; Krienen, Tu, & Buckner, 2010), and sociometry (i.e., the monitoring of other individual's status; Klein & Platt, 2013) add a degree of contextuality, and therefore modulation, to these behaviors.

(Spengler et al. 2009) have argued for two potential mechanisms of regulatory control on social behavior: (1) executive function, a domain-general approach that involves general control functions such as response inhibition and interference control and (2) common representational systems, a more domain-specific approach. Their view assumes that control of social behavior requires common nonspecific as well as specific mechanisms that allow for a self–other distinction. Furthermore, they conclude that controlling automatic representations draws on key subprocesses needed in higher level social cognition (Spengler, Von Cramon, & Brass, 2009). Similar arguments are provided by (Cross and Iacoboni 2014) who showed that unlike reactive control systems, which tend to be automatically engaged and appear to rely more on specialized mechanisms, preparatory control mechanisms use more general mechanisms involving prefrontal cortex. Although significantly more research is needed in terms of the control of all sociocognitive functions, what little research is currently available appears consistent with the H–H model.

CONCLUSIONS

In this chapter, we have argued for a set of principles to place social cognition in a framework that can help simplify and explain its evolution, development, and organization. Underlying this is the assumption that social cognition, both the understanding of and interaction with conspecifics, is not simply a hallmark of human and nonhuman social behavior but may indeed be a basic, perhaps default mode of processing—one deeply embedded in its biology (Hari, Henriksson, Malinen, & Parkkonen, 2015). Brain structure-function relationships evolved phylogenetically and ontogenetically to produce networks capable of reliable computational performance that were at once adaptive to changing circumstances. Such cognitive architectures maintain consistent, recognizable, and reproducible responses across individuals and yet retain many additional degrees of freedom for context-, stimulus-, and task-dependent reconfiguration (Petersen & Sporns, 2015). Different configurations of these networks make different contributions—some involved in domain-general functions, others more engaged in domain-specific behaviors, while still others are more involved in integrating multimodal information or for task switching and control.

The view that emerges, and one consistent with our argument, is one in which elementary building blocks of social cognitive architecture coalesce into ever more complicated processes as a function of circumstances and challenges. These dynamically determined responses are hierarchically and heterarchically organized, interdependent, and interpenetrating with the most sophisticated aspects localized to higher order structures in the frontal cortex, but modulated and influenced by lower level representations, including affective valence. We believe that this conceptualization, which is an elaboration of that proposed by a number of investigators, including most recently (Happé, Cook, & Bird 2017), could be pragmatic in organizing a variety of functions into a rational, phylogenetically and ontogenetically consistent approach. Furthermore, we hope that such an effort can also bootstrap the goal of developing a standard taxonomy and vocabulary. As Paul Nunez has expressed in his new book *The New Science of Consciousness* (Nunez, 2016), "consciousness is rooted in the dynamic patterns of multiple interacting scales." The same can be said for social cognition in general and about empathy, its canonical subcomponent.

References

Adlard, P. A., Perreau, V. M., & Cotman, C. W. (2005). The exercise-induced expression of BDNF within the hippocampus varies across life-span. *Neurobiology of Aging*, *26*, 511–520. doi: 10.1016/j.neurobiolaging.2004.05.006.

Adolphs, R. (2003a). Cognitive neuroscience of human social behaviour. *Nature Reviews Neuroscience*, *4*(3), 165–178. doi: 10.1038/nrn1056.

Adolphs, R. (2003b). Investigating the cognitive neuroscience of social behavior. *Neuropsychologia*, *41*, 119–126. doi: 10.1016/S0028-3932(02)00142-2.

Aragon, O. R., Sharer, E. A., Bargh, J. A., & Pineda, J. A. (2014). Modulations of mirroring activity by desire for social connection and relevance of movement. *Social Cognitive Affective Neuroscience*, *9*(11), 1762–1769. doi: 10.1093/scan/nst172.

Bartz, J. A., Zaki, J., Bolger, N., Hollander, E., Ludwig, N. N., Kolevzon, A., & Ochsner, K. N. (2010). Oxytocin selectively improves empathic accuracy. *Psychological Science*, *21*(10), 1426–1428. doi: 10.1177/0956797610383439.

Beer, J. S., & Ochsner, K. N. (2006). Social cognition: A multi level analysis. *Brain Research*, *1079*, 98–105. doi: 10.1016/j.brainres.2006.01.002.

Blair, R. J. R. (2005). Responding to the emotions of others: Dissociating forms of empathy through the study of typical and psychiatric populations. *Consciousness and Cognition*, *14*, 698–718. doi: 10.1016/j.concog.2005.06.004.

Brothers, L. (1996). Brain mechanisms of social cognition. *Journal of Psychopharmacology*, *10*, 2–8 10/1/2[pii]\r10.1177/026988119601000102.

Bruni, L. E., & Giorgi, F. (2015). Towards a heterarchical approach to biology and cognition. *Progress in Biophysics and Molecular Biology*, *119*, 481–492. doi: 10.1016/j.pbiomolbio.2015.07.005.

Byrne, R. W., & Russon, A. E. (1998). Learning by imitation: A hierarchical approach. *The Behavioral and Brain Sciences*, *21*, 667–684. doi: 10.1017/S0140525X98001745 discussion 684-721..

Cacioppo, S., Capitanio, J. P., & Cacioppo, J. T. (2014). Toward-a-Neurology-of-Loneliness. *Psychol Bull*, *140*, 1464–1504.

Cross, K. A., Iacoboni M. (2014). Neural systems for preparatory and reactive imitation control. *Dissertation Abstracts International: Section B: The Sciences and Engineering*, 74.

De Jaegher, H., Di Paolo, E., & Gallagher, S. (2010). Can social interaction constitute social cognition? *Trends in Cognitive Sciences*, *14*, 441–447. doi: 10.1016/j.tics.2010.06.009.

Decety, J., & Cowell, J. M. (2015). Empathy, justice, and moral behavior. *American Journal Of Bioethics Neuroscience*, *6*, 3–14. doi: 10.1080/21507740.2015.1047055.

Decety, J., & Jackson, P. L. (2004). The functional architecture of human empathy. *Behavioral and Cognitive Neuroscience Reviews*. doi: 10.1177/1534582304267187.

Decety, J., & Svetlova, M. (2012). Putting together phylogenetic and ontogenetic perspectives on empathy. *Developmental Cognitive Neuroscience*, *2*, 1–24. doi: 10.1016/j.dcn.2011.05.003.

Dietrich, A. (2003). Functional neuroanatomy of altered states of consciousness: The transient hypofrontality hypothesis. *Consciousness and Cognition*, *12*, 231–256. doi: 10.1016/S1053-8100(02)00046-6.

Edelman, G. M., & Gally, J. A. (2013). Reentry: A key mechanism for integration of brain function. *Frontiers in Integrative Neuroscience, 7*, 63. doi: 10.3389/fnint.2013.00063.

Fiske, S., & Taylor, S. E. (2013). *Social cognition from brains to culture* (2nd ed.). London: Sage.

Frith, C. D., & Singer, T. (2008). The role of social cognition in decision making. *Philosophical Transactions of the Royal Society of London. Series B, Biological Sciences, 363*, 3875–3886. doi: 10.1098/rstb.2008.0156.

Gintis, H. (2003). The Hitchhiker's guide to altruism: Gene-culture coevolution, and the internalization of norms. *Journal of Theoretical Biology, 220*, 407–418. doi: 10.1006/jtbi.2003.3104.

Green, M. F., Horan, W. P., & Lee, J. (2015). Social cognition in schizophrenia. *Nature Reviews Neuroscience, 16*, 620–631. doi: 10.1038/nrn4005.

Happe, F., & Frith, U. (2014). Annual research review: Towards a developmental neuroscience of atypical social cognition. *Journal of Child Psychology and Psychiatry and Allied Disciplines, 55*, 553–577. doi: 10.1111/jcpp.12162.

Happé, F. G., Cook, J., & Bird, G. (2017). The structure of social cognition in(ter)dependence of sociocognitive processes. *Annual Review of Psychology, 68*, 1–25. doi: 10.1146/annurev-psych-010416-044046.

Hari, R., Henriksson, L., Malinen, S., & Parkkonen, L. (2015). Centrality of social interaction in human brain function. *Neuron, 88*, 181–193. doi: 10.1016/j.neuron.2015.09.022.

Hauser, M. D., & Nelson, D. A. (1991). 'Intentional' signaling in animal communication. *Trends in Ecology and Evolution, 6*, 186–189. doi: 10.1016/0169-5347(91)90211-F.

Heyes, C. (2012). New thinking: The evolution of human cognition. *Philosophical Transactions of the Royal Society B: Biological Sciences, 367*, 2091–2096. doi: 10.1098/rstb.2012.0111.

Heyes, C., & Pearce, J. M. (2015). *Not-so-social learning strategies*. doi: 10.1098/rspb.2014.1709.

Hoffman, M. L. (1984). Interaction of affect and cognition in empathy. In C. E. Izard, J. Kagan, & R. B. Zajonc (Eds.), *Emotions, cognition and behavior*. New York: Cambridge University Press.

Ickes, W. (1997). *Empathic accuracy*. New York: The Guilford Press.

Jones, A. C., & Josephs, R. A. (2006). Interspecies hormonal interactions between man and the domestic dog (*Canis familiaris*). *Hormones and Behavior, 50*(3), 393–400. doi: 10.1016/j.yhbeh.2006.04.007.

Klein, J. T., & Platt, M. L. (2013). Social information signaling by neurons in primate striatum. *Current Biology, 23*, 691–696. doi: 10.1016/j.cub.2013.03.022.

Krienen, F. M., Tu, P. -C., & Buckner, R. L. (2010). Clan mentality: Evidence that the medial prefrontal cortex responds to close others. *The Journal of Neuroscience, 30*, 13906–13915. doi: 10.1523/JNEUROSCI.2180-10.2010.

Langford, D. J. (2006). Social modulation of pain as evidence for empathy in mice. *Science, 312*, 1967–1970. doi: 10.1126/science.1128322.

Lawrence, P. R., & Lorsch, J. W. (1967). Differentiation and integration in complex organizations. *Administrative Science Quarterly, 12*(1), 1–47.

McClung, C. A., & Nestler, E. J. (2008). Neuroplasticity mediated by altered gene expression. *Neuropsychopharmacology, 33*, 3–17. doi: 10.1038/sj.npp.1301544.

McElreath, R. (2003). Reputation and the evolution of conflict. *Journal of Theoretical Biology, 220*, 345–357. doi: 10.1006/jtbi.2003.3166.

Miklósi, a. (1999). The ethological analysis of imitation. *Biological Reviews of the Cambridge Philosophical Society, 74*, 347–374. doi: 10.1111/j.1469-185X.1999.tb00190.x.

Miklósi, Á., Topál, J., & Csányi, V. (2004). Comparative social cognition: What can dogs teach us? *Animal Behaviour, 67*, 995–1004. doi: 10.1016/j.anbehav.2003.10.008.

Miller, G. (2006). Animal behavior: Signs of empathy seen in mice. *Science, 312*, 1860b–1861b. doi: 10.1126/science.312.5782.1860b.

Moeller, A. H. A., Foerster, S., Wilson, M. L., Pusey, A. E., Hahn, B. H., & Ochman, H. (2016). Social behavior shapes the chimpanzee pan-microbiome. *Science Advances, 2*. doi: 10.1126/sciadv.1500997 e1500997.

Morton, J., & Frith, U. (1995). Causal modeling: A structural approach to developmental psychopathology. In *Developmental psychopathology, theory and methods* (pp. 357–390). (1). Oxford, England: John Wiley.

Nelson, E. D., & Monteggia, L. M. (2011). Epigenetics in the mature mammalian brain: Effects on behavior and synaptic transmission. *Neurobiology of Learning and Memory, 96*, 53–60. doi: 10.1016/j.nlm.2011.02.015.

Noë, R. (2006). Cooperation experiments: Coordination through communication versus acting apart together. *Animal Behaviour, 71*, 1–18. doi: 10.1016/j.anbehav.2005.03.037.

Nunez, P. (2016). *The new science of consciousness: Exploring the complexity of brain, mind and self.* Amherst, New York: Prometheus Books.

Panksepp, J., & Panksepp, J. B. (2013). Toward a cross-species understanding of empathy. *Trends in Neurosciences, 36*, 489–496. doi: 10.1016/j.tins.2013.04.009.

Petersen, S. E., & Sporns, O. (2015). Brain networks and cognitive architectures. *Neuron, 88*, 207–219. doi: 10.1016/j.neuron.2015.09.027.

Plotnik, J. M., & de Waal, F. B. (2014). Asian elephants (*Elephas maximus*) reassure others in distress. *PeerJ, 2*, e278. doi: 10.7717/peerj.278.

Preston, S. D., & de Waal, F. B. M. (2002). Empathy: Its ultimate and proximate bases. *The Behavioral and Brain Sciences, 25*, 1–20. doi: 10.1017/S0140525X02000018 discussion 20–71.

Sebanz, N., Bekkering, H., & Knoblich, G. (2006). Joint action: Bodies and minds moving together. *Trends in Cognitive Sciences, 10*, 70–76. doi: 10.1016/j.tics.2005.12.009.

Seyfarth, R. M., & Cheney, D. L. (2015). Social cognition. *Animal Behaviour, 103*, 191–202. doi: 10.1016/j.anbehav.2015.01.030.

Silva, K., Bessa, J., & de Sousa, L. (2012). Auditory contagious yawning in domestic dogs (*Canis familiaris*): First evidence for social modulation. *Animal Cognition, 15*, 721–724. doi: 10.1007/s10071-012-0473-2.

Spengler, S., Von Cramon, D. Y., & Brass, M. (2009). Resisting motor mimicry: Control of imitation involves processes central to social cognition in patients with frontal and temporo-parietal lesions. *Social Neuroscience, 5*(4), 401–416 http://dx.doi.org/10.1080/17470911003687905.

Stoesz, B. M., Hare, J. F., & Snow, W. M. (2013). Neurophysiological mechanisms underlying affiliative social behavior: Insights from comparative research. *Neuroscience and Biobehavioral Reviews, 37*, 123–132. doi: 10.1016/j.neubiorev.2012.11.007.

Thioux, M., Gazzola, V., & Keysers, C. (2008). Action understanding: How, what and why. *Current Biology, 18*(10), R431–R434 http://dx.doi.org/10.1016/j.cub.2008.03.018.

Tomasello, M., Carpenter, M., Call, J., Behne, T., & Moll, H. (2005). Understanding and sharing intentions: The origins of cultural cognition. *The Behavioral and Brain Sciences, 28*, 675–691. doi: 10.1017/S0140525X05000129 discussion 691–735.

Tricomi, E., Delgado, M. R., McCandliss, B. D., McClelland, J. L., & Fiez, J. A. (2006). Performance feedback drives caudate activation in a phonological learning task. *Journal of Cognitive Neuroscience, 18*(6), 1029–1043.

Vazquez-Sanroman, D., Sanchis-Segura, C., Toledo, R., Hernandez, M. E., Manzo, J., & Miquel, M. (2013). The effects of enriched environment on BDNF expression in the mouse cerebellum depending on the length of exposure. *Behavioural Brain Research, 243*, 118–128. doi: 10.1016/j.bbr.2012.12.047.

Völter, C. J., Rossano, F., & Call, J. (2016). Social manipulation in nonhuman primates: Cognitive and motivational determinants. *Neuroscience and Biobehavioral Reviews.* doi: 10.1016/j.neubiorev.2016.09.008.

Wood, J. N. (2003). Social cognition and the prefrontal cortex. *Behavioral and Cognitive Neuroscience Reviews, 2*, 97–114. doi: 10.1177/1534582303253625.

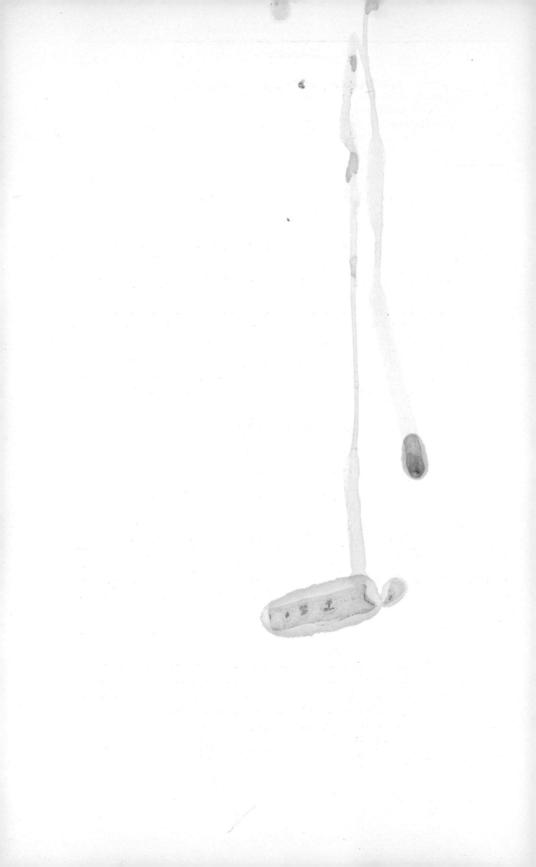

Where Caring for Self and Others Lives in the Brain, and How It Can Be Enhanced and Diminished: Observations on the Neuroscience of Empathy, Compassion, and Self-Compassion

C. Chad Woodruff, Larry Stevens

Northern Arizona University, Flagstaff, AZ, United States

By now, if the reader has journeyed with us through all 10 of the chapters of this book, s/he has perhaps found him/herself on something akin to Mr. Toad's Wild Ride[1], in Chapter 1 hopping aboard Toady's vintage motorcar with Stevens and Woodruff exploring the library of terms, concepts, and arguments swirling around society's understandings of these critical animal attributes. Then crashing through the fireplace into Toad Hall where Flasbeck, Gonzalez-Liencres, and Brüne in Chapter 2 clarify

[1]Mr. Toad's Wild Ride is one of the original attractions that was featured with the grand opening of Disneyland Park in 1955. Based on Walt Disney's adaptation of *The Wind in the Willows*, a well-received 1908 children's novel by Kenneth Grahame, the ride involved a cast of anthropomorphized animal characters, including toads, *voles*, weasels, and badgers, participating in a broad variety of crazy high jinks across a pastoral Edwardian background. The scenes in the narrative to follow are loosely drawn from this Disneyland ride for all ages (you yourself may still enjoy this ride by visiting Fantasyland, Anaheim, California, or by reading further).

The Neuroscience of Empathy, Compassion, and Self-Compassion. http://dx.doi.org/10.1016/B978-0-12-809837-0.00011-8

the definitional, phylogenetic, ethological, contextual, experimental, and neuropsychiatric boundaries of Empathy. Next, our adventurers break through a doorway into Chapter 3 with Stevens and Benjamin into the inner sanctum of Compassion, exploring the temporal and spatial topography of this celebrated human construct behind affective, motivational-intentional, interpersonal, and regulatory teakwood panels. And there, off to the side behind a particularly ornate, baroque panel, hidden in a thick haze of self-esteem but encouraged forward by Stevens, Gauthier-Braham, and Bush, Toady and friends find themselves plunging into the obscure, Chapter 4 world of Self-Compassion neuroscience, with at first only vagaries, uncertainties, and disembodied constructs before them, but far in the distance a dendritic glow beckoning them forward (Whew!).

Still careening further into the depths of the chaos of Toad Hall, our intrepid searchers find themselves entering the dark hall of Cruelty, escorted by the ghoulish West, Savery, and Goodman into Chapter 5 where empathy and compassion are suspended helplessly from the ceiling and dehumanized, personality disordered, psychopathic weasels swing wildly from rococo chandeliers. And off on the southwest wall in Chapter 6, we see our reflection in a vast Mirror of entangled neurons carefully stirred to perfection by the hand of Woodruff and betraying the deepest meanings behind our reckless actions. Our travelers then enter the festive dining chamber, where Birkett and Sasaki whip up a neuroendocrine stew of the finest imported Oxytocin and Vasopressin, while voles and their rodent kin scamper in the dark shadows of the Chapter 7 banquet hall.

At last, Toady and company break free of the labyrinthine chambers of Toad Hall and find themselves careening through the Disneyland countryside, variously terrorizing visitors and workers alike, until they crash against an ancient banyan tree festooned with Asian lanterns and awash with the hypnotic chords of Tibetan golden bowls as our travelers are lulled into the deepest reverie and instilled Compassion by Calderon, Ahern, and Pruzinsky in Chapter 8. Our travelers then find themselves marching entranced into the union of the four tributaries of the River of Brahmaviharas where Goodman, Plonski, and Savery entreat them to a tour of the neuroscience of these ancient headwaters in Chapter 9. Unfortunately, their peace is shattered as they emerge from these tranquil waters and enter a vast warehouse of Social Cognition constructed by Pineda, Singh, and Chepak in Chapter 10, a warehouse which explodes in swirling notions of hierarchically and heterarchically organized cortical and subcortical mechanisms intricately involved in the complexities of becoming another.

Fortunately now, this intellectual explosion catapults our travelers into the streets of the present Chapter 11 and thence down to a warm and inviting tavern, the Mother Road Brewery so the weathered sign proclaims, in which Woodruff and Stevens, over choice ales, attempt to pull all of this mystery and majesty together into an integrated portrait of the neuroscience of empathy, compassion, and self-compassion. So now, in Chapter 11, come Woodruff and Stevens attempting to make some sense and order out of all of this mayhem and mischief. We have chosen to do so not by boiling and bubbling this swirling mass of neuroscience into a foaming and singularly intoxicating brew that in one draught imbues the reader with the totality of the neuroendocrinology of empathy, compassion, and self-compassion. That bit of alchemy is well beyond our cerebral resources at the present time. No, instead, we here will take each chapter in its turn, attempt to summarize the main observations and findings of each, and then round out our treatises with, by then, hopefully informed reflections on how and where our brains experience these phenomena. We hope, by applying our understandings of this ride made wild by empirical neuroscience, to ultimately conclude with suggestions for how to increase the experiences of empathy, compassion, and self-compassion both in individuals and in societies. As stated throughout this book, our ultimate objective is to inform our public, to contribute our parts toward creating a more empathic, compassionate, and self-compassionate world, and to stop the inane, horrific, and ubiquitous cruelties that we humans perpetrate upon one another. We begin this integration with Chapter 1.

EMPATHY, COMPASSION, AND SELF-COMPASSION

Chapter 1 begins with a tracing of the origins of the concepts and terms for the experiencing of empathy, compassion, and self-compassion. Thus, Stevens and Woodruff find the origin of empathy stretching back over a 100 million years in the *mimicry* of birds, in the *emotional contagion* of packs of coyotes joining in a haunting chorus together in the farness of evening, and in the blind display of *preconcern* from the frantic congregation of young rhesus monkeys to the mournful cries of a wailing peer. Such expressions of pre-empathy are suggested to have survival value in promoting group cohesiveness, kin and mate selection, and ultimate evolutionary fitness. Similarly, with their bases in empathy, compassionate and altruistic behaviors have likely been around for over a million years and co-occurred with the development of the prosocial species-preservative system described by Wang (2005). According to Stevens and Woodruff, compassion emerged as a formalized construct in ancient Vedic writings over 2000 years ago and has become one of the most popular teachings of modern religious and spiritual pursuits. And, self-compassion can also be traced to early spiritual practices, if not earlier to self-grooming behaviors in animals. Self-compassion has more recently been popularized in the teachings and research of Dr. Kristin Neff who, along with her colleagues and other researchers, has produced a very large body of clinical and research literature concerning this important personal construct.

Next, Stevens and Woodruff tackle a number of definitional issues surrounding empathy, compassion, and self-compassion in which the evolutionary origins and current conceptual ambiguities are confronted. The authors of Chapter 1 follow the evolution of the Greek expression *Empatheia*, or "in passion," through the German expression *Einfühlung*, or "feeling into," and up to the modern English term Empathy, with its direct connections to the automatic and involuntary contagion with the emotions of another. They explain that this affective response comprises an isomorphic emotional sharing involving a mental representation of the other's experiences, but with a clear differentiation of the observing self from the experiencing other. Stevens and Woodruff, in keeping with contemporary extrapolations, further analyze empathy as composed of an affective and a cognitive component, with more recent attention directed to the cognitive modulation of the other's emotional experience.

Compassion is similarly reduced to its Latin roots, *in compati* or "suffering with" another, and is defined by our authors as "a sensitivity to the suffering of another and a desire to alleviate that suffering." They argue that compassion begins with empathy but only long enough for the observer to determine cognitively that the other is suffering and to contemplate ways of alleviating that suffering. Thus, with compassion there is a more immediate self-other differentiation and top-down mentalizing than with empathy alone, a "feeling with" of the former compared to a "feeling into" of the latter. The authors also differentiate altruism, empathic concern, sympathy, and pity from compassion and agree with Singer and Klimecki (2014) that compassion is a subtype of empathy. They further explain that the degree of self-other differentiation determines whether experiences with the suffering of another become empathic concern or empathic distress.

Stevens and Woodruff then present self-compassion as composed of three bipolar components from the extrapolations of Neff (2003a, b). Those components are (1) Self-Kindness versus Self-Judgment, (2) Mindfulness versus Over-Identification, and (3) Common Humanity versus Isolation (Neff, 2003b). Thus, self-compassion becomes the practice of loving-kindness toward the self without negative self-evaluations, an effort to be present in the moment free of undue overattention to particularly unpleasant experiences, and a sense of union with the community of personkind without isolating oneself from others.

The Chapter 1 authors briefly consider what the world would be like in the absence of these critical human virtues. They cite the tragic examples in life of a lack of empathy in certain animal species, employ the concept of "empathy erosion" (Baron-Cohen, 2011) to explain examples of cruelty in humans, and attribute the numerous examples in history of human atrocities to a similar lack of compassion. And citing the research of Neff and colleagues, they recite a list of mental and physical health consequences of a dearth of self-compassion. They refer the reader to Chapter 5 in this textbook for a detailed presentation of the neuroscience of cruelty.

Stevens and Woodruff then wrap up this exploration of the concepts of empathy, compassion, and self-compassion by engaging the reader in a series of questions and debates concerning some hot topics in this area of investigation. Issues considered are whether compassion is a mental or a behavioral state, how one can feel true compassion for another with whom s/he has had no personal experience (as for common humanity), if there are circumstances in which one can cause harm and still be compassionate, if compassion requires empathy, the nuances of self-other differentiation in the experience of empathy, if empathy necessarily leads to compassion, the importance of the emotional and cognitive components of empathy, the roles of personal distress and perspective-taking in empathy and compassion, and if empathy is necessarily prosocial. The authors are clear in presenting their dialogues not so much as definitive or authoritative answers to these questions but more as a way of engaging the reader in these important social concerns and of generating continued discussion and investigation of the critical social virtues of empathy, compassion, and self-compassion.

Empathy

Flasbeck, Gonzalez-Liencres, and Brüne (Chapter 2) tackle one of the most difficult issues in studying empathy, namely, its definition. Defining empathy has been a bit like trying to pick up a river in that, as soon as you think you've picked it up, the water escapes between your fingers and there is nothing there—it is truly a Herculean task. The authors make a clever attempt at plugging the leaks of this nearly impossible endeavor by constraining their definition phylogenetically. They further support their view of empathy by elaborating on contexts under which empathy is promoted and demoted, making use of the latest cognitive neuroscience and neuropsychiatric research to support them.

Discussion of the definition question begins by addressing mental/behavioral states that are similar to empathy but lack features like self-other discrimination and causal attribution. Instead, these states are seen as precursors to empathy, such as *emotional contagion* and *imitation*, both of which involve representing the feelings and/or intentions of another, but representing them more as if they belonged to the self rather than to the other. We, the editors, add to this, the claim that empathy should be viewed as existing on a continuum with maximal, or *genuine*, empathy relating to a generation of rich, allocentric representations—that are made possible by the observer's own experiences and resultant knowledge, but that represent these as belonging to the other. To the extent that activated representations involve increasing self-referential information, they are further from genuine empathic representations. As indicated by Flasbeck, Gonzalez-Liencres, and Brüne, a key component of empathy is causal attribution, arguing that understanding the causes of another's emotions is equally important to feeling and recognizing those emotions.

Regarding the phylogeny of empathy, Chapter 2 discusses the concept of life history strategies and mentions two types, *K-strategy*, describing species that have relatively few offspring but long life cycles compared to *r-strategy* species whose individuals have shorter life spans but larger numbers of offspring. Members of K-strategy species are said to experience greater natural selection pressure to care for offspring given the relatively few offspring they have and the greater parental return-on-investment that results from a longer offspring life span. It is argued that these selection pressures have favored animals that are capable of maintaining attentional focus on their offspring, feeling what their offspring feel, thinking what they think, and understanding that it is the offspring feeling and thinking that way and not the parent themselves. As Flasbeck and colleagues point out, the evolutionary precursors to empathy may have been functions like emotional contagion, which was likely selected due to the adaptive alerting potential that comes from one individual's perception of a threat and resultant emotional response. In this example, contagion leads each individual who observes any conspecific emoting this alarm to experience it himself, as if it were the observer's own emotional response to some threat toward which, thanks to emotional contagion, he is about to orient and against which he will then be able to defend.

There are of course, in any mammalian population, variations in severity of individual responses to threats, with some creatures proving overreactive to threats, causing nearby conspecifics to experience distress that is disproportionate to the threat. A potential solution to this would be the development of self-identity, enabling the observer to experience the contagious emotions of a conspecific, but disobliging acting on those emotions by recognition that one is only experiencing said emotions because he is observing them in another. This self-other discrimination now affords the observer the ability to focus on the other and to react in a way that is motivated by knowledge of the conspecific's, not the observer's, behavior.

Flasbeck and colleagues go on to discuss contextual influences on empathy, beginning with discussion of how state-dependent aspects, such as stress levels, can have a nonlinear influence on the expression of empathy, whereby both low and high levels of stress are said to be suboptimal for empathizing while the "sweet spot" lies somewhere in the middle, creating enough arousal to motivate engagement, but not so high that the observer reacts with fight or flight impulses (an empathic Yerkes–Dodson Law; Yerkes & Dodson, 1908). Regarding trait-dependent aspects of context effects on empathy, the authors note that, of the "big five" personality traits, agreeableness and conscientiousness relate most strongly. In addition to the big five, the authors discuss investigations of the relationships between empathy deficits and "the dark triad" of psychopathic, narcissistic, and Machiavellian traits, all of which relate to the big five trait of disagreeableness. The authors also point to research showing that occupation affects how one processes another's pain, with doctors apparently attenuating their experiences of their patients' pain, as reflected by decreased vicarious activation of the pain matrix, when performing painful procedures. The conversation of trait characteristics and their relationships to empathy ends with in- and out-group effects, even noting that oxytocin (OT) can enhance in-/out-group differences (see Chapter 7).

Regarding the development of empathy, Chapter 2 discussed the importance of early childhood interactions with caregivers, particularly as concerns emotional responsiveness and the caregiver's ability to help regulate emotional reactions. Further, development of empathy is critically dependent on development of joint attention, self-awareness, self-other discrimination, and theory of mind (ToM). As for measuring empathy in adults, commonly used self-report questionnaires include the Interpersonal Reactivity Index (Davis, 1983) and the Empathy Quotient (EQ; Baron-Cohen & Wheelright, 2004). More direct measures of empathy comprise pain estimation techniques as well as one introduced by the authors, the Social Interaction Empathy Test, in which a distinction is made between empathy for bodily versus psychological pain.

Given all of this, Flasbeck et al. proceed to discuss the brain mechanisms related to empathic processing, including OT, which appears to downregulate amygdalar activity and associated stress hormone release, presumably reducing personal distress in the observer, allowing resources to be devoted to understanding the other. Given OT's generally prosocial effects, it is perhaps surprising that nasal administration not only enhances empathy, trust, and cooperation but also in-group favoritism—not necessarily a prosocial effect. The authors conclude that OT appears to increase the salience of social targets, thereby improving empathic accuracy. They further point out that this OT effect must also be understood in the context of its interactions with dopaminergic as well as serotonergic processes in the nucleus accumbens (NAcc). This effect represents reward circuitry that reinforces social approach.

An aspect of empathy on which much of the social neuroscience of empathy has focused is empathy for pain. Since brain regions associated with the first-person experience of pain, the so-called pain matrix, are somewhat understood, the hypothesis can be tested that empathizing with someone involves activation of the same regions associated with first-person experience. Indeed, activation in regions such as medial prefrontal, anterior cingulated, and the anterior insula (AI) represents just such over-lapping brain areas and therefore supports, though not unequivocally (see Lamm, Decety, & Singer, 2011), that empathizing with another in pain involves some of the same brain regions as the first-person experience of pain. Interestingly, some of these same brain regions dissociate cognitive (cuneus/precuneus [PCun], ventromedial PFC [vmPFC]) from affective (prefrontal cortex [PFC], posterior cingulate cortex [PCC], AI, dorsal cingulate cortex [dACC]) empathy.

Regarding electroencephalographic (EEG) investigations of empathy, Chapter 2 discusses two main lines of research—event-related potentials and spectral analysis of the mu rhythm (mu suppression). The former reveals empathy-related modulation of both early and late components while the latter is correlated with empathic effort and self-other discrimination. Interestingly, correlations between self-report measures of empathy and mu suppression appear to be negative, with increased mu suppression related to decreased perspective-taking scores (Horan et al., 2014; Milston et al., 2013; Neufeld et al., 2016; Woodruff & Klein, 2013; but see Brown et al., 2013 for opposite findings) and decreased EQ scores (Perry, Troje, & Bentin, 2010).

This negative relationship is surprising at first blush because the most obvious hypothesis would be that, to the extent that mu suppression reflects empathic processes, more empathy should be associated with more mu suppression. Of course, it might be the case that brain processes associated with mu suppression are ones that actually attenuate with increasing empathy. This seems unlikely to be the case however, given findings such as those of Oberman et al. (2005) who found that impaired empathy, as seen in their participants with autism, is associated with a lack of mu suppression, whereas the apparent negative relationship alluded to above would predict maximal mu suppression in a population with minimal empathic abilities. We suggest instead that empathy has a nonlinear relationship to mu suppression whereby both low and high levels of mu suppression are associated with lower levels of empathy, but moderate levels of mu suppression are associated with high levels of empathy. In other words, we suggest that the relationship between mu suppression and empathy may be an inverted-U, similar to that proposed by Flasbeck et al. for the relationship between stress and empathy.

Lastly, Flasbeck et al. (Chapter 2) distinguish empathy from compassion by asserting that the latter requires the observer to "disengage" from what they refer to as "the shared or imagined feeling of the other," what the editors would call allocentric representations of the other. To what end is this disengagement from empathic, allocentric representations? We suggest that it results in a freeing of resources to focus attention on the observer's own feelings/intentions in the service of motivating prosocial behavior. By this definition, empathy is a necessary precursor to compassion.

Compassion

In Chapter 3, Stevens and Benjamin define compassion as a sensitivity to the suffering of others and a desire to alleviate that suffering. Contemporary neuroscience research suggests that compassion comprises four components which may be ordered temporally and hierarchically. These components are (1) affective, (2) motivational-intentional, (3) self-other differentiation, and (4) cognitive regulatory. Research supporting each component is presented and an integrated model is offered to explain how opportunities for compassionate acts can be distorted into malicious and cruel behaviors toward others.

First, in order to be sensitive to the suffering of another, Stevens and Benjamin assert that there must be some emotional reaction to their suffering, if only very brief. Notwithstanding the poorer temporal resolution of MRI relative to EEG, research by Ochsner et al. (2004) and Immordino-Yang, McColl, Damasio, and Damasio (2009) indicates that less cognitively demanding empathic experiences (upregulating vs. downregulating negative emotions for the former study and compassion for physical pain relative to social pain for the latter) occur on the order of 2–6 s before more cognitively demanding tasks. And, these responses have been found to occur in more primitive neurological structures associated with the processing of basic arousal responses (i.e., amygdale [Amg], anterior insular cortex, and anterior cingulate cortex [ACC]) (Lindquist, Wager, Kober, Bliss-Moreau, & Barrett, 2012). Similar temporal sequencing has been observed in cortical electrode placements in primates (Buschman & Miller, 2007). Stevens and Benjamin argue that, although more temporally sensitive investigations need to be conducted to better establish this time course in humans, these studies are consistent with suggestions of a more immediate affective response to negative stimuli relative to later cognitive processing of such events.

Brain localizations for this primary emotional responding have been more extensively researched, according to the authors, and a body of literature has been assembled not only strongly implicating these above sites but also better delineating their functional and structural components. In brief, investigations of the localizations of negative affect (Ochsner et al., 2004; Ochsner et al., 2009), psychological and bodily pain (Immordino-Yang et al., 2009), emotional vocalizations (Lutz, Brefczynski-Lewis, Johnstone, & Richard Davidson, 2008), and silent video documentaries of real, distressing scenarios (Klimecki, Leiberg, Lamm, & Singer, 2013) all have revealed activation of components of a circuit composed of the Amg, insular cortex, and ACC along with more distal task-specific sites. Singer and associates (Lamm & Singer, 2010; Singer, Critchley, & Preuschoff, 2009) have further delineated the insular cortex (In) as composed of an anterior portion more involved in social emotions, in empathy, and in the representation and integration of present and future affective experiences, a medial portion involved in the experience of compassion and love, and a posterior portion more dedicated to the manifestation of nociceptive experiences.

Stevens and Benjamin point to de Waal's (2009) compelling description of "preconcern" in nonhuman and human primates as they run almost reflexively toward a conspecific in distress. De Waal considers such preconcern a precursor of empathic understanding, an impulse that becomes inhibited by higher order processes, and the authors wonder if a motor vestige of this automatic responding resides in compassionate humans, even in the absence of overt responding. To date, this motivational-intentional component critical to our definition of compassion has not been clearly identified. However, Lamm and Singer (2010) have suggested that observed motor connections between medial and lateral PFC on the one hand and dorsal anterior In on the other provide a pathway for the motor conversion of affective states. The authors further speculate that the increasingly delineated Mirror Neuron (MN) System (described in detail in Chapter 6 of this book) and its proximal connections through the primary speech area in humans may reflect manifestations of such "intention understanding" for the desire to help one in need. Certainly it is time for studies of MN activity during compassionate perceptions.

The ability to differentiate self from other and perspective-taking in general, has an extensive and quite intellectually colorful history. One need only review the ToM research briefly surveyed in Chapter 3 to obtain a feel for the breadth and richness of this literature. Neurologically, such perspective-taking on the motivations, intentions, emotions, and thoughts of others, often called _mentalizing_, has been localized to a rather diffuse set of structures including the temporoparietal junction (TPJ), the ACC, the superior temporal sulcus (STS), the medial prefrontal cortex (mPFC), the PCun, the medial frontal gyrus, and the temporal poles (TP). It is not too surprising that such a complex mental operation would be arrayed anteriorly to posteriorly along the cortex. Stevens and Benjamin agree that perhaps this broad display of ToM functions would be better managed and understood by differentiating it functionally into basic processes and more localized sites specific to those functions, as suggested by Schaafsma, Pfaff, Spunt, and Adolphs (2015). Needless to say, the ability to separate one's own perceptions and experiences from those of another is critical to the experience of compassion, and the broad dedication of the cortex to this complex process is perhaps a reflection of the importance of this function.

As noted earlier, Stevens and Benjamin argue that some brief empathic experience is critical to a compassionate understanding of another's suffering. This automatic and rather immediate reaction occurs on exposure to the stimulus, but is rather quickly processed at a "higher," more recently evolved level, primarily in frontal cortical structures. Our authors applied the well-worn cognitive psychology terms *bottom-up* and *top-down*, respectively, to functionally conceptualize these components. This differentiation was highlighted in the studies by Ochsner and colleagues (Ochsner et al., 2004, 2009) in their identification of PFC, ACC, TPJ, medial temporal gyrus (mTG), putamen, as well as caudate, thalamus, and cerebellar areas in the top-down appraisal of negative human images mentioned earlier.

Perhaps the most telling investigations presented for the pre-eminent role of higher cortical processing of more basic emotional responses within the context of compassion were the studies by Kédia, Berthoz, Wessa, Hilton, and Martinot (2008) and by Fehse, Silveira, Elvers, and Blautzik (2015). Kedia et al. cleverly stratified their independent variables along two orthogonal moral dilemma dimensions, predator/prey (agent/victim) and self/other scenarios and recorded functional Magnetic Resonance Imaging (fMRI). Their results revealed the involvement of primarily prefrontal and TPJ regions, along with the insular and AMG arousal circuit, in top-down processing of emotional conditions, the activation of primarily ToM regions in other-as-agent processing, and a prominent role of ToM mentalizing in the experience of compassion. These outcomes are consistent with the subsequent Buhle et al. (2014) meta-analysis of the cognitive appraisal of emotions which found, among other things, a modulation of AMG emotional arousal by frontal (dorsolateral prefrontal cortex [dlPFC], ventrolateral prefrontal cortex [vlPFC], dorsomedial prefrontal cortex [dmPFC]) and temporoparietal regions.

However, the final study reviewed in this chapter which perhaps sheds the most light on our abilities to differentially process the suffering of others toward or away from compassionate perceptions and behaviors was that conducted by Fehse, Silveira, Elvers, and Blautzik (2015). In brief, these authors created careworthy and blameworthy endings to human suffering scenarios and recorded fMRIs of participants as they observed and contemplated these written scenes. While not only obtaining behavioral ratings of compassion in the predicted directions, Fehse et al. also found, for the *careworthy* conditions, increased activation of cortical regions involved in affective empathy (mPFC, insula, and ACC) and in sensory, motor, and mnemonic representations of the scenarios (somatosensory cortex, primary motor cortex, fusiform gyrus, hippocampus, and parahippocampus), and, for the *blameworthy* conditions, greater involvement of ToM self-other differentiation and mentalizing regions (TPJ, PCun, dlPFC). In other words, Stevens and Benjamin suggest that for the careworthy compassion scenarios, participants appeared to engage cortical regions more involved in empathizing with and acting upon (assisting?) the victims, whereas for the blameworthy scenarios, participants appeared to activate regions more involved in the cognitive otherization (see Chapter 5) of the victim. Furthermore, a subsequent connectivity analysis in this study revealed, for the blameworthy conditions, a tuning down of compassion centers by direct activation of the ToM rheostat. Stevens and Benjamin then suggest, in the Fehse et al. study, a clear mechanism for the modulation of affective compassion by one's thoughts.

Our authors round out their Chapter 3 by following up this review of the neuroscience of compassion literature by presenting an integrated model for the human expression of compassion and for its attenuation in certain circumstances. That model is as follows:

On witnessing the suffering of another, one first experiences automatically an empathic sharing of the suffering of the other by engaging neural representations of that suffering in an affective circuit composed of the *Amg, the insular cortex*, and the *ACC*. This reaction is followed almost immediately by manifestations of vestigial motor circuits of preconcern stored in motor pathways in *inferior arcuate sulcus* and *intraparietal sulcus/inferior parietal lobule*, and likely other motor circuits, and in humans manifested as motor and verbal impulses to approach the other in order to render assistance. These more instinctual and involuntary responses to the suffering other are then followed by a near simultaneous engagement of top-down, cognitive processing, and mentalizing structures which allow up- (careworthy) or down-regulation (blameworthy) of the affective/motivational component. Sites activated include *dlPFC* (selective attention and processing in working memory), *vlPFC* (response selection and inhibition), and *dmPFC* (affective monitoring and processing), perhaps followed by semantic representations in *posterior temporal cortex* and further self-other differentiation in *temporoparietal junction*, PCun, and back to *dmPFC*, from whence this reverberating neural circuit repeats itself. Depending on the nature of activation within this fronto-temporo-parietal pathway, one's response to the suffering of another can become enhanced or suppressed in its entirety. Our authors anticipate continued neuroscience research on the various components of this model in order to validate and to refine it further.

Self-Compassion

At the time of writing this book, the Neuroscience of Self-Compassion is sorely wanting. Stevens, Gauthier-Braham, and Bush labor under this deficiency in Chapter 4, opting to dig a little deeper for the purpose of this book, to conduct a component analysis and to examine that neuroscience for its parts. Kristin, (2003a, b), the most visible contemporary spokesperson for the practice of self-compassionate attitudes and behaviors, conceptualizes self-compassion as a sensitivity to one's own suffering and a desire to alleviate that suffering. She differentiates self-compassion from self-esteem, the latter as more self-evaluative and more based on social comparisons, and she divides self-compassion into the three bipolar components of *Self-Kindness versus Self-Judgment, Mindfulness versus*

Over-Identification, and *Common Humanity versus Isolation* (Neff, 2003b). Stevens et al. take each of these components in turn and explore the related neuroscience in order to make inferences and predictions regarding the topography that a neurological investigation of self-compassion could well take.

Thus, for the component of Self-Kindness, Stevens et al. consider the neuroscience of self-referential processing, self-criticism, self-enhancement, and self-judgment and briefly summarize the studies of multiple distinguished researchers who have helped to delineate these self-referential constructs. The inferences of Stevens et al. regarding the component of self-kindness are that (1) a collection of structures christened by Northoff and Bermpohl (2004) as Cortical Midline Structures (CMS), which include orbitomedial prefrontal cortex, supragenual ACC, dmPFC, PCC, and precuneus (PCun) are convincingly involved in the processing of self-related input, with specialized functions for each of these sites, (2) mPFC appears to be a locus of self-reflective processing, with dmPFC and vmPFC having differential functions in the processing of cognitive and affective self-referential information respectively, (3) a similar cognitive/affective functional differentiation can be seen in the processing of self-referential information in the dACC and ventral ACC, (4) the anterior insular cortex (AI), having direct connections to the Amg and PFC, monitors the interoceptive bodily status of the organism, and (5) the PCC and PCun, with projections to the TPJ and angular gyrus (Ang), are consistently involved in self-other differentiation, social cognition, and autobiographical memory retrieval.

Fortunately, the component of Mindfulness has a growing neuroscience research history, although there seem to be some disagreements regarding a clear definition of this construct. For our purposes, Neff (2003a) defines mindfulness as being open to and recognizing the positive and negative at any given moment in life. Holzel et al. (2011) divide mindfulness into three interacting components: attentional control, emotional regulation, and a shifting away from CMS self-referential processing to more body awareness, and Stevens et al. in Chapter 4 trace the neuroscience of mindful self-compassion along this template. Thus, they conceptualize such contemplations as beginning with mindfulness-based increased attentional effort and affect modulation associated with enhanced dlPFC, dmPFC, vlPFC, and ACC activations during an initial mindful focus. With practice and skill development, a shift in activation would begin to occur from mPFC toward greater AI and more posterior, somatosensory CMS components, with enhanced connectivity between dlPFC and PCun. This shifting in activation and connectivity would be associated phenomenologically with prototypical body self-awareness. Continued practice and mindfulness expertise would be followed by further posterior CMS shifts, decreased activation of self-referential processing in the default mode network, and a blurring of self-other boundaries.

This above progression through mindfulness practice from frontal to more posterior CMS activations then evolves into expressions of the third component of self-compassion, that being Common-Humanity, or the realization that one is a member of the community of personkind, all with similar successes and failures, joys and disappointments, strengths and weaknesses, etc. shared by everyone. At its extreme, common-humanity is conceptualized as becoming one with the other, what the Vedic Samhitas call "Universal Oneness", d'Aquili and Newberg (1993) call "Absolute Unitary Being", and Manocha (2011) calls "Mental Silence". The authors of Chapter 4 acknowledge that very little research has been conducted on this construct, in part because of the difficulty in quantifying consciousness, or its absence. However, they cite the research of Josipovic, Dinstein, Weber, and Heeger (2012), Josipovic (2013), and Berman and Stevens (2015) which has attempted to quantify this state of nonduality and suggest increased connectivity in "the central precuneus network" (PCun, dlPFC, dmPFC, and Ang) (Josipovic, 2013) and significant EEG cortical slowing (Berman & Stevens, 2015) during the experience of such states of consciousness.

This speculation on the possible neuroscience of self-compassion concludes with presentation of a self-compassion meditation that progresses from contemplations on kindness, caring, and love for the self, through mindful inattention, emotional modulation, and enhanced somatic awareness, toward a joining with common-humanity, a blurring of self-other boundaries, and the experience of nonduality. It is further speculated that neuroimaging of such a meditation would see progressions from the initial enhancement of frontal activations in *dlPFC, dmPFC, vlPFC,* and *ACC*, thence toward a shifting of this activation away from frontal sites, through *AI* to more posterior CMS localizations of *PCun* and *PCC*, with associated increases in connectivity and EEG slow wave propagations from *dlPFC* through central *PCun* and into *TPJ* extensions. The authors await a formal test of this model for the neuroscience of self-compassion.

Cruelty

A distressing topic is broached by authors West, Savery, and Goodman (Chapter 5) in the form of cruelty—perhaps the antithesis, or *far enemy*, of compassion. Citing Taylor (2009), they offer that cruelty is "unjustified voluntary behavior that causes foreseeable suffering toward an undeserving victim or victims." They note that this is a *spectral* definition whereby *callousness* is said to lie on one end of the spectrum with the other end occupied by sadistic *cruelty*, the difference essentially being whether imposed suffering was a means to some other end or whether it was the end in, and of, itself. Further, it is argued that cruelty is best seen not as behaviors characteristic of a particular sort of person, for example, an "evil person", but rather as behaviors in which most humans are capable of engaging under conditions of *empathy erosion, dehumanization,* and *otherization.* Recognition of the fact that we all have some disposition toward cruelty and that engagement in cruel behavior is less a question of character and more a question of the situation means that we are less likely to experience empathy erosion, to otherize and to dehumanize perpetrators of cruelty. As such, we are less likely to treat perpetrators with cruelty because understanding what caused another's behavior *is* empathy.

One particularly interesting point raised concerns the sensitivity to disgust, which is related to amygdalar and insular activation and which is strongly implicated in dehumanization. The latter can come in two forms. *Animalistic dehumanization* is most associated with disgust and is said to occur under conditions in which one views another as lacking the key qualities, whatever those may be, that make one uniquely human, while *mechanistic dehumanization* refers more to the denial of warmth and to attribution of cold and superficial characteristics. Otherization and dehumanization are precursors to empathy erosion insofar as empathizing with another depends on perceived similarity—coming to view another as different from the self in animalistic or mechanistic dehumanizing terms sets up this perceived lack of overlap between self and other making behavior less likely to be determined by "seeing the world through the other persons eyes." Additionally, moral judgments can come into play, leading to disengagement of the "psychosocial and cognitive mechanisms" that generate, or activate, moral beliefs so that one's beliefs are less likely to be expressed in his behavior. Add to this the phenomenon of *diffusion of responsibility* and one has a recipe for occurrences like genocide.

One determinant of otherization and dehumanization is in-group/out-group membership which is marked by reward-related ventral striatal activity in response to successes within one's in-group and failure in an out-group—indeed, those with greater ventral striatal activity generally expressed greater urge to do harm. While this pattern is consistent with *compassion* toward the in- but *schadenfreude* (taking pleasure in another's pain) for the out-group, the reverse pattern, a failure for the in- and success for the out-group elicits anterior cingulate and AI—regions identified by Singer and colleagues as involved in empathy for pain.

Cruelty can affect one's ability to act fairly. Neuroimaging research suggests that structures such as the STS (biological motion detection and social perception) and the TPJ (self-other discrimination and ToM) are recruited in situations where a participant intends to punish another individual. Taken together, the work reviewed in Chapter 5 is suggestive of a neural network that includes structures associated with motivation and reward processes such as in the ventral striatum, promoting schadenfreude and even sadistic cruelty.\In otherwise psychologically healthy individuals, it is believed that social categorization (e.g., in-/out-group, otherization, dehumanization) leads to empathy erosion, perhaps visible in changes in the STS (social perception) and TPJ (self-other discrimination), and lesser activation of empathy-for-pain-related areas (ACC, AI). Other brain regions likely contribute, at least indirectly, to cruelty, including the orbital frontal cortex (OFC) and mPFC. The OFC is important for moral judgments and decision-making, particularly when they involve disgust. While the Amg is more active during disgust, the mPFC is less active, possibly related to a diminishing of empathic processing and to empathy erosion. Next, West et al. point out that cruelty is defined, at least partially, by moral beliefs, and they discuss some neural processes associated with moral "judgments, evaluations, and decisions." They further point out that disorders of moral reasoning, such as psychopathy, are associated with frontal lobe dysfunction, particularly in the OFC and vmPFC.

Following this, the authors discuss *everyday cruelty*, referring to the fact that each of us is capable of some cruelty in some situations, and how it is related to anger, aggression, hatred, jealousy, trauma, social rejection and how these may "reduce empathy and result in cruel behavior." After distinguishing anger as a mental state and aggression as a behavior, noting that aggressive behavior need not be associated with anger (e.g., sports), it is pointed out that aggression can be classified as *reactive* (e.g., *lashing out*) or *instrumental* (e.g., robbery). Though the relationship between anger and aggression is not straightforward, it is noteworthy that anger is associated with dACC, OFC, and the TP when healthy men experience anger. Regarding genetics, an abnormality in the monoamine oxidase A gene that affects multiple neurotransmitters, particularly in combination with head trauma, can lead to aggression.

A potential cause of aggression is social rejection, which is related to some of the same neural structures as bodily pain, namely, the AI and the dACC. Another cause, hatred, similarly involves not only the insula but also premotor cortex. And, self-loathing can be a cause of cruelty toward the self and is related to activity in the dACC and dlPFC. Another potential cause of cruel behavior is jealously, which appears to involve, among other regions, the Amg. The dACC also seems to be associated with the experience of envy, while schadenfreude appears linked to reward-related processing in the ventral striatum and OFC.

The authors then go on to review some psychological disorders in which individuals exhibit cruel behaviors, such as Machiavellianism, conduct disorder and callous-unemotional traits, antisocial personality disorder, psychopathy, and sexual violence. While each of these disorders has their own relationships to cruelty, one common brain region associated with atypical activation is the Amg, perhaps related to the ability to understand others emotions—or an impairment in doing so.

MIRROR NEURONS

MNs respond both when one performs an action and when she observes someone else make that movement. As these neurons were originally discovered in the premotor cortex of macaque monkeys, a region involved in processing intentions, it appears that these neurons are well situated to contribute to action understanding. Woodruff (Chapter 6) discusses some of the latest MN research, beginning with single cell and multisite linear arrays used in research with macaque monkeys, fMRI and EEG, ending with theoretical accounts of MNs and their putative roles in social cognition.

In Chapter 6, we learn about evidence in favor of the action understanding hypothesis, which is, simply stated, that MN activation constitutes our understanding of actions. We also learn reasons to be skeptical of this hypothesis. For example, some MNs in the premotor cortex are congruent, meaning the same action goal that drove the neuron during execution of an action is the same action goal required to drive that neuron during action observation. However, there are many so-called MNs that are incongruent, meaning the action that activates the neuron during observation is a different action than the one that activates it during execution. As noted by Catmur (2015), for these neurons to be involved in action understanding, there must be strict congruency between execution and observation goals. It was also claimed in Chapter 6 that, in order to constitute action understanding, these neurons need to discriminate self from other. However, while MNs do show reliable differences between execution and observation, self-other discrimination is arguably a cognitive, not a motor process (if the two are to be cleanly separated), and MNs therefore would seem unlikely to be involved in that inferential process.

fMRI and EEG studies were also discussed in which claims about measuring MNs have been made, even though it is strictly not possible to make this inference with current neuroimaging resolution. By definition, an MN is a neuron that responds to both execution and observation. Single-cell studies work wonderfully—indeed it was a single-cell study that discovered MNs. But noninvasive neuroimaging requires the summation of postsynaptic potentials across tens of thousands of neurons in order to generate a signal strong enough to be recorded outside the head. And, it is difficult to know whether the same tens of thousands active during execution were the same tens of thousands activated during observation.

Nonetheless, neuroimaging studies have advanced our understanding of mirroring and self-other processing by limiting claims about the extent to which the measured signals reflect MNs. For example, in the *early days* (circa 2000 CE), obtained activation in regions believed to contain MNs (i.e., premotor cortex (PMC), inferior parietal cortex [IPC]) was assumed to reflect those MNs. However, per the logic above, there is currently no way of knowing whether activation in a given voxel in, say, the PMC, was due to the same neurons active for execution and observation, or whether they were due to separate, though possibly overlapping, subsets of neurons. Similarly, some early claims about EEG mu suppression reflecting MNs were overly certain.

This does not mean however, that these techniques should be discarded when attempting to record MNs. One can use techniques like *repetition suppression* to increase certainty that the same subset of neurons was active during both execution and observation. And, these techniques should continue to look for correlations between characteristics of neuroimaging signals and known properties of MNs.

HORMONES

In Chapter 7, Birkett and Sasaki present a review of current literature on the neuroendocrine influences on prosocial behavior. They organize their presentation around two key neuroendocrine systems that play a role in prosocial behavior: Arginine Vasopressin (AVP) and Oxytocin (OT). They explore these neurohormonal systems from a review of preclinical and clinical studies, drawing on neuroendocrinology, behavioral pharmacology, and behavioral genetics.

First to be considered is the AVP system. According to Birkett and Sasaki, AVP is synthesized in hypothalamic suprachiasmatic, paraventricular, and supraoptic nuclei, olfactory bulb, locus coeruleus, medial Amg, and bed nucleus of the stria terminalis, and is transported to posterior pituitary neurosecretory cells, from which it is passed into systemic circulation. Comparative research in invertebrate and vertebrate nonhuman species indicates that AVP plays an important role in social behavior. Because of remarkable affiliative behavioral differences across otherwise nearly identical species of voles, a rodentia order animal living across the world, these field mice have been studied extensively (Insel & Shapiro, 1992; Insel, 2010). These investigations have revealed that paternal behavior, territory defense, mate guarding, pair bonding, partner preference, and other social differences between monogamous and promiscuous species can be influenced variously by number, expression, and distribution of AVP receptors, levels of serum AVP, and administration of AVP agonists and antagonists.

Birkett and Sasaki further report that in human clinical studies, the AVP 1a receptor has been associated with altruism and social interactions (Ebstein, Knafo, Mankuta, Chew, & Lai, 2012; Israel et al., 2008). And, intranasal administration of AVP has been associated with increased facial threat responses to neutral faces in men and reduced facial threat responses to happy and angry faces and increased affiliative responses to neutral faces in women (Thompson et al., 2006). Still, in another cited study by Rilling et al. (2012), intranasal AVP increased reciprocal cooperative behavior and activation of affiliative brain regions, increased connectivity in ACC and ventral anterior insular somatic areas, and decreased activation of autonomic nervous system arousal areas. However, another study by Zink and Meyer-Lindenberg (2012) has reported no effects on Amg in adult males. Thus, although there is contradictory evidence, the Birkett and Sasaki review suggests important roles for AVP in the expression of prosocial behavior.

OT is also synthesized in paraventricular and supraoptic nuclei of the hypothalamus. However, according to the Birkett and Sasaki review, OT is released from posterior pituitary in response to a variety of social as well as stress-related stimuli, and most remarkably to sexual stimuli, uterine dilations, and nursing. Thus, OT has been shown to play a prominent role in maternal reproductive behavior as well as in male trust and empathic behavior. For example, OT has been shown to increase in mothers and fathers involved in affectionate interactions with their infants (Feldman, Gordon, Schneiderman, Weisman, & Zagoory-Sharon, 2010).

Similar to AVP, OT research with monogamous voles has found increased pair bonding and parental behavior with administration of OT and their disruption with an OT antagonist (Lieberwirth & Wang, 2016). Birkett and Sasaki report that many of these effects can last a lifetime following OT administration early in development. Such effects in animal models have been closely tied to the oxytocin receptor and to mediate consolation behaviors in response to stressors.

In humans, OT has a complex relationship to both empathic and compassionate prosocial behaviors and to negative social acts such as withdrawal and intergroup biases. For example, Birkett and Sasaki report that OT-related genes have been associated with positive social interactions and with empathic behavior (Baron-Cohen, Wheelwright, Hill, Raste, & Plumb, 2001; Rodrigues, Saslow, Garcia, John, & Keltner, 2009; Smith, Porges, Norman, Connelly, & Decety, 2014). However, some studies have shown that some OT-related genes may be associated with diminished self-esteem and perceived meaningfulness in response to social ostracism or rejection (McQuaid, McInnis, Matheson, & Anisman, 2015).

Birkett and Sasaki offer a gene-environment interactionist model for reconciling these apparent discrepancies. They suggest that carriers of OT-related genotypes may be more socially sensitive to environmental cues, such that they respond to nonthreatening stimuli with opportunities to affiliate with others and are prone to express empathic and compassionate behaviors in such contexts. However, in the presence of potentially threatening cues, they may be more inclined to social withdrawal and to diminished self-esteem. They further offer that the cultural context of such interactions shapes their perspectives and explains the cultural differences often observed in such gene-environment interactions.

Since the 1990s, OT has been available through a nasal mist administration, making human administration studies quite practical. Many such studies have been conducted and the authors' reviews suggest that results have been generally supportive of increased trust, generosity, empathic behavior, reduced social stress responses, and more prosocial biases in decision-making paradigms (MacDonald & MacDonald, 2010). However, some studies indicate that these relationships may be weak and that effects of intranasal OT administration can be negative in certain contexts (De Dreu, Greer, Van Kleef, Shalvi, & Handgraaf, 2010; Nave, Camerer, & McCullough, 2015; Shalvi & De Dreu, 2014).

Birkett and Sasaki allude early in their review to effects of OT stimulation release studies. Toward the end, they cite a number of investigations that have prompted OT release through mother–infant and father–infant affectionate contact, massage, and companion animal stimulation. Although results of massage studies have been mixed, companion animal studies have been most encouraging, generally resulting in positive physiological changes along with increases in OT in both handlers and animal companions. An interesting finding from several of these studies was that human–animal eye gazes may mediate this relationship.

Birkett and Sasaki conclude this OT section by pointing out that, in contrast to popular lore, OT is not a "love hormone" and that effects are quite contextually and culturally sensitive. They again offer their gene-culture interactionist model for understanding how context can moderate the relationship between environment-gene interactions and behavior.

Regarding the neuroendocrinology of Self-Compassion, Birkett and Sasaki point out that to date there is no research examining the direct causal relationships between AVP or OT and self-compassion. However, they do examine self-grooming behavior in nonhuman animals, as a potential animal model for self-compassion. They point to research with monogamous Mandarin voles indicating that self-grooming in dominant males appears to be related to decreased OT and increased AVP release, whereas in dominant females, self-grooming may be related only to increased AVP activity. However, research results in mice appear to be less certain and more research with both species is clearly indicated.

A scant number of studies of the roles of AVP and OT with humans have been suggestive but certainly not decisive. One perhaps encouraging study found increased self-compassion and salivary OT in a sample of cancer survivors with sleep disturbances following a 3-month mind-body intervention (Lipschitz et al., 2015). Birkett and Sasaki encourage the development of animal models for self-compassion and the examination of genetic polymorphisms associated with this construct, AVP/OT administration studies, and the application of AVP/OT antagonists in the investigation of self-compassionate behaviors and attitudes. Additional directions for research into the relationships between neuroendocrine systems and empathy, compassion, and self-compassion are offered.

TRAINING

Calderon, Ahern, and Pruzinsky in Chapter 8 begin by offering a series of questions they hope to address in their review of the neuroscience of systematic compassion training. They then embark upon a comparative review of four primary training programs developed in consultation with Buddhist geshes (Cognitive-Based Compassion Training [CBCT] and Compassion Cultivation Training [CCT]), academic educators (Project for Empathy and Compassion Education [PEACE]), or His Holiness The Dalai Lama (lifetime Buddhist practitioners). The authors point out that both CBCT and CCT were derived from the Lojong (mind training) tradition of Tibetan Buddhism but are secular in their presentations. Both follow structured weekly classes involving pedagogical instructions, active practice both in classes and in homework exercises, and training across cognitive, affective, motivational, attentional, and behavioral domains. And, both have shown positive effects in psychological (CCT: measures of compassion, mindfulness, well-being, worry, and emotional suppression; CBCT: loneliness, depression, and psychological stress) and physiological (CBCT: immune measures and cortisol; CCT: pain sensitivity and acceptance) dimensions.

Calderon et al. also spotlight the newly developed PEACE program, created as a way to advance compassionate practices within the public school system. PEACE is a 6-week course designed to be taught within the educational system in the form of classroom lectures and discussions on compassion, empathy, and positive psychology, guided group compassion meditation and interactive exercises, and community service, academic, and personal meditative homework activities. PEACE has been implemented within a college classroom context with neurophysiological and behavioral data collected and currently under analysis.

Lastly, the authors describe the lifelong compassion training program taught by The Dalai Lama to his students in Dharamsala, India and around the world. This program has been extensively described and studied longitudinally and is presented across many of The Dalai Lama's books (see for example The Dalai Lama, 1984, 2011, 2015). Practitioners engage in daily practices of intensive compassion meditations and activities involving sustained focused attention and deepened concentration and mindfulness, heightened awareness of and sensitivity to the suffering of all sentient beings, and attention to ways to alleviate this suffering. Although Calderon et al. report no psychological or well-being benefits of such long-term compassion practice in accomplished Tibetan meditators, a growing neuroscience literature has developed around this lifestyle compassion training program and is described.

Accordingly, Calderon et al. first review published neuroscience studies on the highly experienced meditators. Their presentation of outcomes of a few small EEG and MRI investigations with expert meditators suggests that prefrontal (PFC) and TPJ cortical regions show increased MRI activation and elevated gamma EEG waveforms, indicating enhanced attention and integration of sensory input across multiple modalities during compassion meditation. Additionally, these studies have found increased activation of ACC, In, and Amg differentially in expert compared to novice compassion meditators, suggesting an increased sensitivity to the suffering of others as well.

Reviews of the relatively few compassion training studies with novice meditators suggest a similar network of cortical and subcortical activations. For example, Calderon et al. report outcomes of a study by Mascaro, Rilling, Negi, and Raison (2013) which found increases in inferior frontal gyrus (IFG), STS, dmPFC, and anterior paracingulate cortex following CBCT. And Klimecki, Leiberg, Ricard, and Singer (2014), in comparing compassion with empathy training, found differential activation of mOFC, pregenual ACC (pACC), and striatum following compassion training in contrast to AI, ACC, temporal gyrus, dlPFC, operculum, and basal ganglia with empathy training. Calderon et al. point out that this latter study comparing empathy training with compassion training found relatively decreased activation of pain matrix areas of mACC and In and increased activation of more frontal executive processing areas of mOFC, ACC, and NAcc with compassion training focus on relief of suffering.

The Chapter 8 authors summarize their review with an integration of these studies into a mapping of a sequence of brain areas composed of cortical (dlPFC, IFG, mOFG, temporal gyrus, STS, and TPJ), embedded (In and Amg), subcortical (NAcc, striatum, and ventral tegmental area [VTA]), and midline (mACC, pACC, and dmPFC) structures activated during compassion training. They present quite colorful brain maps of these regions as well. Calderon et al. further organize these areas by negative affective, reward/pleasure, and mentalizing functions and suggest that these functions follow the progression in compassion training from the awareness of the suffering of another toward feelings of pleasure (sympathetic joy) with the focus on mechanisms for the alleviation of their suffering.

BRAHMAVIHARAS

Goodman, Plonski, and Savery in Chapter 9 introduce us to the ancient esoteric practices of the four Brahmaviharas, or pre-Buddhist divine contemplations: Loving-Kindness (*Metta*), Compassion (*Karuna*), Sympathetic Joy, (*Mudita*), and Equanimity (*Upekkha*). Following an in-depth description of each, and their "enemies," they then articulate critical foundational research on the roles of the contemplative skills of sustained attention and of open awareness, citing the research of Jazaieri et al. (2013); Mascaro,

Rilling, Negi, and Raison (2012); Mascaro, Darcher, Negi, and Raison (2015); and Ozawa-de Silva and Dodson-Lavelle (2011) utilizing CCT and CBCT to train prerequisite attentional capacities prior to formal compassion training. Goodman et al. elaborate these attentional refinements by describing the importance of developing a balance between *Samatha*, or sustained focused attention to a particular object (a mantra or mandala), and *Vipassana*, or the mindful and insightful awareness of passing moment-to-moment experiences and of the ever-changing nature of existence. They explain that such skills are essential for a residence within the four abodes of the Brahmaviharas and particularly to the experience of compassion. These attentional subsystems may be divided into (1) *alerting* to relevant stimulus input, involving frontal and parietal cortical regions, (2) *orienting* to new perceptual cues, involving parietal and frontal lobes and the TPJ, and (3) *monitoring and conflict resolution* involving dACC and lateral PFC. Goodman et al. cite a growing and impressive body of research supporting these topographic distinctions and indicating that training in focused attention and open monitoring activities may in fact enhance these neural networks and, in so doing, modulate attentional resources, regulate affective control and processing, and influence self-referential processing in the default mode network. Such foundational changes may then provide the infrastructure for more efficient acquisition of the Brahmaviharas.

Goodman et al. next embark upon an exploration of the neuroscience of the four divine abodes, on these boundless ways of living in the practice of abiding Buddhist soteriology, or salvation from suffering. They skillfully expose the reader to the neurological alterations that result from explicit practice in components of the Brahmaviharas. However, they note that their review of this literature reveals no published research investigating neural outcomes of directed training in Sympathetic Joy or Equanimity and they strongly encourage researchers to pursue this line of inquiry. Loving-Kindness and Compassion research, on the other hand, has been underway for quite some time and considerable research has accumulated. Operating from their conceptual frame of such practices increasing receptivity to others' emotions, reward processing and positive affect, and prosocial approach intentions and behaviors, Goodman et al. examine each of these possible outcomes through the lens of loving-kindness and compassion training.

Their review suggests that combined loving-kindness and compassion training can modulate amygdaloid and IPC/IFG activity during the experience of emotional states of others. These findings are intriguing indeed, for these areas are involved in states of emotional arousal and action/intention understanding through the human MN system, respectively (Desbordes et al., 2012; Lee et al., 2012; Leung et al., 2015; Leung et al., 2017; Lutz et al., 2008; Mascaro et al., 2012; Weng et al., 2013).

Similarly, for reward processing and positive affect, numerous studies of loving-kindness and compassion meditation have shown effects on striatal areas including caudate nucleus, globus pallidus, putamen, NAcc, VTA, and other components of the mesolimbic dopamine system, regions of the brain implicated in pleasure and reward (Phan, Wager, Taylor, & Liberzon, 2002). For example, Klimecki et al. (2013) and Klimecki et al. (2014) found increased activity in ventral striatum, NAcc, putamen, and VTA along with more positive subjective reports while viewing distressing videos following compassion training. Despite these supportive outcomes involving reward structures, the authors of Chapter 9 caution about the necessity of controlling for potential "schadenfreude," or enjoyment of the suffering of others, in such studies.

And regarding prosocial approach behaviors, Goodman and colleagues suggest potential involvement of the dlPFC and mesolimbic dopamine system during compassion-induced frontal executive control of potentially overwhelming negative affect from the suffering of others. They cite the study of Weng et al. (2013) in demonstrating activation of the dlPFC and increased connectivity with NAcc in response to distressing pictures following compassion training. Goodman et al. also present a series of studies supporting the involvement of the social bonding and maternal nurturing areas of periaqueductal gray and septal regions activated following compassion training.

In summary, Goodman, Plonski, and Savery present converging and quite convincing evidence from a broad variety of cross-sectional, training effects, and acute state investigations that directed contemplative engagement of at least two of the four domains of the Brahmaviharas has effects on specific brain areas predicted from a functional analysis of these practices. Loving-kindness and compassion training programs were shown to impact *amygdaloid activity* involved in detection and appraisal of the emotions of others, components of the *MN system* involved in action/intention understanding, the *mesolimbic dopamine system* potentially involved in reward and pleasure at the "sympathetic joy" of another's relief from suffering, *prefrontal cortical systems* involved in cognitive and emotional control, and *septal and midbrain periaqueductal gray* involved in parental care and nurturing. These authors conclude by pointing out the not-too-surprising consistency between these neurological networks and their functions on the one hand and the 2500 years of Buddhist practice of the Brahmaviharas on the other.

SOCIAL COGNITION

Pineda, Singh, and Chepak (Chapter 10) take a relatively macroscopic approach to their topic, providing us with a sophisticated model of social cognition—one in which *becoming* the other is a means of understanding the other. Using concepts like hierarchical and heterarchical organization (their H-H model) and interdependent versus interpenetrating mechanisms, the authors present a model of social cognition. Of particular importance are the terms *differentiation*, a drive to develop self-recognition, how one differs from others, and *integration*, referring to the opposite process of bonding and social engagement.

As a case study of social cognition, the authors refer to empathy, noting multiple possible definitions and the need for a standardized taxonomy, and the role that neurobiology can play in such a process of standardization. While the distinction between cognitive and emotional/affective empathy is widely discussed, the authors cite Blair (2005) as invoking a third form, motor empathy. They go on to make the appeal that empathy is a "superordinate category" insofar as it subsumes processes like emotional contagion, sympathy, and helping behavior, with associated neural processes operating in parallel. It might be argued that empathy is an emergent process insofar as it is what happens when each of these subprocesses interacts in a specific way. It can be seen as lying on a continuum, from basic forms of empathy (e.g., emotional contagion) to more sophisticated elaborations (e.g., ToM).

Noting the large number of species that possess at least the most rudimentary forms of empathy, the authors discuss Panksepp and Panksepp (2013) who proposed a three-tiered hierarchy of empathy that explains the conservation of empathy-like processes across species. Primary processes are said to depend on phylogenetically older subcortex and relate to processes like emotional contagion. They thus provide a bootstrap from which subsequent species could evolve to the secondary level, which involves learning and memory. At the tertiary level are the most sophisticated forms of empathy involving conscious experience of others' mental states. They even extend their H-H model to compassion, suggesting that compassion involves a dissolution of self-other distinctions (in contradiction to the positions of the authors of Chapters 1, 2, and 3) and that it adds to empathy insofar as it entails a motivation to help.

A key evolutionary component of their model involves the idea that evolution cannot select for superordinate categories such as the one in which empathy exists, but that such categories can emerge from the evolutionarily simpler mechanisms alluded to above. One suggested unit of selection is mirror processing, as such a mechanism can be seen as underlying mimicry and imitation, leading to a new method of learning. Combining these more elementary functions is then said to lead to the emergence of empathy and ToM.

AN INTEGRATED PORTRAIT OF COMPASSION

At least two of the aims of the present chapter are to suggest, from separate independent reviews of the most current neuroscience research literature, areas in the human brain where empathy, compassion, and self-compassion are expressed and the mechanisms of these neurological manifestations. We hope to shed light on the sites of unique hemodynamic alterations and differential electromagnetic frequency characteristics coincident with empathic, compassionate, and self-compassionate experiences. In so doing, we aspire not only to advance basic research leading to a further understanding of these processes but also to suggest applied investigations toward increasing these characteristics in those desiring to do so and in others burdened with the "enemies" of these virtues. Our observations from this review follow.

For the experience of compassion, the reviews of Stevens and Benjamin in Chapter 3, of Calderon, Ahern, and Pruzinsky in Chapter 8, and of Goodman, Plonski, and Savery in Chapter 9 provide converging evidence for a sequence of neurological events that embody the components of compassionate experiencing. We may assemble these components into a chain of responses which at this stage of the neuroscience must be considered tentative and speculative and certainly in need of further research verification. These events would appear to start with a brief, automatic, and vestigial affective empathic response originating from experience with the suffering of another and expressed through increased activation of an *amygdaloid, anterior insular,* and *ACC* circuit. This circuit very quickly activates a similarly ancestral, neurologic vestige of more primitive preconcern, premotor activation in *inferior arcuate sulcus* and *intraparietal sulcus/inferior parietal lobe* regions recognized as part of the MN system. These premotor activations give rise to an impulse to approach the sufferer and to render assistance, quite likely accompanied by autonomic nervous system arousal and the experience of personal distress. An implication of these arousal responses early in the compassion chain is that these responses are automatic and involuntary, occur prior to cognitive awareness, and are universal across human beings, with the possible exception of neurologically based personality and behavioral/perceptual anomalies as suggested in Chapter 5 on Cruelty.

Next in this sequence of responses to the suffering of another, we would expect to see increased involvement of a cognitive processing circuit in the PFC. This cognitive system would be composed of *dlPFC, vlPFC,* and *dmPFC* activated differentially dependent upon the nature of the event processing. Considering the singular outcomes of the Fehse et al. (2015) study, if perception of the suffering scenario were followed by a careworthy perspective, we might see greater activation of mPFC leading to further excitation of the Amg, AI, ACC circuit, and more compassion; if perception of the scenario were followed by a more blameworthy perspective, we would expect to see activation of dlPFC leading to inhibition of the mPFC, Amg, AI, ACC circuit, and diminished compassion for others. These frontal circuits could likewise modulate personal distress arousal through self-other differentiation and a psychological distancing of self from other.

Notwithstanding the perceived preeminence of thoughts and words in the modulation of this prefrontal function, a more parsimonious explanation of dlPFC and mPFC activation might be similar to that of Melzack and Wall's (1965) identification of an inhibitory neurological gate in the dorsal horn of the spinal cord which modulates the perception of pain; activate the gate with descending periaqueductal gray or local A-Beta fibers and you inhibit the perception of pain. Except, for the mechanism described here in PFC, these sophisticated inhibitory and excitatory neural networks would open or close a gate on our perception of compassion, as described above. And, in this model, our thoughts and words might be more of a premotor epiphenomenon in IFG or posterior temporal cortex of this PFC processing. (See Davis & MacNeilage, 2004; Falk, 2004; Grezes & Decety, 2001; Holden, 2004; and MacNeilage & Davis, 2005 for a discussion of this exciting literature on the evolution of language in the development of motor circuits.)

Additionally, a further modulation of this frontal system might be seen with collateral activations of more posterior *TPJ* and PCun sites contributing to important self-other differentiation and to a sorting out of perceived experiences of the observer from the suffering other. This differentiation coupled with the emergence of "sympathetic joy" and associated reward centers in mesolimbic dopaminergic sites of *globus pallidus, putamen, NAcc,* and *VTA* could result in feelings of pleasure at the contemplation of alleviated suffering. With sustained activation of this network within the context of prosocial bonding and parental care and nurturing, we might also see activations of *hypothalamic, septal,* and *periaqueductal gray* regions involved in the release of OT and vasopressin, as alluded to by Birkett and Sasaki in Chapter 7 and Goodman et al. in Chapter 9.

Although each of our authors has been quite thoughtful in suggesting directions for future research involving the foci of their respective chapters, we would like to propose an additional test of this integrative model. Such an investigation would involve a constructive replication of the Fehse et al. study, but in this redesigned study taking advantage of the superior temporal resolution and neuroimaging capabilities of contemporary EEG technology to study the time-course and localizations of the experience of compassion. Our study would utilize the clever presentation of careworthy/blameworthy stimulus dyads as in the Fehse et al. study, with EEGs recorded continuously throughout stimulus exposure, and with subjective compassion ratings, in prescreened compassion-strong (perhaps, with added complexity, compared with compassion-weak) research participants. EEGs would be analyzed for a testing of the above compassion sequencing and modulation, and observed electrocortical frequency characteristics of each sequence, as well as localizations of each component. Our laboratory is currently gearing up for the conduct of such a study.

THE EMPATHY-TO-COMPASSION (ETOC) MODEL

Empathy and Compassion each on their own are difficult enough to conceptualize, and trying to understand the way they relate to one another only adds a higher order of complexity. Nonetheless, we suggest that this complexity can be managed by modeling the route from empathy-to-compassion (EtoC) as a continuous modulation of self-other representational states. The model assumes that the process from empathy, to sympathy, to compassion is marked by a dynamical shifting of attentional resources between egocentric (other as self) and allocentric (other as other) representations whereby the observer represents the other as the self, the other as the other, then rapidly oscillates between these two representational states across sympathy and into compassion, the difference between the last two oscillatory phases being a baseline shift biased toward self for sympathy and toward the other for compassion.

In Fig. 11.1, we have attempted to explain this process of coming to understand, and subsequently care for, another. This is intended to model but one of a variety of ways that an individual could come to know another, experience compassion for another, or neither. The model is unidimensional, conceiving of the EtoC process as a dynamic oscillation of attention between self- and other-focused representations whereby the observer's initial experience is an egocentric representation of an affective and/or cognitive state, transitioning, via self-other discrimination, to allocentric

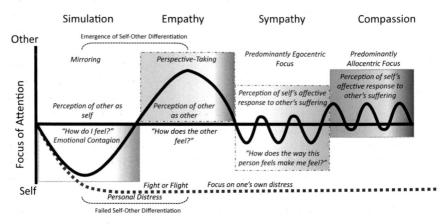

FIGURE 11.1   **The Empathy to Compassion Model (EtoC).** A model of the time course of attentional focus to self and other representations as an individual progresses from simulating the other's emotions, to perceiving those emotions as belonging to the other (empathy), to a comparator process in which sympathy emerges from the consideration of how the other's emotions affect the self and finally to compassion as the observer focuses mainly on the other's feelings with some consideration of the observer's own desire to alleviate suffering. This model is intended to be only one possible route from empathy to compassion.

representations, then to a rapidly oscillating phase of alternating empathy and self-analysis, with a slight shift of this oscillation toward self (we will call this *sympathy*), followed by a shift of this oscillation toward the other during the compassion phase.

The process begins with perception of another person's suffering, which is assumed to involve simulation (e.g., in MN areas). The model assumes at this point that representations of the social target's affective and cognitive states are activated in the observer's brain, as well as in the rest of her body (affect), as if those states belonged to her. In other words, if the affective state is one of fear, then the observer experiences her own expression of fear in her own body, without initially recognizing that the fear belongs to the social target. In Fig. 11.1, this is described as "perceiving the other as self" and is akin to emotional contagion and/or personal distress. As indicated by the dotted red line, one possibility is that the resulting personal distress leads to a sympathetic nervous system response (fight or flight) and the person's actions are aimed at relieving her own distress. Note, under this model, that even if she decides to help the other person, if this is done out of motivation to lessen her own distress, according to the model, she has side-stepped the rest of the EtoC process because the remaining stages (empathy, sympathy, and compassion) of her actions are now determined by representations of her own distress rather than those of the others.

Alternatively, if the observer is able to shift attention to allocentric representations of the other, then she can engage in genuine empathy, having shifted to representing the affective/cognitive state as belonging to the other. In this empathic phase, activated representations are assumed to contain minimal (though probably not zero) information about the self. Unlike some models of empathy that would include in the set of empathic states even those in which the observer experiences personal distress (hence, a self-dominated representational state), here personal distress is modeled as very different from the other-focused state of empathy as it involves settling into somewhat of a steady state of self-focus, characterized by the obligatory focus on self, more specifically, self-preservation.

The issue is clouded by the fact that there are at least two senses of "attending to the other." The first involves the attending to the other represented *as the other*, while the second would be attending to the other represented *as the self*. The latter is the one referred to in the simulation phase of the model, while the former is reserved for the second stage in which the observer has transitioned from a state of viewing the other's experience as her own, to viewing the other's experience as belonging to the other (an allocentric representation is attended). Once the empathy phase concludes, the sympathy phase occurs as attention is switched rapidly back and forth between egocentric and allocentric representations in a comparator process whereby the observer takes aspects of the social target's affective/cognitive states, alternating between allocentric and egocentric representations to generate a representation of how the observer would feel were she in the same affective/cognitive states.

These oscillations are hypothesized not to be centered on the self-other baseline, but shifted more toward egocentric representations such that those representations spend more time activated than allocentric representations, representing the idea, "How does the way she feels make me feel?" Notice that this question, while requiring some allocentric awareness, is primarily about how the self feels. Similarly an oscillation between egocentric and allocentric representations is hypothesized for compassion, but shifted more toward allocentric representations, reflecting the idea that compassion, while requiring some degree of egocentric processing (e.g., sympathetic joy), is an experience dominated by awareness of the other.

This model affords a certain amount of anatomical specification. One could derive from the model the hypothesis that some neurophysiological signal should vary in a way correlated to the model's function. For example, fMRI might be a candidate tool for testing the hypothesis that the model's function could be convolved with a hemodynamic response function. However, two problems present themselves.

1. This technique assumes that there is a single brain region, voxel for that matter, that displays this time course. This may not be the case—instead, as suggested multiple times in this book, high-level constructs, even self-other discrimination, may not *reside* in a single brain region but rather emerge from the interaction of multiple brain regions.
2. The time course of the model function is likely less than 2 s, perhaps making the relatively low temporal resolution of fMRI incapable of modeling this variance.

EEG may be able to get around both of these problems. One such EEG signal is mu suppression. Though mu suppression studies generally use blocked analysis techniques, mu rhythm desynchronization can be measured with the millisecond resolution of event-related desynchronization (ERD). Using a blocked design, Woodruff, Martin, and Bilyk (2011) found that mu suppression was reliably greater for executing an action relative to observing another perform that action, and the size of the self-other difference scores was positively related to self-reported perspective-taking. In other words, the greater the mu suppression self-other difference, the better the participant reported his/her perspective-taking abilities. As such, this mu suppression self-other difference approach could be used with mu rhythm ERDs to assess the extent to which ERD difference waves correlate with the time course of egocentric/allocentric attentional allocation proposed in the above model. If the model is accurate, then there may be a brain signal that tracks this dynamic shifting of attention across the EtoC process.

Regarding number 2 above, while EEG's relatively low spatial resolution makes it difficult to identify brain regions (again, this could be seen as a plus given the emergent property argument above), the exquisite temporal resolution would allow for the examination of time series correlations between the time course of the model and the time course of various EEG signals such as event-related potentials and/or ERD, which allow for millisecond resolution. The central vertex electrode, Cz, is commonly used to measure mu suppression. The hypothesis could then be expressed as the prediction that the difference wave of mu ERD to self, minus mu ERD to other, will significantly correlate with the EtoC model function.

FINAL THOUGHTS

Research into the neuroscience of empathy, compassion, and self-compassion is important to our understanding of these prosocial constructs and to our ability to promote them in society and to demote the far enemy of these, cruelty. Each one of these constructs is in need of further definitional clarity and it is the hope of this book's editors that some progress in that direction has been made here. We suggest that future research continue to attempt to clarify these definitions as well as to research the important roles that processes like self-other differentiation, ToM, and personal distress play in each of these constructs, as well as in their neurological manifestations. And, we sincerely hope that you have enjoyed your Wild Ride into the Neuroscience of Empathy, Compassion, and Self-Compassion.

References

Baron-Cohen, S. (2011). *The science of evil: On empathy and the origins of cruelty*. New York: Basic Books.

Baron-Cohen, S., & Wheelwright, S. (2004). The Empathy Quotient: An Investigation of Adultswith Asperger Syndrome or High Functioning Autism, and Normal Sex Differences. *Journal of Autism and Developmental Disorders, 34*(2), 163–175.

Baron-Cohen, S., Wheelwright, S., Hill, J., Raste, Y., & Plumb, I. (2001). The "Reading the Mind in the Eyes" test revised version: A study with normal adults, and adults with Asperger syndrome or high-functioning autism. *Journal of Child Psychology and Psychiatry, 42*(2), 241–251.

Batson, C. D. (2009). These things called empathy: Eight related but distinct phenomena. In J. Decety, & W. Ickes (Eds.), *The social neuroscience of empathy* (1st ed., pp. 3–15). Cambridge, MA: MIT Press.

Berman, A. E., & Stevens, L. (2015). EEG manifestations of nondual experiences in meditators. *Consciousness and Cognition, 31*, 1–11.

Blair, R. J. R. (2005). Responding to the emotions of others: Dissociating forms of empathy through the study of typical and psychiatric populations. *Consciousness and Cognition, 14*, 698–718. doi: 10.1016/j.concog.2005.06.004.

Brown, E., Wiersema, J., Pourtois, G., & Brüne, M. (2013). Modulation of motor cortex activity when observing rewarding and punishing actions. *Neuropsychologia, 51*, 52–58.

Buhle, J. T., Silvers, J. A., Wager, T. D., Lopez, R., Onyemekwu, C., Kober, H., et al. (2014). Cognitive reappraisal of emotion: A meta-analysis of human neuroimaging studies. *Cerebral Cortex, 24,* 2981–2990.

Buschman, T., & Miller, E. K. (2007). Top-down versus bottom-up control of attention in the prefrontal and posterior parietal cortices. *Science, 315,* 1860–1862.

Catmur, C. (2015). Understanding intentions from actions: Direct perception, inference and the roles of mirror and mentalizing systems. *Consciousness and Cognition, 36,* 426–433.

d'Aquili, E. G., & Newberg, A. B. (1993). Liminality, trance, and unitary states of ritual and meditation. *Studia Liturgica, 23,* 2–34.

Davis, B. L., & MacNeilage, P. F. (2004). The frame/content theory of speech evolution: From lip smacks to syllables. *Primatologie, 6,* 305–328.

Davis, M. H. (1983). Measuring individual differences in empathy: Evidence for a multidimensional approach. *Journal of Personality and Social Psychology, 44*(1), 113–126.

De Dreu, C. K. W., Greer, L. L., Van Kleef, G. A., Shalvi, S., & Handgraaf, M. J. J. (2010). Oxytocin promotes human ethnocentrism. *Proceedings of the National Academy of Sciences, 108,* 1262–1266.

de Oliveira, D. C., Zuardi, A. W., Graeff, F. G., Queiroz, R. H., & Crippa, J. A. (2012). Anxiolytic-like effect of oxytocin in the simulated public speaking test. *Journal of Psychopharmacology, 26,* 497–504.

De Vries, G. J. (2004). Minireview: Sex differences in adult and developing brains: Compensation, compensation, compensation. *Endocrinology, 145*(3), 1063–1068.

de Waal, F. (2009). *The age of empathy.* New York: Three Rivers Press.

Denny, B. T., Kober, H., Wager, T. D., & Ochsner, K. N. (2012). A meta-analysis of functional neuroimaging studies of self- and other-judgments reveals a spatial gradient for mentalizing in medial prefrontal cortex. *Journal of Cognitive Neuroscience, 24*(8), 1742–1752.

Desbordes, G., Negi, L. T., Pace, T. W., Wallace, B. A., Raison, C. L., & Schwartz, E. L. (2012). Effects of mindful-attention and compassion meditation training on amygdala response to emotional stimuli in an ordinary, non-meditative state. *Frontiers in Human Neuroscience, 6,* 1–15. doi: 10.3389/fnhum.2012.00292.

Desbordes, G., Gard, T., Hoge, E. A., Hölzel, B. K., Kerr, C., Lazar, S. W., et al. (2015). Moving beyond mindfulness: Defining equanimity as an outcome measure in meditation and contemplative research. *Mindfulness, 6*(2), 356–372.

Doerig, N., Schlumpf, Y., Spinelli, S., Spati, J., Brakowski, J., Quednow, B. B., et al. (2014). Neural representation and clinically relevant moderators of individualised self-criticism in healthy subjects. *Social, Cognitive, and Affective Neuroscience, 9*(9), 1333–1340.

Ebstein, R. P., Knafo, A., Mankuta, D., Chew, S. H., & Lai, P. S. (2012). The contributions of oxytocin and vasopressin pathway genes to human behavior. *Hormones and Behavior, 61,* 359–379. doi: 10.1016/j.yhbeh.2011.12.014.

Falk, D. (2004). Prelinguistic evolution in early hominins: Whence motherese? *Behavioral and Brain Sciences, 27,* 491–541.

Fehse, K., Silveira, S., Elvers, K., & Blautzik, J. (2015). Compassion, guilt and innocence: An fMRI study of responses to victims who are responsible for their fate. *Social Neuroscience, 10*(3), 243–252.

Feldman, R., Gordon, I., Schneiderman, I., Weisman, O., & Zagoory-Sharon, O. (2010). Natural variations in maternal and paternal care are associated with systematic changes in oxytocin following parent–infant contact. *Psychoneuroendocrinology, 35*(8), 1133–1141.

Gonzalez-Liencres, C., Shamay-Tsoory, S. G., & Brüne, M. (2013). Towards a neuroscience of empathy: Ontogeny, phylogeny, brain mechanisms, context and psychopathology. *Neuroscience & Biobehavioral Reviews, 37*(8), 1537–1548.

Grezes, J., & Decety, J. (2001). Functional anatomy of execution, mental simulation, observation, and verb generation of actions: A meta-analysis. *Human Brain Mapping, 12,* 1–19.

Handlin, L., Nilsson, A., Ejdebäck, M., Hydbring-Sandberg, E., & Uvnäs-Moberg, K. (2012). Associations between the psychological characteristics of the human–dog relationship and oxytocin and cortisol levels. *Anthrozoös, 25*(2), 215–228.

Holden, C. (2004). The origin of speech. *Science, 303*, 1316–1319.

Holzel, B. K., Lazar, S. W., Gard, T., Schuman-Olivier, Z., Vago, D. R., & Ott, U. (2011). How does mindfulness meditation work? Proposing mechanisms of action from a conceptual and neural perspective. *Perspectives on Psychological Science, 6*(6), 537–559.

Horan, W. P., Pineda, J. A., Wynn, J. K., Iacoboni, M., & Green, M. F. (2014). Some markers of mirroring appear intact in schizophrenia: evidence from mu suppression. *Cognitive, Affective, & Behavioral Neuroscience, 14*(3), 1049–1060.

Immordino-Yang, M. H., McColl, A., Damasio, H., & Damasio, A. (2009). Neural correlates of admiration and compassion. *Proceedings of the National Academy of Sciences of the United States of America, 106*(19), 8021–8026.

Insel, T. R. (2010). The challenge of translation in social neuroscience: A review of oxytocin, vasopressin, and affiliative behavior. *Neuron, 65*(6), 768–779.

Insel, T. R., & Shapiro, L. E. (1992). Oxytocin receptor distribution reflects social organization in monogamous and polygamous voles. *Proceedings of the National Academy of Sciences of the United States of America, 89*, 5981–5985.

Israel, S., et al. (2008). Molecular genetic studies of the arginine vasopressin 1a receptor (AVPR1a) and the oxytocin receptor (OXTR) in human behaviour: From autism to altruism with some notes in between. *Progress in Brain Research, 170*, 435–449.

Jazaieri, H., Jinpa, T. L., McGonigal, K., Rosenberg, E., Finkelstein, J., Simon-Thomas, E., et al. (2013). Enhancing compassion: A randomized controlled trial of a compassion cultivation training program. *Journal of Happiness Studies, 14*, 1113–1126. doi: 10.1007/s10902-012-9373-z.

Josipovic, Z. (2013). Neural correlates of nondual awareness in meditation. *Annals of the New York Academy of Sciences, 1307*, 1–10.

Josipovic, Z., Dinstein, I., Weber, J., & Heeger, D. J. (2012). Influence of meditation on anti-correlated networks in the brain. *Frontiers in Human Neuroscience, 5*, 1–11.

Kédia, G., Berthoz, S., Wessa, M., Hilton, D., & Martinot, J. -L. (2008). An agent harms a victim: A functional magnetic resonance imaging study on specific moral emotions. *Journal of Cognitive Neuroscience, 20*(10), 1788–1798. http://doi.org/10.1162/jocn.2008.20070.

Kim, J. W., Kim, S. E., Kim, J. J., Jeong, B., Park, C. H., Son, A. R., et al. (2009). Compassionate attitude towards others' suffering activates the mesolimbic neural system. *Neuropsychologia, 47*(10), 2073–2081.

Kjaer, T. W., Nowak, M., & Lou, H. C. (2002). Reflective self-awareness and conscious states: PET evidence for a common midline parietofrontal core. *NeuroImage, 17*, 1080–1086.

Klimecki, O. M., Leiberg, S., Lamm, C., & Singer, T. (2013). Functional neural plasticity and associated changes in positive affect after compassion training. *Cerebral Cortex, 23*(7), 1552–1561.

Klimecki, O. M., Leiberg, S., Ricard, M., & Singer, T. (2014). Differential pattern of functional brain plasticity after compassion and empathy training. *Social Cognitive and Affective Neuroscience, 9*(6), 873–879.

Lamm, C., & Singer, T. (2010). The role of anterior insular cortex in social emotions. *Brain Structure and Function, 214*, 579–591.

Lamm, C., Decety, J., & Singer, T. (2011). Meta-analytic evidence for common and distinct neural networks associated with directly experienced pain and empathy for pain. *NeuroImage, 54*(3), 2492–2502.

Lee, T. M., Leung, M. K., Hou, W. K., Tang, J. C., Yin, J., So, K. F., et al. (2012). Distinct neural activity associated with focused-attention meditation and loving-kindness meditation. *PLoS One, 7*(8), e40054. doi: 10.1371/journal.pone.0040054.

Leung, M. K., Chan, C. C., Yin, J., Lee, C. F., So, K. F., & Lee, T. M. (2015). Enhanced amygdala–cortical functional connectivity in meditators. *Neuroscience Letters, 590*, 106–110.

Leung, M. K., Lau, W. K., Chan, C. C., Wong, S. S., Fung, A. L., & Lee, T. M. (2017). Meditation-induced neuroplastic changes in amygdala activity during negative affective processing. *Social Neuroscience*, 1–12. https://doi.org/10.1080/17470919.2017.1311939.

Lieberwirth, C., & Wang, Z. (2016). The neurobiology of pair bond formation, bond disruption, and social buffering. *Current Opinion in Neurobiology, 40*, 8–13.

Lindquist, K. A., Wager, T. D., Kober, H., Bliss-Moreau, E., & Barrett, L. F. (2012). The brain basis of emotion: A meta-analytic review. *Behavioral and Brain Sciences, 35*(3), 121–143.

Lipschitz, D. L., Kuhn, R., Kinney, A. Y., Grewen, K., Donaldson, G. W., & Nakamura, Y. (2015). An exploratory study of the effects of mind–body interventions targeting sleep on salivary oxytocin levels in cancer survivors. *Integrative Cancer Therapies, 14*(4), 366–380.

Longe, O., Maratos, F. A., Gilbert, P., Evans, G., Volker, F., Rockliff, H., et al. (2010). Having a word with yourself: Neural correlates of self-criticism and self-reassurance. *NeuroImage, 49*, 1849–1856.

Lutz, A., Brefczynski-Lewis, J., Johnstone, T., & Davidson, R. J. (2008). Regulation of the neural circuitry of emotion by compassion meditation: Effects of meditative expertise. *PloS One, 3*(3), e1897.

MacDonald, K., & MacDonald, T. M. (2010). The peptide that binds: A systematic review of oxytocin and its prosocial effects in humans. *Harvard Review of Psychiatry, 18*(1), 1–21.

MacNeilage, P. F., & Davis, B. L. (2005). The frame/content theory of evolution of speech: A comparison with gestural-origins alternative. *Interaction Studies, 6*(2), 173–199.

Manocha, R. (2011). Meditation, mindfulness, and mind-emptiness. *Acta Neuropsychiatrica, 23*(1), 46–47.

Mascaro, J. S., Rilling, J. K., Negi, L. T., & Raison, C. L. (2012). Compassion meditation enhances empathic accuracy and related neural activity. *Social Cognitive and Affective Neuroscience, 8*(1), 48–55.

Mascaro, J. S., Rilling, J. K., Negi, L. T., & Raison, C. L. (2013). Pre-existing brain function predicts subsequent practice of mindfulness and compassion meditation. *NeuroImage, 69*, 35–42. doi: 10.1016/j.neuroimage.2012.12.021.

Mascaro, J. S., Darcher, A., Negi, L. T., & Raison, C. L. (2015). The neural mediators of kindness-based meditation: A theoretical model. *Frontiers in Psychology, 6*(109), 1–12. doi: 10.3389/fpsyg.2015.00109.

McQuaid, R. J., McInnis, O. A., Matheson, K., & Anisman, H. (2015). Distress of ostracism: Oxytocin receptor gene polymorphism confers sensitivity to social exclusion. *Social Cognitive and Affective Neuroscience, 10*, 1153–1159.

Melzack, R., & Wall, P. D. (1965). Pain mechanisms: A new theory. *Science, 150*(3699), 971–979. doi: 10.1126/science.150.3699.971. PMID 5320816.

Milston, S., Vanman, E., & Cunnington, R. (2013). Cognitive empathy and motor activity during observed actions. *Neuropsychologia, 51*(6), 1103–1108.

Murray, R. J., Schaer, M., & Debbane, M. (2012). Degrees of separation: A quantitative neuroimaging meta-analysis investigating self-specificity and shared neural activation between self- and other-reflection. *Neuroscience and Biobehavioral Reviews, 36*, 1043–1059.

Nave, G., Camerer, C., & McCullough, M. (2015). Does oxytocin increase trust in humans? A critical review of research. *Perspectives on Psychological Science, 10*, 772–789.

Neff, K. (2003a). Self-compassion: An alternative conceptualization of a healthy attitude toward oneself. *Self and Identity, 2*, 85–101.

Neff, K. (2003b). The development and validation of a scale to measure self-compassion. *Self and Identity, 2*, 223–250.

Negi, L. T. (2013). *Emory compassion meditation protocol: Cognitively-based compassion training manual*. Atlanta, GA: Emory University.

Neufeld, E., Brown, E. C., Lee-Grimm, S. -I., Newen, A., & Brüne, M. (2016). Intentional action processing results from automatic bottom-up attention: An EEG-investigation into the Social Relevance Hypothesis using hypnosis. *Consciousness and Cognition, 42*, 101–112.

Northoff, G., & Bermpohl, F. (2004). Cortical midline structures and the self. *Trends in Cognitive Science, 8*(3), 102–107.

Northoff, G., Heinzel, A., de Greck, M., Bermpohl, F., Dobrowolny, H., & Panksepp, J. (2006). Self-referential processing in our brain: A meta-analysis of imaging studies on the self. *NeuroImage, 31,* 440–457.

Oberman, L., Hubbard, E., McCleary, J., Altschuler, E., Ramachandran, V., & Pineda, J. (2005). EEG evidence for mirror neuron dysfunction in autism spectrum disorders. *Cognitive Brain Research, 24,* 190–198.

Ochsner, K. N., Bunge, S. A., Gross, J. J., & Gabrieli, J. D. (2002). Rethinking feelings: An fMRI study of the cognitive regulation of emotion. *Journal of Cognitive Neuroscience, 14*(8), 1215–1229.

Ochsner, K. N., Ray, R. D., Cooper, J. C., Robertson, E. R., Chopra, S., Gabrieli, J. D. E., et al. (2004). For better or for worse: Neural systems supporting the cognitive down- and upregulation of negative emotion. *NeuroImage, 23,* 483–499.

Ochsner, K. N., Ray, R. R., Hughes, B., McRae, K., Cooper, J. C., Weber, J., et al. (2009). Bottom-up and top-down processes in emotion generation: Common and distinct neural mechanisms. *Psychological Science, 20*(11), 1322–1331.

Ozawa-de Silva, B., & Dodson-Lavelle, B. (2011). An education of heart and mind: Practical and theoretical issues in teaching cognitively based compassion training to children. *Practical Matters, 4,* 1–28.

Pace, T. W., Negi, L. T., Adame, D. D., Cole, S. P., Sivilli, T. I., Brown, T. D., et al. (2009). Effect of compassion meditation on neuroendocrine, innate immune and behavioral responses to psychosocial stress. *Psychoneuroendocrinology, 34*(1), 87–98.

Panksepp, J., & Panksepp, J. B. (2013). Toward a cross-species understanding of empathy. *Trends in Neurosciences, 36*(8), 489–496.

Perry, A., Troje, N. F., & Bentin, S. (2010). Exploring motor system contributions to the perception of social information: Evidence from EEG activity in the mu/alpha frequency range. *Social Neuroscience, 5*(3), 272–284.

Phan, K. L., Wager, T., Taylor, S. F., & Liberzon, I. (2002). Functional neuroanatomy of emotion: A meta-analysis of emotion activation studies in PET and fMRI. *NeuroImage, 16*(2), 331–348. doi: 10.1006/nimg.2002.1087.

Phan, K. L., Taylor, S. F., Welsh, R. C., Ho, S. -H., Britton, J. C., & Liberzon, I. (2004a). Neural correlates of individual ratings of emotional salience: A trial-related fMRI study. *NeuroImage, 21,* 768–780.

Phan, K. L., Wager, T. D., Taylor, S. F., & Liberzon, I. (2004b). Functional neuroimaging studies of human emotions. *CNS Spectrums, 9*(4), 258–266.

Qiao, X., Yan, Y., Wu, R., Tai, F., Hao, P., Cao, Y., et al. (2014). Sociality and oxytocin and vasopressin in the brain of male and female dominant and subordinate mandarin voles. *Journal of Comparative Physiology A, 200*(2), 149–159.

Qin, P., & Northoff, G. (2011). How is our self related to midline regions and the default-mode network. *NeuroImage, 57,* 1221–1233.

Rilling, J. K. (2013). The neural and hormonal bases of human parental care. *Neuropsychologia, 51*(4), 731–747.

Rilling, J. K., Sanfey, A. G., Aronson, J. A., Nystrom, L. E., & Cohen, J. D. (2004). The neural correlates of theory of mind within interpersonal interactions. *NeuroImage, 22*(4), 1694–1703. http://doi.org/10.1016/j.neuroimage.2004.04.015.

Rilling, J. K., DeMarco, A. C., Hackett, P. D., Thompson, R., Ditzen, B., Patel, R., et al. (2012). Effects of intranasal oxytocin and vasopressin on cooperative behavior and associated brain activity in men. *Psychoneuroendocrinology, 37*(4), 447–461.

Rodrigues, S. M., Saslow, L. R., Garcia, N., John, O. P., & Keltner, D. (2009). Oxytocin receptor genetic variation relates to empathy and stress reactivity in humans. *Proceedings of the National Academy of Sciences, 106*(50), 21437–21441.

Schaafsma, S. M., Pfaff, D. W., Spunt, R. P., & Adolphs, R. (2015). Deconstructing and reconstructing theory of mind. *Trends in Cognitive Sciences, 19*(2), 65–72. http://doi.org/10.1016/j.tics.2014.11.007.

Shalvi, S., & De Dreu, C. K. W. (2014). Oxytocin promotes group-serving dishonesty. *Proceedings of the National Academy of Sciences, 111*, 5503–5507.

Singer, T., & Klimecki, O. M. (2014). Empathy and compassion. *Current Biology, 24*(18), R875–R878.

Singer, T., Critchley, H. D., & Preuschoff, K. (2009). A common role of insula in feelings, empathy and uncertainty. *Trends in cognitive sciences, 13*(8), 334–340.

Smith, K. E., Porges, E. C., Norman, G. J., Connelly, J. J., & Decety, J. (2014). Oxytocin receptor gene variation predicts empathic concern and autonomic arousal while perceiving harm to others. *Social Neuroscience, 9*(1), 1–9.

Sperduti, M., Delaveau, P., Fossati, P., & Nadel, J. (2011). Different brain structures related to self- and external-agency attribution: A brief review and meta-analysis. *Brain Structure and Function, 216*, 151–157.

Tang, Y-Y., Holzel, B., & Posner, M. (2015). The neuroscience of mindfulness meditation. *Nature Reviews Neuroscience, 16*(4), 213–225.

The Dalai Lama. (1984). *Kindness, Clarity, and Insight.* Boston, MA: Snow Lion.

The Dalai Lama. (2011). *How to be compassionate: A handbook for creating inner peace and a happier world.* New York: Atria.

The Dalai Lama. (2015). *The world of Tibetan Buddhism: An overview of its philosophy and practice.* Somerville, MA: Wisdom Publications.

Thompson, R. R., George, K., Walton, J. C., Orr, S. P., & Benson, J. (2006). Sex-specific influences of vasopressin on human social communication. *Proceedings of the National Academy of Sciences, 103*(20), 7889–7894.

van der Meer, L., Costafreda, S., Aleman, A., & David, A. S. (2010). Self-reflection and the brain: A theoretical review and meta-analysis of neuroimaging studies with implications for schizophrenia. *Neuroscience and Biobehavioral Reviews, 34*(6), 935–946.

Wang, S. (2005). A conceptual framework for integrating research related to the physiology of compassion and the wisdom of Buddhist teachings. In P. Gilbert (Ed.), *Compassion: Conceptualisations, research, and use in psychotherapy* (pp. 75–120). New York: Routledge.

Weng, H. Y., Fox, A. S., Shackman, A. J., Stodola, D. E., Caldwell, J. Z., Olson, M. C., et al. (2013). Compassion training alters altruism and neural responses to suffering. *Psychological Science, 24*(7), 1171–1180.

Woodruff, C. C., & Klein, S. (2013). Attentional distraction, μ-suppression and empathic perspective-taking. *Experimental Brain Research, 229*(4), 507–515.

Woodruff, C. C., Martin, T., & Bilyk, N. (2011a). Differences in self- and other-induced mu suppression are correlated with empathic abilities. *Brain Research, 1405*, 69–76.

Yerkes, R. M., & Dodson, J. D. (1908). The relation of strength of stimulus to rapidity of habit-formation. *Journal of Comparative Neurology and Psychology, 18*, 459–482.

Zink, C. F., & Meyer-Lindenberg, A. (2012). Human neuroimaging of oxytocin and vasopressin in social cognition. *Hormones and Behavior, 61*(3), 400–409.

Index

Printed in the United States
By Bookmasters